FORTRAN IV FOR BUSINESS AND GENERAL APPLICATIONS

FORTRAN IV FOR BUSINESS AND GENERAL APPLICATIONS

HARICE L. SEEDS
Los Angeles City College

JOHN WILEY & SONS, INC.
NEW YORK
LONDON
SYDNEY
TORONTO

Library of Congress Cataloging in Publication Data:

Seeds, Harice L

FORTRAN IV for business and general applications.

Includes index.

1. FORTRAN (Computer program language) 2. Electronic data processing—Business.
I. Title.
HF5548.5.F2S344   001.6′424   74-34058
ISBN 0-471-77109-0

Printed in the United States of America

10-9 8 7 6 5 4

Preface

The FORTRAN language is a tool for solving problems. Its versatility, especially as developed in the version known as FORTRAN IV, is limited only by the imagination of its users. Many computer languages have been developed in recent years for special purposes, but FORTRAN IV remains one that is applicable to a wide variety of purposes. It is also the most common computer language and is found on almost all digital computers.

Manufacturers, software companies, and other businesses are becoming more and more aware of FORTRAN's usefulness. They see advantages in the comparatively short initial learning period required for programmers. They also see that less time is needed for developing individual programs because less coding and fewer commands are required than in the traditional business languages.

This book deals mainly with business problems, but students in the social sciences, humanities, and other nonmathematical disciplines will find it useful and easy to understand. Laymen's terms explain concepts that are too often hidden in technical jargon. Technical terms are introduced and explained as they are used so that students will become familiar with them. Each new concept is presented as simply as possible, both as a separate development and in relation to its use with other FORTRAN capabilities.

This is accomplished partly by presenting a programming problem that begins as a card-to-printer listing and develops through several additions into various billing programs for a business firm. The programs incorporate most of the features of business data processing and of FORTRAN IV. Although other applications are also developed, the concentration on one basic program enables the student to see the new, increased capabilities most advantageously. It also enables him to compare and contrast FORTRAN IV techniques by seeing different solutions to the same basic problem.

Another unique feature of program development is the consistent use of card layout forms, printer spacing charts, and flowcharts. These programmer aids show the student the various considerations involved in commercial programming and the necessity for complete documentation.

Several programming assignments follow each programming chapter. All assignments demonstrate the instruction being studied as it is encountered in actual programming, and they were carefully developed to require only the FORTRAN IV capabilities already studied. Although the assignments are realistic, they are purposely simple so that the student can develop and execute several programs during the course.

A list of chapter objectives introduces each chapter. Review questions are interspersed throughout the chapters for study checkpoints. At the end of each chapter, just before the programming assignments, students are asked to review the chapter objectives. Thus the objectives not only introduce the FORTRAN capability but also are a chapter summary and an aid for review.

When the FORTRAN IV language is studied concurrently with, or follows, a general computer science or business data processing course, Chapters 1 and 2, which are introductory, can be skipped and programming can be introduced immediately. When the instructor introduces the FORTRAN language, he can start with either Chapter 3 or Chapter 5. Chapter 3 explains and develops a short, complete FORTRAN IV program to input and output data. Chapter 4 extends this program so that unlimited amounts of data can be read and printed. Chapter 5, on the other hand, concentrates on literals in printed output.

The study of Chapter 5 before Chapters 3 and 4 enables the student to write programs at the first class meeting. He becomes familiar with computer output before encountering the intricacies of field specifications. Thus he has high enthusiasm from seeing the results of his programming efforts so quickly, and this interest extends into the study of the more complicated concepts of Chapter 3. The student also learns many aspects of formatting while at the height of his enthusiasm. This is a distinct advantage because report form is important in business data processing. The book's flexibility allows the instructor to choose the approaches that he prefers.

The arrangement of FORTRAN IV instructions and the importance placed on actual programming exercises give students a usable tool no matter how far the course extends. For business survey courses or for general education classes, this is particularly valuable. By the time the student has completed Chapter 11, he can program any FORTRAN IV problem, although the program may be longer than it will be when all of the language capabilities are learned. He also knows what tasks computers can perform. This is an educational requirement not only for businessmen but for all laymen in the 1970s.

Harice L. Seeds

Contents

FORTRAN IV FOR BUSINESS AND GENERAL APPLICATIONS

Chapter Objectives

1. Understand the difference between computer hardware and computer software.
2. Recognize the basic elements of computer systems and the functions of each element.
3. Know the interrelationships and differences among characters, fields, records, and files.
4. Know the differences between machine and assembly languages and compiler languages.
5. Know the difference between program compilation and program execution.

1

Introduction to Programming

FORTRAN is a language that requires very little knowledge of the inner manipulations of a computer. The FORTRAN language itself takes care of most of the details a computer requires. Some computer knowledge helps, however, in understanding terms and procedures, and most people who are interested in programming want to know how the computer accomplishes its amazing feats. Therefore this introductory chapter presents an overview of (1) the computer, (2) data as stored and used by computers, and (3) the development of computers and computer programming languages. Each of these topics is presented briefly to introduce the reader to basic concepts of computer development and to initiate him to computer-oriented vocabulary terms. Each computer concept has many aspects. Books ranging from easily understood laymen's language to highly technical terminology are available if the reader wishes to explore these aspects more fully.

Computer Hardware

In computer terminology, the physical equipment or devices of a computer are called *hardware*. Computer programs of instructions are called *software*. A quick survey of computer hardware and software provides background for a study of the FORTRAN language.

FORTRAN IV is the most modern version of the FORTRAN language. Programs in FORTRAN IV can be processed by virtually all modern computers, such as IBM S/360, S/370, 1130, and System 3 computers, Xerox, Burroughs, CDC, and Univac computers. These are virtually all third- and fourth-generation computers that can perform intricate manipulations unknown to earlier computers.

The word computer gives the impression of one machine. Actually, *computer system* is a more accurate term because computers consist of several devices. Each device is a machine consisting of its own electronic circuitry but connected to the other computer equipment.

Computer systems vary in size according to manufacturer, series, model, and amount of storage. Their physical shapes differ, depending upon which equipment is utilized. Some devices may not even be physically in the same area as the rest of the system. They may be a few feet away (in the next office or upstairs, for example) or they may be hundreds of miles away from the central system.

REVIEW QUESTIONS

1. In computer terminology, what is computer equipment called?
2. Why is the term "computer system" more accurate than the word computer?
3. What factors determine the physical appearance of a computer?

Central Processing Unit

Because physical appearance can differ so widely, Figure 1 demonstrates the way computers function regardless of specific devices.

Of all parts of a computer, the *Central Processing Unit* (CPU) performs the greatest number and the greatest variety of tasks. It is one

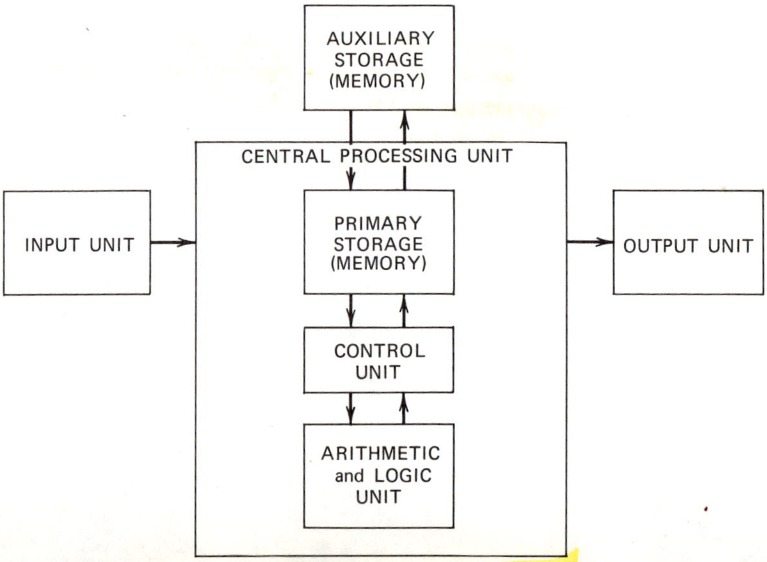

Figure 1 Schematic diagram of computer systems.

piece of equipment, but it contains the Arithmetic-Logic Unit, the Control Unit, and primary storage. The "face" or front of the CPU is a visual display unit called the *console*. By its lights, the console gives information to the operator about operations being performed by the computer. Many of the dials, switches, and keys on the console can be used by the operator to give operational instructions to the CPU itself. Thus, in a special way, the Central Processing Unit is also an input/output device.

The most essential parts of the CPU, however, are within it. The *arithmetic-logic* section performs the basic arithmetic processes of addition and subtraction, multiplication and division. (Technically, multiplication and division are variations of addition and subtraction.) No matter how complicated mathematical calculations are, computers break them down to these arithmetic processes. The Arithmetic-Logic Unit of the CPU also stores (briefly), shifts, and transfers data. It compares data and makes decisions that depend upon whether the two compared items are equal or unequal. This last process of comparing and branching is the essence of "logical" operations.

The *control section* of the CPU is the computer's "traffic manager." The Control Unit coordinates the interaction between units of the computer. It directs the order by which operations will be performed. It also determines when input/output devices will transmit and when data will be transferred to and from storage.

Storage in the CPU (and on disk in fourth-generation virtual storage computers) is often termed "main" or "primary" memory. Until the late 1960s, primary storage usually consisted of magnetic cores. These are tiny iron rings (Figure 2). They can be magnetized in millionths of a second, and they keep the magnetism until it is deliberately changed. The cores are either "on" (magnetized clockwise usually) or "off" (magnetized counterclockwise usually).

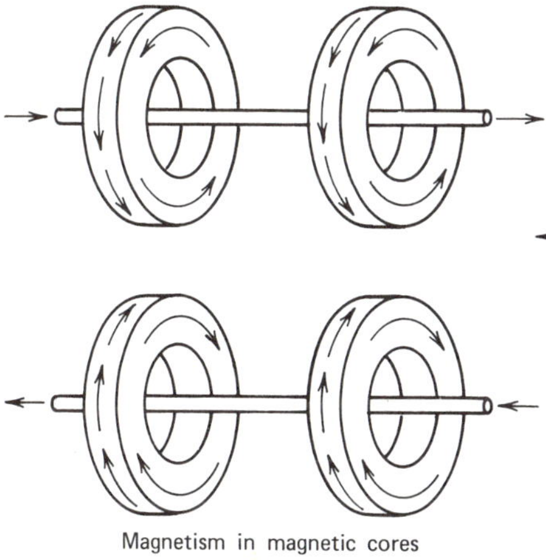

Magnetism in magnetic cores

Two half—currents activate a core

Figure 2 Binary states of magnetic core.

These states of magnetic core are binary because only two conditions are possible: clockwise or counterclockwise, "on" or "off," 1 or 0. Thus the clockwise/counterclockwise or on/off state of a core in memory is represented numerically by a binary digit, either 0 or 1. In discussing computer storage, 0 represents the off condition, and 1 represents the on condition. Such discussions frequently refer to binary digits as "bits."

Today most primary storage is composed of miniaturized circuitry. Although more difficult to visualize than core, its components also utilize the principle of binary conditions and are represented by binary digits.

REVIEW QUESTIONS

4. Which part of a computer performs the greatest number and greatest variety of tasks?
5. What is the "face" or front of the CPU called?
6. What does the control unit coordinate?
7. Which part of the CPU performs addition, subtraction, multiplication and division?

Auxiliary Storage Units

Additional storage units increase the memory capacity of a computer. They usually are called *auxiliary* or *secondary storage*. Storage that is separate from the CPU takes many forms, but each uses the binary principle. That is, a spot either is or is not magnetized; a punch either is or is not present. Punched paper tape, magnetic tape, magnetic disk, magnetic drum, and magnetic strips in data cells are all forms of auxiliary storage. So are punched data cards. Each form needs its own special "reader" or drive. However, an installation can use different devices in any combination that is deemed best for its own jobs.

Before information in auxiliary storage can be utilized, however, it must be transferred into the primary storage area of the Central Processing Unit. Only in the CPU can any processing except input/output occur. Figure 3 shows the devices and media that are most frequently used for auxiliary storage.

REVIEW QUESTIONS

8. Name three types of auxiliary storage.
9. What is the meaning of a "binary" condition?
10. How is all computer storage a form of binary states or conditions?
11. Where must data be stored before they can be processed?

Input/Output Devices

Input/output devices all have the same purpose: to get information into or out of the Central Processing Unit. Computer programs fre-

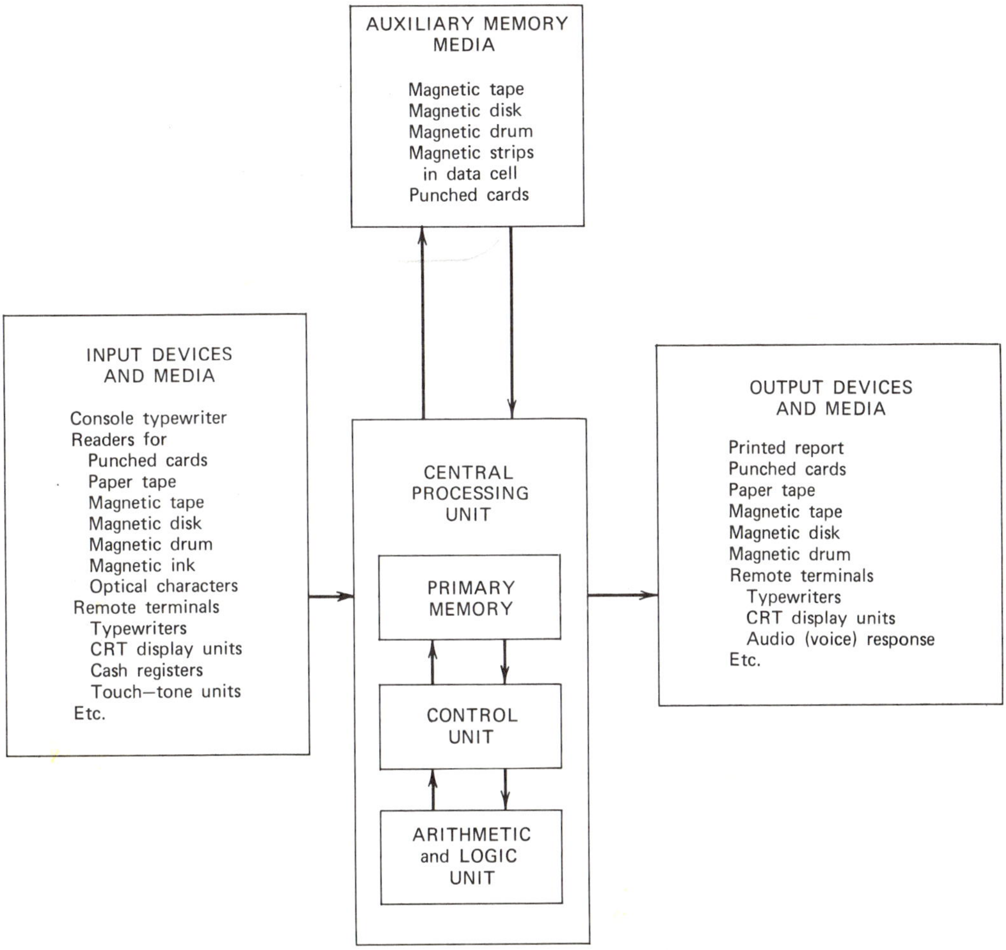

Figure 3 *Devices and media in computer systems.*

quently print reports, but computer output is increasingly intended for later use as input for another computer program. The most common medium that can be both input and output is still punched cards. The uses of magnetic tape and magnetic disks are growing, however, because they require little handling and are fast in operation. Storage on magnetic tapes, magnetic disks and drums, and in data cells also takes far less space than card storage does.

The most dramatic advances in recent computer development involve such input/output devices as voice recognition units, optical character scanners for handwritten or printed characters, microfilm printers, and cathode ray tube (CRT) display units that look like small television screens. No matter what medium is used, however, every input device must perform the task of transmitting data that the CPU can utilize finally in machine-understandable (binary) form, and every output device must transmit from binary form into human-understandable or machine-understandable form.

Many input/output media, such as punched cards or magnetic tape, are auxiliary storage until the data records are required for input.

Characters, Fields, Records, and Files

The basic element of computer input or output is called a *record*. It is all the information related to one subject. That subject can be an inventory item, a customer, or an employee, for example. A record can be a punched card report of a purchased item, a line of print in a payroll report, or data input or output on a magnetic tape or disk. Minimum and maximum record lengths depend on the input or output medium (card, tape, disk, etc.) transmitting the data.

A record is made up of one or more pieces of information called data fields or simply *fields*. A punched card record, for instance, could contain the identifying number, price, and quantity of an item for sale. Each of these three units of information related to the sale item is a numeric field. *Numeric fields* contain only numeric characters. That is, they can contain only numbers, plus or minus signs, and decimal points. Dollar signs and commas cannot be part of a FORTRAN numeric field. If a sign is not part of a numeric field, the field is assumed to be positive.

If the name of an item is present, that field is *alphameric*. This means that its characters can be alphabetic, numeric or special characters. FORTRAN alphabetic characters include not only all the letters of the English alphabet, but also the dollar sign ($). *Special characters* include everything else in the computer printer set of characters, such as punctuation marks, symbols like the percentage sign (%) and ampersand (&), and the blank (usually signified in writing as b̸). Alphameric fields have many special capabilities as well as special rules in FORTRAN. These are discussed and demonstrated at considerable length throughout the text.

Fields are always part of a record. A collection of records is called a *file*. Time cards for all employees form a time card file. A magnetic tape or disk with all customers' names and addresses is a file. A printed report is an output file to the computer. Ordinarily, a business program processes one complete file of records.

REVIEW QUESTIONS

12. What are the basic purposes of input/output devices?
13. Why are magnetic tapes and magnetic disks used increasingly?
14. What is a record?
15. What is a field?
16. What is the difference between a numeric and an alphameric field?
17. What is a file?

Bytes

A number, letter, or special character ordinarily takes one column in a punched card or one print position on a printed report. In IBM S/360 and S/370 and System 3 computers, and in other third- and fourth-generation computers, a character occupies one byte of computer storage. These computers are often called "8-bit byte" computers because each character is represented by 1 byte consisting of 8 bits or binary digits.[1] These bits are the numeric representations of magnetic core or other units of computer storage that have only 2 possible states: "off" (0) or "on" (1). Fortunately for the FORTRAN programmer he rarely needs to be aware of these internal storage details. He should know that the storage unit for a character is a byte since the term is often used in discussions.

Software

In order to utilize the capabilities of a computer, a person must analyze his problem to see how a computer can solve it. Then he must instruct the machine to do the required processing. At first, such instructions were wired into a computer, and only data were "read" by an input device so that it could be stored and processed.

Not long after electronic computers were first in operation, however, the great mathematician John von Neumann observed that computer memories could store not only data but programs of instructions as well. His "stored program concept" developed into series of instructions stored in computer memory to manipulate data also stored in the computer. Each group of instructions is called a computer program, and each program normally processes a data file.[2] Thus two separate kinds of input are entered into computer storage: (1) instructions to the computer and (2) data that the computer will process by directions given in the program of instructions.

Today these programs can be very complex. They can be written by the computer installation personnel or a programming service bureau, or they can be supplied by the computer manufacturer. The computer's own programs of operating instructions and procedures are usually called the *supervisor* or *nucleus*. These programs ordinarily are supplied by computer manufacturers or software specialists.

Although industrywide agreement has not been reached about

[1]Nine bits actually make up each byte, but the "parity" or self-checking bit is known only to the computer. So programmers refer only to the 8 bits with which they work.

[2]Such mathematical programs as creating random numbers or searching for prime numbers are usually performed without input data, however.

whether or not to include user application programs, the term software generally refers to professionally prepared stored programs of instructions.

Machine Language

Instructions in the early stored programs were given in numeric form. The programmer gave decimal number instructions that the computer easily translated into usable binary form. An instruction usually consisted of two or three numeric parts, representing an arithmetic or manipulating operation and one or two addresses in computer storage. In this "machine language," which was different for almost every kind of computer, the number 4 might represent the instruction to add one field to another field. The complete instruction could be:

```
4    105    207
```

This machine language instruction directs the computer to add (4) data beginning at position 105 of computer storage to data beginning in storage position 207.

The machine languages were a big step above wired instructions, but every tiny detail had to be programmed, the instructions were difficult to remember, and the language varied with each computer.

Assembler Languages

Computers respond quickly to numeric commands, but human beings have difficulty remembering the numeric symbols. This situation was eased when the programmers writing instructions for the computer substituted a letter for the numeric operation code in an instruction. For instance, instead of

```
4    105    207
```

the instruction could be

```
A    105    207
```

This was a big advance in programming because letters meaningful to humans, such as A for *add,* are more easily remembered than numbers. For the computer, the translation from A to 4 to the binary digits required only a little extra preliminary instructions.

Next came the realization that alphabetic characters can represent more than just operation codes. Instead of being limited to the actual numeric storage addresses, programmers can use names or labels as addresses in storage. Data fields can be referred to by such humanly meaningful names as BONUS or PAY instead of being addressed by their numeric locations in storage. For example, the instruction

```
A    BONUS    PAY
```

adds data from the two storage locations labeled BONUS and PAY.

In order to convert the alphabetic operation codes and data field labels to their numeric addresses, the computer must already have stored instructions on how to perform the conversions. A large program, called an *assembler,* translates or converts the operation codes and labeled fields into the numeric commands required by the computer.

Assembly language instructions are in a 1-to-1 ratio with machine language commands. This means that one assembly language command translates into one machine language command. Assembly languages were an important step in the development of computer programming, but their detailed instructions and rigid requirements demand great time and care in both logic development and instruction writing.

REVIEW QUESTIONS

18. What is a byte?
19. What is computer software?
20. Why do programmers rarely write in machine languages?
21. What is meant by the statement that machine and assembly language commands have a 1-to-1 ratio?

Compiler Languages

After assembly (or symbolic programming) languages were established, programmers began to develop highly sophisticated sets of commands for converting instructions. These conversion programs usually are called *compilers,* although there are also generators, which have certain technical differences. Like assemblers, compilers convert or translate statements understood by humans into machine commands that a computer can execute. Compiler language instructions, however, are closer to the English language than to machine language. This is largely possible because compiler language instructions are not on a 1-to-1 ratio with machine language commands. One compiler language instruction generates several machine language commands, so that there is a 1-to-several ratio. This also means that the programmer need not worry about most of the internal computer movements since the compiler is assuming those details. Therefore compiler language programming is much easier and faster than assembler or machine language programming.

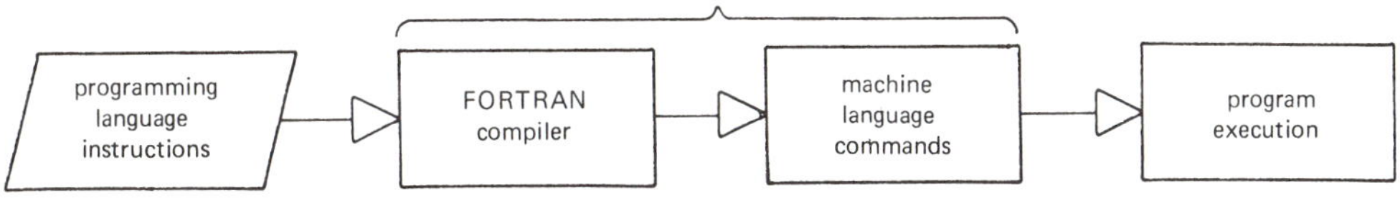

Figure 4

Because new tasks are constantly being found for computers, and because people differ about the best way to develop computer languages, many different compilers have been designed and are in use today. Some compiler languages are designed primarily for scientific use, others mainly for business reports. Some languages are developed for general computer usage; others are meant for limited, special computer tasks. Almost all are written so that they can be used on many different computers, regardless of the specific machine language of the computer. The most common, and therefore best known, compiler languages are FORTRAN, COBOL, ALGOL, PL/I, RPG (with a generator rather than a compiler), APL, and BASIC. They all have elaborate sets of instructions so that the programmer can easily utilize a computer's power and versatility.

Nonmachine languages, particularly compiler and generator languages, are often referred to as "source" languages. Source languages, except for assembly languages, frequently are divided into two categories: problem-oriented languages and procedure-oriented languages. In *procedure-oriented languages,* the programmer develops his program according to the types of tasks that the computer is to perform. For instance, the first instructions might describe all the forms of data to be fed to the computer by punched cards, paper tape, magnetic tape, or magnetic disk, during any part of the program. These are all covered by the general term "input." The next instructions detail all calculations that are to be performed on any of the data fields during any part of the program. Last might be specifications for all data printed, punched, or otherwise output by a device of the computer. All instructions are grouped by procedural divisions of input, calculations, and output. The compiler or generator translates these procedure-oriented instructions into machine commands that are to be executed in the computer's actual order of procedures. COBOL and RPG are both procedure-oriented languages.

In *problem-oriented languages,* such as FORTRAN, the programmer arranges instructions basically in the order by which they are to be executed. An instruction for reading occurs when the program needs input information. Calculations are described when the logic of the problem requires these calculations. Output instructions are given when information is to be printed, punched, or otherwise output. Ordinarily input, output, and calculation instructions are interspersed throughout the entire problem-oriented language program.

REVIEW QUESTIONS

22. What is a source language?
23. What are the advantages of compiler languages over machine or assembler languages?
24. What are the two basic categories of compiler or generator languages?
25. Name three compiler languages.

Program Compilation and Execution

In both problem- and procedure-oriented languages, a successful program goes through two phases. The first phase is called program *compilation.* In this phase the compiler checks the instructions for errors in the language rules. Logic of the programmer's instructions cannot be checked, but each instruction is analyzed to make certain that it does not break any rules of the computer language. If no serious errors are found, the source language instructions are converted into machine language commands. These machine language commands, called the *object program,* are the output of the compiler program. This object program may simply be stored by the computer until after completion of the second phase of the program, or it can be punched by the computer into cards, now called an object deck, and saved for later processing.

The second phase is *execution* of the program. During this phase, records are input, calculations are performed, and reports are output. In business programs particularly, execution time is often seen as a series of cycles, one for each data record processed. Execution may begin either immediately after an errorless compilation or after submitting a previously punched object deck. The first method is used when a program is being developed and tested. The second method cuts the time of production runs. Figure 5 shows the process from problem identification to solution.

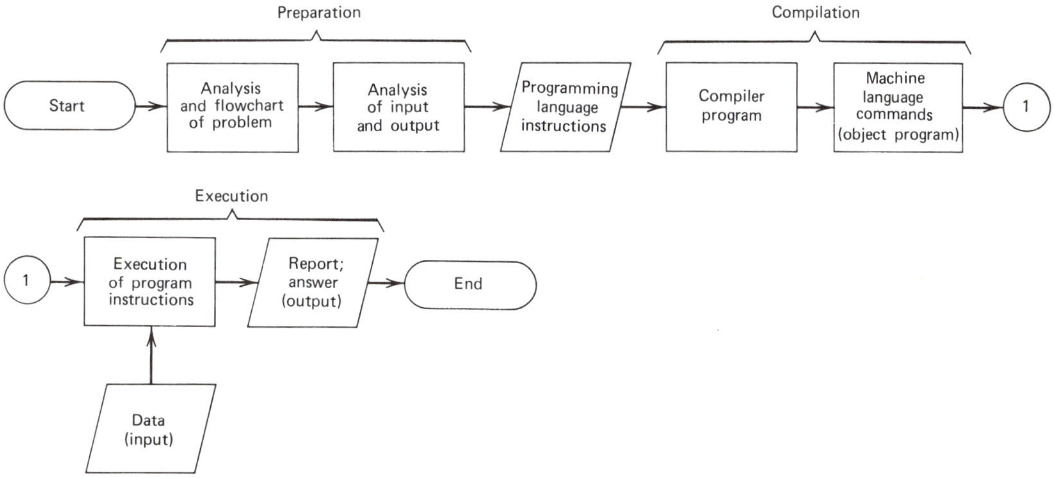

Figure 5

Error Detection

If programming language errors are found during the compilation phase, the compiler outputs explanatory messages. If an error is so serious that the compiler cannot ignore or accommodate to it, the program terminates without entering the second phase. Even during the execution phase the compiler can detect other types of errors. Again error messages are printed to aid the programmer, and sometimes the program is terminated before execution is completed.

Even when the computer gives no error messages and the entire program is processed, a programmer should check his results carefully. Faulty logic in problem solving can create a technically acceptable program that does not do what the programmer really wants. Sometimes the computer gives an answer, but not to the question the programmer intended to ask. This program checking process is called "debugging." It is an important step that should not be overlooked. Thus, programming consists of analyzing a problem, developing the input and desired output, instructing the computer how to solve the problem, and then checking the output to make certain that the problem was both analyzed and solved correctly with the output in the required form.

REVIEW QUESTIONS

26. What occurs during program compilation?
27. What occurs during program execution?

OBJECTIVES REVIEW

Study the objectives at the beginning of this chapter. Check each one to be certain you have achieved it. Restudy the chapter sections related to any objective that you cannot perform.

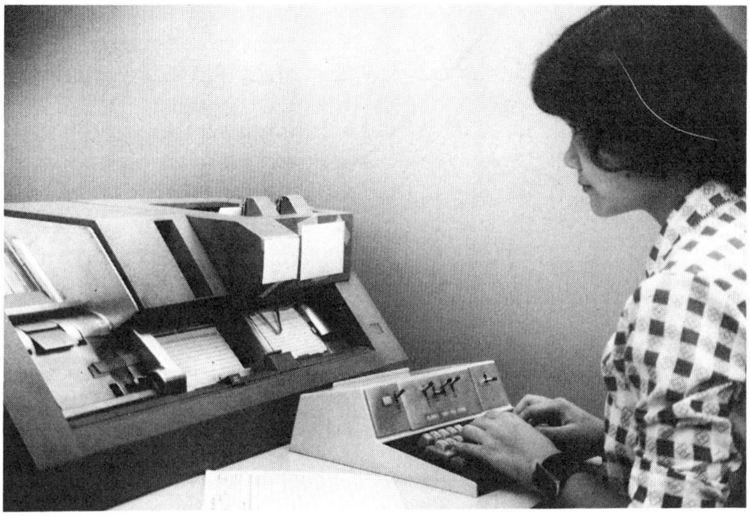

IBM 29 Keypunch. Commonly used to prepare FORTRAN instructions (and data) for computer.

Chapter Objectives

1. Be able to read a flowchart for a card-to-printer program.
2. Be able to draw a flowchart for a card-to-printer program.
3. Be able to read a card layout form to input numeric fields.
4. Be able to draw a card layout form with numeric fields.
5. Be able to read a printer spacing chart with numeric fields.
6. Be able to design a printer spacing chart with numeric fields.

2[1]

Programming Preliminaries: Flowcharts, Printer Spacing Charts, and Card Layout Forms

When a program is very simple, a programmer can easily analyze his problem and know how his program can solve it. Because FORTRAN is a problem-oriented language, the sequence or order in which instructions should be arranged is easily seen. As problems become more complex, however, the analysis of a problem and the logical development of instructions become more difficult. Yet a programmer must understand exactly what he wants his program to do before he begins writing the program instructions. He must know the type and form of information (data) to be input, and the kind of output wanted. He must also be aware of all the processing needed to achieve that output.

Various techniques and devices have been developed to help the programmer in these preliminary steps. The most universally accepted are the multiple-card layout form, the printer spacing chart, and the flowchart. All of these aids are used and explained in programs developed in this book.

Introduction to the Program

The first demonstration program is a card-to-printer listing. This means that certain information is read from one data card and then the same information is printed. This type of short program can print inventories, lists, and other data stored on punched cards. With only slight

[1]If the instructor wants students to write and submit computer programs as soon as possible, Chapter 5, Literals in FORMAT Statements, can be studied before Chapter 2 or before Chapter 3.

changes in the program instructions, the input and/or output could be on other media such as paper tape, magnetic tape, or magnetic disk.

The program is for a utility company. A punched data card contains customer identification number, meter reading of the previous month, and meter reading for the current month. The same fields are output on the computer printer.

The program is developed step by step. First, input fields are represented on a multiple card layout form. Next, the printed report form is developed on a printer spacing chart. The problem of how to obtain the output is analyzed and flowcharted. In actual practice, these preliminary tasks are often developed concurrently, but they should all be completed before the FORTRAN program instructions are written.

The card-to-printer FORTRAN program introduces READ, WRITE, and FORMAT statements. STOP, CALL EXIT, and END statements are also demonstrated. Comment cards provide documentation by explaining the instructions. The sequence of instructions in FORTRAN programs and the differences between comment statements and regular FORTRAN statements are explained. Integer and real numbers are illustrated and defined.

After instructions are written on a FORTRAN coding sheet, they must be keypunched into cards. Then the program and the data cards are submitted together to the computer for processing.

The card layout form, printer spacing chart, sample input data, computer listing of instructions, and the printed report are all presented as they are developed for the utility company program. Listings that contain typical errors of keypunching and programming are also shown. In this way, students learn to recognize common types of errors and error messages so that they can correct their own programs.

Program Input

Sometimes the programmer is given data in a form he must follow. For example, data fields and their placement are established if information is already on data cards or magnetic tape or disk. At other times, however, data are being gathered for the first time. Then the programmer often helps in designing the data card. In either situation, however, the fields to be read and their placement on the record must be known before program instructions can be written.

As soon as the data card fields are known, the programmer draws their size and location on a multiple card layout form, available from most computer manufacturers and forms manufacturers. The data card for the first program contains three fields to be stored: customer identification number in columns 1-5, meter reading of the previous month in columns 30-35, and current meter reading in columns 38-43. The fields are on the completed layout form for the data card:

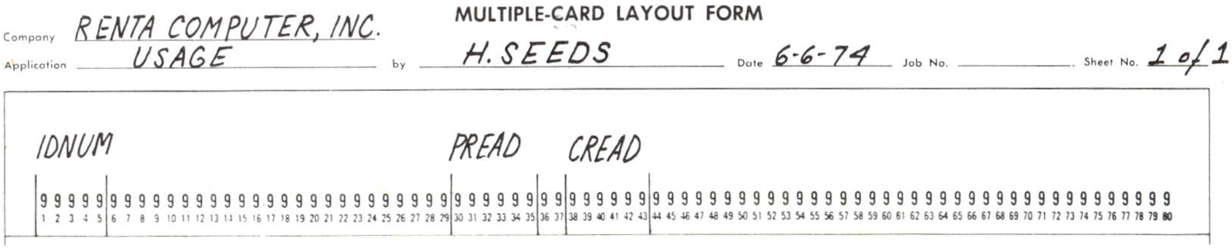

Decimal points are not punched in the meter reading fields of the data card. Instead, the usual business practice of saving space in input records by omitting decimal points is followed. The decimal points are implied by the FORTRAN instructions.

The multiple card layout form serves a double purpose. First, it aids the programmer by representing the data while the program is being written, and, second, it documents the program for later reference.

To illustrate the relationship between layout forms and data cards, a sample card illustrates the layout form:

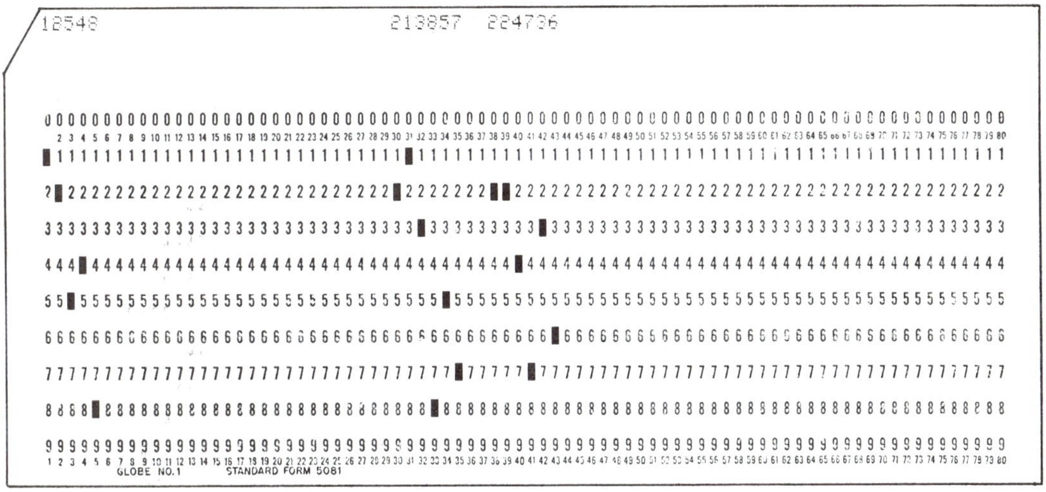

The numbers 12548, punched in columns 1-5, are the customer identification number; digits 213857 (representing 2138.57), in columns 30-35, are the previous month's meter reading; digits 224736 (representing 2247.36), in columns 38-43, are the current meter reading. Other columns may or may not contain other information, but only the three fields listed in the READ statement are stored.

REVIEW QUESTIONS

1. What information is on a completed multiple card layout form?
2. For what two purposes should the multiple card layout form be used?
3. What is the purpose of a card-to-printer computer program?

Program Output

The programmer must next decide about the appearance of the printed report. He must know the fields to be printed on each line of the report, and the spacing between lines of the report.

To help arrange printed output in the desired form, printer spacing charts are issued by virtually all computer manufacturers. Printer spacing charts establish the positions of data to be printed and indicate the spacing between printed lines. Thus they help programmers attain the desired appearance of the printed report.

Each line of the chart represents one line on the printer paper. Numbers at the top of the chart indicate print positions across the paper. The total number of print positions is determined by the paper being used and by the model of printer.

The programmer for the utility company decides on the following output form:

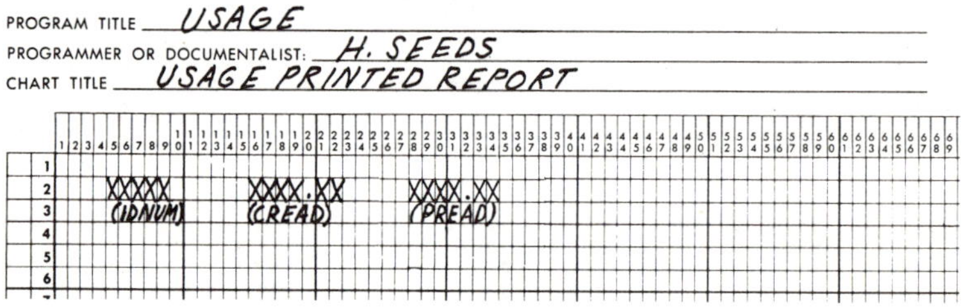

Customer identification number will be in print positions 5-9. Current meter reading will be in print positions 16-22. Previous month's meter reading will be in print positions 28-34.

REVIEW QUESTIONS

4. How is a printer spacing chart used?
5. What does each line of a printer spacing chart represent?

Flowcharting

Flowcharting is a technique for representing the solution of a problem in picture form.[1] When correctly used, a flowchart is doubly useful because (1) it is a picture of the logical analysis and development of a program the computer is to execute, and (2) it is a record of that process.

Figure 6 shows the standard symbols utilized in program flowcharting. Although minor variations occur in symbol definitions, most templates now contain symbols conforming to the International Organization for Standardization (IOS) Draft Recommendation on

[1]IBM manual C20-8152 deals solely with the techniques of flowcharting. It is an excellent reference for in-depth study of flowcharting.

Flowchart Symbols for Information Processing, and consistent with the fewer symbols adopted by the U.S.A. Standards Institute (USASI). These groups have issued standard *system* flowcharting symbols also, but they are not included since that subject is beyond the scope of this book.

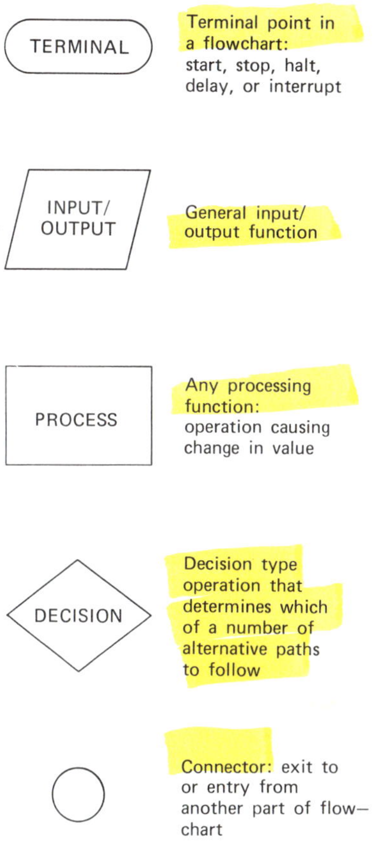

Figure 6 Basic program flowcharting symbols.

A flowchart is read by first locating the terminal symbol labeled BEGIN or START.

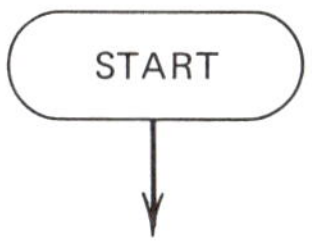

Arrows indicate the flow or movement of the program from symbol to symbol. If an arrow leads to a connector symbol containing only a number, letter, or name, another connector symbol with that same number, letter, or name must be found with an arrow leading from it to another stop in the program. There the program continues.

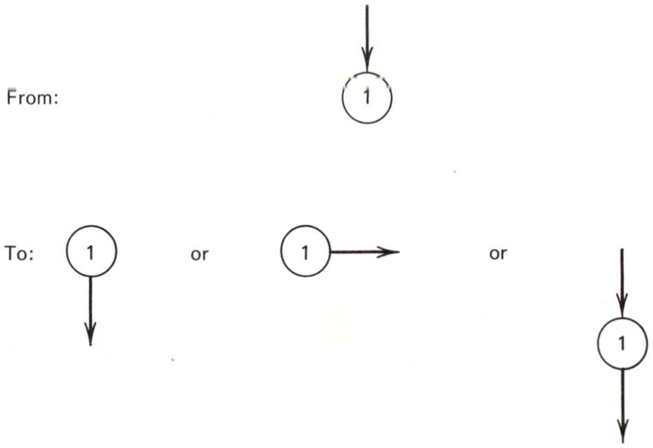

The arrow-directed paths are followed until HALT, STOP, or END is encountered in a terminal symbol.

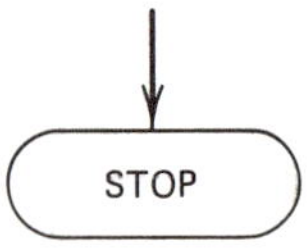

Any path that does not lead to a HALT, STOP, or END symbol reveals an error in program logic. If a program follows such a flowchart and the computer processes until the point of error, it does not know how to proceed. It has no instructions to follow. Depending on the type of error and the computer model, it either prints an error message or just "sits" in a state of idling. If there is no point of error where the program stops, another type of flowcharting error might send the program into an endless search for a termination point. Thus the flowchart not only provides documentation; it also aids the programmer in finding and correcting possible logic errors.

Flowcharting templates are readily available, and one of the student's preliminary steps in all assignments should be the development of a program flowchart.

REVIEW QUESTIONS

6. What is the purpose of a printer spacing chart?
7. What is a flowchart?
8. What are two basic reasons for developing a flowchart?

Flowcharting the Program

The first program reads three fields from a data card and then prints the same three fields on the computer printer. Only two flowcharting symbols are required to flowchart this problem. They are the terminal and input/output symbols. Two versions of the problem, both acceptable, illustrate differing views of the amount of detail to be included in a flowchart:

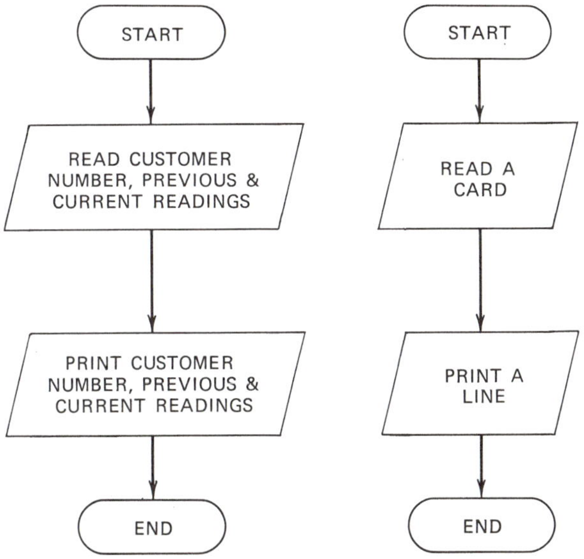

Terminal symbols show the beginning and end of the program. The first input/output symbol indicates that customer identification number, previous meter reading, and current meter reading will be input to the computer. The second input/output symbol shows the same three fields output by the computer. As the rightmost flowchart demonstrates, input and output fields are not always identified in flowcharts. The amount of detail drawn is a matter of personal or instructor preference.

A flowchart is usually drawn on one or more sheets of paper for documentary purposes. Often a short description of the program appears on the same sheet. This description usually is developed before, or together with, the flowchart, but in final documentation form, the program description appears either on a separate page or just below the flowchart. An example of this type of documentation is the following description of the first program:

> This program inputs customer number, meter reading for the previous month, and meter reading for the current month from a punched data card. The three fields are then output on the computer printer.

This type of descriptive explanation should be brief enough to be read quickly but detailed enough to be meaningful to the original programmer or to another programmer at a later time. Sometimes the program description is also keypunched into comment cards and placed at the beginning of the source deck so that documentation is always present when the program is listed by the computer printer.

REVIEW QUESTIONS

9. What is the name of the flowcharting symbol that indicates the beginning or end of a program? What is its shape?
10. What is the name of the flowcharting symbol that indicates a card is to be read or a line is to be printed? What is its shape?
11. Why is a descriptive summary often placed with the problem flowchart?

Coding Forms

When the programmer is satisfied that the input and the output data are well organized, and that the program logic is both accurate and complete, he is ready to write the FORTRAN program instructions. These are written on FORTRAN coding forms. Each line on the coding sheet represents one punched *program* card. That is, each line of the coding sheet must be keypunched into a separate punched card. These program cards constitute the program, or source language, deck. They are not to be confused with *data* cards. Data cards contain the information that the computer will process according to the program instructions. Data can also be input from paper tape, magnetic tape, magnetic disk, or other devices, but punched data cards are still so common that they are utilized in most of the demonstration programs. When programmers want to use different input media, changes required in FORTRAN instructions are minor.

Several varieties of FORTRAN coding sheets are available from computer manufacturers and from suppliers of computer paper. Figure 7 is a typical FORTRAN coding form. Numbers above the first line indicate the corresponding card columns. As the coding sheet illustrates, FORTRAN forms set off columns 1-5, 6, 7-72, and 73-80 into four separate areas.

Columns 1-5; Statement Numbers

Columns 1-5 contain statement numbers. Many FORTRAN statements do not require a statement number, but almost all FORTRAN statements *can* be numbered. Statement numbers, which are called

23
COLUMNS 1-5:
STATEMENT
NUMBERS

Figure 7

"labels" in FORTRAN compiler messages to the programmer, are keypunched anywhere within these columns.

Any number from 1 to 99999 can be used so long as it is not used as a statement number for another statement in the same program. Two identical labels would be as confusing as the same street address for two different places in the same town.

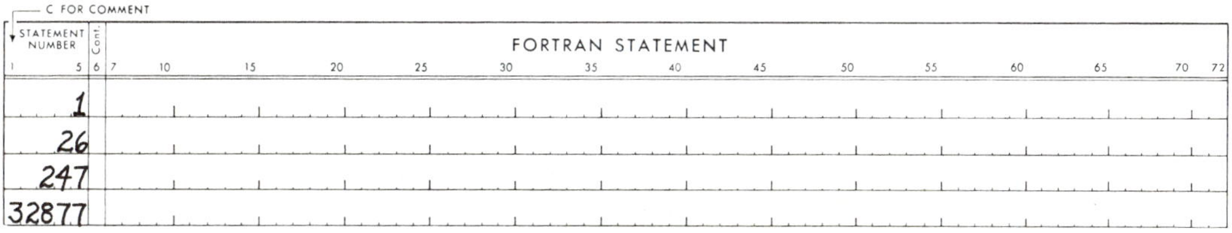

Statements are often numbered for the programmer's convenience. In case a deck of program cards falls, the programmer can reassemble statements quickly and accurately if they are numbered in sequence. Insofar as the computer is concerned, however, statements need not be numbered sequentially. In fact, FORTRAN statements require numbers only when other FORTRAN statements refer to them. For example, input and output statements refer to FORMAT statements, as you will soon discover. Therefore, FORMAT statements always must be numbered so that the computer will know which FORMAT statement is being referenced. If the program is to branch to a certain statement, that statement must be numbered. Special rules about statement numbering are given as they are encountered.

Sometimes column 1 performs a special function in a program card. When cards in a program only document or comment upon a program, they are not numbered. Instead, card column 1 contains the letter C, indicating that the card is a comment statement rather than an instruction.

C FOR COMMENT

STATEMENT NUMBER (1–5)	Cont. (6)	FORTRAN STATEMENT (7–72)
C		THIS PROGRAM INPUTS CUSTOMER IDENTIFICATION NUMBER (IDNUM).

The usefulness of this feature is illustrated further in the section on Comment Statements in the next chapter.

Column 6: Continuation of Instruction

Ordinarily in FORTRAN statements, column 6 must be blank. A character in column 6 indicates that a card continues the instruction of the previous card.

C FOR COMMENT

STATEMENT NUMBER (1–5)	Cont. (6)	FORTRAN STATEMENT (7–72)
1		READ (5,2) NUMBER, RATE, HOURS, FICAYD, BONUS, COMISH, DEPEND,
	/	TAXRAT, RETIRE, AID

Most computers accept any character except zero or blank as a continuation signal in column 6. Comment cards cannot be continued, however. The letter C must be punched in the first column of every comment card.

Columns 7-72: FORTRAN Instruction

Columns 7-72 contain the actual FORTRAN statement or instruction.

1–5	6	7–72
	6	READ (5,7) IDNUM

A FORTRAN instruction can be punched anywhere within columns 7 and 72. This flexibility results from the fact that the FORTRAN compiler ignores program card blanks, except for special cases that will be explained as they occur. Some programmers begin their instructions in column 8 simply to decrease the chance of accidentally keypunching column 6.

Columns 73-80: Program Identification

Many FORTRAN coding forms have only one place for columns 73-80—at the top of the form. This practice developed because those columns usually are either blank or the same for all cards in the source deck. For example, the programmer might keypunch USAGE 74 or PAYROLL into columns 73-80 of every program card so that it can be easily identified.

Program		Graphic	Card Form #	Identification
Programmer	Date	Punch		USAGE 74 (73–80)

Sometimes columns 73-80 are not even shown on the form since they are punched only when the programmer wants his source deck identified.

Comment cards can utilize columns 73-80 either for comments or for program identification.

REVIEW QUESTIONS

12. A line on the coding form represents how many punched cards?
13. On FORTRAN instruction cards, columns 1-5 are used for what purpose?
14. When does column 1 have a special purpose? How is it fulfilled?
15. What is the special purpose of column 6? What characters may be used for this purpose?
16. FORTRAN instructions are contained within which card columns?
17. Program identification can be placed in which card columns?

OBJECTIVES REVIEW

Study the objectives at the beginning of this chapter. Check each one to be certain you have achieved it. Restudy the chapter sections that are related to any objective you cannot perform.

Chapter Objectives

1. Be able to write comment FORTRAN statements to document programs.
2. Be able to distinguish between integer and real (decimal) numeric fields.
3. Be able to write a READ statement to input integers, real numbers, and/or blank spaces from cards, tape, or sequential disk records.
4. Be able to write a WRITE statement to output integers, real numbers, and/or blank spaces for printer, card punch, tape, or sequential disk records.
5. Be able to write a FORMAT statement with I, F, and/or X format specifications.
6. Be able to distinguish between integer and real field names.

3

Comment, READ, WRITE, and FORMAT STATEMENTS

Comment Statements

FORTRAN programs are written with three basic types of statements: (1) comment statements, (2) executable instructions, and (3) nonexecutable or descriptive statements. Comment statements, the first type, are a special kind of nonexecutable statement. Comment statements are listed when the computer prints the program instructions, but they are not stored in the computer as other instructions are. Although comment statements are not required by the computer, they are valuable to programmers and employers for documentation. They explain a program or a program section so that it can be understood by others or remembered by the programmer later. Comments should be written as the program develops instead of waiting until it is perfected. Too often another program demands the programmer's attention then, and he never returns to document the earlier program.

Comment statements require the letter C in column 1, but then any number, letter, blank, or other special character can be in any other card column. Occasionally programmers are dismayed to find that the reverse is also true: if a C is keypunched accidentally into column 1, the FORTRAN statement in the rest of the card is treated as a comment, and is neither stored nor executed.

Unless discussion particularly applies to comment statements, they are not included in the term "FORTRAN statements" throughout this text. That term applies only to executable and nonexecutable statements that are stored by the computer.

In the first demonstration program, comment statements document both the full program and sections of the program. This use of comment cards guarantees that some documentation is always included with the program source deck. The first seven comment cards state the general purpose of the program, identify the programmer and the date of programming, and provide spacing for easier reading. They also give full explanations of field name abbreviations.

```
C THIS PROGRAM INPUTS CUSTOMER IDENTIFICATION NUMBER (IDNUM), METER
C READING FOR THE PREVIOUS MONTH (PREAD), AND METER READING FOR THE
C CURRENT MONTH (CREAD) FROM A PUNCHED DATA CARD. THE 3 FIELDS ARE THEN
C OUTPUT ON A PRINTER.
C
C PROGRAMMED BY H. SEEDS, JUNE 1974
C
```

Because the C in column 1 of each of these lines establishes it as a comment statement rather than an instruction, the message can begin in any column after the C. Many programmers find it best to begin either in columns 3 (as in the example) or 4, or to indent to columns 10-15. In all these instances, the eye can easily separate the comments from instructions when the computer prints the source program. The seven punched comment cards are shown in Figure 8.

Incidentally, the computer demands neither correct punctuation nor correct spelling in comment statements, but prospective employers are often interested in these features. They particularly appreciate good documentation because there is a high rate of turnover in programmer jobs, and employers are concerned about maintaining programs.

REVIEW QUESTIONS

1. What are the three basic types of FORTRAN statements?
2. What is the purpose of the two comment cards that are blank except for the C's in column 1?
3. In what other ways are comment statements valuable to programmers?
4. How are comment statements valuable to employers?

The READ Statement

When a programmer is ready to write the program instructions, he first studies the problem flowchart. Because the FORTRAN compiler takes care of "housekeeping" details that are often required in starting and ending programs in other languages, the FORTRAN programmer can concentrate on the problem logic between the terminal symbols.

In the card-to-printer demonstration program, the flowchart shows that the programmer must first instruct the computer to read a record and store three fields. (This could also be a tape or disk-to-printer

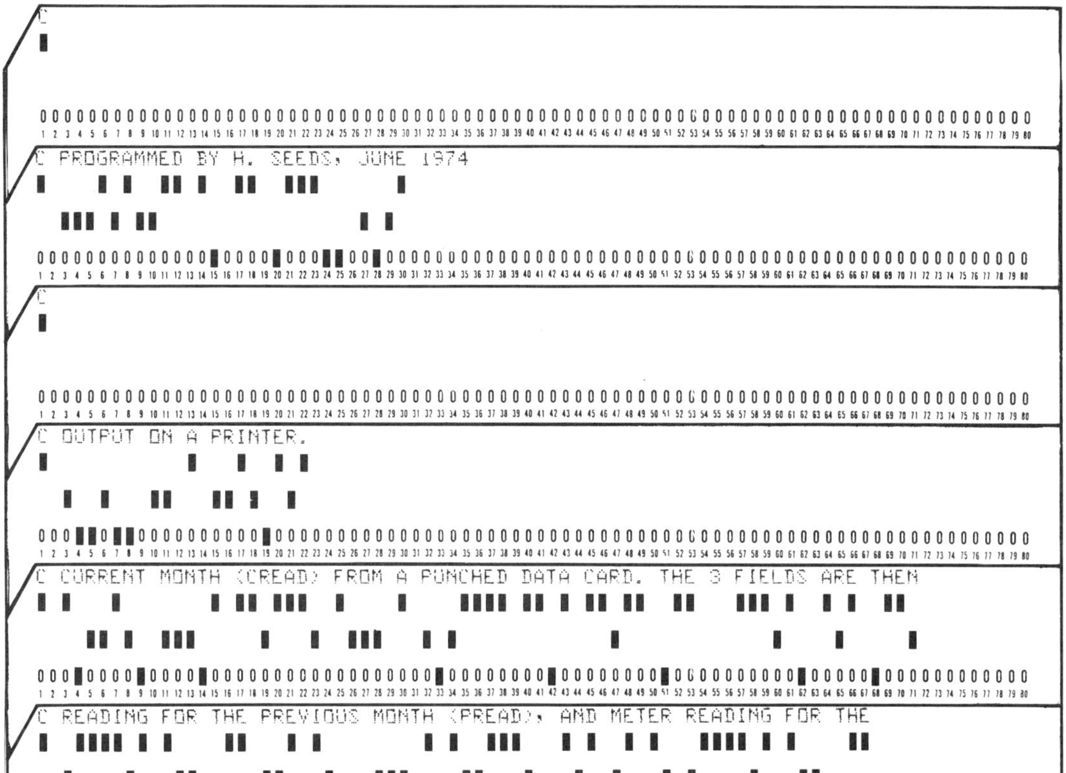

Figure 8

program.) The programmer looks at his Multiple Card Layout Form to find the order in which the fields are punched into the data card (or stored on tape or disk). Then he writes statement number 1:

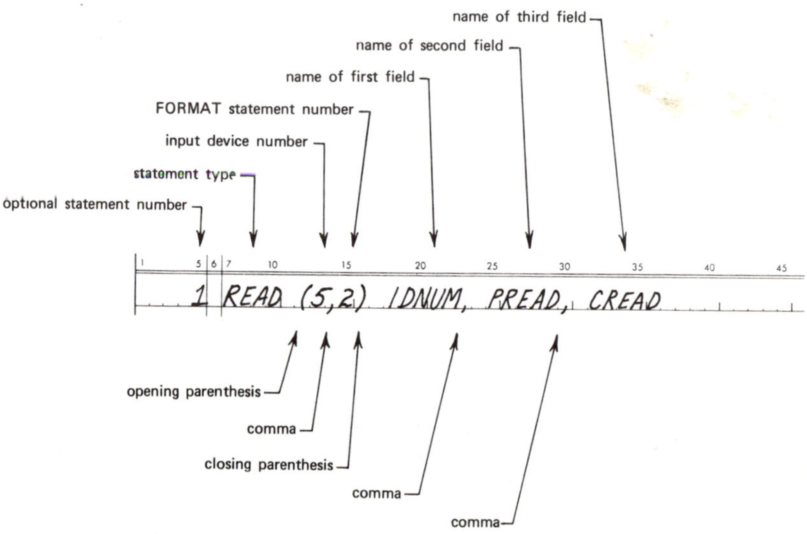

Statement 1, which is numbered only for the programmer's convenience, begins with the word READ in column 7. Actually, READ can begin in any column to the right of column 6 so long as the *entire statement* is within columns 7-72. The word READ instructs the computer to receive data from an input device of the computer. The device can be a card reader or a tape or disk drive. The only restriction is that the records must be processed in sequence.[1]

A pair of opening and closing parentheses containing two numbers follows the word READ:

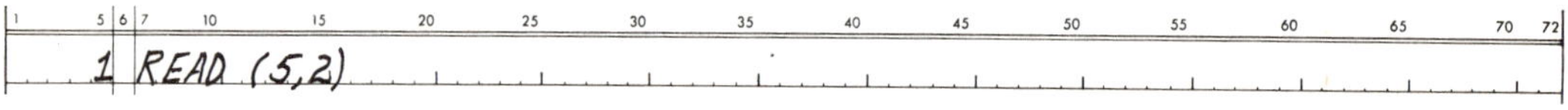

The first number within the parentheses tells the computer *which* device will input the data. The 5 in the parentheses of statement 1 refers to the punched card reader in many installations. This number, technically termed the "data set reference number," varies from one installation to another.[2] The number 1 also is often used for the card reader. Tape and disk drives have individually assigned numbers. Information about data set reference numbers used in specific computer installations, or about ways in which to assign these numbers, ordinarily is obtained from computer center personnel. If difficulties arise in finding the correct number for an input or output device, the computer manufacturer should be consulted.

[1]Random access disk processing is discussed in chapter 25. FORTRAN IV does not support index sequential disk processing.

[2]Integer field names can be used instead of numbers for either the first or second number within the parentheses. See Chapter 6 on assignment statements.

A required comma follows the data set reference number, and then a FORMAT statement number is given. In READ statement 1, FORMAT statement 2 is referenced. FORMAT statement 2 will inform the computer about the record location of fields listed after the parentheses:

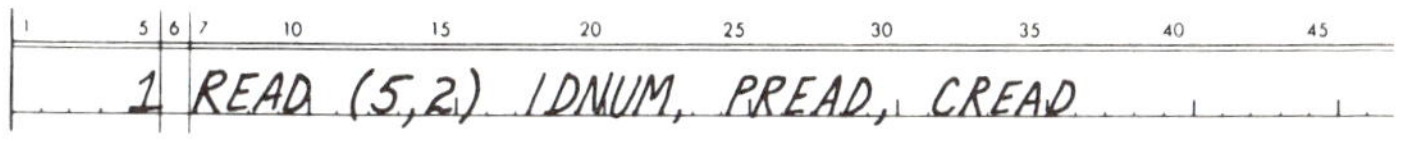

Thus READ statement 1 calls for customer identification number (IDNUM), previous month's meter reading (PREAD), and current month's meter reading (CREAD), to be read from input device 5 according to specifications in FORMAT statement 2.

If compilation of the program is successful, the computer establishes memory space for these three fields even before a card (or tape or disk record) is read. This allocation of space can be visualized in the following manner:

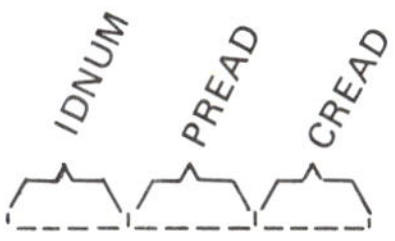

When a record is read, fields read from the record are then stored in these field locations in the computer. Until the fields are input, however, whatever was in these locations from previous programs remains. Field locations are reserved but not automatically cleared in FORTRAN.

Names of the fields, not the contents of the fields, are listed in the READ statement. IDNUM, the first field name listed, is an integer. Integers are whole numbers, sometimes called counting numbers, that do not contain a decimal point. An integer can be a positive, zero, or negative value. In FORTRAN IV, it can be as large as 2,147,483,647, which is $2^{31} - 1$. A FORTRAN IV integer field cannot contain commas, however. The only acceptable contents of integer fields are digits and a positive or negative sign. If neither sign is present, the number is assumed to have a positive value. Inventory and employee numbers, as well as numbers used in counting, are usually integers.

PREAD and CREAD, the second and third fields listed in READ statement 1, are real numbers. That is, they are numbers with decimal points either present or understood. Real numbers can be negative, zero, or positive. Because the range of real numbers is from approximately 10^{-78} to approximately 10^{75}, FORTRAN IV real fields can contain so many digits in storage that nonscientific programmers rarely create a real field too large for the FORTRAN IV compiler.

When a program utilizes such items as pay rates and prices, these fields are real numbers because they represent money, and money normally is written with two digits to the right of a decimal point. A person's age, on the other hand, could be either real or integer, depending on whether or not it is given as a whole number or with a decimal fraction. As the card layout form and the printer spacing chart demonstrate, current and previous meter readings are given in hundredths of a unit. Therefore PREAD and CREAD are fields with real numbers.

REVIEW QUESTIONS

5. Do READ statements require statement numbers? If so, why?
6. What is the earliest column in which the word READ can begin?
7. What is a data set reference number? Give an example.
8. What is an integer? Give an example from the USAGE program.
9. What is a real number? Give an example from the USAGE program.

Field Names

Because the computer stores and locates fields by their names, these names are sometimes called field addresses. Field names can be from one to six (occasionally five) characters long. This limit is arbitrary in a sense. It was set by creators of the FORTRAN compiler so that storage space would not be wasted on unnecessarily long names.

All field names must begin with a FORTRAN alphabetic letter. This means a letter in the English alphabet or the dollar sign ($). If the name is more than one letter long, any alphabetic or numeric characters can be used for the remainder of the name. No special characters (such as #, %, &, c, *, /, etc.) can be a part of a field name, except a blank that is ignored. Therefore ID NUM, I D N U M, and IDNUM are identical names to the FORTRAN compiler. The compiler determines that a field name is ended when it encounters either a comma or column 73. (Because other languages such as COBOL do not permit blanks, some programming instructors feel that it is always wise to avoid blanks in field names.)

The first character of a field name is especially important and must follow certain rules. These rules or "conventions" are important because FORTRAN has various kinds of fields. The two most common types of numeric fields have just been introduced, integer and real. From the first letter of the field name, the FORTRAN compiler can tell whether the field contents are integer or real. Unless informed otherwise[3] the compiler assumes that integer field names *begin* with the letters I, J, K, L, M, or N. A handy hint for remembering: they range from I (integer) through N (number)!

The FORTRAN name convention assumes that real field names begin with the dollar sign or with any alphabetic character except those from I through N. Thus real field names begin with letters from A-H, O-Z, or $.

[3]Special FORTRAN IV statements can override these conventions. For further information, see Chapter 15, type specification statements.

READ statement 1 lists fields IDNUM, PREAD, and CREAD. IDNUM is an integer field name because it begins with the letter I. PREAD and CREAD are real field names because they begin with P and C. The following examples show acceptable and invalid names for integer and real fields.

Acceptable Names for Integer Fields	Unacceptable Names for Integer Fields	
L	CUSTMR	(real first character)
ITEM 1	74ITEM	(numeric first character)
JOBNUM	ID#	(special character used)
NUMBER	$TOTAL	(real first character)
J$1974	LONGEST	(too many characters)

Acceptable Names for Real Fields	Unacceptable Names for Real Fields	
TOTAL	NUMBER	(integer first character)
X	I	(integer first character)
PAYRAT	74PAY	(numeric first character)
TAX 74	PAYROLL	(too many characters)
$VALUE	T&G	(special character used)

REVIEW QUESTIONS

10. What are the two common types of FORTRAN numeric fields?
11. How long can an acceptable field name be?
12. How short can an acceptable field name be?
13. How does the FORTRAN compiler identify an integer field name?
14. How does the FORTRAN compiler identify a real field name?

FORMAT Statement with the READ Statement

A FORMAT statement specifies the arrangement of input or output data. It informs the computer of the size and placement of fields within a record. Because FORMAT statements are always used with input or output statements that refer to them, FORMAT statements require numbers. The FORMAT statement number must be the same as the second number within the parentheses of the input or output statement. More than one READ or WRITE statement can utilize the same FORMAT statement.

FORTRAN statements in the card-to-printer demonstration program are placed in the order by which they are to be processed. FORMAT statements are not executable commands, however. They are nonexecutable statements that *describe* the form of input or output data.

Therefore, in a FORTRAN program they can be placed anywhere before the END statement. Many programmers group them together at either the beginning or end of their programs. If the FORMAT statement can be near the READ or WRITE statement that refers to it, however, the programmer can easily check the pair of statements for inaccuracies.

FORMAT statement 2 describes the lengths, forms, and placement on the data card (or tape or disk record) of the three fields listed in READ statement 1:

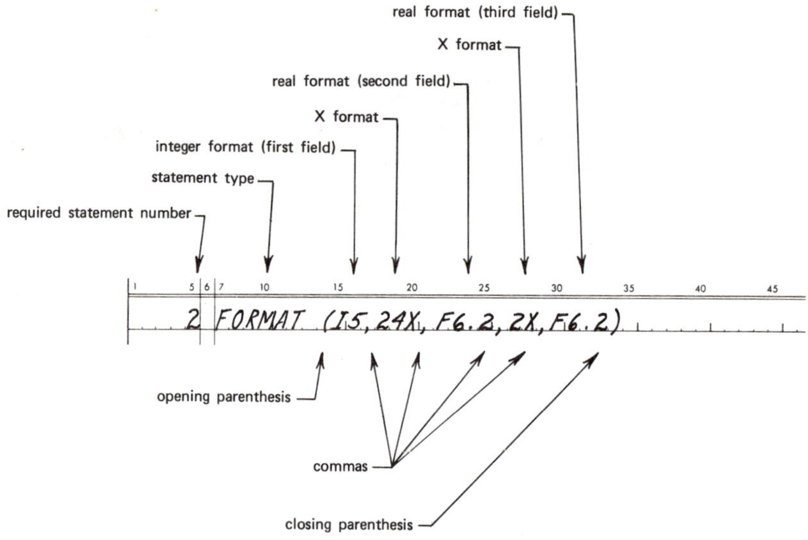

The FORMAT statement contains the required statement number (2) in columns 1-5. The actual statement begins in column 7 or later, with the word FORMAT. Specifications for the fields listed in READ statement 1 follow the word FORMAT, enclosed in a pair of parentheses.

The I Format Specification

Integer fields are specified in FORMAT statements by the I format. This consists of the letter I followed by the number of record positions (card columns, tape, disk, or print positions, etc.) allotted to the field. According to FORMAT statement 2, the first field listed in the input/output statement occupies the first 5 positions in the record. Therefore integer field IDNUM occupies columns 1-5 of the data card.

```
    1 READ (5,2) IDNUM,
    2 FORMAT (I5,
```

The location is established by the specification I5 at the first position within the parentheses. This position at the opening of the parentheses represents the first position of the data record, which is column 1 in card input.

If one of the columns reserved for this numeric field is blank, that position will be interpreted as a zero by the compiler. The largest possible number that can be read as IDNUM by the I5 specification is 99999. The I5 specification also limits a negative number so that it cannot extend beyond the negative −9999.

As shown earlier, the sample data card contains 12548 in columns 1-5. After execution of the READ statement, the area in computer storage reserved for IDNUM contains the binary form of this number. Although the computer actually stores in binary or base 2 numbers, the FORTRAN compiler does all the necessary conversions so that the programmer need not even be aware of the form change and can visualize storage in the normal decimal or base 10 number system.

IDNUM

12548

The letter I and the length designation following it constitute a format element. Because other format specifications are also present, a comma must follow the I5 specification. A comma separates format elements within parentheses. Blank spaces can be present between any of the format elements and commas.

The X Format Specification

FORMAT statement 2 contains two X format specifications. The first is the 24X specification following the I5 specification:

```
    2 FORMAT (I5,24X,
```

This specification establishes the 24 positions after the I5 positions (columns 6-29 in the data card) as blanks.

The X format specification consists of the letter X with a number *before* it. The X signifies a blank position in the data record; the number tells how many blanks there are. The number of blanks is limited only by the size of the record. That is, a card containing 80 columns cannot have elements for one record totaling more than 80 positions. Even if the input record contains characters in the positions designated as part of the X format specification, the computer is instructed to assume that those positions are blank and not part of any field in the program.

Therefore the presence of information not pertinent to the program does not make the input record unusable.

Not all FORTRAN IV compilers require a comma *after* the X format. These compilers permit the next format element to begin immediately after the X. When the X element follows another format element, however, a comma is required to separate them.

Some FORTRAN IV compilers permit an X without a number when only one blank space is wanted, but many always require a digit before the X. Even with a compiler that does not require a 1, the programmer is not in error if he uses 1X.

FORMAT statement 2 also contains a 2X specification informing the computer that columns 36-37 are blank.

The F Format Specification

The third and fifth elements within the parentheses of FORMAT statement 2 are F format specifications.

```
    2 FORMAT (I5,24X, F6.2, 2X, F6.2)
```

The F reflects the earlier descriptive term "floating point" numbers for what are now termed real numbers. The F format, used to specify real fields, consists of the letter F followed by a number, a decimal point, and another number. For example, both F format elements in FORMAT statement 2 are F6.2.

The F indicates that the field contains a real number. The first digit following the F tells the number of record positions (6) allotted to the field. On a data card, each position is a card column. These columns include all significant digits to the left of the decimal point and as many digits as are wanted to the right of the decimal point. They must also include columns for a positive or negative sign or for a decimal point if any of these is present. The second number (2) represents only the number of digits to the right of the decimal point in the field.

Thus the second field listed in the READ statement, PREAD, is matched by the FORTRAN compiler with the second field specification, F6.2.

```
    1 READ (5,2) IDNUM, PREAD
    2 FORMAT (I5,24X,F6.2,
```

Real field PREAD is allotted six columns immediately following the 24 blanks in columns 6-29. Therefore PREAD occupies columns 30-35 of the data card, with the two low-order columns (34-35) assigned to the right of the implied decimal point. In FORTRAN IV, a decimal point is always implied according to the F format specification whenever it is not punched. Card columns 30-35, allotted to PREAD, contain 213857. The computer stores PREAD as 2138.57.

CREAD, the third field listed in READ statement 1, is matched with the third field specification in FORMAT statement 2.

```
    2 FORMAT (I5,24X,F6.2,2X,F6.2)
```

CREAD occupies the six columns following the 2X specification. Thus columns 38-46 of the data card contain CREAD, with the contents of columns 45-46 assigned to the right of the implied decimal point. The columns, which are keypunched with 224736, are stored in real field CREAD as 2247.36.

Although FORTRAN is one of the few programming languages that permits decimal points in input data, space on the card is saved by not punching any. Even without a keypunched decimal point, the compiler stores the field in the form specified in the FORMAT statement, as demonstrated by the values stored for real fields PREAD and CREAD. Including a decimal point in the contents of these fields would require an extra card column and an F7.2 format specification. Standard business data processing practice omits decimal points from input data fields.

When a field does not occupy all its allotted columns, the compiler stores the blanks as zeros. For example, if PREAD contained a blank in column 30, its first position, the field would be stored as 0138.57. If column 35 contained a blank also, PREAD would be stored as 0138.50.

Because no other fields are listed in the READ statement, the remainder of the data card is assumed to be blank. The X format is not necessary in such a situation. In fact, if the FORMAT statement contains other specifications, they are ignored after all fields listed in the input statement have been matched with field specifications.

REVIEW QUESTIONS

15. How does the FORTRAN compiler interpret a blank in a column allotted to a numeric field on a data card?
16. What format specification type indicates an integer field?
17. What format specification type indicates a real field?
18. What format specification element indicates blanks?
19. What do the two numbers in an F format specification represent?

The WRITE Statement

After the three fields have been input, the third symbol of the flowchart calls for the same fields to be printed. Once values have been stored for fields, they can be output separately or together and in any sequence.

The WRITE statement instructs the computer to output information to an output device on the computer.

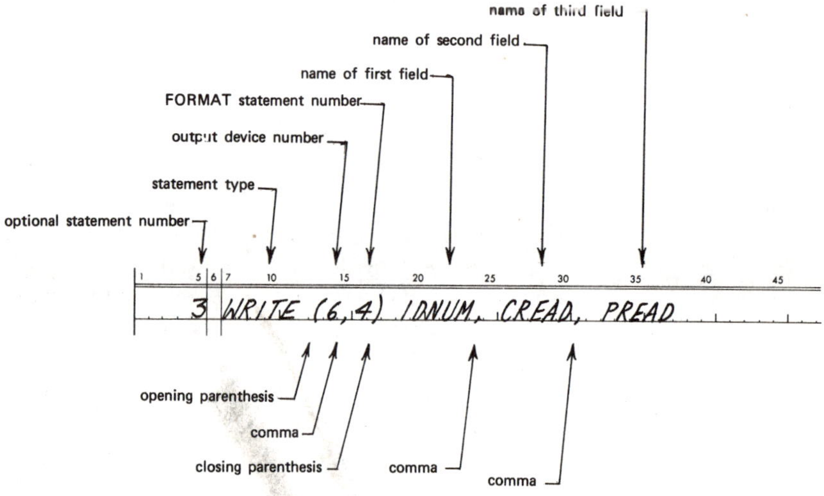

Although statement 3 has a label, the statement number is not required.

The word WRITE, beginning no earlier than column 7, instructs the computer to produce characters on printer or typewriter paper, on punched cards, magnetic tape or disk, or on any other output media of the computer.

Like the READ statement, the WRITE statement contains 2 numbers in parentheses. The first is the device or data set reference number. In many installations (especially those with IBM Operating Systems), data set reference number '6' is assigned to the printer. It refers to a printer in statement 3. In other installations, the printer is often assigned '3.' Any input/output device can be assigned a different data set reference number. Computer center personnel, instructors, and manufacturers' manuals ordinarily provide information about these assigned numbers.

The second number in parentheses of the FORMAT statement is a '4.' This indicates that FORMAT statement 4 specifies the placement and form of the output. Names of the fields to be printed are listed after the parentheses in the WRITE statement, just as names of input fields are listed in the READ statement.

FORMAT With the WRITE Statement

No matter which device is used, the FORTRAN compiler assumes that input or output will begin in position 1. This is often referred to as "tab" position 1. Printed output involves a complicating feature because tab position 1 is automatically assigned not to the first position on the printed page but to the position in storage just *ahead* of the first print position. Thus tab position 1 on the printer is the carriage control position which controls line spacing. Carriage control is discussed more fully in the next chapter, but now the programmer must remember to guarantee a blank (to produce single spacing) in tab position 1 of the printed line.

In FORMAT statement 4, a 5X specification in the opening position creates blanks in the first five tab positions.

```
    4 FORMAT (5X,
```

The 5X specification inserts blanks in tab position 1 for carriage control and in the first four (leftmost) positions of the printed line. This is an easy way to combine carriage control and spacing. Because carriage control is so important, however, some programmers always have a separate element for tab position 1. For example, they might divide the 5X element into two parts, one for carriage control and the other for spaces in the first four print positions of the line:

```
    4 FORMAT (1X,4X,
```

In this way they always remember to allow for carriage control.

In FORMAT statement 4, the X format is also utilized to separate the printing of listed fields.

```
    4 FORMAT (5X,I5,6X,F7.2,5X,F7.2)
```

The X format specification is the simplest method of achieving the spacing required by the printer spacing chart on page 18.

Output of Integer Fields

According to the printer spacing chart, integer field IDNUM is to be printed in print positions 5-9. Since the contents of this customer identification field are five digits long, and five print positions are allotted to the field by the I5 specification, all five print positions of the field will be filled. If, however, the exact size of an integer field is not known, the largest size reasonably possible must be specified.

Numeric fields, both integer and real, are always right-justified. That is, even if the field has fewer nonzero digits than print positions allotted, the low-order (rightmost) digit always is in the rightmost column of the field. For example, if an I6 field is to begin in print position 4 but the field contains only three significant digits, print positions 4, 5, and 6 will be blank. The three digits will be in print position 7, 8, and 9.

```
                          I6 field
                         _________  1
Print positions:    1 2 3 4 5 6 7 8 9 0
Field contents:                 1 2 3
```

As this illustrates, when a field is larger than necessary, leading zeros do not print. Instead, the leftmost positions of the field contain blanks.

If the contents of an integer field are negative, the sign is part of the field. It will print in the position immediately to the left of the high-order (leftmost) nonzero digit. If the contents of the field are positive, most FORTRAN IV compilers do not require a position for the sign.

The following table shows output of different integer field contents with various I format specifications.

Field Contents	I2 Format	I3 Format	I4 Format	I5 Format
1	1	1	1	1
−1	−1	−1	−1	−1
12	12	12	12	12
−12	**	−12	−12	−12
123	**	123	123	123
1234	**	***	1234	1234
−1234	**	***	****	−1234
12345	**	***	****	12345

As these examples show, when there are not enough positions to display the full contents of a field, asterisks are printed in positions assigned to the field.

REVIEW QUESTIONS

20. What is a data set reference number?
21. Where are data set reference numbers given in FORMAT statements?
22. What is the purpose of the X format specification?
23. What type of field uses the I format specification?

Output of Real Fields

The I specification for integer field IDNUM had the same length specification (5) for both input and output of the field. However, the F specifications for real fields PREAD and CREAD require each field to be at least one position larger than it was for input specifications. This extra position is required for the printed decimal point. Therefore FORMAT statement 4 requires the F7.2 length for both PREAD and CREAD.

```
    3 WRITE (6,4) IDNUM, CREAD, PREAD
    4 FORMAT (5X,I5,6X,F7.2,5X,F7.2)
```

In printed output, the F7.2 specification means that real fields CREAD and PREAD are each allotted seven print positions. Of these positions, the four high-order (leftmost) positions are for digits to the left of the decimal point. The required decimal point is in the fifth position, and the two low-order positions will contain two digits to the right of the decimal point. Thus, with FORMAT statement 4, the positions for real fields CREAD and PREAD can contain a positive number as large as 9999.99. and a negative number to −999.99.

Like integers, real number fields in FORTRAN do not print leading zeros and they are right-justified in the printed field. The following table shows the output of several real fields with various F format specifications.

Field Contents	F2.1 Format	F3.1 Format	F3.2 Format	F4.2 Format	F5.2 Format	F5.3 Format	F8.4 Format
0.2200	.2	.2	.22	.22	.22	.220	.2200
0.278	.3	.3	.28	.28	.28	.278	.2780
1.2300	**	1.2	***	1.23	1.23	1.230	1.2300
−1.23	**	***	***	****	−1.23	*****	−1.2300
12.3460	**	***	***	****	12.35	*****	12.3460

As the table illustrates, the compiler adds zeros or truncates digits to the *right* of the decimal point to make the contents fit the second number of the F specification. The table also shows how FORTRAN compilers ordinarily round up (half-adjust) automatically for output if the leftmost truncated (cut-off) digit is from 5 through 9.[4] Also like integer fields, real fields print asterisks if the format specification is not large enough. The F format must be able to hold all significant digits to the *left* of the decimal point, the decimal point, and the designated number of digits to the right of the decimal point.

Following the printer spacing chart, FORMAT statement 4 specifies that the contents of CREAD will be output in print positions 16-22. Real field PREAD will occupy print positions 28-34. Notice that

[4]For greater accountability and accuracy in crossfooting and other accounting techniques, see the section on double precision in Chapter 15, type specification statements.

CREAD is output before PREAD, although they were input in the reverse order. Once a field is stored, it can be output at any time, in any order, singly or combined with other stored fields.

The size of the computer printer determines the maximum number of tab and print positions available. Some printers have only 80 print positions. Usually, however, printers have either 120, 132, or 144 print positions. The computer used for the demonstration programs has a 132 position printer; therefore with its widest paper it has 132 print positions and 133 tab positions.

The STOP Statement

The *logical* conclusion of a FORTRAN program is ordinarily indicated by a STOP statement. This statement consists of the word STOP, which must be within columns 7-72.

```
    5 STOP
```

The STOP statement can be numbered, but numbers are optional unless required by other statements within the program.

Because the execution of STOP statements sometimes slows production time, some computer installations do not use them. Such centers prefer CALL EXIT, a special (subroutine) command.[5] The two statements achieve the same results, but CALL EXIT involves a different form of execution that is sometimes preferred.

```
    5 CALL EXIT
```

Notice that the CALL EXIT statement also is numbered 5. This emphasizes the fact that *either* CALL EXIT or STOP is used but not *both* for the same point of conclusion. Like STOP, CALL EXIT does not require a statement number.

The END Statement

The last instruction of a FORTRAN source program must be an END statement. Because many FORTRAN compilers will not execute if the END statement is numbered, it ordinarily consists only of the word END within columns 7-72.

[5] If further technical information is wanted, see Chapter 21, Subprograms: Subroutines.

In most programs, the END statement follows the STOP statement. Because the logical conclusion (STOP or CALL EXIT statement) and the physical conclusion (END statement) of a program are not always the same, STOP or CALL EXIT sometimes occurs other than at the end of a program. The END statement, however, must be the physical conclusion of the FORTRAN program.

REVIEW QUESTIONS

24. When is the F format specification used?
25. What is printed when an F field specification is not large enough for all digits to the left of the decimal point?
26. What statements can indicate the logical end of a FORTRAN program?
27. What statement indicates the physical end of a FORTRAN program?

When the output device is a magnetic tape or disk, an additional instruction is required. END FILE must be placed in the program after output to the device is completed and before the CALL EXIT or STOP statement. For example, when data set reference number 10 is assigned to a magnetic tape device, statement 6 informs the compiler that output to device 10 is completed:

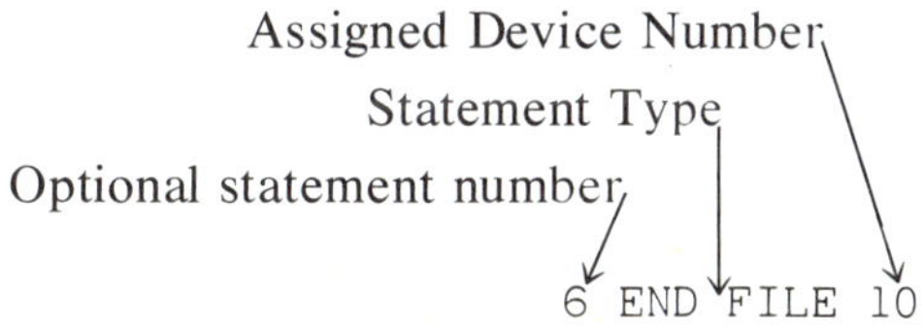

This instruction normally is placed just before the STOP or CALL EXIT statement. If the data records are to be used later in the same program, however, the END FILE statement must appear before the records are made available by a REWIND statement:

```
REWIND 10
```

Keypunching and Submitting a Program

When a programmer has finished coding his program and has checked it for possible duplicate statement numbers or other errors, he must either give his coding sheet to someone else to keypunch or he must keypunch his instructions himself.

```
C FOR COMMENT
STATEMENT NUMBER | Cont. | FORTRAN STATEMENT
1   5 | 6 | 7  10  15  20  25  30  35  40  45  50  55  60  65  70  72

C THIS PROGRAM INPUTS CUSTOMER IDENTIFICATION NUMBER (IDNUM), METER
C READING FOR THE PREVIOUS MONTH (PREAD), AND METER READING FOR THE
C CURRENT MONTH (CREAD) FROM A PUNCHED DATA CARD. THE 3 FIELDS ARE THEN
C OUTPUT ON A PRINTER.
C
C PROGRAMMED BY H. SEEDS, JUNE 1974
C
C RECORD (PUNCHED CARD) INPUT
    1 READ (5,2) IDNUM, PREAD, CREAD
    2 FORMAT (I5,24X,F6.2,2X,F6.2)
C
C RECORD (PRINTED LINE) OUTPUT
    3 WRITE (6,4) IDNUM, CREAD, PREAD
    4 FORMAT (5X,I5,6X,F7.2,5X,F7.2)
C
C END OF PROGRAM
    5 STOP
      END
```

Each line of the coding form represents one punched card in the source language (FORTRAN) deck of cards. Column placement, particularly before and after column 6, must be accurately entered.

If data cards are not already in existence, that deck also must be keypunched. In most installations, certain cards are also required to instruct the computer that a FORTRAN program is to be run and, hopefully, executed. These are called Job Control or JCL cards. Appendix A has two typical sets of Job Control cards, for IBM S/360 and S/370 DOS and OS systems. Job Control card information usually is distributed by computer center personnel, an instructor, or the computer manufacturer.

When Job Control cards, FORTRAN source language program, and data cards (or tape or disk records) are assembled in the correct order, they are submitted to the computer card reader by the student, instructor, or a member of the computer installation. As the card reader inputs the FORTRAN program cards, each instruction and comment card ordinarily is listed on the computer printer. For example, the card-to-printer program produced the following listing:

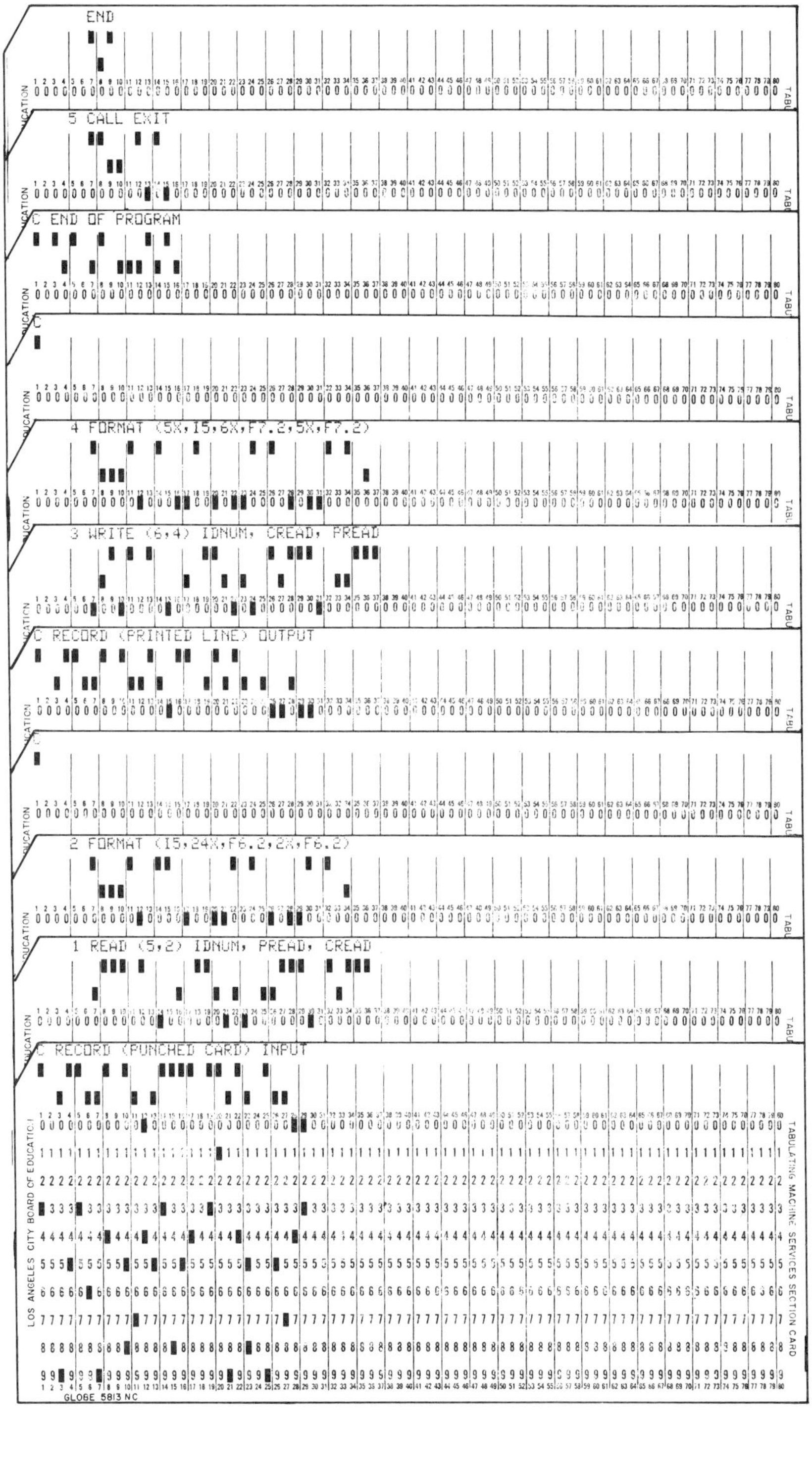
END
5 CALL EXIT
C END OF PROGRAM
C
4 FORMAT (5X,I5,6X,F7.2,5X,F7.2)
3 WRITE (6,4) IDNUM, CREAD, PREAD
C RECORD (PRINTED LINE) OUTPUT
C
2 FORMAT (I5,24X,F6.2,2X,F6.2)
1 READ (5,2) IDNUM, PREAD, CREAD
C RECORD (PUNCHED CARD) INPUT
LOS ANGELES CITY BOARD OF EDUCATION
TABULATING MACHINE SERVICES SECTION CARD
GLOBE 5813 NC

```
      C THIS PROGRAM INPUTS CUSTOMER IDENTIFICATION NUMBER (IDNUM), METER
      C READING FOR THE PREVIOUS MONTH (PREAD), AND METER READING FOR THE
      C CURRENT MONTH (CREAD) FROM A PUNCHED DATA CARD. THE 3 FIELDS ARE THEN
      C OUTPUT ON A PRINTER.
      C
      C PROGRAMMED BY H. SEEDS, JUNE 1974.
      C
      C RECORD (PUNCHED CARD) INPUT
0001      1 READ (5,2) IDNUM, PREAD, CREAD
0002      2 FORMAT (I5,24X,F6.2,2X,F6.2)
      C
      C RECORD (PRINTED LINE) OUTPUT
0003      3 WRITE (6,4) IDNUM, CREAD, PREAD
0004      4 FORMAT (5X,I5,6X,F7.2,5X,F7.2)
      C
      C END OF PROGRAM
0005      5 STOP
0006        END
```

Error Detection

The program listing is an essential part of program documentation. Particularly when a program error occurs, the listing should be examined with special care. Misplaced cards and keypunching errors can be seen more easily from a printed list of instructions than from the actual punched cards. In addition, FORTRAN compilers send messages when an error is detected. The details given in the message depend upon the version of FORTRAN compiler executing. On most systems, however, a dollar sign indicates that an error has been detected in the line above. The dollar sign is as close to the error as the compiler can determine it to be. For example:

```
0001            1 REED (5,2) IDNUM, PREAD, CREAD
                   $ $
          01)  ILF001I ILLEGAL TYPE          02)  ILF013I SYNTAX
0002            2 FORMAT (I5,24X,F6.2,2X,F6.2)
```

The keypunching of the word READ must be corrected and the program resubmitted. Notice the help that the compiler gives by diagnosing the error. READ is declared an illegal type of command, and an opening parenthesis is a syntax error unless it follows special commands. Some compilers give even more detailed explanations.

A different type of common error occurs when a field name is too long:

```
0001            1 READ (5,2) IDNUMBER, PREAD, CREAD
                                 $
          01)  ILF003I NAME LENGTH
```

The program will run successfully when the programmer shortens field name IDNUMBER. The dollar sign is just below the sixth letter of the field name, and the next line lists name length as the error. The name should, of course, be changed to IDNUM to match the name used in WRITE statement 3.

These are typical of the types of errors (bugs) that the compiler frequently detects in programs. The machine cannot know what the programmer wanted the program to produce, however, and so the programmer must check the logical progression of his instructions himself. This is the area in which a flowchart has tremendous value.

Successful Execution

When a program is without compiler errors, the printed report, or output, is printed after the program listing. Card-to-printer program USAGE1, when processed with the data card shown, prints the following:

```
12548        2247.36       2138.57
```

Fields IDNUM, CREAD, and PREAD, which represent customer identification number, current meter reading, and previous meter reading, are printed in the form and location designated on the printer spacing chart.

Output can be a sequential tape or disk record instead of a printed line. In the WRITE statement, the installation tape or disk data set reference number would be used instead of the 6 for printer. In the FORMAT statement, blanks in tab position 1 and elsewhere probably would be eliminated to conserve space. Otherwise the instructions for WRITE and FORMAT statements apply to sequential output on any available device.

REVIEW QUESTIONS

28. One line of a FORTRAN coding sheet represents how many punched cards?
29. What is a program listing?
30. Give two examples of program listing uses.
31. What is a program printout?

OBJECTIVES REVIEW

Look at the objectives at the beginning of this chapter. Check each one to be certain you have achieved it. Restudy the chapter sections related to any you cannot perform.

REVIEW TEST

Study the following FORTRAN program carefully. Using the "data card" that is given, "process" the program just as the FORTRAN compiler does. On scratch paper, keep a record of what is in memory for every field as the program proceeds. On a printer spacing chart or in the space below, print the output of the test program as it would appear on the printer. Watch both the contents and the placement of fields.

Data Card

```
                    1         2         3         4
Columns:  1234567890123456789012345678901234567890

Card:     2378 312  2579
```

Program

```
1 READ (5,2)NUMBER, KOUNT, PRICE
2 FORMAT (I4, 1X, I3, 2X, F4.2)
3 WRITE (6,4) NUMBER, PRICE, KOUNT
4 FORMAT (10X,I4, 5X, F5.2, 5X, I3)
5 STOP
  END
```

Printout

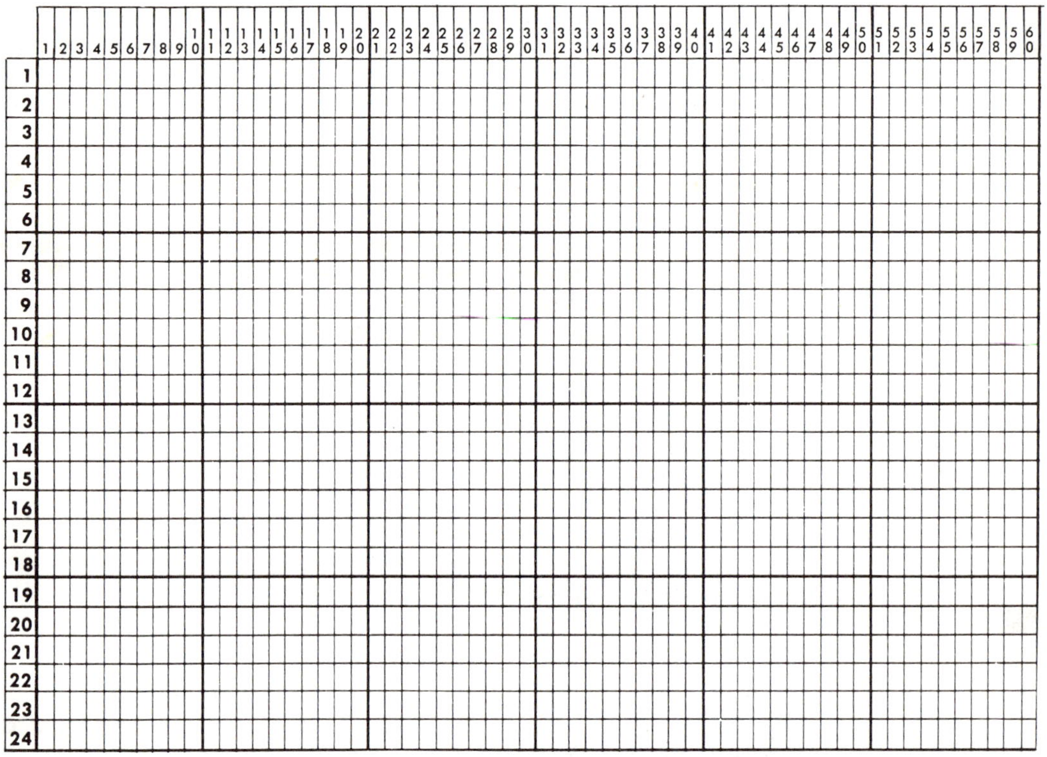

ASSIGNMENTS

Select one of the following card-to-printer problems. Use either a data card you create to fit the requirements or the first card from the demonstration data set.[6] Complete a multiple card layout form and printer spacing chart according to the specifications given. Flowchart the prob-

[6]See Appendix B, the data records usable for all assignments in this book.

lem. Following the flowchart, write a FORTRAN program of instructions to read and print the data card fields. Keypunch and submit your program cards and data card for program processing.

	Data Card Fields	Tab Positions	Type
1. Input:	Department major	21-22	I2
	Student identification number	23-27	I5
	Units completed	28-31	F4.1
	Units in progress	64-66	F3.1
Output:	Student identification number	2-6	I5
	Department major	9-10	I2
	Units completed	20-24	F5.1
	Units in progress	31-34	F4.1
2. Input:	Employee number	21-25	I5
	Hours worked	29-31	F3.1
	Rate of pay	34-36	F3.2
Output:	Employee number	6-10	I5
	Hours worked	20-23	F4.1
	Rate of pay	30-33	F4.2
3. Input:	Library branch number	23-25	I3
	Books checked out this week	37-42	I6
	Books returned this week	52-57	I6
Output:	Library branch number	5-7	I3
	Books checked out this week	15-20	I6
	Books returned this week	25-30	I6
4. Input:	Inventory number	21-25	I5
	Price per item	33-36	F4.2
Output:	Inventory number	4-8	I5
	Price per item	15-19	F5.2
5. Input:	Stock company number	21-25	I5
	Sales price per share	52-57	F6.2
	Number of shares sold (in 100's)	62-68	I7
Output:	Stock company number	15-19	I5
	Number of shares sold (in 100's)	34-40	I7
	Sales price per share	61-67	F7.2

Chapter Objectives

1. Be able to program a "loop" by using the GO TO statement.
2. Be able to use the END= option of the READ statement if the FORTRAN compiler can utilize it.
3. Be able to write a FORTRAN printer program that lists records from data cards, or tape or disk sequential files.
4. Be able to write a FORTRAN program that outputs records to tape or disk or printer.

4

GO TO Statement and END= Option in READ Statement

One of the characteristics of business data processing is the large number of records input and then output. A READ and a WRITE statement for each record would be a waste of both human time and computer storage. Therefore the computer's ability to read and write records is fully realized only when the computer can input and output many records with few instructions. This ability to perform a task or a series of tasks repeatedly is one of the great capabilities of the computer. Unlike humans, the computer is just as accurate (or inaccurate) the fiftieth, five hundredth, or five thousandth time it performs a task as it is the first time. This repetition of tasks is called "looping."

A loop in programming involves the repeated execution of one or more instructions. This requires more instructions than the first program that executed each instruction once until all instructions were processed sequentially to the end of the program.

The next step in the card-to-printer program uses a loop to repeat the READ and WRITE statements until all records are read and printed. This break in the sequential pattern of instruction execution introduces the flowchart entry and exit connectors. Since there must be a way to conclude the loop so that it will not cycle endlessly, the flowcharting decision symbol must also be utilized.

The flowchart and descriptive statement are developed for the card-to-printer expanded program, USAGE2:

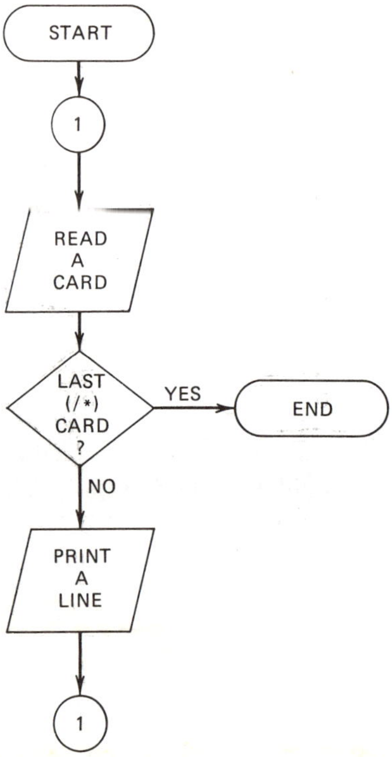

Program USAGE2 inputs customer identification number (IDNUM), meter reading for the previous month (PREAD), and meter reading for the current month (CREAD) from a data card (or tape or sequential disk record). The three fields are then output on a printer (or tape or sequential disk record). After printing the detail line, the program branches back to the READ statement until the END= option of the READ statement branches it to CALL EXIT after the last card is processed.

As the flowchart demonstrates, the card-to-printer program now cycles repeatedly from the connector after the print symbol to the connector before the read symbol. The cycle or loop continues until the last card is input. Then the logical decision symbol instructs the program to end. In this, as in most third- and fourth-generation computer programs, "last card" really means the card following the last true data card. On the IBM S/360 and S/370 computers, a card containing /* in the first two columns follows the data deck. In some smaller or older machines, it is a "dummy" or false data card following the last valid data card.[1]

The input and output data format for program USAGE2 are identical to the data format shown on the multiple card layout form

[1]If a "dummy" last card must be utilized to determine the last card test, this technique is explained in the chapter on the IF statement.

53
GO TO STATEMENT
AND END = OPTION
IN READ
STATEMENT

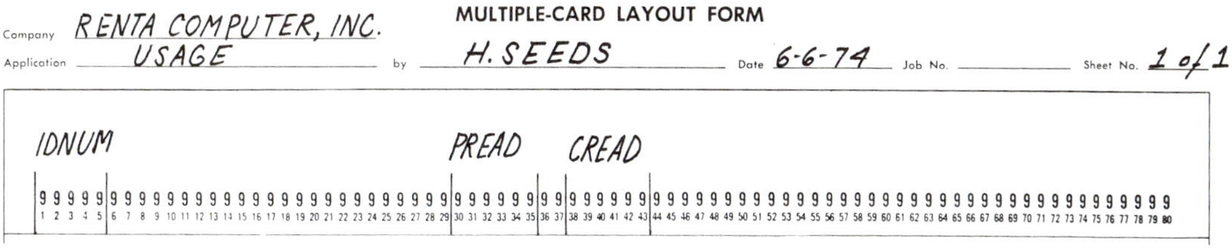

and printer spacing chart for program USAGE1 in the previous chapter. In the case of the printer spacing chart,

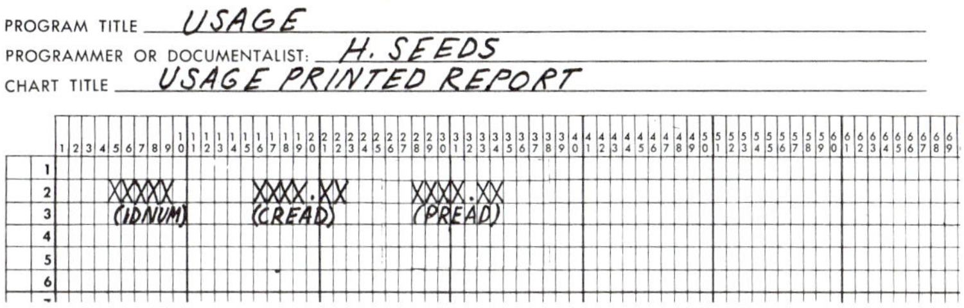

the printed line format is repeated for several cards instead of for just one card, but field placements remain unchanged in all the data cards.

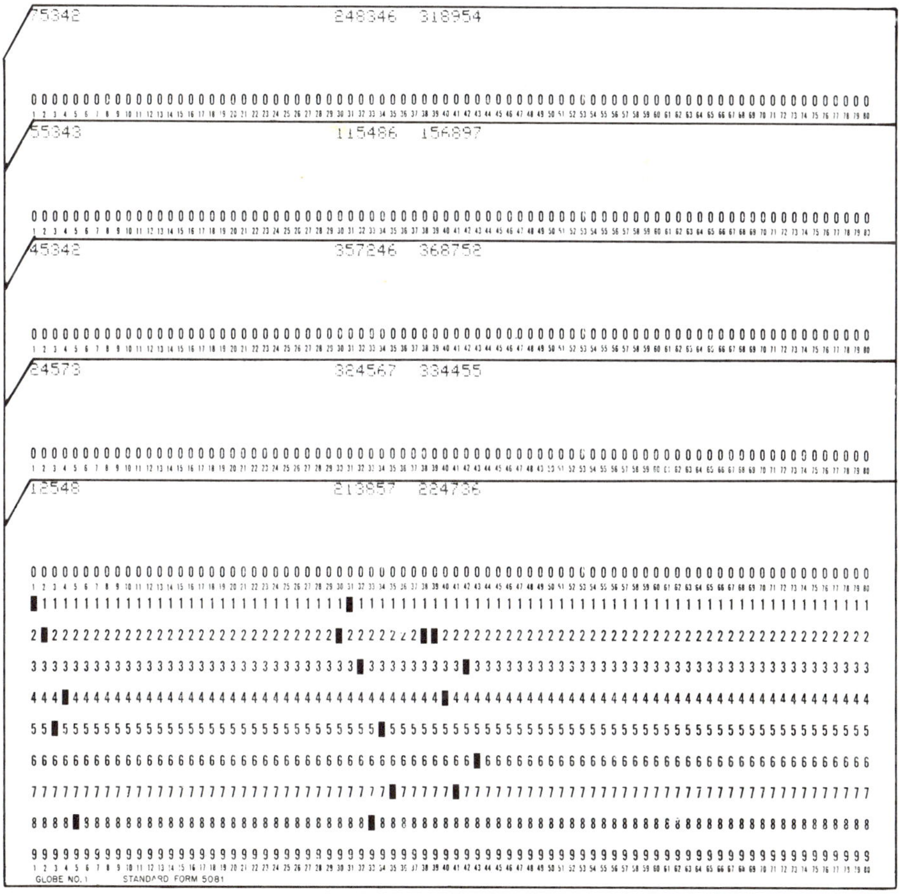

Therefore, immediately after flowcharting the problem, the programmer can proceed to code the FORTRAN program for USAGE2.

Looping with the GO TO Statement

In order to carry out the flowchart for program USAGE2, the programmer must be able to instruct the computer not to end after the first card but to branch back and repeat the same processing steps for each data card. In FORTRAN, the simplest form of looping is accomplished by the GO TO instruction.

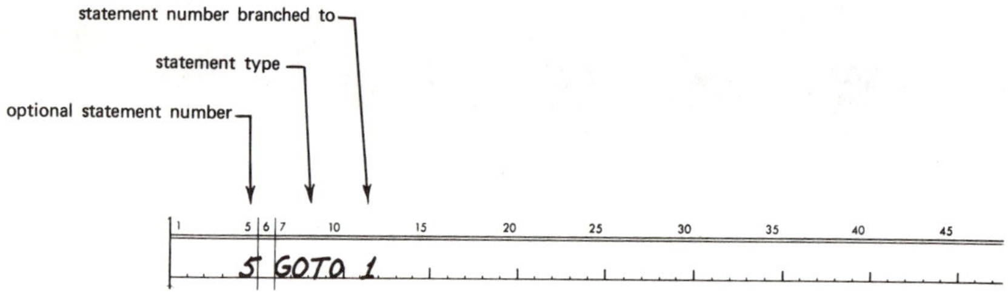

The GO TO (or GOTO since blanks are ignored) statement is an *unconditional branching* instruction. This means that when the compiler encounters a GO TO instruction, the program must branch to the statement listed in the GO TO statement and continue processing from that statement.

The branched-to statement must be a numbered, executable statement. Program USAGE2 branches back to the READ instruction after each execution of the WRITE instruction. Therefore numbering the READ statement is no longer optional but required.

Program USAGE2
Programmer H. SEEDS — Date 6-74

```
    1 READ (5,2,END=6) IDNUM, PREAD, CREAD
    2 FORMAT (I5,24X,F6.2,2X,F6.2)
    3 WRITE (6,4) IDNUM, CREAD, PREAD
    4 FORMAT (5X,I5,6X,F7.2,5X,F7.2)
    5 GO TO 1
    6 CALL EXIT
      END
```

Every time the computer completes execution of WRITE statement 3, GO TO statement 5 automatically branches the program to READ statement 1. The program repeats the loop (statements 1 through 5) for each data card. In each cycle of the loop, a data card is read and the three data fields are printed. Thus the entire file of data cards is processed by adding GO TO statement 5.

This action is better understood when the programmer realizes that every time the READ instruction is executed, contents of the three fields in computer storage are completely replaced by data just input by the newly read card. After each line is printed, the FORTRAN compiler automatically clears the output area in storage in preparation for the next line of print.

A statement listed in the GO TO instruction can be anywhere in the program, but it must be an executable statement. The most common non-executable statements are FORMAT and END. Because END statements usually cannot be numbered, they do not present a problem. The programmer must be careful, however, to avoid listing a FORMAT statement number in the GO TO instruction. For example, if GOTO statement 5 tried to branch to FORMAT statement 2

```
    5 GO TO 2
```

or to FORMAT statement 4

```
    5 GOTO 4
```

the program would cancel without beginning the execution phase. The compiler would realize that the statement listed in the GO TO instruction was not an executable instruction; so the program could not begin execution.

Because GO TO statements are unconditional branching instructions, a program never "falls through" to the statement after a GO TO command. Therefore FORTRAN logic requires the *first executable statement* following a GO TO command to be numbered.

```
    5 GO TO 1
C END OF PROGRAM
    6 CALL EXIT
```

The comment statement is nonexecutable, but the CALL EXIT command is executable and therefore requires a number.

Numbering the first executable statement following a GO TO

statement allows another instruction to branch to it. Otherwise, the CALL EXIT instruction never could be executed.

REVIEW QUESTIONS

1. Why is the GO TO instruction called an unconditional branch?
2. A GO TO instruction must branch to what type of statement?
3. What is required of the first executable statement following a GO TO instruction?

END = Option in the READ statement

The flowchart for the multiple card-to-printer program includes the decision symbol for determining the last data card. Otherwise the flowchart would show the read-write loop circling endlessly. The determination of the last card is especially easy when a FORTRAN compiler contains an END= option for the READ statement. This option instructs the computer to branch to the statement listed in the option when READ is executed but the /* card following the last valid data card is read or the end of file mark is encountered on tape or disk.

```
    1 READ (5,2,END=6) IDNUM, PREAD, CREAD
```

The option END= 6 is coded after the data set reference number and FORMAT statement number within the parentheses of READ statement 1. It instructs the computer to branch to statement 6 when "last card" (/* in columns 1 and 2) is read.

The program now executes statements 1 through 5, then branches back to statement 1 to execute the statements again. This loop continues until the card reader senses the /* card. When this card is read, control is transferred to statement 6, the executable instruction listed in the END= option. Because statement 6 is CALL EXIT, this instruction terminates the program.

The statement listed in the END= option need not be a CALL EXIT or STOP statement. In later demonstration programs, total calculations and total printing will occur when the END= option branches to instructions for these activities. The END= option may branch to any executable instruction anywhere in the program. The programmer has the responsibility to lead the program eventually to a CALL EXIT or STOP command.

Using the data cards listed, the multiple card-to-printer program USAGE2 produces the following printed output:

END= OPTION IN THE READ STATEMENT

```
12548          2247.36        2138.57
24573          3344.55        3245.67
45342          3687.52        3572.46
55343          1568.97        1154.86
75342          3189.54        2483.46
```

If the END= option is not available on the FORTRAN compiler, a program without the option in the READ statement will simply terminate when the input device reaches the /* card. All data will be processed, but a message warning of an illegal ending will be printed at the conclusion of the regular processing. To avoid this "illegal" ending, a "dummy" or false data card is used with an IF statement. This test for last card is illustrated in the chapter on the IF statement.

REVIEW QUESTIONS

4. What is the purpose of the END= option?
5. The END= option is a part of which FORTRAN statement?
6. What type of statement must be listed in the END= option?

OBJECTIVES REVIEW

Study the objectives listed at the beginning of this chapter. Check each one to be certain you have achieved it. Restudy the chapter sections related to any objective that you cannot perform.

REVIEW TEST

Study the following FORTRAN program carefully. Using the "data cards" that are given, "process" the program just as the FORTRAN compiler does. On scratch paper, keep a record of what is in memory for every field as the program proceeds. On a printer spacing chart or in the space below, print the output of the test program as it would appear on the printer. Watch both the contents and the placement of fields.

Data Cards

```
                   1         2         3
Columns:  123456789012345678901234567890
Card 1:   1684 25 645
Card 2:   2759 15 850
Card 3:   4217 18 775
Card 4:   /*
```

Program

```
1 READ (5,2,END=6) IDNUM, KIDS, COST
2 FORMAT (I4, 1X, I2, 1X, F3.2)
3 WRITE (6,4) IDNUM, KIDS, COST
4 FORMAT (6X, I4, 5X, I2, 4X, F4.2)
5 GO TO 1
6 STOP
  END
```

Printout

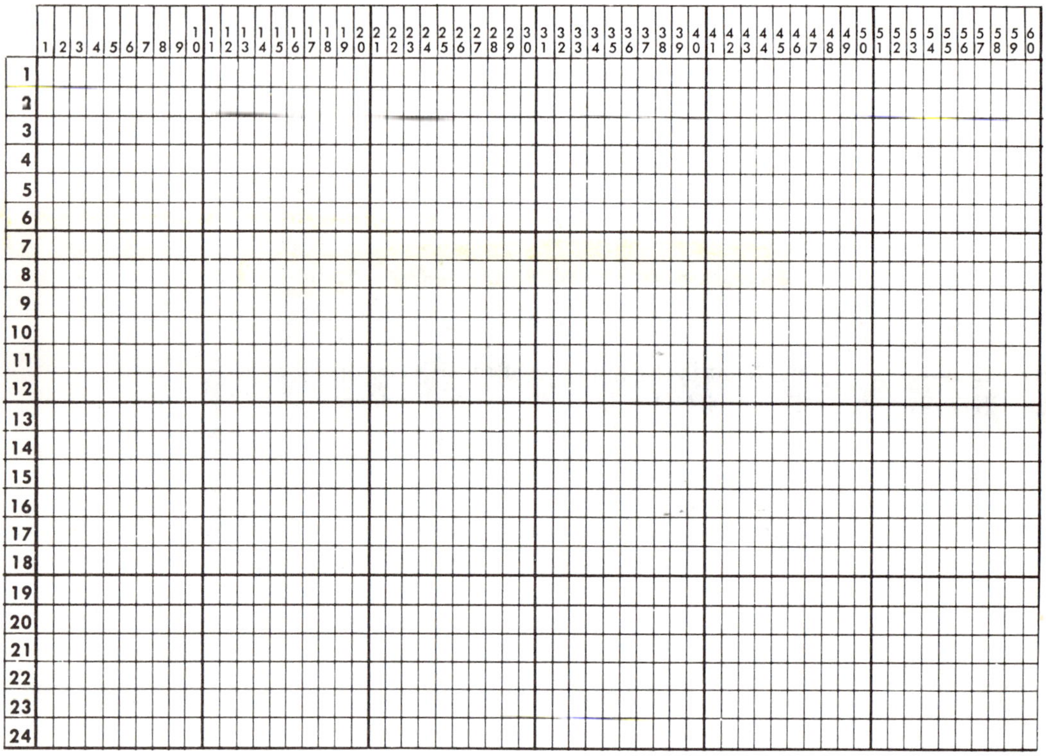

ASSIGNMENTS

Select one of the following multiple card-to-printer problems. Using the demonstration data cards[2], complete a multiple card layout form and printer spacing chart according to the specifications given. Flowchart the problem. Following the flowchart, write a FORTRAN program of instructions to read and print the fields from the deck of data cards. Keypunch and submit your program cards and data cards for program processing.

	Record Fields	Tab Positions	Type
1. Input:	Department major	21-22	I2
	Student identification number	23-27	I5
	Units completed	28-31	F4.1
	Units in progress	64-66	F3.1
Output:	Student identification number	2-6	I5
	Department major	9-10	I2
	Units completed	20-24	F5.1
	Units in progress	31-34	F4.1

[2]See Appendix B, the data records usable for all assignments in this book.

2.	Input:	Inventory number	21-25	I5
		Number on hand	33-36	I4
		Cost value per item	38-42	F5.2
	Output:	Inventory number	3-7	I5
		Number on hand	15-18	I4
		Cost value per item	25-30	F6.2
3.	Input:	Company assets account number	21-25	I5
		Cash on hand	30-36	F7.2
		Merchandise on hand value	39-45	F7.2
		Accounts receivable	52-57	F6.2
		Furniture and fixtures value	62-68	F7.2
		Buildings and land value	74-80	F7.2
	Output:	Company assets account number	11-15	I5
		Cash on hand	20-27	F8.2
		Merchandise on hand value	38-45	F8.2
		Accounts receivable	56-62	F7.2
		Furniture and fixtures value	73-80	F8.2
		Buildings and land value	91-98	F8.2
4.	Input:	Company account number	23-26	I4
		Net profit for month	38-42	F5.0
		Gross profit for month	53-57	F5.0
	Output:	Company account number	10-13	I4
		Gross profit for month	21-28	F8.2
		Net profit for month	41-48	F8.2
5.	Input:	Family identification number	21-25	I5
		Number of persons in family	74-75	I2
		Average age of persons in family	34-36	F3.1
	Output:	Family identification number	5-9	I5
		Number of persons in family	21-22	I2
		Average age of persons in family	34-37	F4.1

Chapter Objectives

1. Be able to use literals in headings and other explanatory printed material.
2. Be able to utilize a continuation card in FORMAT statements.
3. Be able to establish spacing by the T format specification.
4. Be able to regulate line spacing by using carriage control characters.
5. Be able to use the slash for skipping input or output records.
6. Be able to use either apostrophes (single quotation marks) or Hollerith format specifications for literals.

5

Literals in FORMAT Statements

The multiple card-to-printer program USAGE2 printed all the integer and real fields as established in the card layout form and the printer spacing chart. The printed report is meaningful only to the programmer, however, because the numbers appear without any explanations. This situation is remedied by introducing the use of literals and carriage control in FORMAT statements.

Headings—Literals in FORMAT Statements

A flowchart is drawn for problem USAGE3. This flowchart contains an additional input/output symbol.

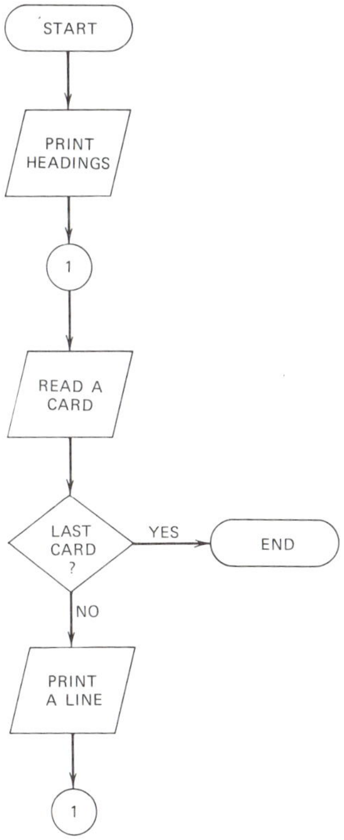

The new input/output symbol indicates that headings will be printed. Because this occurs only once during the program, the symbol is placed between the START symbol and the connector symbol beginning the read-write loop.

Headings are written with WRITE and FORMAT statements, but ordinarily the WRITE statements for headings do not list field names after the parentheses. Instead the computer prints literals (nonfield messages) included in the FORMAT statement. The literal can be enclosed in apostrophes—sometimes called single quotation marks—or can be part of a Hollerith format specification.

Literals Enclosed in Apostrophes

The apostrophe or single quotation mark is the numeric shift of the H key on IBM 029 and 129 keypunches. It punches the 5 and 8 rows of a card column. The characters enclosed between two apostrophes form a literal. Any letters, digits, or special characters on the computer's printer can be used in a literal. Because blanks in literals are considered special characters, they are not ignored in literals as they usually are in FORTRAN statements. Digits within a literal cannot be used in arithmetic calculations because they are not stored as part of a field.

To make the card-to-printer program more meaningful, the printer spacing chart (showing tab positions) includes literals as headings.

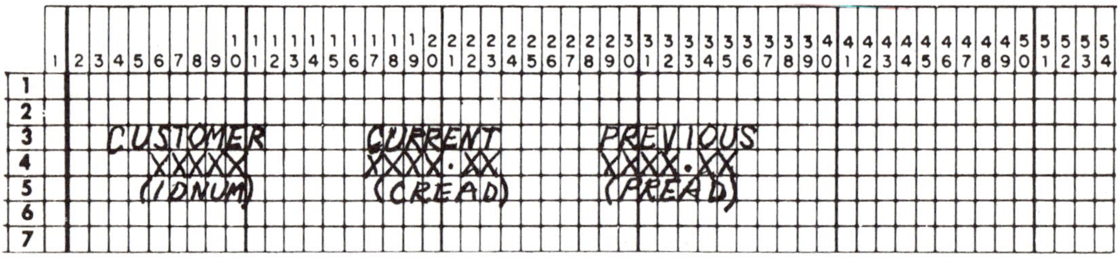

In order to carry out this plan, the programmer develops a pair of WRITE and FORMAT instructions. He remembers that the first position on the printer is reserved for carriage control and that he wants a blank in it for single spacing. He follows the chart for the rest of the positions. (See p. 38 on use of '6' for printer.)

```
   10 WRITE (6,11)
   11 FORMAT (3X,'CUSTOMER',5X,'CURRENT',5X,'PREVIOUS')
```

The WRITE and FORMAT statements are numbered 10 and 11 even though they will come at the beginning of the program. Sequencing statement numbers is only for the convenience and orderliness of the programmer. Because all the statements from program USAGE2 can be used in program USAGE3, their numbers are retained and statements 10 and 11 are simply placed before statement 1.

The three literals in statement 11 are 'CUSTOMER', 'CURRENT', and 'PREVIOUS'. When WRITE statement 10 calls for FORMAT statement 11 to be executed, the 3X specification is in the opening position. This instructs the printer to leave three blank spaces, the first in the *off-page* carriage control position. Two blanks are left in the first two *print* positions. Then, beginning in the third print position, the literal CUSTOMER is printed. Note that the apostrophes do not print. They are special signals to the compiler that a literal is to be established in memory.

Immediately following CUSTOMER, the 5X specification allots five blank spaces before the literal CURRENT is printed. Another 5X specification provides five more blank spaces, and then the literal PREVIOUS is printed.

REVIEW QUESTIONS

1. In which kind of FORTRAN statement are literals specified?
2. The numeric (upper) shift of which keypunch key contains the apostrophe?
3. How do literals make a printed report more meaningful?

Since blanks are special characters in literals, FORMAT statement 11 could achieve the identical output when written as one long literal:

```
   11 FORMAT('   CUSTOMER     CURRENT     PREVIOUS')
```

After WRITE statement 10 is executed, the program proceeds as before:

```
C THE PROGRAM BRANCHES BACK TO THE READ STATEMENT AFTER
C PROCESSING EACH CARD.  THE END = OPTION TESTS FOR LAST CARD.
C COLUMN HEADINGS ARE PRINTED.
C PROGRAMMED BY H. SEEDS, JUNE 1974
   10 WRITE (6,11)
   11 FORMAT (3X, 'CUSTOMER     CURRENT     PREVIOUS')
    1 READ (5,2,END=6) IDNUM, PREAD, CREAD
    2 FORMAT (I5, 24X, F6.2, 2X, F6.2)
    3 WRITE (6,4) IDNUM, CREAD, PREAD
    4 FORMAT (5X,I5,6X,F7.2,5X,F7.2)
C BRANCH BACK TO READ STATEMENT
    5 GO TO 1
    6 CALL EXIT
      END
```

The program prints the headings, enters the read-write loop, and terminates when the END= option in READ statement 1 branches the program to statement 6, the CALL EXIT statement. The program produces the following printed report:

```
CUSTOMER        CURRENT        PREVIOUS
  12540         3247.36        2138.57
  24573         3344.55        3245.67
  45342         3687.52        3572.46
  55343         1568.97        1154.86
  75342         3189.54        2483.46
```

Apostrophe Within Literals

If the programmer wants an apostrophe or single quotation mark to print within a literal, he must punch an apostrophe in each of 2 successive columns (' '). The double quotation mark cannot be used for this purpose. FORMAT statement 22 illustrates the correct way to print an apostrophe:

```
   22 FORMAT (T10,'ERIC''S SPORTS CARS')
```

FORMAT statement 22 will print ERIC'S SPORTS CARS, beginning in print position 9 (tab position 10).

Two apostrophes next to each other in a literal expression cause one apostrophe to be printed. If only one apostrophe is punched within the literal, the computer assumes that it signals the end of the literal. This creates errors for the remaining characters of the intended literal.

If the programmer wants an apostrophe (or single quotation mark) at the beginning and/or end of a literal, three adjacent apostrophes are required:

```
   32 FORMAT (T20,'''THE STORY''')
```

When a WRITE statement calls FORMAT 32, the printer will begin to print 'THE STORY' in print position 19.

FORMAT Continuation Card

Although one printed line cannot extend beyond the number of positions on the printer, FORMAT statements can be continued onto one or more cards. If the first card of the FORMAT statement is filled, column 6 in the next card is punched to indicate that the statement of the first card is continued. On most computers, any character except blank or zero can be used as a continuation signal. If several continuation cards are required, the numbers 1,2,3, etc. in column 6 of the successive cards are helpful for showing sequence to the programmer. FORMAT statement 31 requires two cards.

```
   31 FORMAT ('    THE ELECTRONIC INSTRUMENT COMPANY OF WESTERN LOS ANGEL
     1ES COUNTY')
```

If the first card of FORMAT statement 31 continued the literal beyond column 72, the characters in columns 73-80 would not print. If the closing apostrophe was punched in columns 73-80, it would create an error for the compiler. Since statement 31 is within the 132 print positions but too long for one FORMAT card, the character in column 6 of the second card informs the FORTRAN compiler that it continues the FORMAT statement. Notice that column 72 of the first card and column 7 of the continuation card are treated as adjacent columns with no space between.

REVIEW QUESTIONS

4. What special coding is required if the programmer wants to print an apostrophe or single quotation mark?
5. How are FORMAT statements continued beyond a first card?
6. What characters can be used as continuation signals?
7. What determines the maximum length of a printed literal?

Hollerith Format

Not all FORTRAN IV compilers can accept a literal enclosed in apostrophes. Compilers lacking this capability require the use of the Hollerith or H format specification for printing literal expressions. The Hollerith format specification can appear anywhere within the parentheses of a FORMAT statement. It consists of three basic parts: (1) the number of positions or columns occupied by the literal, (2) the letter H, and (3) the literal itself:

literal expression
type of format specification
length of literal

```
   33 FORMAT (10X, 26HTHE RENTA COMPUTER COMPANY)
```

The H identifies the type of format specification for the FORTRAN compiler. The count of characters begins immediately after the H. Like literals enclosed within apostrophes, literals in Hollerith formats regard a blank as a special character rather than ignoring it.

In FORMAT statement 33, the Hollerith format contains a literal 26 characters long. This literal can include alphabetic, numeric, or special characters. If the characters are numeric, they cannot be used in arithmetic calculations. The literal in statement 33 begins in tab position 11 (print position 10):

```
THE RENTA COMPUTER COMPANY
```

Care must be used in determining the length of the Hollerith literal. Otherwise errors will keep the program from executing. For example, if the count had been punched in the FORMAT statement as 25 instead of 26, the FORTRAN compiler would not understand the Y in the twenty-sixth position. Thus the extra letter would create an error. If, on the other hand, the count is too long because 27 was punched before the H, the closing parenthesis becomes part of the literal. The statement lacks a closing parenthesis, and so a compilation error results. The latter type of error can be easily avoided by one or more precautionary blanks after the Hollerith literal. FORMAT statement 34 illustrates this technique:

```
   34 FORMAT (10X, 26HTHE RENTA COMPUTER COMPANY  )
```

If the count of the Hollerith literal is one or two positions too long, the blanks at the end of the literal keep the statement error free. This technique can also be used if the Hollerith format specification is followed by a separating comma and other format elements.

```
   35 FORMAT (10X, 26HTHE RENTA COMPUTER COMPANY  ,5X,11HLOS ANGELES  )
```

REVIEW QUESTIONS

8. What types of characters can a Hollerith literal contain?
9. What precautions should be taken to avoid errors in the use of Hollerith literals?

T Format Positions

Another method of writing headings or other literals results in the same output but eliminates the necessity for counting blank spaces before or between elements of a FORMAT statement. This capability is achieved by using the T or Tab format specification to indicate the leftmost position of each element, including literal expressions of either type.

Most FORTRAN IV compilers can use tab position numbers to indicate specific positions in input or output records. Punched card, magnetic tape, and magnetic disk input and output utilize tab position 1 to indicate the first position of the record, tab position 2 for the second position, etc. There are as many tab positions as there are record positions. For instance, tab position 1 is the first or leftmost position on a punched card, while tab position 80 is the last or rightmost tab position on the card.

When the output device is the printer, a special situation occurs: tab position 1 is the automatically assigned position in storage just *ahead* of the first print position. Thus *print* position 1 is *tab* or T position 2. The size of the computer printer determines the number of tab and print positions available. Some printers have only 80 print positions. Then T positions range from 1-81, and print positions from 1-80. Printers usually have either 100, 120, or 144 print positions. The computer used for demonstration programs has a 132 position printer. Therefore with its widest paper, it has 132 print positions and 133 tab positions.

T or tab positions are indicated by the T format specification. This consists of the letter T followed by the tab position at which the next element is to begin. For example, the printer spacing chart for problem USAGE3 shows that the three words of the column heading begin in print positions 3, 16, and 28. This heading line can be printed by WRITE statement 110 and FORMAT statement 111.

```
110 WRITE (6,111)
111 FORMAT(T4,'CUSTOMER',T17,'CURRENT',T29,'PREVIOUS')
```

Each literal begins at the tab (*not print*) position indicated by the T specification immediately before it.

Because a T format specification is considered a separate element of the FORMAT statement, commas set off T formats from other elements in a FORMAT statement. Of course all elements of the FORMAT statement must be between the opening and closing parentheses. This is illustrated in WRITE statement 112 and FORMAT statement 113 when the T format is used with both literals and field specifications.

```
112 WRITE(6,113) IDNUM
113 FORMAT(T10,'CURRENT CUSTOMER NUMBER:',T40,I5)
```

CURRENT CUSTOMER NUMBER: will be printed beginning in tab position 10. The contents of field IDNUM will print, beginning in tab position 40.

```
CURRENT CUSTOMER NUMBER:      12548
```

Although it is more orderly for the programmer, tab positions need not be in sequential order. FORMAT statement 113 would create the same output if it were written in reverse order.

```
113  FORMAT(T40, I5, T10, 'CURRENT CUSTOMER NUMBER')
```

REVIEW QUESTIONS

10. Which tab position is card column 1?
11. Which tab position is print position 1?
12. Which punctuation mark is required immediately after a T format specification?

Printer Carriage Control Characters

When output is on the printer, the contents of special tab position 1 control the vertical skipping of lines on the page. That is, single spacing, double spacing, skip to the top of a new page, etc., are determined by the character in tab position 1. The following are the carriage control codes for tab position 1:

(blank) = single space before printing
0 (zero) = double space before printing
−(minus) = triple space before printing
+(plus) = no spacing before printing
1(one) = skip to top of next page before printing

Single Spacing

A blank in tab position 1 causes the printer to skip one line and then print any fields listed in the WRITE statement and/or any literals listed in the FORMAT statement. Because the FORTRAN compiler ordinarily assumes line skipping only *before* printing, this has the effect of single spacing the printed report.

This is illustrated every time statement 3 is printed according to FORMAT statement 4.

SINGLE SPACING

Program USAGE2
Programmer H. SEEDS Date 6-74

```
    1 READ (5,2,END=6) IDNUM, PREAD, CREAD
    2 FORMAT (I5,24X,F6.2,2X,F6.2)
    3 WRITE (6,4) IDNUM, CREAD, PREAD
    4 FORMAT (5X,I5,6X,F7.2,5X,F7.2)
    5 GO TO 1
    6 CALL EXIT
      END
```

Because the first position after the opening parenthesis is tab position 1 unless other instructions are given, the 5X in the opening positions place a blank in the carriage control position as well as in the first four print positions.

The blank for single spacing can be placed with the X format specification, or with a blank in the opening position of a literal

```
   25 FORMAT ('   GROKETT CAMPING SUPPLIES')
```

or simply by skipping over the opening position with a higher tab position number.

```
   26 FORMAT (T35,'PROGRAMMED BY A. BELKIN')
```

Because the FORTRAN compiler clears the entire output area to blanks at the beginning of each program and after executing each WRITE statement, every print position is blank unless a nonblank character is inserted. The line described in FORMAT statement 26 begins to print in tab position 35, the 34th print position. Tab position 1 and the first 33 print positions all contain blanks since no other nonblank characters were inserted in these positions. Thus the most common form of printed output, single spacing before printing, is again achieved.

In order to remember this important tab position 1 in printer output, many programmers begin all printing formats with a special literal for the carriage control position. Three examples of this technique are given in FORMAT statements 27, 28, and 29.

```
27 FORMAT (1X,T19,'DAILY REPORT')
28 FORMAT (' ',15X,'FIRST STREET MARKET')
29 FORMAT (1H0,15X,'TED JACOBS, MANAGER')
```

Because statements 27 and 28 contain blanks in tab position 1, each of them causes single spacing before printing. Statement 29 causes the printer to space twice before printing because tab position 1 contains a zero. When the three FORMAT statements are called out in order by three WRITE statements, the following is printed:

```
        DAILY REPORT
     FIRST STREET MARKET

     TED JACOBS, MANAGER
```

When the printer spacing chart calls for two blank lines between the second and third lines, FORMAT statement 29 has a minus sign in tab position 1.

```
29 FORMAT ('-',15X,'TED JACOBS, MANAGER')
```

The minus sign in tab position 1 causes the printer to space three lines and then print the literal on the third line. Thus two lines are left blank.

Sometimes a printer begins to print a report immediately after output of program storage information. To guarantee that the report does not begin in the middle of such a page, the digit 1 specifies that the printer skip to the top printing line of a new page before printing.

```
30 FORMAT ('1',T50,'THE REALLY NEW COMPANY')
```

Sometimes a new page is required at various places in the program. Then a FORMAT statement can instruct the printer to skip to a new page without printing anything. The printer is resting in the top line position when the next WRITE instruction is executed.

```
31 WRITE (6,32)
32 FORMAT('1')
33 WRITE (6,34)
34 FORMAT(T50,'THE J. & S. SWIMSUIT COMPANY')
```

The two FORMAT statements are called out, one after the other, and so the computer skips to the top of a new page and then spaces one line before printing the literal in the second FORMAT statement. This same technique of moving the printer without printing anything can also be used with the other carriage control characters.

On rare occasions the programmer does not want the printer to advance before printing. A + (plus sign) is then inserted in tab position 1.

```
41 WRITE (6,42)
42 FORMAT (' ',5X,'REGULAR HEADINGS ARE IN TAB POSITIONS 2-81')
43 WRITE (6,44)
44 FORMAT('+',T82,'LATER MESSAGES GO IN POSITIONS 82-133')
```

Even if other, *nonprinting* instructions are executed between statements 41 and 43, the literals in FORMAT statements 42 and 44 will print on the same line. The + in tab position 1 of FORMAT 44 instructs the printer *not* to advance before printing.

REVIEW QUESTIONS

13. Where is the carriage control character located?
14. Which character creates double space reports?
15. Which character creates single space reports?
16. Which character causes the printer to skip to the top of a new page?
17. Which character instructs the printer not to advance before printing?

Slash for End-of-Record

One pair of WRITE and FORMAT statements can be used for printing and spacing more than one line. This is accomplished by using a slash (/) to indicate the end of a physical record, which in this case is a line of print. For example, a 2-line, single spaced heading can be written with one WRITE statement and one FORMAT statement containing a slash.

```
50 WRITE (6,51)
51 FORMAT('1',T25,'RENTA COMPUTER, INC.'/T30,'JUNE, 1974')
```

The printer begins the first literal at the top of a new page because the carriage control character is 1. Then in tab position 25, the literal begins. Immediately after the closing apostrophe, a slash indicates the end of the record. This signals the printer to begin a new line. The T30 specification both places a blank in the carriage control position for single spacing and begins the second literal in tab position 30 of the second line. The following two lines are printed:

```
RENTA COMPUTER, INC.
     JUNE, 1974
```

The slash must be outside the apostrophes enclosing the literal. Commas are not required to separate the slash from other FORMAT specifications, and they cause no errors when included in the statement.

The compiler reads the slash as the end of a record, and specifications following the slash refer to the next record (line). Tab position 1 is automatically assumed to be the opening position of the next record unless other specifications are given. Thus the T30 specification following the slash in statement 51 leaves a blank in carriage control position 1 and in the first 28 print positions.

If double spacing is wanted between two printed lines, it can be achieved in either of two ways. In the first method, a zero is inserted in the carriage control position immediately after a slash.

```
52 FORMAT(T28,'GREAT PROGRAMMING CO.'/'0',T29,'SUNRISE, MINNESOTA')
```

The '0' in tab position 1 of the second record instructs carriage control to double space. Then the T format begins the literal in tab position 29.

The second method of double spacing utilizes two consecutive slashes and a blank in tab position 1.

```
53 FORMAT(T28,'GREAT PROGRAMMING CO.'//T29,'SUNRISE, MINNESOTA')
```

The first slash ends the first record. The second slash ends the second record before it prints anything. The blank in tab position 1 following the two slashes instructs the printer to space another line on which it will print. Thus a blank line is between the two printed lines, achieving double spacing.

When the compiler encounters a slash between or before or after elements in a FORMAT statement, the printer is instructed that the end of a record has been reached. Any number of blank lines can be achieved in this manner. When several slashes are wanted, they can be written economically by using a double pair of parentheses. For example, FORMAT 4 signals 20 slashes:

```
3 WRITE (6,4)
4 FORMAT('1',10X,'ABC CO.',(20(/)),8X,'DAILY REPORT')
```

REVIEW QUESTIONS

18. How does the printer interpret a slash in a FORMAT statement?
19. After a slash, what tab position is assumed by the printer?
20. How many blank lines are created by four slashes between literals in a FORMAT statement?

REVIEW TEST

Study the following FORTRAN program carefully. "Process" the program just as the FORTRAN compiler does. On a printer spacing chart or in the space below, print the output of the test program as it would appear on the printer.

Program

```
1 WRITE (6,2)
2 FORMAT ('1', T18, 'FORTRAN UNIVERSITY')
3 WRITE (6,4)
4 FORMAT (T20, 'MIDTOWN, IDAHO')
5 WRITE (6,6)
6 FORMAT ('0', 9X, 'STUDENT', 3X,'UNITS',T35,'CHARGES' /
 1 10X, 'NUMBER', T37, 'DUE')
7 STOP
  END
```

Printout

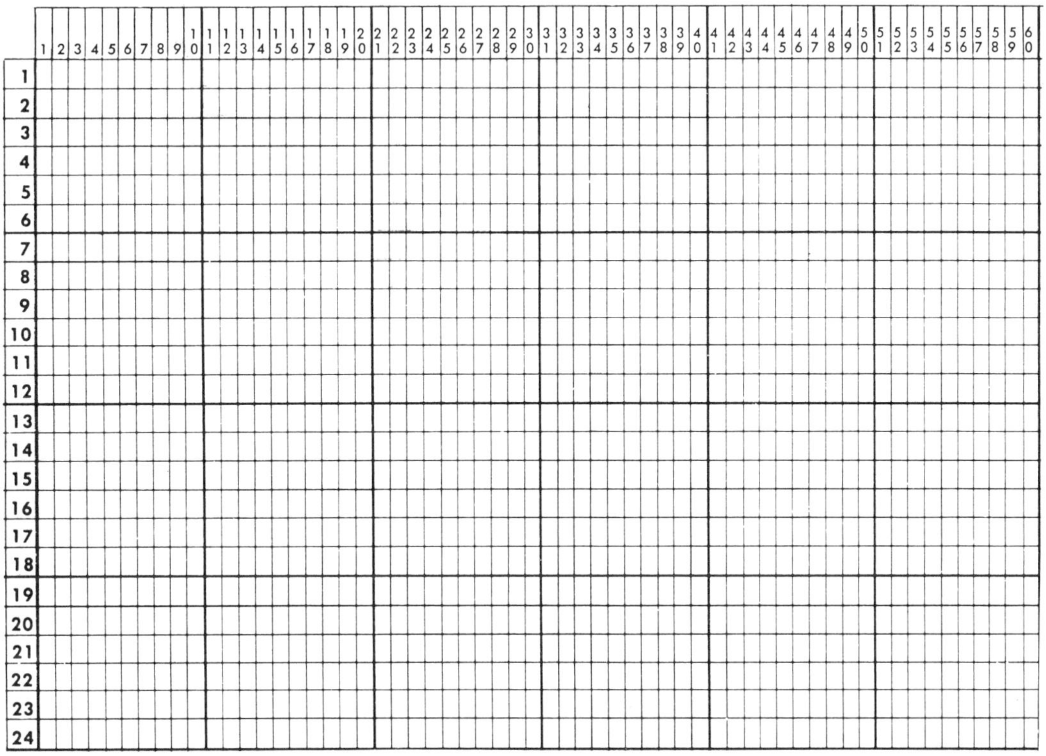

OBJECTIVES REVIEW

Study the objectives listed at the beginning of this chapter. Check each one to be certain you have achieved it. Restudy the chapter sections related to any objectives you cannot perform.

ASSIGNMENTS

Set 1 (if this is the first programming chapter assigned). Complete flowchart, printer spacing chart, and coding for one of the following programs. Then keypunch and submit the program for processing.

1. Create an attractive heading for three lines of print, with single spacing between the first two lines, and double spacing between the second and third lines. The first line contains the name of the company. The second prints the location. The third has your name as president.

2. Write a letter with a salutation and at least three lines of message. Double space before your name at the end of the message.

3. Write your name and address so that it can be a three-line address label.

4. Write the name of your school. Double space and then write the full address of the school. Center the information on the page.

ASSIGNMENTS

Set 2 (if chapters 3 and 4 have been studied). Choose one of the assignments at the end of chapter 4. In addition to the earlier instructions, write appropriate company headings and column headings. Use a printer spacing chart to create accurate placements of fields and literals.

IBM S/360 model 30, CPU console.

Chapter Objectives

1. Be able to specify addition, subtraction, multiplication, and division in FORTRAN arithmetic statements.
2. Be able to specify exponentiation (to the power of) in FORTRAN statements.
3. Be able to use FORTRAN assignment (replacement) statements to establish or reset the value of fields.
4. Be able to explain the order by which arithmetic expressions are executed.
5. Be able to use parentheses to determine the order by which arithmetic expressions are executed in arithmetic statements.

6

Arithmetic Statements

The computer was used basically as a programmable printer in programs USAGE, USAGE2, and USAGE3. Such uses are important, especially in business data processing that requires many printed reports. But the ability of the computer to perform arithmetic calculations at spectacular speed with remarkable accuracy (if instructed accurately) is essential to computer programming.

In FORTRAN an arithmetic statement establishes the contents of a field (1) by either giving the value itself or by giving the name of another field with the same value or (2) by calculating the value of the field, using one or more of the five arithmetic operation signs.

In addition to the general name of arithmetic statement, an instruction using the first method is often called an assignment or a replacement statement. Both types of arithmetic statements are illustrated in program USAGE4.

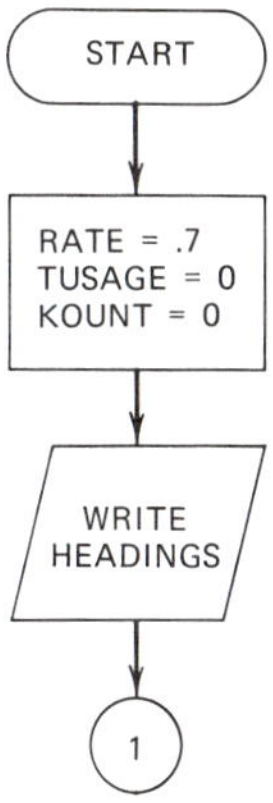

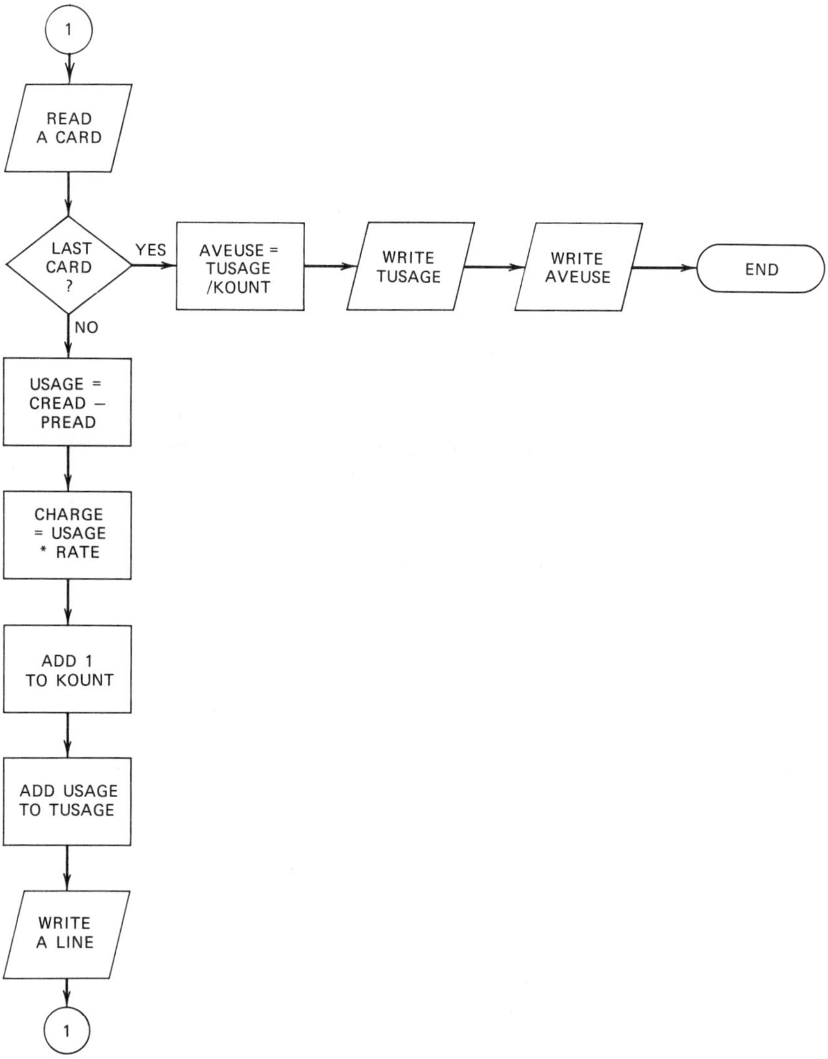

Input utilizes the same data input format as programs USAGE2 and USAGE3. Output now has more fields, however, as shown in the printer spacing chart.

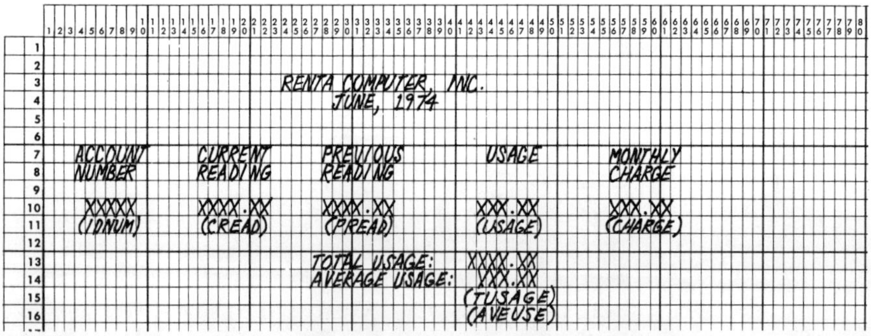

Assignment Statements

Sometimes a program requires information that is constant rather than variable. That is, the field does not change with each data card. Instead it either remains unchanged throughout the program or is changed by calculations or by another arithmetic statement. For example, in program USAGE4, the rate charged for usage is the same for all customers. Therefore the rate is given only once, at the beginning of the program. When a field is established in this way, with an immediate value, the process is usually called "initializing" a field. Statement 1 initializes RATE with the value of .7, representing 70 per cent.

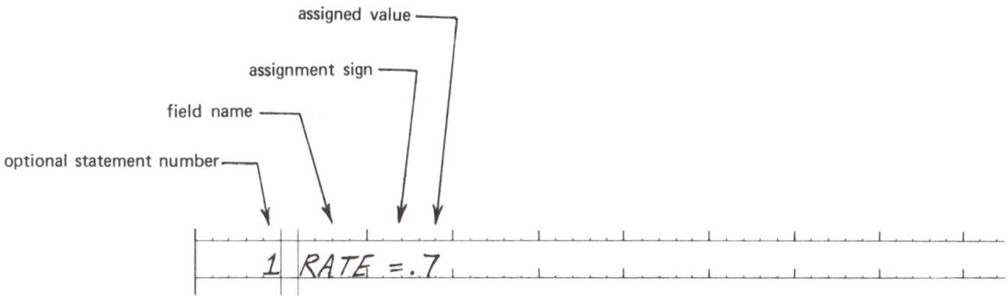

The = sign is called the assignment or replacement sign in FORTRAN. It is not an "equal" sign in the arithmetic sense. In FORTRAN it means "is now assigned the value of" or "is replaced by" instead of the arithmetic meaning of "is equal to." This is an important point to remember because the two sides of the = sign are *not* interchangeable in FORTRAN as they are in the arithmetic meaning. The name of the field receiving the new value must be on the *left* side of the = sign. Digits, field names, arithmetic expressions, or combinations of these can be on the *right* side of the FORTRAN = sign. If a field name is on the right side of the = sign, the computer must have a value *already stored* for that field. Statement 1 uses the decimal point and digit 7 on the right side of the = sign. The decimal point can be used in assignment statements, but dollar signs and commas are not permitted.

When an item is counted or totaled, a special counting or accumulating field for the item requires an initial value of zero. As quantities are added to this field, its value changes, but accuracy demands that the field begin as 0. In expanded program USAGE4, customers are counted and total usage is accumulated. In order to achieve accurate results, both a customer counting field (KOUNT) and a total usage field (TUSAGE) must be established with initial values of 0.

```
2 TUSAGE = 0.
3 KOUNT = 0
```

In statement 2, real field TUSAGE is assigned the value 0. The forms 0.0 or .0 are also acceptable for initializing real fields to zero. Integer field KOUNT is assigned the value 0 without a decimal point in statement 3. Because blanks are ignored before and after operational signs, blank spaces can be on either or both sides of the = sign in statements 1, 2, and 3. An assignment statement can have, but does not require, a statement number.

The values established for RATE, TUSAGE, and KOUNT will remain in storage until input, calculations, or another assignment statement replaces the contents with a new value.

When a field name is on the right side of the = sign, two precautions must be taken. The programmer must first check to make certain that the field on the right already has a value in storage. The second precaution concerns the difference between real and integer numbers. If a real number duplicates a real or an integer number, the field remains essentially the same, and if an integer is made equal to another integer, the fields are identical. If, however, an integer duplicates a real field, all digits to the right of the decimal in the original field are dropped in the integer field. For example:

```
51 REAL = 123.45
52 INTGER = 123
53 R1 = REAL
54 R2 = INTGER
55 I1 = REAL
56 I2 = INTGER
```

After statements 51-56 are all processed, the following values are in storage:

Field Name	Field Contents
REAL	123.45
INTGER	123
R1	123.45
R2	123.0
I1	123
I2	123

Integer field I1 has dropped the decimal fraction in field REAL. In later calculations, this "deficiency" will be demonstrated as an asset in certain types of differentiations.

REVIEW QUESTIONS

1. Why is "=" called the assignment or replacement sign in FORTRAN?
2. What must always be on the left side of the = sign?
3. How is a FORTRAN assignment statement different from an arithmetic equality statement?

Arithmetic Statements with Operation Signs

Five arithmetic signs or operators are used in FORTRAN arithmetic statements.

+ means "plus"—addition
− means "minus"—subtraction
* means "times"—multiplication
/ means "divided by"—division
** means "to the power of"—exponentiation

Arithmetic statements can contain expressions using one or more of these operators with either field names or numbers or a combination of both. The arithmetic expressions must be on the right side of the = sign because the name of the field receiving the new value is required as the only entry on the left side.

The flowchart shows that after each data card is read, four calculations are made. The first of these calculations establishes real field USAGE by giving it the value obtained when the previous meter reading is subtracted from the current meter reading.

Subtraction

FORTRAN uses the −(the 11-punch, minus sign) to signal the subtraction operation.

```
12 READ (5,13,END=21) IDNUM, PREAD, CREAD
13 FORMAT (I5, 24X, F6.2, 2X, F6.2)
14 USAGE = CREAD - PREAD
```

To calculate the value of USAGE, the computer locates the stored values of CREAD (current meter reading) and PREAD (previous meter reading) that were obtained when the data card was read. These values are substituted for the field names in the arithmetic instruction, so that real field USAGE receives the value of CREAD minus the value of PREAD. For example, if CREAD contains 37.00 and PREAD contains 12.50, USAGE receives the value of 24.50. The computer actually stores more digits than these, but all to the right of the rightmost nonzero digit are assumed to be 0's, such as 24.5000000000. Neither CREAD nor PREAD changes its contents by the subtraction process. Only the field named on the left of the = sign receives a new value. Every time statement 14 is executed, values currently stored for CREAD and PREAD are used to establish a new value for USAGE.

The FORTRAN compiler follows algebraic rules in regard to positive and negative values. When the difference (answer field) requires a negative sign, the sign will be output as part of the field contents, immediately to the left of the first nonzero digit. Therefore, if there is a possibility of a negative answer, the field format size must be large enough to hold the sign. Otherwise only asterisks (*) will be output.

Although some FORTRAN compilers will not permit integer and real fields in the same arithmetic statement, most FORTRAN IV compilers now accommodate this "mixed mode."

Multiplication

The next calculation required by the USAGE4 flowchart establishes real field CHARGE by multiplying the contents of fields USAGE and RATE:

```
15 CHARGE = USAGE * RATE
```

RATE is a constant established in statement 1. USAGE is a variable calculated during the processing of each data card when statement 14 is executed. CHARGE is also calculated for each data card. In statement 15, the * (11-4-8 punch, asterisk) instructs the computer to multiply the contents of USAGE by the contents of RATE, with the product (answer) placed in field CHARGE.

For example, assume the following field contents before statement 15 is executed:

Field Name	Field Contents
USAGE	24.50
RATE	0.7
CHARGE	XXXXXXXXXXXX. (unknown)

When the statement is to be executed, the computer finds the stored values for USAGE and RATE and multiplies them.

24.50	(USAGE)
* .7	(RATE)
17.15	(CHARGE)

Real field CHARGE is now equal to 17.15. The FORTRAN compiler automatically adjusts decimal points in arithmetic operations.

As the multiplication operation shows, fields listed on the right side of the arithmetic statement do not change values. Only the field listed on the left of the = sign changes value.

Field Name	Field Contents
USAGE	24.50
RATE	0.7
CHARGE	17.15

Most FORTRAN compilers accept "mixed mode" in multiplication. The field type of the product determines the form of the answer. For example, if the statement multiplies the contents of USAGE and RATE, but stores the product in integer field ICHARG, the decimal fraction is lost.

```
55 ICHARG = USAGE * RATE
```

The compiler again finds the values for the fields USAGE and RATE and multiplies them.

```
 24.50    (USAGE)
   *.7    (RATE)
 ------
    17    (ICHARG)
```

Because an integer cannot have a fraction, the answer is truncated (cut off) to the whole number value of 17. Thus field names, which ordinarily determine field type, should be watched in creating all fields.

Addition

The most frequent calculations in business data processing are counting and totaling. In problem USAGE4, customers are counted and usage is accumulated or totaled. These operations are indicated by the + (12-6-8 punch, plus sign) in FORTRAN.

Both counting and accumulating require that the fields begin with zero values. Statements 2 and 3 initialize real field TUSAGE and integer field KOUNT to zeros.

```
2 TUSAGE = 0.
3 KOUNT = 0
```

Thus, immediately before statements 16 and 17 are executed for the first time, the computer stores the following values.

Field Name	Field Contents
KOUNT	0
TUSAGE	0.0
USAGE	24.50

Then statement 16 is executed for the first time.

```
16 KOUNT = KOUNT + 1
```

In order to carry out this instruction, the computer finds the current 0 value of KOUNT and adds 1 to it. The sum of the addition (0 + 1 = 1) is assigned as the new value for KOUNT.

Field Name	Field Contents
KOUNT	1

This process of adding 1 to the current value of KOUNT is repeated every time statement 16 is executed. Since it is executed every time a record is input, KOUNT is an accurate reflection of the number of data cards (hence customers) read. If a deck of data cards contains 35 records, field KOUNT has a stored value of 35 after all cards are processed. The same result is obtained if tape or disk records are input.

Statement 17 illustrates the second common use of addition in business data processing, accumulating totals.

```
17 TUSAGE = TUSAGE + USAGE
```

Like the instruction for counting, the field named on the left of the = sign must also be one of the fields on the right side of the = sign. Instead of adding the value 1, however, the *contents* of the field being accumulated are added to the totaling field.

The computer finds the current values of fields listed on the right side of the = sign. Just before statement 17 is executed for the first time, the following values are in storage.

Field Name	Field Contents
KOUNT	1
TUSAGE	0.0
USAGE	24.50

The computer adds the current value of TUSAGE to the current value of USAGE. The sum is the new value of TUSAGE.

Field Name	Field Contents
KOUNT	1
TUSAGE	24.50
USAGE	24.50

Assume that USAGE for the second customer processed is 10.25. The computer now stores the following:

Field Name	Field Contents
KOUNT	2
TUSAGE	24.50
USAGE	10.25

When statement 17 is executed for the second customer, again the current value of TUSAGE is added to the current value of USAGE.

```
  24.50   (TUSAGE)
+ 10.25   (USAGE)
  -----
  34.75
```

The sum is the new value of TUSAGE.

Field Name	Field Contents
KOUNT	2
TUSAGE	34.75
USAGE	10.25

This process is repeated for every data card. When the last record is processed, KOUNT contains the number of cards processed, and TUSAGE contains the total amount of USAGE for all cards processed.

The third type of addition operation adds two fields and places the sum in a third field. For example, if the RENTA COMPUTER COMPANY had a base charge in addition to the usage charge, an instruction would add BASE to CHARGE and place the answer in COMCHG.

```
60 COMCHG = BASE + CHARGE
```

Every time statement 60 is executed, a new value is stored for field COMCHG. This new value is dependent upon the current values of BASE and CHARGE, but neither of these fields is changed by the execution of statement 60. This is a perfectly valid addition operation, but it cannot be used for counting or totaling because it receives a new value each execution without regard to the previous contents of COMCHG.

REVIEW QUESTIONS

4. What operators (signs) are used to indicate multiplication, subtraction, and addition?

5. When an arithmetic statement creates an integer field from contents of real fields, what happens to the decimal fractions?

6. In an arithmetic statement with fields on both sides of the = sign, which field contents are changed by execution of the instruction?

Division

The flowchart for USAGE4 shows that when the last (/*) card is sensed, average usage is calculated. This is achieved by using the integer field KOUNT, which has been counting customers, and real field TUSAGE, which has been accumulating the total amount of usage for all customers.

When the /* card is read, the END= option in READ statement 12 branches the program to statement 21:

```
12 READ (5, 13, END=21) IDNUM, PREAD, CREAD
```

To execute statement 21, the computer first finds the stored values of TUSAGE and KOUNT:

```
21 AVEUSE = TUSAGE / KOUNT
```

The stored value of TUSAGE is divided by the stored value of KOUNT. The quotient (answer) is stored in real field AVEUSE. AVEUSE need not be initialized to 0. before the statement is executed, because the new value is established regardless of any previous contents.

Assume that when the /* card is input and the program branches to statement 21, the following values are in storage:

Field Name	Field Contents
KOUNT	35
TUSAGE	1133.00
USAGE	23.11
AVEUSE	XXXXX.X (unknown)

The computer divides 1133.00 by 35, and places the quotient in real field AVEUSE.

Field Name	Field Contents
KOUNT	35
TUSAGE	1133.00
USAGE	23.11
AVEUSE	32.37104+

Despite the fact that AVEUSE is a real field, it is important for TUSAGE also to be a real field. Otherwise the stored quotient would not contain any possible fraction. If both fields on the right side of the = sign are integers, the integer answer (32) is calculated and *then* converted to real form (32.0) and stored as AVEUSE.

Exponentiation

The last FORTRAN arithmetic operator specifies exponentiation—to the power of. In mathematical expressions, a number raised to the power of 2 is said to have an exponent of 2, to be squared, or to be multiplied times itself. All these expressions refer to the operation exponentiation. In arithmetic, a number with an exponent of 2 is written $NUMBER^2$. In FORTRAN the same expression is written NUMBER**2. For example, SQUARE is a field equal to NUMBER squared:

```
65 SQUARE = NUMBER ** 2
```

If, for example, NUMBER equals 15, SQUARE equals 225.0 because 15 times 15 equals 225. Another example calculates CUBE, which is NUMBER raised to the third power ($NUMBER^3$):

```
66 CUBE = NUMBER ** 3
```

Real field CUBE now has the value of 3375.0, the equivalent of NUMBER times NUMBER times NUMBER.

Instead of a numeric constant such as '3', the exponent can be a field name:

```
67 ANSWER = ANUM ** N
```

In statement 67, ANSWER is equal to the contents of real field ANUM raised to the power of integer field N. As with all arithmetic statements, fields listed on the right side of the = sign must have values *already stored* in the computer before the statement is executed. Some FORTRAN compilers also require the exponent to be an integer or integer field name. The other fields can be either real or integer types. Like the other arithmetic operations, the type of field listed on the left of the = sign determines whether the answer will be stored as either a real or an integer field.

Once a value is stored in the memory of a computer, it is simply a value for that field. That is, the computer does not "remember" how the value was obtained. No relationship with another field is retained. For example, if CHARGE is determined by multiplying USAGE times RATE, CHARGE is not automatically altered when the contents of USAGE or RATE are altered. Only when the instruction multiplies RATE times USAGE to obtain a value for CHARGE is there an interrelationship.

This independence of fields also means that fields need not be output in the order by which they were first stored. They can be output in any order the report requires.

REVIEW QUESTIONS

7. How is an exponent expressed in FORTRAN?
8. What sign expresses the operation of division?
9. Does a computer "remember" how a field originates? If so, how?

Program USAGE4, with comment cards for documentation, is completed:

```
C THIS PROGRAM INPUTS CUSTOMER IDENTIFICATION NUMBER (IDNUM),
C METER READING FOR THE PREVIOUS MONTH (PREAD), AND METER
C READING FOR THE CURRENT MONTH (CREAD) FROM PUNCHED DATA CARDS.
C TUSAGE AND CHARGE ARE CALCULATED. TOTAL AND AVERAGE USAGE ARE
C PRINTED AFTER ALL CARDS ARE PROCESSED.
C PROGRAMMED BY H. SEEDS, JUNE 1974.
C
C INITIAL VALUES ESTABLISHED FOR RATE, CARD COUNT, AND TOTAL USAGE
    1 RATE = .7
    2 TUSAGE = 0.
    3 KOUNT = 0
C HEADINGS ARE PRINTED
    4 WRITE (6,5)
    5 FORMAT ('1',T25,'RENTA COMPUTER, INC.'/T30,'JUNE, 1974')
    6 WRITE (6,7)
    7 FORMAT ('0',3X,'ACCOUNT',5X,'CURRENT',5X,'PREVIOUS',8X,
     /'USAGE',7X,'MONTHLY')
    8 WRITE (6,9)
    9 FORMAT (4X,'NUMBER',6X,'READING',5X,'READING',21X,'CHARGE')
   10 WRITE (6,11)
   11 FORMAT(' ')
C PROCESSING LOOP BEGINS WITH RECORD (CARD) INPUT
   12 READ (5,13,END = 21) IDNUM, PREAD, CREAD
   13 FORMAT (I5, 24X, F6.2, 2X, F6.2)
C DETAIL CALCULATIONS
   14 USAGE = CREAD - PREAD
   15 TUSAGE = TUSAGE + USAGE
   16 CHARGE = USAGE * RATE
   17 KOUNT = KOUNT + 1
C RECORD (PRINTED LINE) OUTPUT
   18 WRITE (6,19) IDNUM, CREAD, PREAD, USAGE, CHARGE
   19 FORMAT (5X,I5,6X,F7.2,5X,F7.2,8X,F6.2,7X,F6.2)
C BRANCH BACK TO READ STATEMENT
   20 GO TO 12
C TOTAL AND AVERAGE CALCULATED AND PRINTED AFTER LAST CARD
   21 AVEUSE = TUSAGE / KOUNT
   22 WRITE (6, 23) TUSAGE
   23 FORMAT ('0',26X,'TOTAL USAGE: ', 2X,F7.2)
   24 WRITE (6,25) AVEUSE
   25 FORMAT (27X, 'AVERAGE USAGE: ',1X,F6.2)
C END OF PROGRAM
   26 CALL EXIT
      END
```

With the five demonstration data cards, program USAGE4 prints the following report:

```
                    RENTA COMPUTER, INC.
                        JUNE, 1974

ACCOUNT      CURRENT      PREVIOUS        USAGE      MONTHLY
NUMBER       READING      READING                    CHARGE

 12548       2247.36      2138.57        108.79       76.15
 24573       3344.55      3245.67         98.88       69.22
 45342       3687.52      3572.46        115.06       80.54
 55343       1568.97      1154.86        414.11      289.88
 75342       3189.54      2483.46        706.08      494.26

                       TOTAL USAGE:     1442.92
                       AVERAGE USAGE:    288.58
```

Hierarchy of Operations

Arithmetic statements often involve more than one operation. When executing statements with more than one arithmetic sign, the FORTRAN compiler has its established order of operations, called a hierarchy of operations. Its most basic rule is always to search arithmetic expressions from left to right. The first search looks for operations within parentheses. Operations within parentheses are executed, observing FORTRAN's order of operations. After all arithmetic expressions within parentheses have been executed, the compiler searches the remainder of the expression for any exponential operations. After exponents are processed, the third search is for multiplication and division operations. The last search is for addition and subtraction operations.

In summary, the FORTRAN compiler searches from left-to-right four times, processing in the following hierarchy of operations:

1. Parenthetical expressions.
2. Exponentials.
3. Multiplication, division.
4. Addition, subtraction.

To illustrate this order, especially the use of parentheses, let us assume that after a programmer works through the program calculations, he sees that he could use fewer instructions. He sees that statements 14 and 15 can be combined to obtain the value of field CHARGE. Instead of the present statements,

```
 14 USAGE = CREAD - PREAD
 15 CHARGE = USAGE * RATE
```

PREAD can be subtracted from CREAD and the difference multiplied times RATE.

```
114 CHARGE = (CREAD - PREAD) * RATE
```

The parentheses set off the subtraction operation so that it will be processed first. Then the result is multiplied by RATE. Thus statement 114 accomplishes what previously required two statements to calculate.

This process of combining operations can continue until it becomes clumsier than it is practical. For instance, a payroll problem with hours, rate, bonus, taxes and fica can produce statement 200:

```
200 PAY=(HOURS*PAYRAT)+((HOURS*PAYRAT)*.08)-(((HOURS*PAYRAT)
   1+((HOURS*PAYRAT)*.08))*TAXRAT-(((HOURS*PAYRAT)+((HOURS
   2*PAYRAT)*.08))*FICART)
```

The programmer must be certain to match pairs of parentheses. There must be a closing parenthesis for each opening parenthesis, and an opening parenthesis for each closing parenthesis.

This method of writing instructions has one serious limitation. Because they do not have individual field names, bonus, taxes, and fica payment cannot be output as separate fields, nor can they be accumulated into total fields.

REVIEW QUESTIONS

10. What are the four levels in FORTRAN's hierarchy of operations?

11. In which direction does the FORTRAN compiler search when determining the order of operations?

OBJECTIVES REVIEW

Study the objectives listed at the beginning of this chapter. Check each one to be certain you have achieved it. Restudy the chapter sections related to any objectives you have not achieved.

REVIEW TEST

Study the following FORTRAN program carefully. Using the "data cards" that are given, "process" the program just as the FORTRAN compiler does. On scratch paper, keep a record of what is in memory for every field as the program proceeds. On a printer spacing chart or in the space below, print the output of the test program as it would appear on the printer. Watch both the contents and the placement of fields and headings.

Data Cards
Columns:

```
         1         2
12345678901234567890
1347 011   2450
2568 200   0600
3176 025   1174
/*
```

Program

```
    0 KOUNT = 0
    1 TEXTEN = 0.
    2 WRITE (6,3)
    3 FORMAT('1',T21,'RIGHT CLOTHIERS')
    4 WRITE (6,5)
    5 FORMAT('0',T12,'ITEM',4X,'QUANTITY',4X,'COST',3X,'EXTENSION')
    6 READ(5,7,END = 14) ITEM,NUMBER,COST
    7 FORMAT(I4,1X,I3,3X,F4.2)
    8 EXTEN = NUMBER * COST
    9 TEXTEN = TEXTEN + EXTEN
   10 KOUNT=KOUNT +1
   11 WRITE (6,12)ITEM,NUMBER,COST, EXTEN
   12 FORMAT(' ',T12,I4,T23,I3,T31,F5.2,T40,F8.2)
   13 GO TO 6
   14 WRITE(6,15)TEXTEN
   15 FORMAT('0',T38,'$',F9.2)
   16 WRITE(6,17) KOUNT
   17 FORMAT(' ',T38,I4,1X,'ITEMS')
   18 STOP
      END
```

Printout

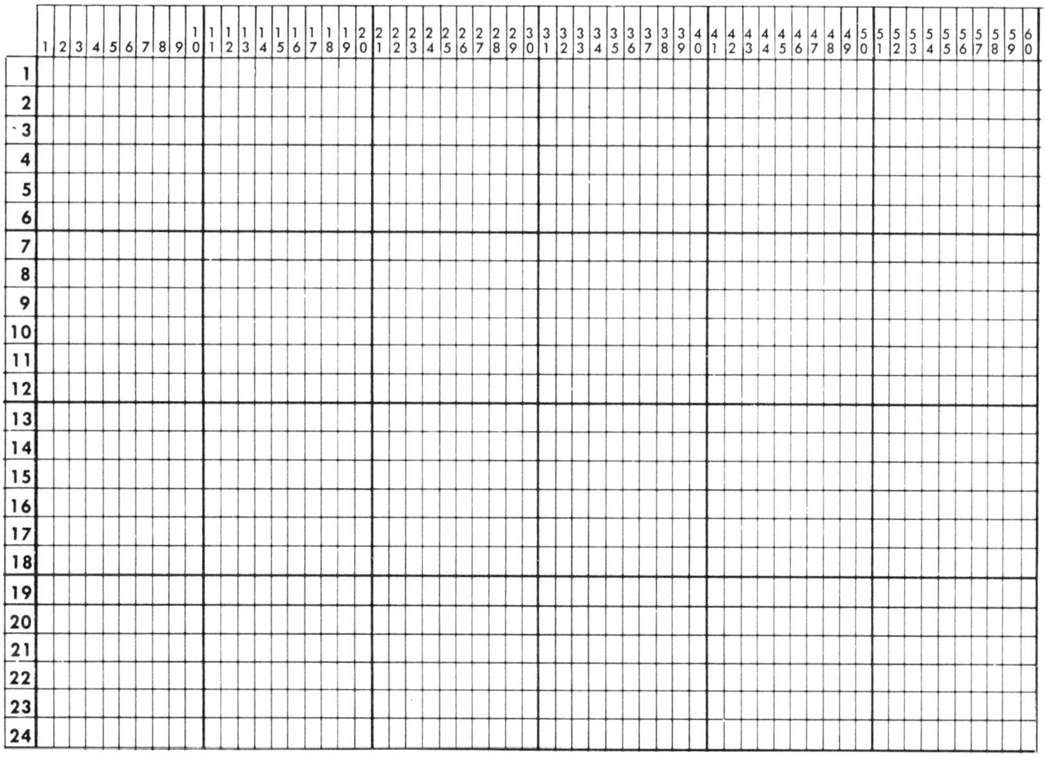

ASSIGNMENTS

Complete a flowchart, printer spacing chart, and coding for one of the following programs. Then keypunch and submit the program for processing.

1. A teacher must know the number of punched cards submitted to the computer by students in a data processing class. The student ID number and the number of cards submitted are recorded for each student. The number of cards is totaled, and students are counted. After all records are processed, the average number of cards per student is calculated.

Input Records

Fields	Card Columns	
Student ID number	21-27	I7
Number of cards	52-54	I3

Headings of printed report contain name and location of school, and column identifications. Detail lines print all input fields. After all records are processed, total lines print the total number of cards read, the number of students counted, and the average number of cards per student.

2. A printed report of the day's sales is prepared for the sales manager.

Input Records

Fields	Card Columns	
Seller's ID number	21-25	I5
Item sales number	38-40	I3
Number of units sold	74-75	I2
Price per unit	62-66	F5.2
Commission rate	52-53	F2.2

Calculate the total amount of sale and the seller's commission for each record. Count all sales records. Total the amount of all sales and of all sales commissions. After all records are processed, find the average amount of sales and the average commission.

Headings contain the company name, company location, and column identification. Detail output lines contain the seller's ID number, item sales number, number of units sold, price per unit, amount of sale, seller's commission rate, and the seller's commission.

Total output lines contain the total amount of all sales, total amount of all sales commissions, average amount of all sales, and average amount of all sales commissions.

3. A printed report for a bank lists short-term loans. Calculations determine the amount due at the date of maturity: Amount due equals the amount borrowed plus interest. Interest equals the amount borrowed multiplied by the annual interest rate, multiplied by the time of the loan (I=Prt). Banks commonly use a 360-day year in loan calculations. Therefore, a 45-day loan is for 45/360 of a year.

Input Records

Fields	Card Columns	
Loan account number	21-25	I5
Amount of loan	52-57	F6.2
Annual rate of interest	74-77	F4.2
Number of days of loan	38-40	I3 or F3.0

Calculate amount of interest and amount due for each account. Total both calculated fields.

Printed report has company and column headings. Detail lines contain all input fields, amount of interest, and amount due. At end of report, total interest and total amount due are printed with identifying message.

4. A report lists all store sales in which a special 8% discount is given.

Input Records

Fields	Card Columns	
Purchaser's account number	21-25	I5
Original price	52-57	F6.2

The net price is calculated by subtracting the amount of the discount from the original price. A state sales tax of 4.5% of the net price is calculated and added to the net price to obtain the cost. Amounts of sales tax, net price, cost are totaled. The printed report contains the company name and location and column headings. Detail lines contain the input fields, net price, amount of sales tax, and cost. After the last card is processed, the three totals are printed.

5. A list of auto insurance policy cancellations is printed. The law requires the company to prorate the premium and keep only the amount for the number of days the policy was in force. The remainder must be returned to the policy owner. The amount retained by the company is calculated by multiplying the amount of the premium by the part of the year the policy was in force. Insurance companies use a 365-day year. Therefore, a policy in effect for 45 days is 45/365 of a year. Both amounts retained and amounts to be returned are calculated and totalled.

Input Records

Fields	Card Columns	
Policy holder's account number	21-25	I5
Dollar value of policy	38-43	F6.2
Number of days policy in force	76-78	I3 or F3.0

Report contains company name and location and column headings. Detail lines contain all input fields, amount retained, and amount to be returned. After the last record is processed, the two total amounts are printed with identifications.

Chapter Objectives

1. Be able to input alphameric information of any length with the most efficient use of storage.
2. Be able to output alphameric information of any length.
3. Be able to write a program printing mailing address lists or other alphameric lists, for labels or standard length paper.
4. Be able to use the "open" Hollerith statement for information to be input and output only.

7

Alphameric Fields and The "Open" Hollerith Format

In business data processing, names of customers, employees, sales items, etc. frequently are required with other detail information. Therefore the programmer must learn how to input and output alphameric data. Alphameric fields (which are often called alphanumeric or A fields) are most frequently used for nonnumeric information, but the "open Hollerith" can also be utilized in special cases. Both techniques are illustrated and explained in this chapter.

Alphameric Fields

An alphameric field can contain alphabetic, numeric, or special characters, or any combination of these types of characters. Normally an alphameric field is used only in input and output operations, not in calculations. When numeric characters are part of an alphameric field, they are not recognized by the compiler as digits, and so they cannot be used for ordinary arithmetic operations. Like literals, alphameric fields regard blanks as characters.

Names of alphameric fields follow most of the rules for numeric field names: (1) names of alphameric fields are one to six characters in length, (2) the first character of the name must be alphabetic, (3) special characters—except the blank and the dollar sign—cannot be part of the name. Names of alphameric fields are not limited in one restriction, however. Any alphabetic character is acceptable as the first character of the field name. The following examples illustrate acceptable and unacceptable names for alphameric fields.

Acceptable Names For Alphameric Fields	Unacceptable Names For Alphameric Fields	
N	123	(number for first character)
N1	1N	(number for first character)
NAME	Q&A	(special character used)
HEAD1	HEADING	(too many characters)
$MONEY	%PERCT	(special character used)

The chief difficulty in understanding and using alphameric fields arises because many FORTRAN compilers are limited in the length of such fields. Unless special instructions are given,[1] an alphameric field in an IBM S/360 or S/370 FORTRAN compiler cannot contain more than four characters. Since most names, descriptions, addresses, etc., extend beyond four characters, the data must be stored in computer memory as several alphameric fields. Although this seems strange at first, most programmers soon see how it is done. Then the technique is easy to use.

For example, a person's name is allotted 20 positions in a data card and on a printer spacing chart. In computer storage, however, the FORTRAN compiler can accept only four characters for each alphameric field. Therefore the 20-character names can most economically be divided into five alphameric fields, each four characters in length. This is the most economical method of storage because the compiler reserves four bytes for each alphameric field even when the programmer asks only for a one, two, or three character field. In fact, unless special instructions are given, it reserves four bytes for fields longer than four characters also, but it stores only the rightmost four characters of the field designated. Therefore the best use of computer storage (without special instructions) is made whenever a 4-character field fills an alphameric specification.

This alphameric field limitation means that although people mentally regard long alphameric information—such as a name—as one unit, the computer requires a separate name for *each* of the required alphameric fields. The programmer can group and remember the fields easily when they are labeled with such names as NAME1, NAME2, NAME3, NAME4, and NAME5. Even shorter are field names N1, N2, N3, N4, and N5.[2]

The data cards used in the USAGE problems now contain customer's names in columns 6-25:

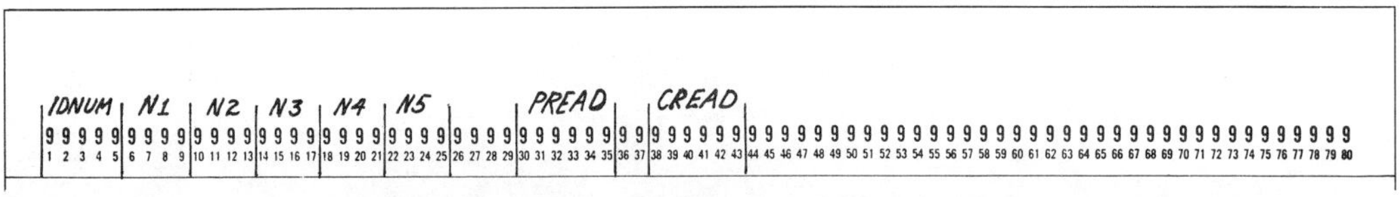

[1]For further information, see Chapter 15, Type Specification Statements.

[2]Multiple field names are most easily handled as arrays, a technique demonstrated in Chapter 11, DIMENSION Statement and Arrays.

The cards now look like this:

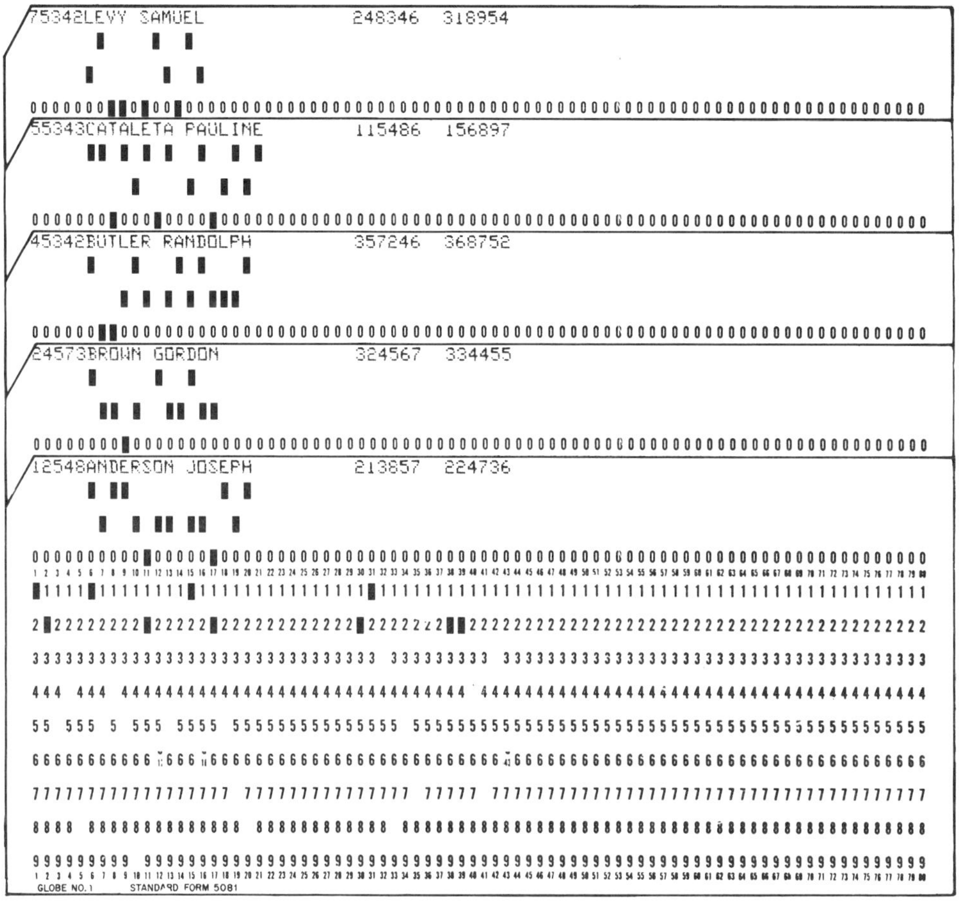

These added names are now part of the printed report form:

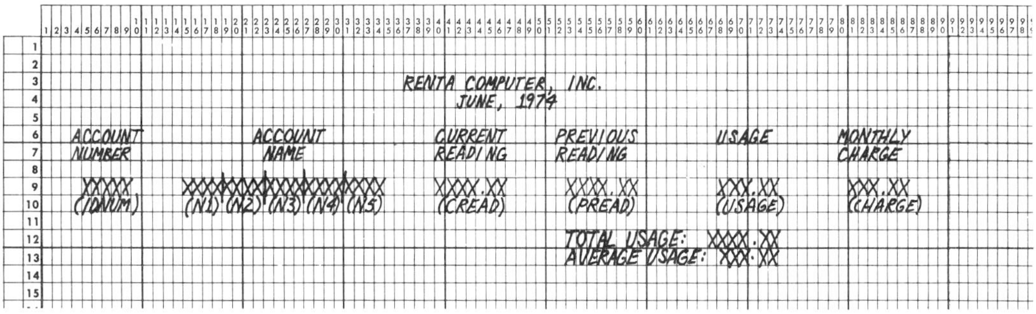

Since the FORTRAN compiler cannot store ANDERSON b̸JOSEPHb̸b̸b̸b̸b̸ as one 20-position alphameric field, the READ and

FORMAT statements create five 4-position A fields. Because the five fields are adjacent to each other and all the same length and type, they need not be listed separately but can instead use a duplicating factor of 5. The duplicating factor instructs the compiler to repeat the A4 specification five times.

```
12 READ(5,13,END=21) IDNUM, N1,N2,N3,N4,N5,PREAD,CREAD
13 FORMAT(I5,5A4,4X,F6.2,2X,F6.2)
```

When statement 12 is executed with FORMAT statement 13, eight separate fields are now stored by the computer. When the first data card is processed, storage contains the following:

Field Name	Field Contents
IDNUM	12548
N1	ANDE
N2	RSON
N3	ƀJOS
N4	EPHƀ
N5	ƀƀƀƀ
PREAD	2138.57
CREAD	2247.36

Four characters, including the blanks, are stored in each of the five alphameric fields. When the fields are to be output in the printed report, the five A fields are again placed adjacent to each other:

```
18 WRITE (6,19) IDNUM,N1,N2,N3,N4,N5,CREAD,PREAD,USAGE,CHARGE
19 FORMAT (5X,I5,5X,5A4,6X,F7.2,5X,F7.2,8X,F6.2,8X,F6.2)
```

In the printed report, the five alphameric fields appear simply as one person's name:

```
ANDERSON JOSEPH
```

Like numeric fields, alphameric fields can be output anywhere on the printed line. Ordinarily, they should not be separated by any other fields or blank spaces.

If only 19 instead of 20 positions are reserved in the data card for the customers' names, five fields are still the simplest way to store the alphameric characters. The 5A4 specification can not be used, however. Instead, the most economical method of storing the 19 alphameric characters is four A4 fields and one A3 field. This same technique can be used in FORMAT statements for any alphameric information not evenly divided into 4-character fields.

REVIEW QUESTIONS

1. What types of characters can be part of alphameric fields?
2. On the IBM S/360 or S/370, what is the largest alphameric field possible without special instructions?
3. Why is the largest size alphameric field the most economical size on the IBM S/360 and S/370?

Computers are used increasingly as printers. Sometimes information is merely input and output, without any field manipulations, calculations, or editing. For example, a store mails advertisements for a special sale to all its credit card customers. The addresses are printed on 6-line adhesive labels with 40 characters to a line. They are on a continuous form paper especially prepared for computer output:

A card file contains all the customers' names and addresses in 3-line formats:

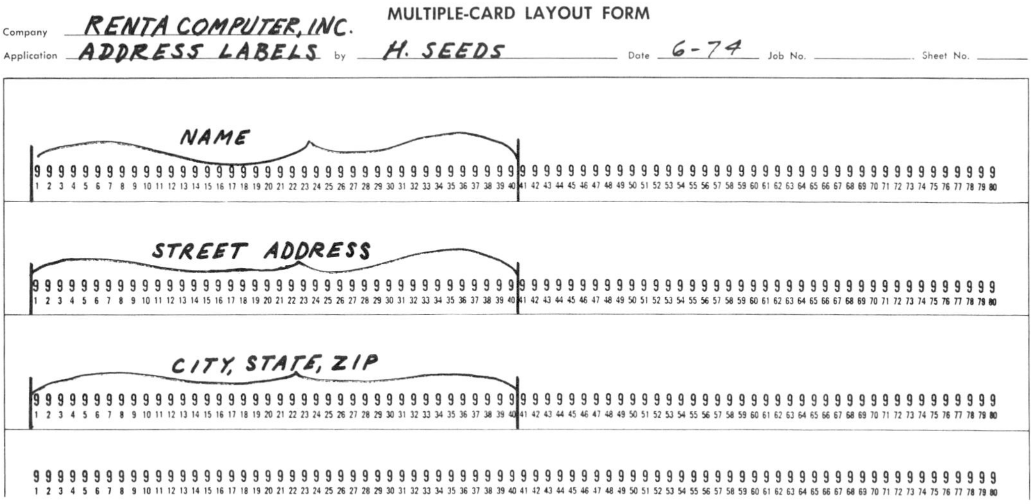

The following cards contain records for two customers:

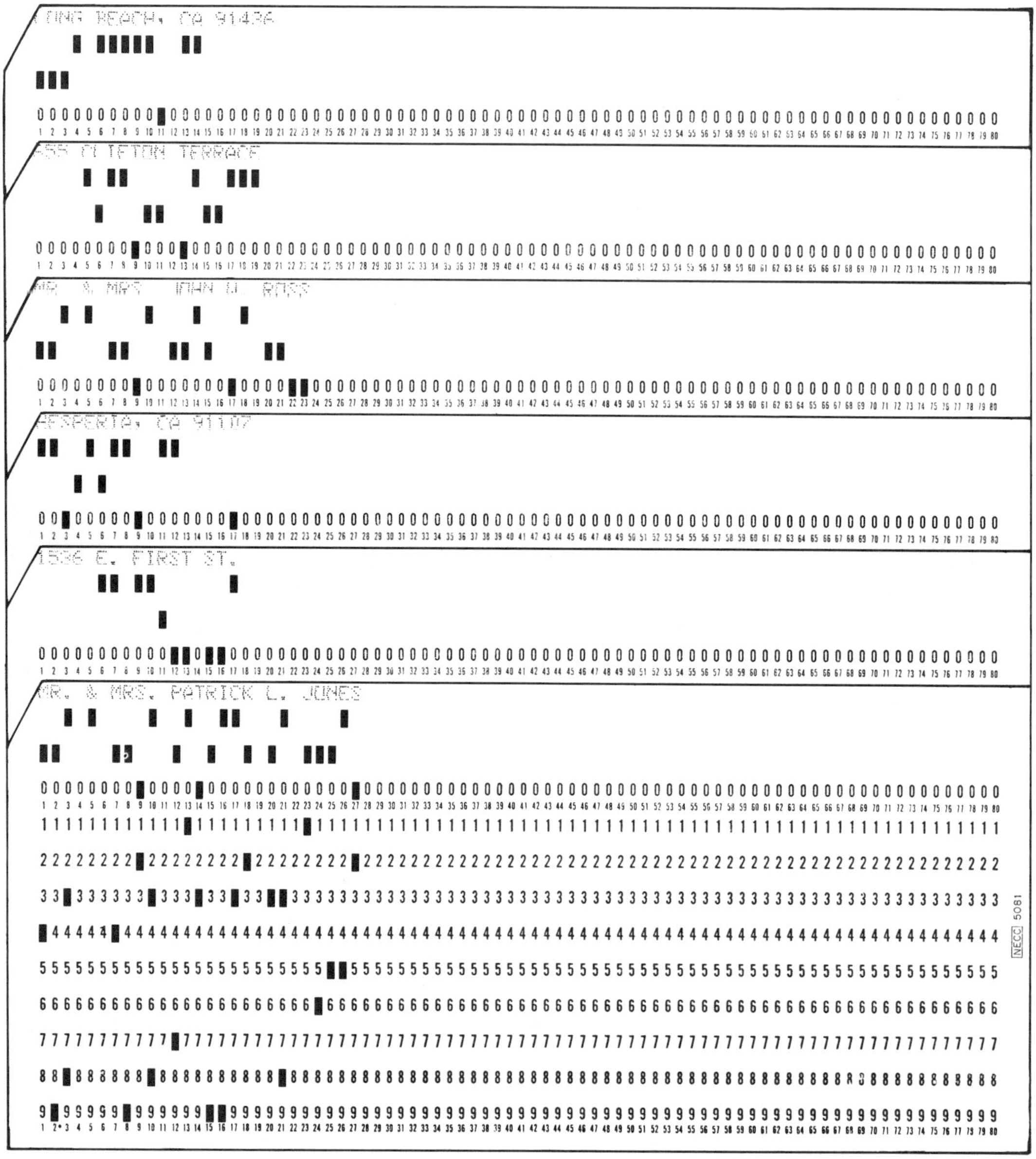

The address labels are to be printed in the following format:

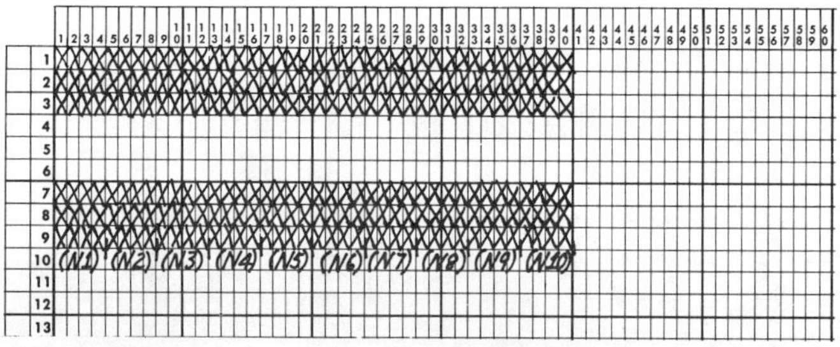

With the input and output formats established, the program is flowcharted.[3]

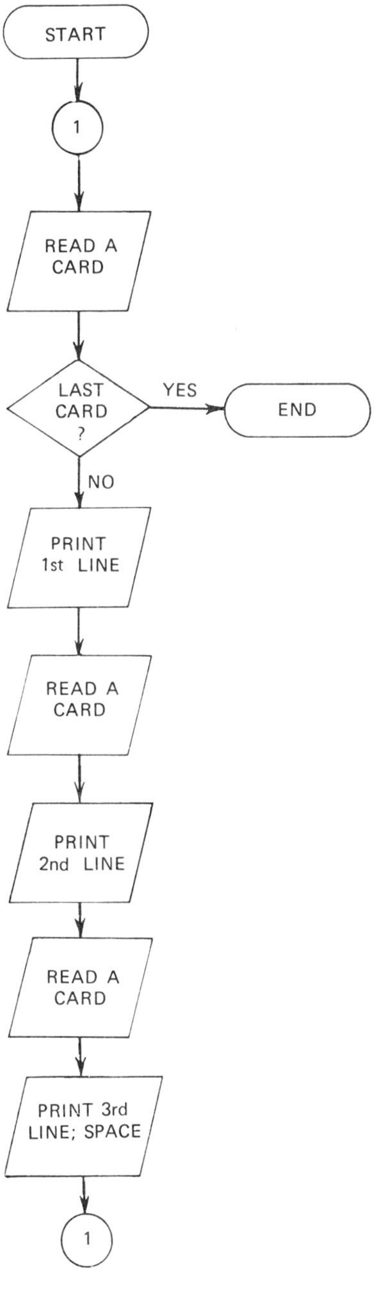

[3]A less repetitious, more flexible flowchart can be used after the introduction of conditional branching by the IF statement.

The first 40 columns of each card are read and printed as 10 alphameric fields of four characters each. The carriage control position in the FORMAT statement for each detail line of print contains a blank for single spacing. After the three lines have been output according to FORMAT statement 4, statements 9 and 10 instruct the printer to triple space. This moves the printer down to the next address label.

```
C PROGRAM TO PRINT 3-LINE ADDRESS LABELS
    1 READ(5,2,END=12)N1,N2,N3,N4,N5,N6,N7,N8,N9,N10
    2 FORMAT (10A4)
    3 WRITE(6,4)N1,N2,N3,N4,N5,N6,N7,N8,N9,N10
    4 FORMAT (' ',10A4)
    5 READ(5,2)N1,N2,N3,N4,N5,N6,N7,N8,N9,N10
    6 WRITE (6,4)N1,N2,N3,N4,N5,N6,N7,N8,N9,N10
    7 READ (5,2)N1,N2,N3,N4,N5,N6,N7,N8,N9,N10
    8 WRITE (6,4)N1,N2,N3,N4,N5,N6,N7,N8,N9,N10
    9 WRITE (6,10)
   10 FORMAT ('-')
   11 GO TO 1
   12 CALL EXIT
      END
```

The program reads and prints three lines of the address and then spaces to a new label. This process continues until the entire file of customer names and addresses is processed:

Sometimes a programmer wants a list of everything in all 80 columns of a deck of data cards. He can use a simple program that divides the 80 columns of each card into 20 A4 fields:

```
C PROGRAM TO READ AND PRINT A FILE OF DATA CARDS
    1 READ (5,2,END=6)N1, N2,N3,N4,N5,N6,N7,N8,N9,N10,N11,N12,
     1 N13,N14,N15,N16,N17,N18,N19,N20
    2 FORMAT (20A4)
    3 WRITE(6,4)N1,N2,N3,N4,N5,N6,N7,N8,N9,N10,N11,N12,N13,
     1 N14,N15,N16,N17,N18,N19,N20
    4 FORMAT (' ',20A4)
    5 GO TO 1
    6 CALL EXIT
      END
```

Again carriage control contains a blank for single spacing in the FORMAT for printing, but a '0' in the first position of statement 4 would provide double spacing for all printed lines if the programmer wanted that.

Field names N1, N2, N3, etc. need not be used for all alphameric fields. As the discussion on alphameric field names stated, such fields follow the basic rules of all field names. Because alphameric fields are required so often in multiple blocks of fields, the numeric grouping such as N1, N2, etc. is often used. In addition, when arrays and implied DO loops are discussed, this type of name is most easily transferred to the more sophisticated techniques.

REVIEW QUESTIONS

4. What FORMAT specification will read and store the entire contents of an 80-column card, regardless of the types of characters present?
5. What FORMAT specification will print a single spaced listing of the contents of 80-column cards, regardless of the types of characters present?

The "Open" Hollerith Format

Sometimes a different technique is used to input and output alphameric data. The data is not stored in labeled fields which must be both input and output by field names. Instead, characters are stored as part of a FORMAT statement and printed whenever the FORMAT statement is used with a WRITE statement. This "open" Hollerith technique can be utilized only if a READ and then a WRITE instruction are executed with the same FORMAT statement, and the FORMAT contains a Hollerith format specification.

```
51 READ (5,52,END=55)
52 FORMAT(' ',79H
  1                            )
53 WRITE (6,52)
54 GO TO 51
55 CALL EXIT
   END
```

Statements 51-54 will read and print all contents of a deck of data cards, with one exception: the first card column will be ignored. Because it is used in printing as well as reading, the first position of FORMAT statement 52 must be reserved for carriage control. Even if the literal ' ' were omitted, and the Hollerith specification changed to 80H, the first position would be regarded as the carriage control instruction when WRITE statement 53 was executed. Therefore the programmer must guard against the accidental insertion of any character except a blank, zero, minus, or plus. Other characters give unpredictable (until tested) results.

If data set reference number 7, representing the card punch, were used in the FORMAT statement, a deck of cards could be duplicated. Then, of course, column 1 would have no special significance because carriage control does not exist for card punching.

```
61 READ (5,62,END=65)
62 FORMAT (80H
  1                            )
63 WRITE (7,62)
64 GO TO 61
65 CALL EXIT
   END
```

Every character punched on every data card is punched into the new deck of cards. After the last card is read and duplicated, the program ends.

The drawback of the "open" Hollerith specification is that characters are restricted to exactly the same positions in input and output. It has a handy versatility at times, however. Assume that several businesses use one computer service bureau for a basic business program. The bureau can use a single program for reports of the various companies if different company names and report dates can appear in the headings. For example, assume that all the reports use 120-column paper. The printer spacing chart shows three heading lines, each having all characters in the first 79 positions.

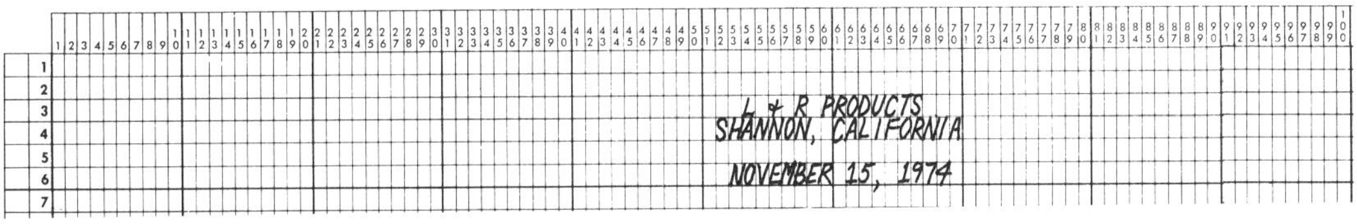

The three lines contain a company name, address, and date of the report. As a card layout form shows, these items are keypunched in the same positions minus 1 in three data cards:

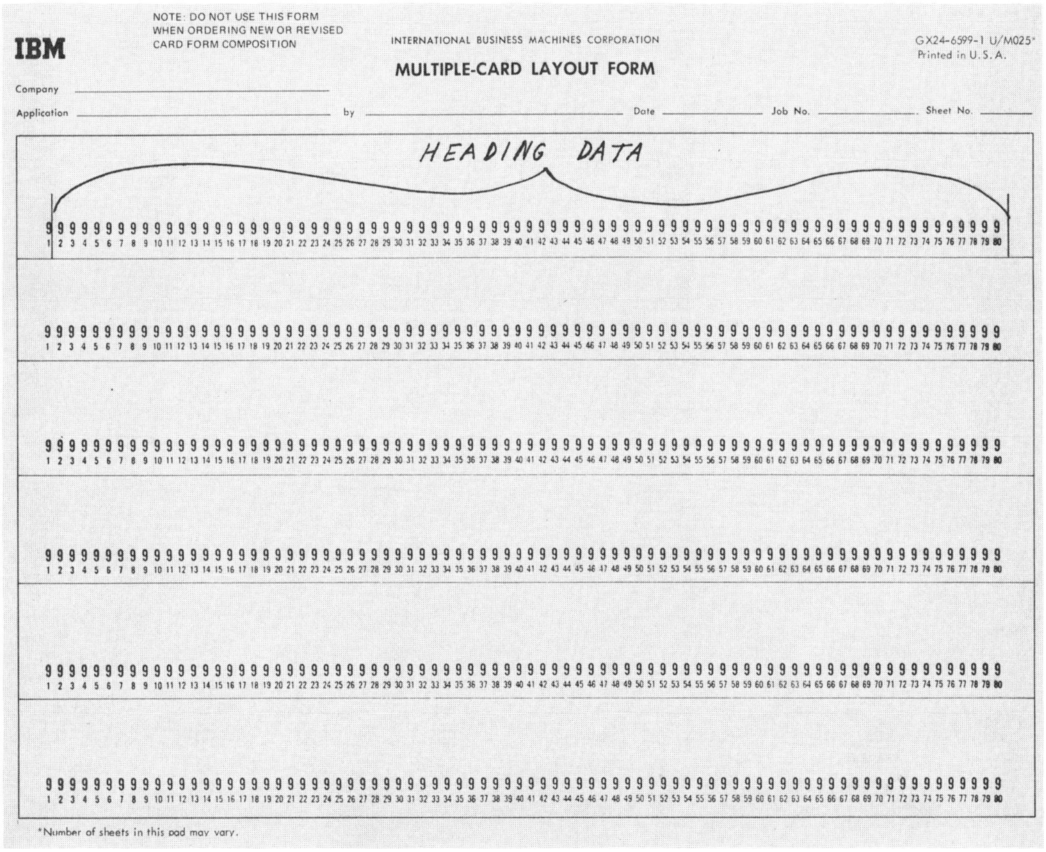

The logic for such a program beginning is seen in the flowchart:

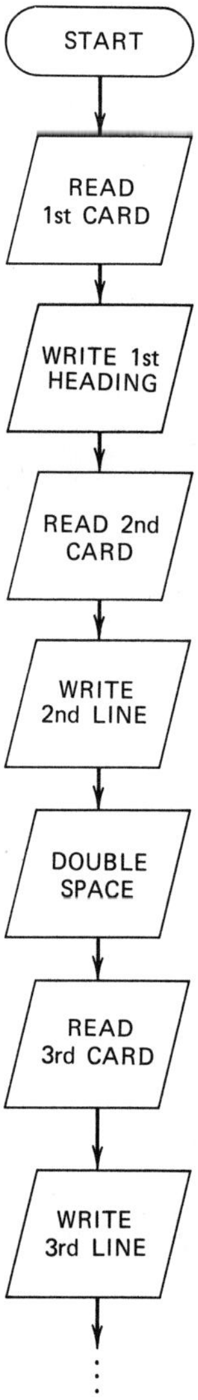

Using the "open" Hollerith specification of FORMAT statement 2, the program inputs, spaces, and outputs the 3-line heading.

```
1 READ (5,2)
2 FORMAT (1X,79H
 /                              )
3 WRITE (6,2)
4 READ (5,2)
5 WRITE (6,2)
6 WRITE (6,7)
```

```
7 FORMAT (' ')
8 READ (5,2)
9 WRITE (6,2)
```

In this program segment, FORMAT statement 2 is used by three READ and three WRITE statements. Statement 2 consists of the precautionary blank in tab position 1, and a 79-position "open" Hollerith specification.

After each data card is read, the contents of columns 2-80 are stored *as part of* FORMAT statement 2. For example, immediately after statement 1 is executed, FORMAT statement 2 contains the following in storage: 1X, 79Hƀƀƀƀƀƀƀƀƀƀƀƀƀƀƀƀƀƀƀƀƀƀƀƀƀƀƀƀƀƀ ƀƀƀƀƀƀƀƀƀƀƀƀLƀ&ƀRƀPRODUCTSƀƀƀƀƀƀƀƀƀƀƀ. When WRITE statement 3 calls for FORMAT statement 2, the Hollerith specification prints as it is currently stored.

The 1X specification to guarantee single spacing cannot be changed during the program. The 79H specification retains the same characters only until another READ statement utilizing FORMAT statement 2 is executed. Therefore, when READ statement 4 is processed, FORMAT statement 2 stores 1X, 79Hƀƀƀƀƀƀƀƀƀƀƀƀƀƀƀƀƀƀƀƀƀƀƀƀƀƀƀƀƀ ƀƀƀƀƀƀƀƀƀƀƀƀƀƀƀƀSHANNON,ƀCALIFORNIAƀƀƀƀƀƀƀƀƀ. WRITE statement 5 prints the literal as stored.

Because the blank provided by the 1X in tab position 1 cannot be altered, WRITE statement 6 and FORMAT statement 7 provide double spacing. This could be achieved by two other methods. In the first, a blank data card is read, stored, and output by READ and WRITE statements using FORMAT statement 2. Then the card containing the last heading data is read, and the date replaces the 79 blanks previously stored. In the second method, an 80H specification is established in FORMAT statement 2 instead of the 79H specification. The third data card creates double spacing by containing a zero rather than a blank in the first column, tab position 1.

After the third heading data card is read by statement 8, FORMAT statement 2 contains 1X, 79Hƀƀƀƀƀƀƀƀƀƀƀƀƀƀƀƀƀƀƀƀƀƀƀƀƀ ƀƀƀƀƀƀƀƀƀƀƀƀƀƀƀƀƀƀƀƀNOVEMBERƀ15,ƀ1974ƀƀƀƀƀƀƀƀ ƀƀ. This literal is output by WRITE statement 9. After statements 1-9 are executed, the following is on the printer, with the first line beginning in print position 54.

```
  L & R PRODUCTS
SHANNON, CALIFORNIA

 NOVEMBER 15, 1974
```

The program then proceeds into its main processing.

By changing the data cards with heading information, the programmer can use the same program for all companies the bureau services. This type of versatility is very useful in commercial establishments.

REVIEW QUESTIONS

6. How can a literal be placed in an "open" Hollerith format?
7. How long does the literal remain as part of the "open" Hollerith format?
8. How is the literal output?
9. What is the limitation of an "open" Hollerith specification?

Sometimes the same literals are used several times during the execution of a program. Separate FORMAT statements can retain the information simultaneously from all the data cards. In the program segment with statements 11-21, READ instructions store data from all three cards into three different FORMAT statements. WRITE instructions are executed whenever necessary.

```
11 READ (5,12)
12 FORMAT (1X,79H
  2                                   )
13 READ (5,14)
14 FORMAT (1X,79H
  4                                   )
15 READ (5,16)
16 FORMAT (1X,79H
  6                                   )
17 WRITE (6,12)
18 WRITE (6,14)
19 WRITE (6,20)
20 FORMAT ('0')
21 WRITE (6,16)
```

The output of the program segment is identical to the segment with statements 1-9, but each of the three FORMAT statements retains its contents throughout the program. Thus all three literals are available for output throughout the entire processing.

When the "open" Hollerith specification is used in this way, the FORTRAN compiler allows another variation that is useful to the programmer. Because the entire Hollerith format area is displaced when READ statements are executed, identifications can be made in the program listings without later complications in output. For example, statements 11-16 could be coded in the following way.

```
11 READ (5,12)
12 FORMAT (1X, 79HCOMPANY NAME
  2                                  )
13 READ (5,14)
14 FORMAT (1X, 79HCOMPANY ADDRESS
  4                                  )
15 READ (5,16)
16 FORMAT (1X, 79HREPORT DATE
  6                                  )
```

After READ statements fill the Hollerith areas these identifications are no longer stored, but the programmer is often aided by program listings that identify the intended contents of "open" Hollerith fields in this manner.

The "open" Hollerith specification need not be used alone, but it is unusual to find integer or real fields that are to be output in identical input and output positions, even though the same fields need not be used for both input and output. The "open" Hollerith can be used for employees' or customers' names, or any other alphameric material, however, if the same FORMAT specifications apply to both input and output.

REVIEW QUESTIONS

10. How do "open" Hollerith statements give a program flexibility?

11. How can the intended contents of "open" Hollerith specifications be identified in program listings?

12. When the same FORMAT statement is used for both READ and WRITE statements, which tab position requires special attention?

OBJECTIVES REVIEW

Study the objectives listed at the beginning of this chapter. Check each one to be certain you have achieved it. Restudy the chapter sections related to any objectives you have not achieved.

REVIEW TEST

Study the following FORTRAN program carefully. Using the "data cards" that are given, "process" the program just as the FORTRAN compiler does. On scratch paper, keep a record of what is in storage for every field as the program proceeds. On a printer spacing chart or in the space below, print the output of the test program as it would appear on the printer. Watch both the contents and placement of fields and headings.

Data Cards

```
                   1         2         3         4
Columns:  1234567890123456789012345678901234567890
Card 1:   SMITHFIELD JANE     6273   155
Card 2:   TAYLOR RALPH        7154   080
Card 3:   UNDERSHAFT GEORGE   9367   197
Card 4:   /*
```

Program

```
1 WRITE (6,2)
2 FORMAT (T37, 'FORTRAN COLLEGE')
3 WRITE (6,4)
4 FORMAT (10X, 'STUDENT', T40, 'UNITS', T55, 'CHARGES')
```

```
 5 READ (5,6,END=11)N1,N2,N3,N4,N5,IDNUM,UNITS
 6 FORMAT (5A4,I4,3X,F3.1)
 7 CHARGE = UNITS * 10.0
 8 WRITE (6,9) N1,N2,N3,N4,N5,IDNUM, UNITS,CHARGE
 9 FORMAT (T10,5A4,2X,I5,T41,F4.1,T54,F8.2)
10 GO TO 5
11 STOP
   END
```

Printout

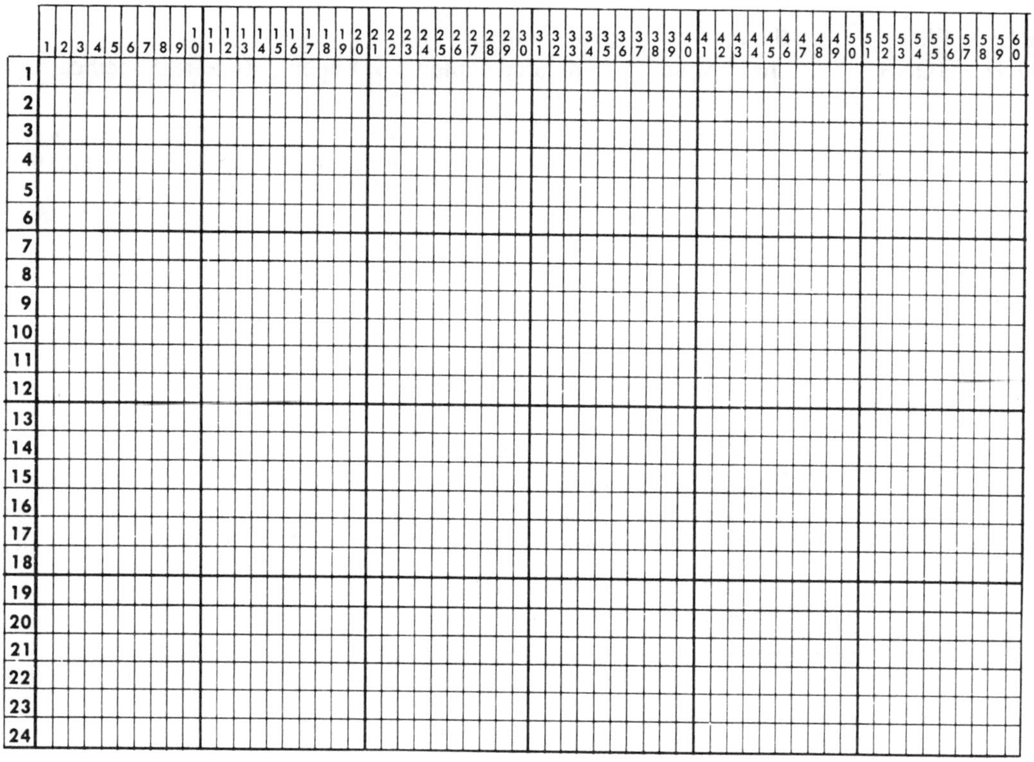

ASSIGNMENTS

Complete a flowchart and printer spacing chart for one of the following programs. Keypunch a set of special data cards containing heading information about the company. This will be input and printed either with A format specifications or with "open" Hollerith specifications. Then code, keypunch, and submit the program with the heading data cards just ahead of the regular data cards.

1. Complete the following inventory program:

Input Cards

Fields	Card Columns	
Item code name	1-4	(A4)
Item number	23-27	(I5)
Number on hand	33-36	(I4)
Price per item	52-56	(F5.2)

Calculate the value of each item by multiplying the price by the number on hand. Count the number of items processed. Total the number on hand and the calculated values. The printed report begins with the special company information and column headings. Detail lines contain the input fields and the calculated value (extension). After the last record is processed, print with identification the number of items processed, the total number of items on hand, and the total value.

2. A printed report calculates tax assessments for property in an unincorporated (noncity) area. For each \$100 of assessed valuation, county taxes are \$2.37, school taxes are \$4.48, and special district taxes are \$.56. Calculate these taxes for each assessment. Calculate the combined amount due for each record, and accumulate totals for each of the three taxes.

Input Cards

Fields	Card Columns	
Property owner	1-20	(5A4)
Assessment property number	21-27	(I7)
Assessed property value (in whole dollars)	30-35	(F6.0)

The printed report begins with the special heading information (name of county and state) and column headings. Detail lines contain the input fields, the amounts of the three taxes, and the combined amount. After the last card is processed, print the totals for each tax.

3. After labor negotiations, all of a company's hourly employees receive a 7% increase in their hourly wage. The new rates are calculated, and a report is printed to show the increase in dollar values.

Input Cards

Fields	Card Columns	
Employee's name	1-20	(5A4)
Employee's ID number	23-27	(I5)
Hourly pay rate	55-57	(F3.2)

After printing the company and column headings, the report lists the input fields and the new hourly pay rate for each employee.

4. A company receives invoices with item weight in pounds and height in inches. For certain processes, the company requires the height in feet and the weight in ounces. Convert the following information into the required measurements.

Input Cards

Fields	Card Columns	
Item number	23-27	(I5)
Height of item (in inches)	63-66	(F4.1)
Weight of item (in pounds)	71-73	(F3.1)

After printing company and column information, the following fields are output: item number, height of item (in inches and feet), and weight of item (in pounds and ounces).

5. A builder calculates the number of 1-foot floor tiles required for a building project. Each card contains the length and width of the area to be tiled in one building. The number of tiles is calculated by multiplying length by width. The number of buildings is counted. The number of tiles for each building, the total number of tiles for the project, and the average per building are calculated.

Input Record

Fields	Card Columns	
Building code number	23-27	(I5)
Length (in feet)	63-66	(F4.1)
Width (in feet)	71-73	(F3.1)

After printing the building company heading and column headings, detail lines are printed with all input fields and the required number of tiles. After the last card is processed, the total number of tiles and the average number per building are printed with identifications.

6. After printing headings, use the "open" Hollerith format to read and print the following data:

Input Record

Fields	Card Columns	
ID number	21-27	(I7)
Type	50	(I1)
Quantity	61-65	(I5)

IBM 1403 line printer.

Chapter Objectives

1. Be able to explain the difference between conditional and unconditional branching.
2. Be able to flowchart the conditional branching or logical decision making condition.
3. Be able to use the arithmetic IF statement to express conditional branching.
4. Be able to use the arithmetic IF statement for either 2-way or 3-way conditional branching.
5. Be able to use the arithmetic IF statement for last card test when the END= option is not available.
6. Be able to use the arithmetic IF statement with a line counter field to provide appropriate printing.
7. Be able to use the arithmetic IF statement with alphameric fields.
8. Be able to use the arithmetic IF statement to match multiple sequentially organized files.

8

Arithmetic IF Statement

The GOTO statement *unconditionally* branches a program to a statement specified in the GOTO instruction. When a GOTO command is encountered, the compiler automatically branches to the statement listed instead of continuing to the next sequential statement. Sometimes, however, a programmer wants to branch to one of two or more different instructions depending upon certain conditions in the program. For example, a bonus is earned if the employee works *more than* 40 hours; or a special discount is given to all orders *greater than* \$500; or a count is taken of all people *older than* 65 years. In each case, a comparison (with 40, 500, or 65) must be made. The program branches to a statement according to the condition (result) of the comparison.

This two-fold process of evaluating and then determining the direction of processing is called *conditional branching*. Sometimes it is referred to as "logical decision making." In computer-related work, the word "logic" has various meanings, but the term "logical decision making" means comparing two quantities and then branching as a result of the comparison.

FORTRAN has three logical decision statements: the arithmetic IF, the logical IF, and the computed GOTO. The arithmetic IF is the most basic and most commonly used of the three. Usually it is simply called the IF statement. That is how it will be referred to in this chapter.

The IF statement enables the programmer to choose the way a program flows. For example, Renta Computer, Inc., gives a special 10% discount to all users with monthly usage greater than 200.0 hours, and a 5% discount to all users with usage equal to 200.0. In order to find whether a customer is eligible for a discount, 200.0 is subtracted from the calculated field USAGE: USAGE − 200.0. This calculation is stated in such a way that the result is either (1) a negative value, (2) a zero, or (3) a positive value. That is, when compared with zero, the expression is either less than, equal to, or greater than 0. The result of this comparison determines to which statement the program branches.

When USAGE is less than 200.0, the result is a negative value. For example, if USAGE equals 135.0, the following calculation has the effect of creating a negative value:

```
  135.0 (USAGE)
 -200.0
 ------
  -65.0 (negative quantity; less than 0)
```

When USAGE is 200.0, the result is zero:

```
  200.0 (USAGE)
 -200.0
 ------
    0.0 (zero value; equal to 0)
```

When USAGE is greater than 200.0, a positive value results:

```
  265.0 (USAGE)
 -200.0
 ------
   65.0 (positive quantity; greater than 0)
```

Special discounts are given only to those customers whose tested value (USAGE − 200.0) gives a zero or positive condition. Therefore a different sequence of instructions is required for each of the three possible conditions. Negative values must branch the program directly to the detail print line. Zero values go to the 5% discount calculations. Positive values must go to 10% discount calculations. Both zero and positive instruction sequences return to the main line of processing by branching to the detail print instruction. This logical decision making is shown in the problem flowchart. At a program point that requires a logical decision, the diamond-shaped decision symbol is used.

After studying the various conditions possible, the programmer uses an IF statement for the conditional branching:

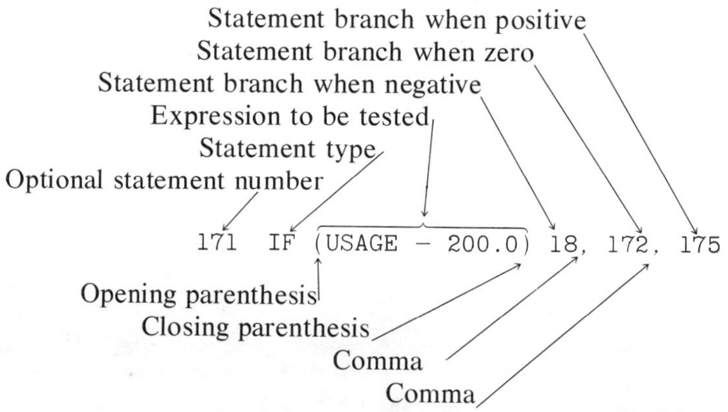

The IF statement begins with the word IF, followed by an arithmetic expression within a pair of parentheses. After the closing parenthesis is a list of three integers separated by commas. Each integer represents the number of an *executable* statement. The order or position of the statement numbers within the IF statement is important because it determines the program branching. The three possible branches are always in the following order: first position, negative; middle position, zero; last position, positive. This means that when the value of the expression within the parentheses is negative, the program branches to the first statement listed. For example, if USAGE equals 135 when statement 171 is executed, the resulting value (USAGE – 200.0) is negative, and so the program branches to statement 18, the first integer listed.

When USAGE equals 200.0, the value of the expression in parentheses is zero. The program branches to statement 172 because it is the second statement number listed. A positive value, when USAGE is greater than 200.0, branches the program to statement 175, the third statement listed. If program logic requires it, any two of the three statement numbers can be the same. No matter which executable statement the program branches to, that instruction is executed and the program proceeds from that point.

The expression in parentheses can be an arithmetic expression with any arithmetic sign (or signs) except the assignment (equal) sign.

Like the GO TO instruction, the IF statement need not be numbered, but the first executable statement *following* it requires a statement number.

REVIEW QUESTIONS

1. What is the difference between conditional and unconditional branches? Give a FORTRAN instruction of each type.
2. What are the two basic steps in logical decision making?
3. Which arithmetic sign cannot be in the parentheses of an IF statement?
4. How many statement numbers must be listed after the parentheses?
5. What branching condition does each statement number represent?

Some examples illustrate the possibilities:

```
50 IF (USAGE - MINUM) 60, 20, 40
51 IF (USAGE * RATE) 13, 14, 3
52 IF (TOTAL / KOUNT) 34, 51, 90
53 IF (PAY + BONUS - TAXES + COMISH - DUES) 45, 43, 47
54 IF (KODE - KTEST) 13, 15, 13
55 IF (VALUE - QUANT ** 2) 32, 56, 12
```

The parenthetical expression can simply be a field name:

```
56 IF (USAGE) 72, 54, 78
```

When a field name is used alone, the field contents are compared to 0, and found to be less than (negative), equal to (zero), or greater than (positive) zero. In each case, the IF statement tests the current value of the expression in parentheses.

Program USAGE—IF

Input data format is studied from the card layout form:

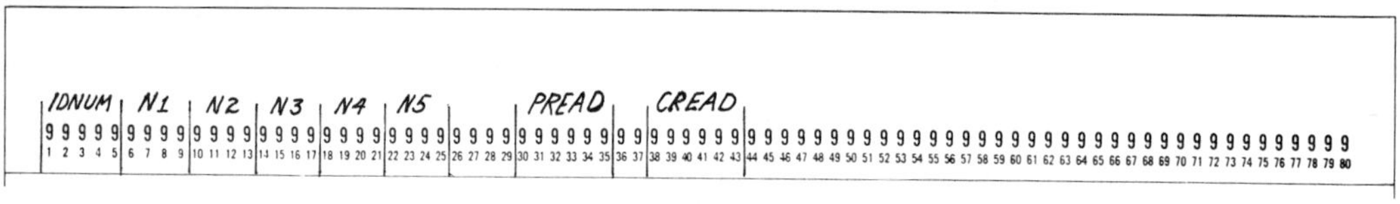

Output is designed on a printer spacing chart:

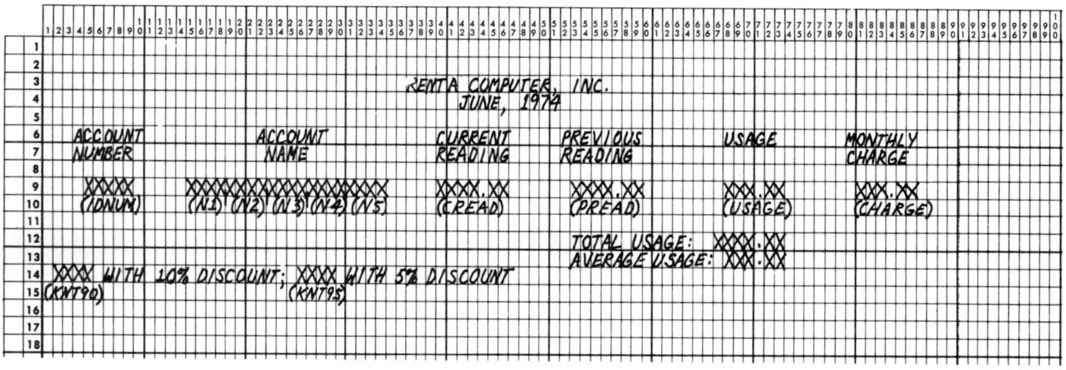

With logical decision making shown by the use of the diamond-shaped decision symbol, problem USAGE-IF is flowcharted.

119
PROGRAM
USAGE—IF

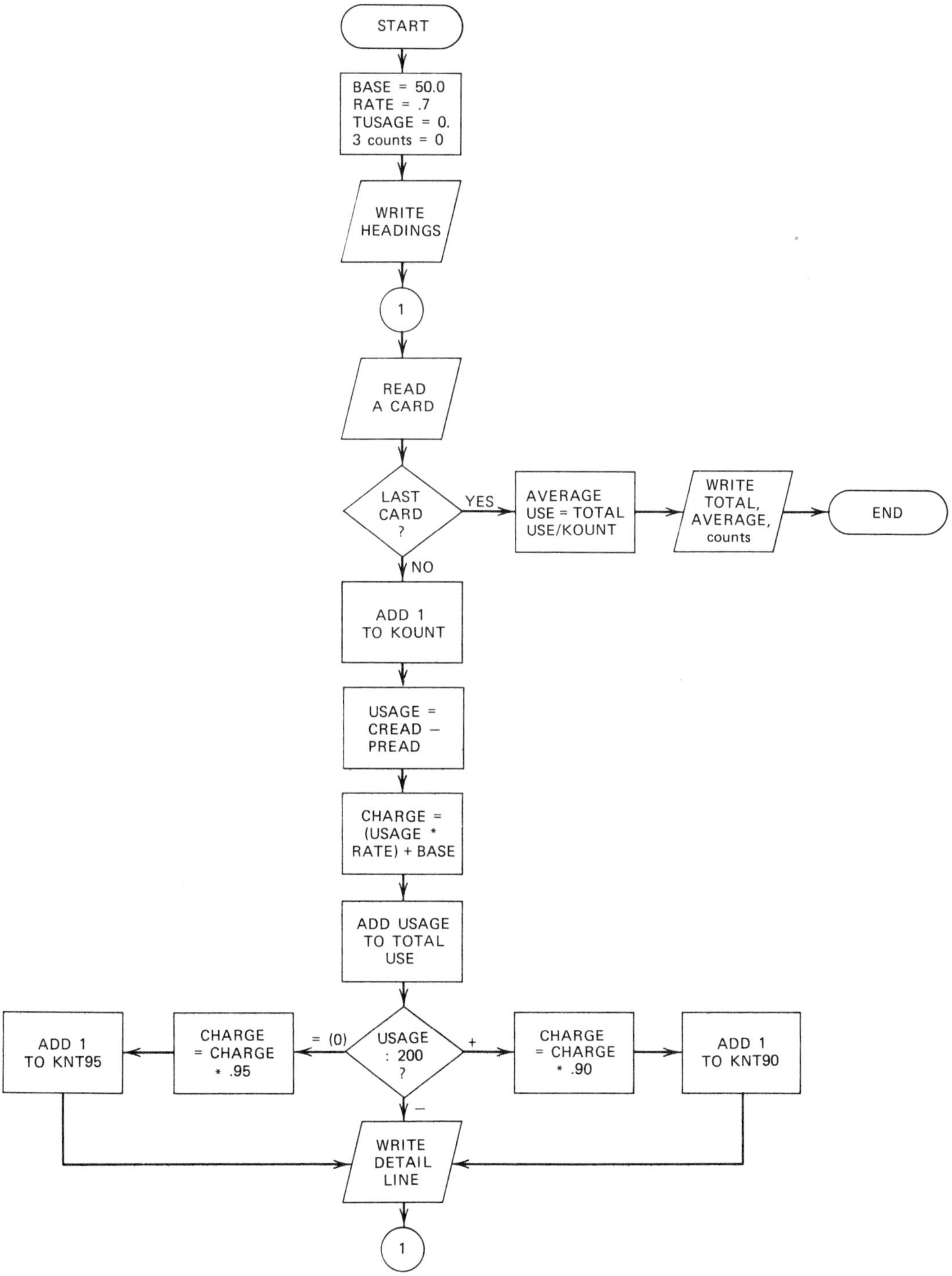

Program USAGE-IF, with a $50.00 base charge in addition to calculated CHARGE, is written:

```
C USAGE AND CHARGE ARE CALCULATED FOR EACH CUSTOMER. CUSTOMER
C COUNT (KOUNT), TOTAL USAGE (TUSAGE), AND AVERAGE USAGE (AVEUSE)
C ARE CALCULATED, USAGE IS TESTED FOR SPECIAL DISCOUNTS.
C CUSTOMERS WITH SPECIAL DISCOUNTS ARE COUNTED. TOTAL AND AVERAGE
C USAGE, AND BOTH COUNTS ARE PRINTED AFTER ALL CARDS ARE PROCESSED.
C PROGRAMMED BY H. SEEDS, JUNE 1974.
C
C BASE CHARGE, RATE, TOTAL USAGE, AND COUNTS ARE INITIALIZED
  101 KNT90 = 0
  102 KNT95 = 0
    0 BASE = 50.00
    1 RATE = .7
    2 TUSAGE = 0.0
    3 KOUNT = 0
C HEADINGS ARE PRINTED
    4 WRITE (6,5)
    5 FORMAT ('1',T38,'RENTA COMPUTER, INC.'/T43,'JUNE, 1974')
    6 WRITE (6,7)
    7 FORMAT ('0',3X,'ACCOUNT',11X,'ACCOUNT',11X,'CURRENT',5X,
     1 'PREVIOUS',8X,'USAGE',7X,'MONTHLY')
    8 WRITE (6,9)
    9 FORMAT (4X,'NUMBER',13X,'NAME',13X,'READING',5X,'READING',
     1 21X,'CHARGE')
   10 WRITE (6,11)
   11 FORMAT (' ')
C READ-CALCULATE-WRITE CYCLE
   12 READ(5,13,END=21)IDNUM,N1,N2,N3,N4,N5,PREAD,CREAD
   13 FORMAT (I5,5A4,4X,F6.2,2X,F6.2)
   14 KOUNT = KOUNT + 1
   15 USAGE = CREAD - PREAD
   16 TUSAGE = TUSAGE + USAGE
   17 CHARGE = BASE + (USAGE * RATE)
C TEST WHETHER USAGE IS LESS THAN, EQUAL TO, OR GREATER THAN 200.00
  171 IF (USAGE-200.0) 18, 172, 175
  172 CHARGE = CHARGE * .95
  173 KNT95 = KNT95 + 1
  174 GO TO 18
  175 CHARGE = CHARGE * .90
  176 KNT90 = KNT90 + 1
   18 WRITE(6,19) IDNUM, N1,N2,N3,N4,N5,CREAD,PREAD,USAGE,CHARGE
   19 FORMAT(5X,I5,5X,5A4,5X,F7.2,6X,F7.2,8X,F6.2,7X,F6.2)
   20 GO TO 12
C TOTAL CALCULATIONS AND OUTPUT AFTER LAST DATA CARD PROCESSED
   21 AVEUSE = TUSAGE / KOUNT
   22 WRITE (6,23) TUSAGE
   23 FORMAT ('0',T54,'TOTAL USAGE: ',T68,F7.2)
   24 WRITE (6,25) AVEUSE
   25 FORMAT (T54,'AVERAGE USAGE: ',T69,F6.2)
```

```
26 WRITE (6,27) KNT90,KNT95
27 FORMAT (T3,I4,' WITH 10% DISCOUNT: ',I4,' WITH 5% DISCOUNT')
28 CALL EXIT
   END
```

The USAGE-IF program outputs the following printed report:

```
                                   RENTA COMPUTER, INC.
                                        JUNE, 1974

ACCOUNT            ACCOUNT             CURRENT       PREVIOUS          USAGE        MONTHLY
NUMBER              NAME               READING       READING                        CHARGE

 12548      ANDERSON JOSEPH            2247.36       2138.57          108.79        126.15
 24573      BROWN GORDON               3344.55       3245.67           98.88        119.22
 45342      BUTLER RANDOLPH            3687.52       3572.46          115.06        130.54
 55343      CATALETA PAULINE           1568.97       1154.86          414.11        305.89
 75342      LEVY SAMUEL                3189.54       2483.46          706.08        489.83

                                                     TOTAL USAGE:    1442.92
                                                     AVERAGE USAGE:  288.58
 2 WITH 10% DISCOUNT;        0 WITH 5% DISCOUNT
```

Often, as in program USAGE−IF, these different branches of the IF statement later merge into the same main stream of processing.

Last Card Test

When a FORTRAN compiler lacks the capability of branching for last card with the END= option in the READ statement, the IF statement has a special task. It is used with a false or "dummy" data card to determine when the last data card has been read. A frequent technique utilizes a number that could not possibly exist in a data card field. For example, NUMBER is a five-digit field that never is greater than 75000. A "dummy" data card placed at the end of the regular data cards is punched with 99999 in the I5 field NUMBER. After each card is read, NUMBER is tested for this "dummy" condition:

```
1 READ (5,2) NUMBER, AMOUNT
2 FORMAT (I5,1X,F6.2)
3 IF (NUMBER - 99999) 4, 20, 4
```

When 99999 is input as NUMBER, a zero condition occurs in the IF statement, and the program branches to statement 20 for last card processing. Otherwise, the main line of programming (statement 4) is followed. This technique usually is flowcharted the same as when the READ statement contains the END= option.

Even when the tested expression in parentheses can never logically be one of the conditions (negative, zero, or positive), all three positions must always be listed with numbers of executable statements. For instance, in the last card test, NUMBER can be only zero or a negative value. Yet the number of an executable statement must be listed in the last or positive position.

Sometimes a "dummy" last card has a number punched in an otherwise unused data card column. Then a field name is given to that column so that it can be tested. The following example tests field LAST in column 80:

```
11 READ (5,2) NUMBER, AMOUNT, LAST
12 FORMAT (I5, 1X, F6.2, T80, I1)
13 IF (LAST) 14, 14, 20
```

If any number is in column 80, the program branches to the final routine at statement 20. All other cards branch the program to statement 14 for routine processing.

REVIEW QUESTIONS

6. What is a "dummy" data card?
7. How can an IF statement be used to detect the last data card?

The IF Statement in Counting

A program frequently counts the number of times each condition occurs. One counter field increases by 1 whenever the tested value is negative, another when the value is zero, and a third when the value is positive. For example, in a special study, a tally is made of all individuals (1) under 21 years of age, (2) 21 years of age, and (3) over 21 years of age.

A flowchart shows the program logic on the facing page. KOUNTP, KOUNTN, and KOUNTZ are counters for the three possible conditions of positive, negative, and zero. As each card is processed, the IF statement determines which counter will be increased. At the completion of the program, the three counters are printed.

Data cards have the following format:

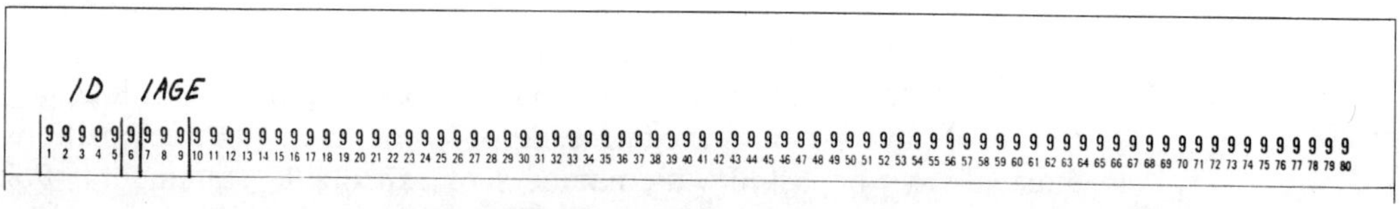

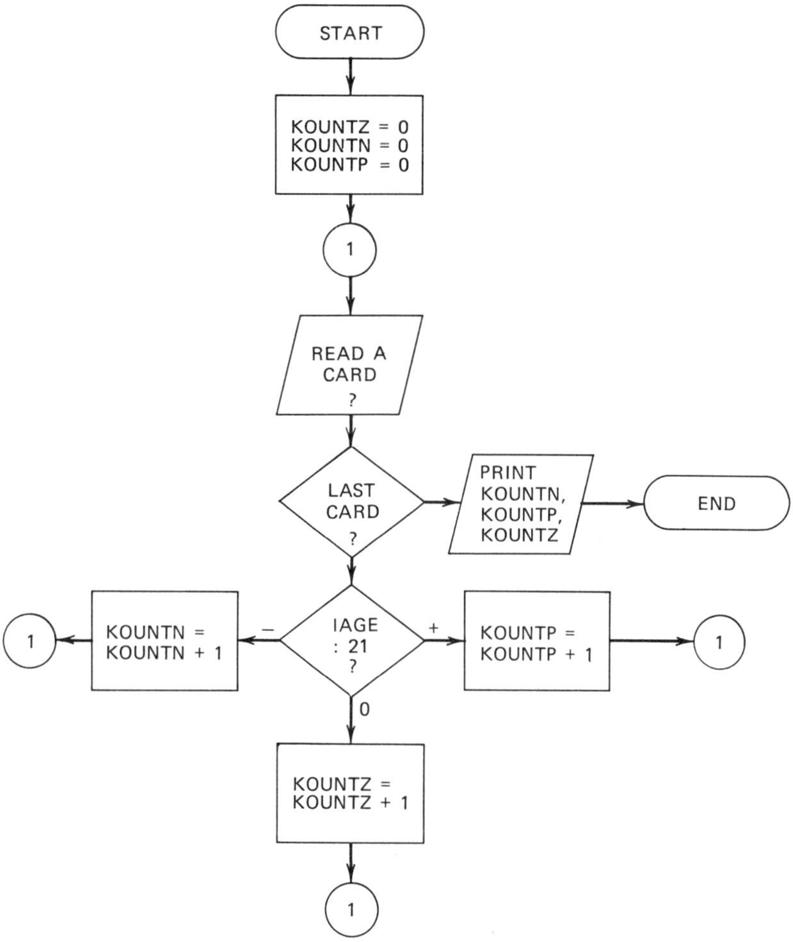

A program to execute the flowchart reading these data cards, is written:

```
C INITIALIZE 3 COUNTERS TO ZERO
    1 KOUNTP = 0
    2 KOUNTZ = 0
    3 KOUNTN = 0
C READ A CARD
    4 READ (5,5,END=13)ID, IAGE
    5 FORMAT (I5,1X,I3)
C TEST IAGE FOR NEGATIVE, POSITIVE, OR ZERO
    6 IF (IAGE - 21) 7, 9, 11
```

```
C BRANCH WHEN NEGATIVE
    7 KOUNTN = KOUNTN + 1
    8 GO TO 4
C BRANCH WHEN ZERO
    9 KOUNTZ = KOUNTZ +1
   10 GO TO 4
C BRANCH WHEN POSITIVE
   11 KOUNTP = KOUNTP + 1
   12 GO TO 4
C BRANCH WHEN LAST CARD IS READ
   13 WRITE (6,14) KOUNTP, KOUNTZ, KOUNTN
   14 FORMAT (T10, I4, ' OVER 21;' ,T25,I4, ' 21; ' ,T35,I4,
     1 ' UNDER 21.')
   15 CALL EXIT
      END
```

At the beginning of the program, the three counting fields, KOUNTP, KOUNTZ, and KOUNTN, are established as integer fields with values of 0. After each data card is read, IF statement 6 tests the condition of field IAGE. When IAGE is negative, the program branches to statement 7. Counter KOUNTN is increased by 1. Then GOTO statement 8 unconditionally branches the program back to READ statement 4.

When IAGE equals 0, the program branches to statement 9. KOUNTZ is increased by 1. GOTO statement 10, the next instruction, sends the program back to READ statement 4. The program branches to statement 11 when IAGE is positive. After KOUNTP is incremented by 1, GOTO statement 12 branches the program to READ statement 4.

When the compiler encounters the /* card after the last data card, the END= option in READ statement 4 causes a branch to WRITE statement 13. Just before the program ends, the three tallies, KOUNTN, KOUNTZ, and KOUNTP, are printed:

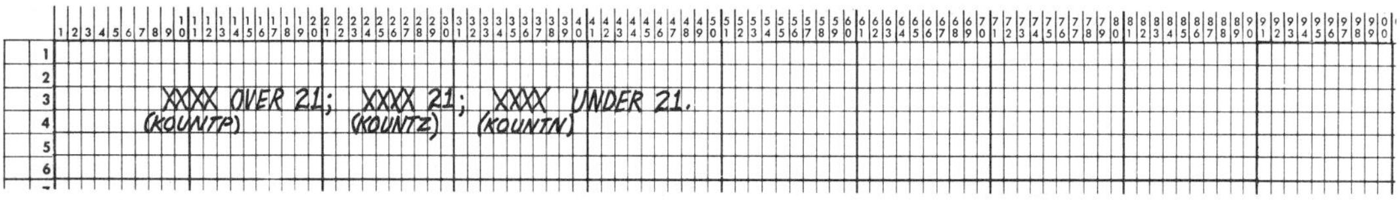

Although each of the three possible conditions of IF statement 6 causes a branch to a different instruction, each branch ends with a GOTO statement returning the program to READ statement 4 so that the next data card can be input. This type of return to a main line of processing does not always occur, however, and it is not required except when demanded by the logic of the program itself. Each branch can contain completely separate procedures with as many instructions as required by the program logic.

Sometimes the ability to count the number of times a statement is executed is valuable in determining when a limit is reached. For example, the study of ages is changed so that it will end whether either of two conditions occurs: 1) the last record is processed or 2) twenty-five 21-year-old individuals are processed.

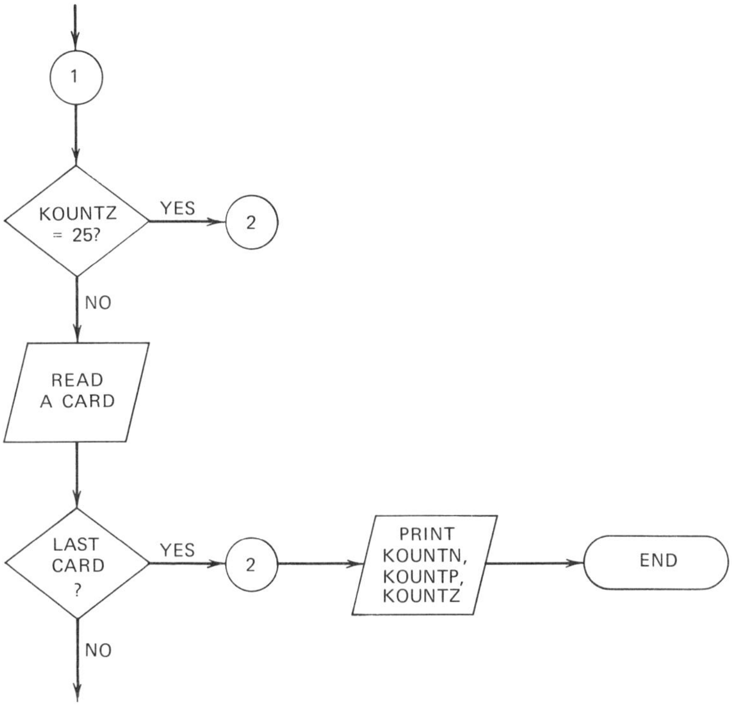

To accomplish this decision making, statement 30 is inserted just before the READ statement:

```
30 IF (KOUNTZ - 25) 4, 13, 13
```

IF statement 30 tests the contents of field KOUNTZ. Until KOUNTZ equals 25, the program branches to READ statement 4. When KOUNTZ equals 25, though, the program branches to statement 13 for the final steps of the program. Thus, the IF statement determines the end of processing when the tested condition is reached before the END= option is used.

REVIEW QUESTIONS

8. When an IF statement value can branch logically to only two possible conditions, how many statement numbers must be listed?
9. How can an IF statement be used in counting the occurrence of certain conditions?

IF Statement With Line Counter

Frequently the IF statement is used when headings and/or totals are printed on every page. To utilize this technique, a field to be used as the line counter is initialized to 0. This field is increased by 1 every time the printer single spaces, and by 2 every time it double spaces. After each line is output, the field is tested to determine whether or not the page limit for lines has been reached or exceeded.

For example, after the 42nd line, page totals are printed, and the printer skips to the top of the next page to print headings. The values of the line counting field and the two page totals are reset before the program resumes the main line processing. A flowchart illustrates the logic of this program segment:

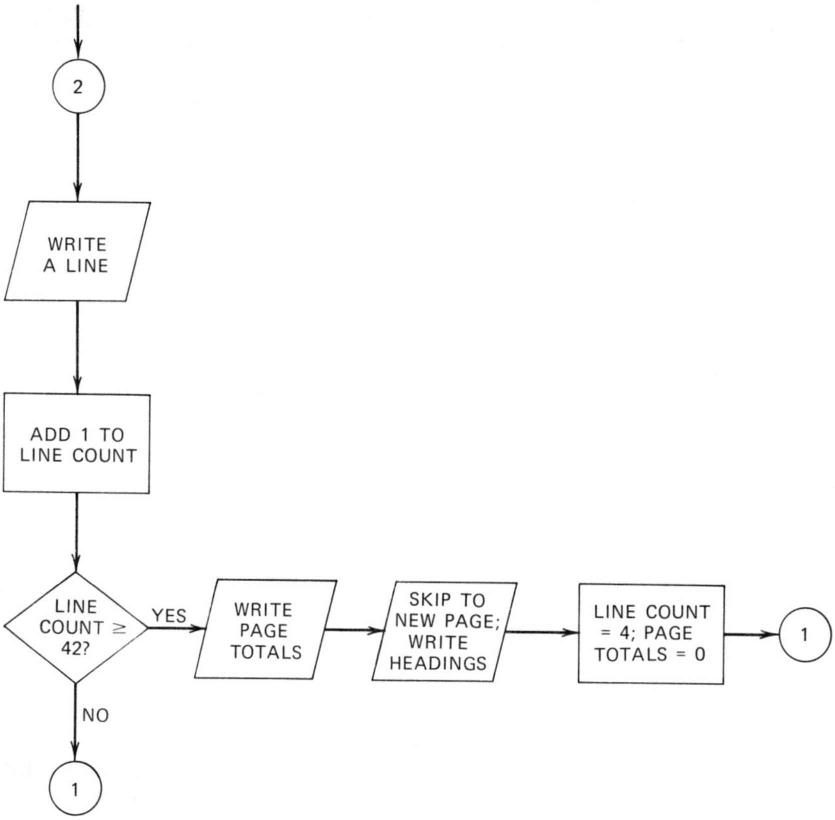

FORTRAN statements execute the line counter test:

```
 1 LINECT = 0
        .
        .
        .
12 WRITE (6,10)ID, COST, ETC
```

```
13 LINECT=LINECT+1
14 IF(LINECT-42) 3,15,15
15 WRITE (6,16)PTOT1, PTOT2
16 FORMAT('0',T60,F7.2,T75,F7.2 /'1',T50,'COMPANY NAME'///)
17 PTOT1=0.
18 PTOT2=0.
19 LINECT=4
20 GO TO 3
```

Every time a line is printed, IF statement 14 tests the line counter field. When the line count is equal to or greater than 42, the program goes to WRITE statement 15, which calls for the output of two page totals, then directs the printer to skip to the top of the next page to print a company heading, with three blank lines after the heading line.

Statements 17 and 18 reset the subtotals so that they will begin with zeroes for the next page. The line count field is reset to the value of 4. GOTO statement 20 returns the program to the mainline processing.

IF Statement to Match Multiple Sequentially Organized Files

Many data processing applications utilize records from more than one file (or "data set" as a file is called in most FORTRAN manuals). For example, one file is a collection of all the master customer cards of a department store. Each record of this file contains information that seldom changes, such as name and address of all charge account customers. Another file is the collection of all transaction records for these customers.

Both these types of record files are most frequently on punched cards, paper tape, magnetic tape, or magnetic disk, with each file arranged in ascending sequence by a "key" field they share. In both the master and transaction records, the customer identification number is the key field because it provides the key that locks the two files together for processing. A FORTRAN programmer can process two or more sequentially organized files by using the IF statement to test whether or not key fields match.[1]

Renta Computer, Inc. demonstrates this use of the IF statement by processing together the transaction cards and a new master file that is on magnetic tape. The customer identification number, which is the key field, is in positions 1-5 of the master file, and in columns 1-5 of the transaction records. Placing the key field in the same positions in records of both files frequently occurs but is not required. A key field can be anywhere within a record.

[1]Direct (randomly arranged) files on devices such as magnetic disk or drum can be processed by DEFINE FILE and direct access READ and WRITE statements, discussed in Chapter 25. Indexed sequential data files are not supported by FORTRAN IV.

In order for both fields to be in storage at the same time, however, each must have a unique name. Therefore the key field is called IDM in the master file records and IDNUM in transaction file records. When the printed report is output, or if a new file is created for output, either field name can be utilized.

Each master record contains not only the customer identification number (key field), but also the customer's name and previous meter reading.

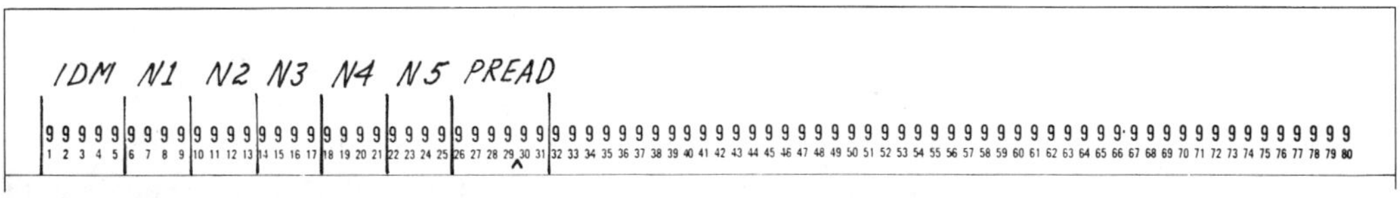

Transaction cards now contain only the customer identification number (key field) and the current meter reading.

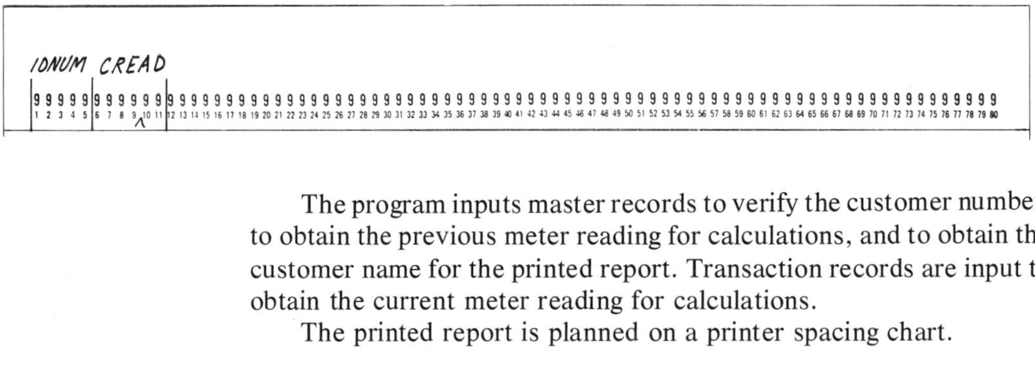

The program inputs master records to verify the customer number, to obtain the previous meter reading for calculations, and to obtain the customer name for the printed report. Transaction records are input to obtain the current meter reading for calculations.

The printed report is planned on a printer spacing chart.

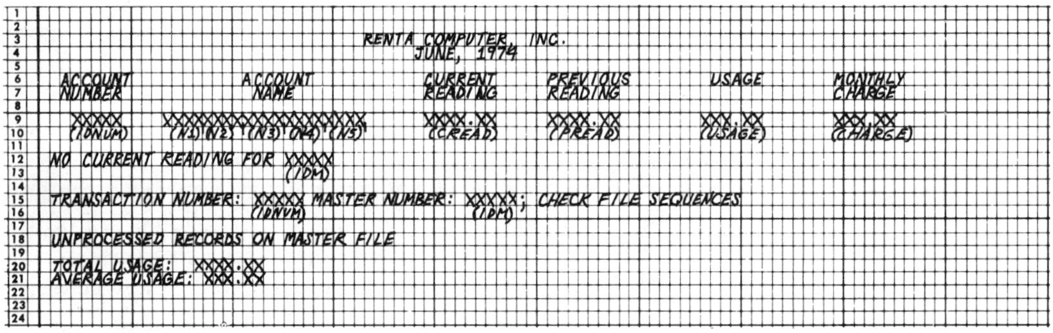

The logic of the problem is flowcharted.

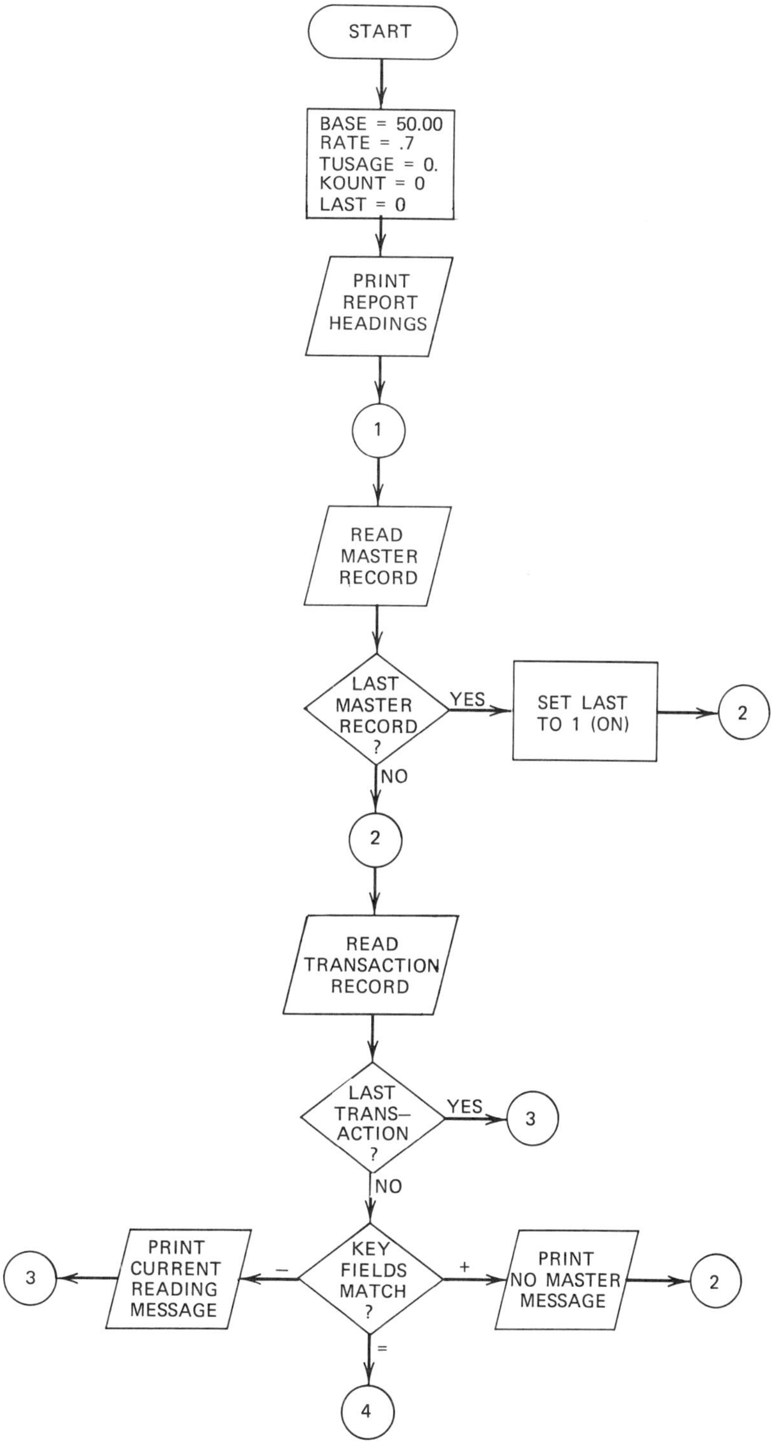
START
BASE = 50.00
RATE = .7
TUSAGE = 0.
KOUNT = 0
LAST = 0
PRINT REPORT HEADINGS
1
READ MASTER RECORD
LAST MASTER RECORD ?
YES
SET LAST TO 1 (ON)
2
NO
2
READ TRANSACTION RECORD
LAST TRANS– ACTION ?
YES
3
NO
KEY FIELDS MATCH ?
–
PRINT CURRENT READING MESSAGE
3
+
PRINT NO MASTER MESSAGE
2
=
4

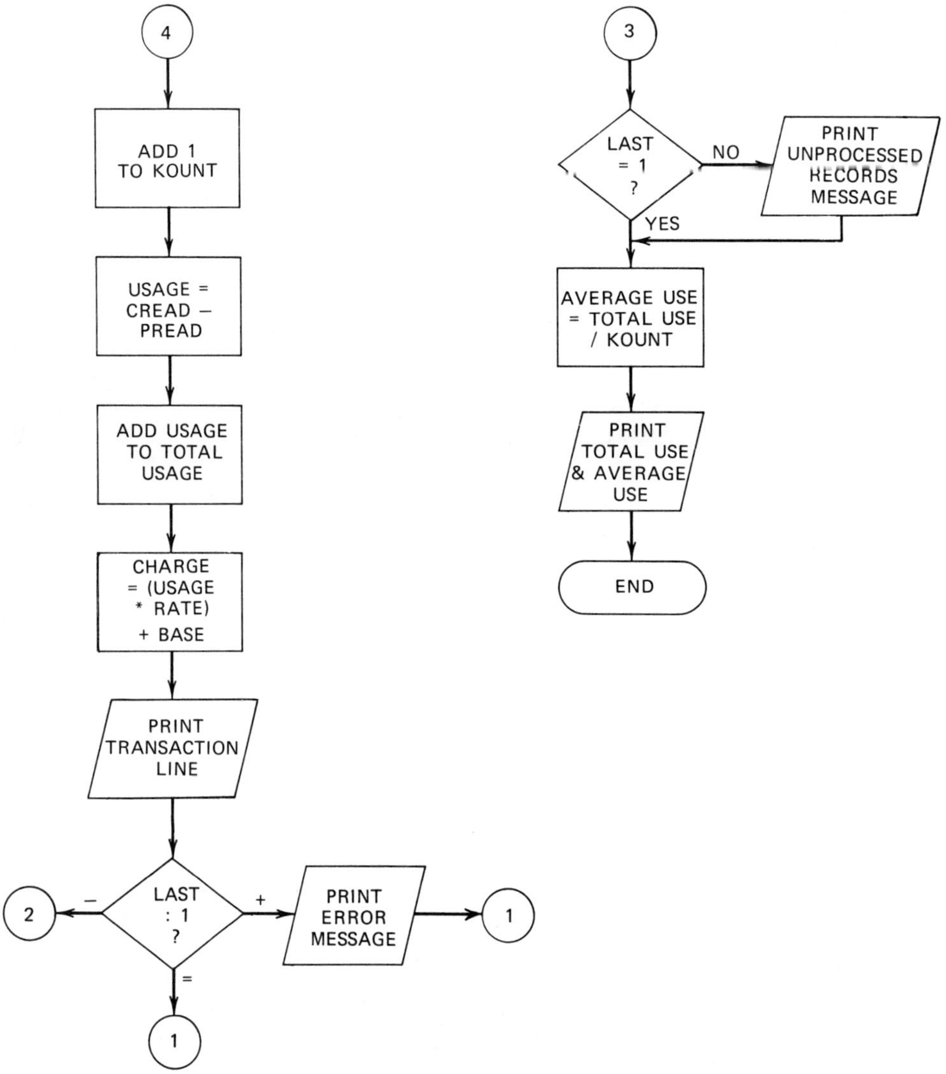

After the "housekeeping" of initializing fields and printing headings, a record from the master file and a record from the transaction file are input:

```
C READ MASTER RECORD FROM MAGNETIC TAPE
    8 READ (10,9,END=29) IDM,N1,N2,N3,N4,N5,PREAD
    9 FORMAT (I5,5A4,F6.2)
C READ TRANSACTION RECORD FROM PUNCHED CARD
   10 READ (5,11,END=31) IDNUM,CREAD
   11 FORMAT (I5,F6.2)
```

An IF statement then tests the key fields to determine whether or not the two fields match:

```
C TEST FOR MATCHING KEY FIELDS
   12 IF (IDM - IDNUM) 13, 19, 16
C OUTPUT WHEN TRANSACTION NUMBER IS LARGER
   13 WRITE (6,14) IDM
   14 FORMAT (T3,'NO CURRENT READING FOR ',I5)
   15 GO TO 25
C OUTPUT WHEN MASTER NUMBER IS LARGER
   16 WRITE (6,17) IDNUM, IDM
   17 FORMAT(T3,'TRANSACTION NUMBER: ',I5,' MASTER NUMBER: ',
     1 I5, '; CHECK FILE SEQUENCES')
   18 GO TO 10
C PROCESSING WHEN KEY FIELDS MATCH
   19 KOUNT = KOUNT + 1
```

The program also utilizes an IF statement to determine whether the entire master file has been input. A special "switch" field, called LAST, is established. Named after a second-generation computer concept of switches, a field that is called a switch is "set" and "tested." The switch, like a metal toggle switch that can be only up or down, or off or on, is a field with only two conditions: 0 (off) or 1 (on). LAST is set "off" at the opening of the program. (Actually programming logic allows either setting, so long as there is a change of setting later.)

```
5 LAST = 0
```

When the last master record is input, LAST is changed to 1, "on."

```
29 LAST = 1
```

To prevent a READ instruction to the master file after it has already been input completely, LAST is tested after a transaction record is processed but before a new record is input:

```
25 IF (LAST - 1) 8, 10, 26
```

IF statement 25 tests whether or not LAST is "on." It determines whether the program branches back to read another master record (statement 8) or another transaction record (statement 10), or branches forward to write an error message.

When the last transaction record is processed, LAST is tested again so that a special message will be output if some master records are still unread:

```
31 IF (LAST - 1) 34, 36, 32
32 WRITE (6,27)
33 GO TO 36
34 WRITE (6,35)
35 FORMAT (T3,'UNPROCESSED RECORDS ON MASTER FILE')
```

The complete program is coded:

```
C INITIALIZE BASE CHARGE, RATE, TOTAL USAGE, COUNT, AND LAST
    1 BASE = 50.00
    2 RATE = .7
    3 TUSAGE = 0.0
    4 KOUNT = 0
    5 LAST = 0
C PRINT HEADINGS
    6 WRITE (6,7)
    7 FORMAT ('1',T35,'RENTA COMPUTER, INC.'/T40,'JUNE, 1974'//
     1 4X,'ACCOUNT',11X,'ACCOUNT',11X,'CURRENT',5X,'PREVIOUS',
     2 8X,'USAGE',7X,'MONTHLY'/4X,'NUMBER',13X,'NAME',13X,
     3 'READING',5X,'READING',21X,'CHARGE'//)
C READ MASTER RECORD FROM MAGNETIC TAPE
    8 READ (10,9,END=29) IDM, N1,N2,N3,N4,N5,PREAD
    9 FORMAT (I5,5A4,F6.2)
C READ TRANSACTION RECORD FROM PUNCHED CARD
   10 READ (5,11,END=31) IDNUM, CREAD
   11 FORMAT (I5, F6.2)
C TEST FOR MATCHING KEY FIELDS
   12 IF (IDM - IDNUM) 13, 19, 16
C OUTPUT WHEN TRANSACTION NUMBER IS LARGER
   13 WRITE (6,14) IDM
   14 FORMAT (T3,'NO CURRENT READING FOR ',I5)
   15 GO TO 25
C OUTPUT WHEN MASTER NUMBER IS LARGER
   16 WRITE (6,17) IDNUM, IDM
   17 FORMAT (T3,'TRANSACTION NUMBER: ', I5,' MASTER NUMBER: ',
     1 I5, '; CHECK FILE SEQUENCES')
   18 GO TO 10
C PROCESSING WHEN KEY FIELDS MATCH
   19 KOUNT = KOUNT + 1
   20 USAGE = CREAD - PREAD
   21 TUSAGE = TUSAGE + USAGE
   22 CHARGE = BASE + (USAGE * RATE)
   23 WRITE (6,24) IDNUM, N1,N2,N3,N4,N5,CREAD,PREAD,USAGE,CHARGE
   24 FORMAT (4X,I5,5X,5A4,6X,F7.2,5X,F7.2,8X,F6.2,7X,F6.2)
C TEST FOR LAST MASTER RECORD
   25 IF (LAST - 1) 8, 10, 26
C OUTPUT WHEN LAST RECORD SWITCH NEITHER 0 NOR 1
   26 WRITE (6,27)
   27 FORMAT (T3, 'ERROR IN LAST RECORD SWITCH')
   28 GO TO 8
```

```
C SET ON LAST RECORD SWITCH WHEN LAST MASTER RECORD INPUT
   29 LAST = 1
   30 GO TO 10
C PROCESSING AFTER LAST TRANSACTION RECORD INPUT
   31 IF (LAST - 1) 34, 36, 32
   32 WRITE (6,27)
   33 GO TO 36
   34 WRITE (6,35)
   35 FORMAT (T3,'UNPROCESSED RECORDS ON MASTER FILE')
   36 AVEUSE = TUSAGE / KOUNT
   37 WRITE (6,38) TUSAGE, AVEUSE
   38 FORMAT ('0',1X,'TOTAL USAGE: ',1X,F7.2/T3,'AVERAGE USAGE: '
     1 ,F6.2)
   39 CALL EXIT
      END
```

REVIEW QUESTIONS

10. What is the function of a key field when processing multiple files?
11. In which record positions can a key field be placed?
12. How is the IF statement valuable in processing with key fields?

IF Statement to Determine Odd or Even Numbers

The IF statement enables the programmer to utilize the difference in the ways integer and real numbers are stored. For example, a program sometimes requires only even numbers or only odd numbers for processing. The programmer must be able to differentiate between even and odd numbers, whether integer or real. A simple technique involving the use of the IF statement not only teaches this method of differentiation but also gives insight into the ways in which fields can be manipulated in FORTRAN for various kinds of tests.

Even and odd number of both real and integer fields illustrate this technique:

Field Name	Field Contents
NUM1	1234
NUM2	2345
REAL1	1234.0
REAL2	2345.0

Whether the number tested is real or integer, it first must be divided by 2, with the result stored as an *integer*.

```
21 NM1 = NUM1 / 2
22 NM2 = NUM2 / 2
```

```
23 IRL1 = REAL1 / 2
24 IRL2 = REAL2 / 2
```

After the execution of statements 21-24, storage contains the following fields:

Field Name	Field Contents
NUM1	1234
NUM2	2345
REAL1	1234.0
REAL2	2345.0
NM1	617
NM2	1172
IRL1	617
IRL2	1172

The second step multiplies by 2 the field that was halved. The result is stored in the same numeric type as the original field:

```
25 N1 = NM1 * 2
26 N2 = NM2 * 2
27 R1 = IRL1 * 2
28 R2 = IRL2 * 2
```

Fields in storage now contain the following:

Field Name	Field Contents
NUM1	1234
NUM2	2345
REAL1	1234.0
REAL2	2345.0
NM1	617
NM2	1172
IRL1	617
IRL2	1172
N1	1234
N2	2344
R1	1234.0
R2	2344.0

After these preliminary steps, the IF statement tests whether the reconstructed numbers are equal to or different from the original numbers.

```
29 IF (NUM1 - N1) 33, 34, 33
30 IF (NUM2 - N2) 35, 36, 35
31 IF (REAL1 - R1) 37, 38, 37
32 IF (REAL2 - R2) 39, 40, 39
```

NUM1 and N1 are identical, and REAL1 and R1 are equal. NUM2 and N2, however, are not equal, and REAL2 and R2 are not equal. When the tested numbers are identical, the subtraction expression results in a zero value. The programmer knows then that the original number was even. If, however, the numbers are not identical, a negative or positive value results from the subtraction. The programmer knows that the original number was odd. The IF statement allows him to branch the numbers for the appropriate processing.

IF Statement With Alphameric Fields

The collating sequences of computers include all characters whether numeric, alphabetic, or special. Therefore, any character that is on the computer's printer set can be used in the IF statement parenthetical expression of most FORTRAN IV compilers. This means that the relationship of two alphameric fields[2] can be determined by an IF statement. For example, an A4 alphameric code is used as a customer identification in an order schedule arranged in sequential order. This program segment is flowcharted on page 136.

Whenever a new customer is processed, the alphameric code is stored. When another card is input, the field in the new card is compared with the stored field by subtracting one from the other. When the two fields are identical, the result of the subtraction is a zero condition. When the two fields are different, the subtraction produces a positive or negative condition. The process, then, is essentially the same as if the fields were numeric instead of alphameric.

The IF statement is written as though the fields were numeric:

```
4 IF (STORED - ACCTID) 5, 7, 5
```

The only precaution the programmer must take is to be certain that the field names are of the same type. This is important because integer and real field names indicate a different method of storing field contents even for alphameric fields in most systems. Two real field names like STORED and ACCTID can be used together, or two integer names like ISTORE and KODE. STORED and ISTORE or STORED and KODE, however, usually give different values to the computer even when the card columns contain identical entries.

The ability of the IF statement to test alphameric as well as numeric fields gives FORTRAN programming a greater versatility.

[2]Except complex fields, discussed in Chapter 15, Type Specification Statements.

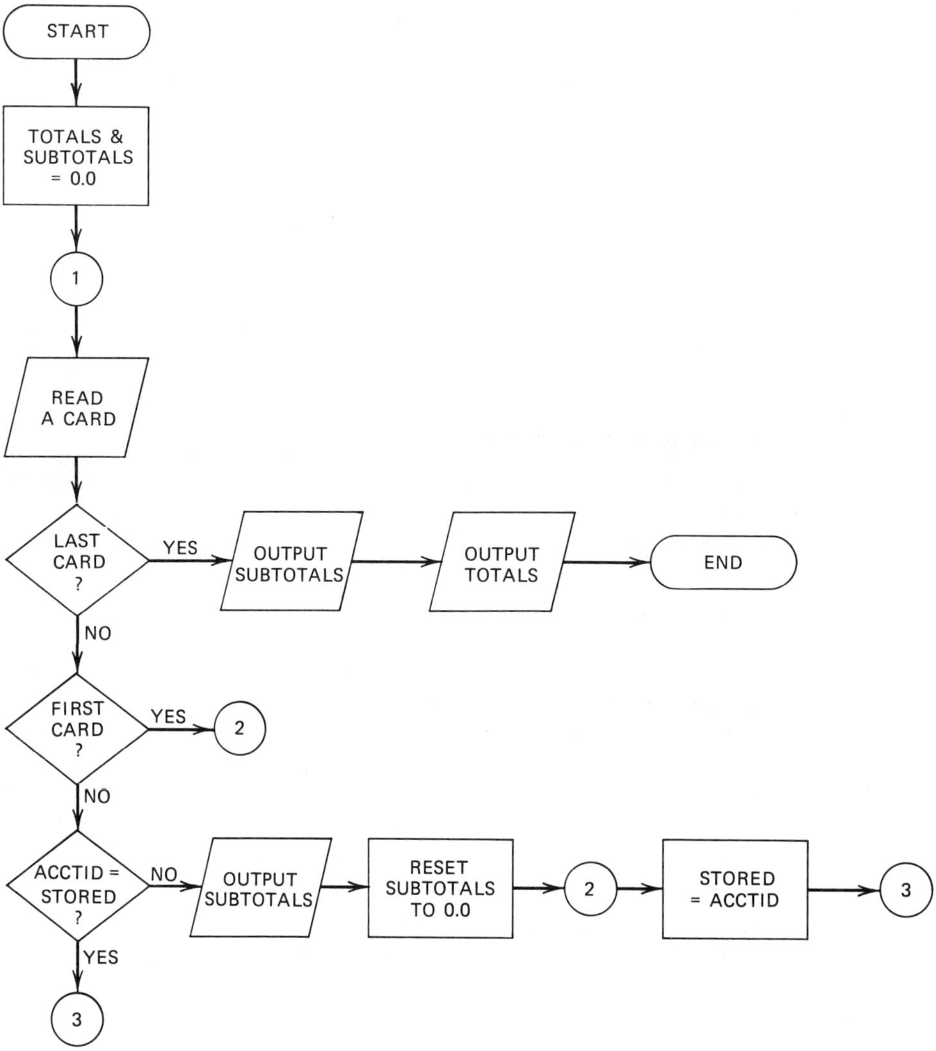

REVIEW QUESTIONS

13. How can an IF statement be used to differentiate between odd and even numbers?
14. What special precautions must be taken when comparing alphameric fields in an IF statement?

OBJECTIVES REVIEW

Study the objectives at the beginning of this chapter. Check each one to be certain you have achieved it. Restudy the chapter sections relating to any objective you cannot perform.

REVIEW TEST

Study the following FORTRAN program carefully. Using the "data cards" that are given, "process" the program just as the FORTRAN compiler does. On scratch paper, keep a record of what is in storage for every field as the program proceeds. On a printer spacing chart or in the space below, print the output of the test program as it would appear on a printer. Watch both the contents and placement of fields and headings.

Data Cards

```
                    1         2         3         4
Columns:  1234567890123456789012345678901234567890
Card 1:   3468  40
Card 2:   4671  32
Card 3:   5210  35
Card 4:   6493  44
Card 5:   /*
```

Program

```
 1 KMINUS = 0
 2 KPLUS = 0
 3 K70 = 0
 4 WRITE (6,5)
 5 FORMAT (T25,'NEW COLLEGE'//T14,'ID',T22,'POINTS', T32,
  1 'SCORE',T42,'GRADE')
 6 READ (5,9,END = 24) ID, IPOINT
 9 FORMAT (I4,2X,I2)
10 ISCORE = IPOINT * 2
11 IF (ISCORE - 70) 12, 16, 20
12 KMINUS = KMINUS + 1
13 WRITE (6,14) ID, IPOINT, ISCORE
14 FORMAT (T13,I4,7X,I2,7X,I3,T42,'FAIL')
15 GO TO 6
16 K70 = K70 + 1
17 WRITE (6,18) ID, IPOINT, ISCORE
18 FORMAT (T13,I4,7X,I2,7X, I3,T42,'D')
19 GO TO 6
20 KPLUS = KPLUS + 1
21 WRITE (6,22) ID, IPOINT, ISCORE
22 FORMAT (T13,I4,7X,I2,7X,I3,T42,'PASS')
23 GO TO 6
24 WRITE (6,25) KPLUS, K70, KMINUS
25 FORMAT ('0',T10,'PASS: ',I2/T10,'D:',4X,I2/T10,'FAIL:',I3)
26 STOP
   END
```

Printout

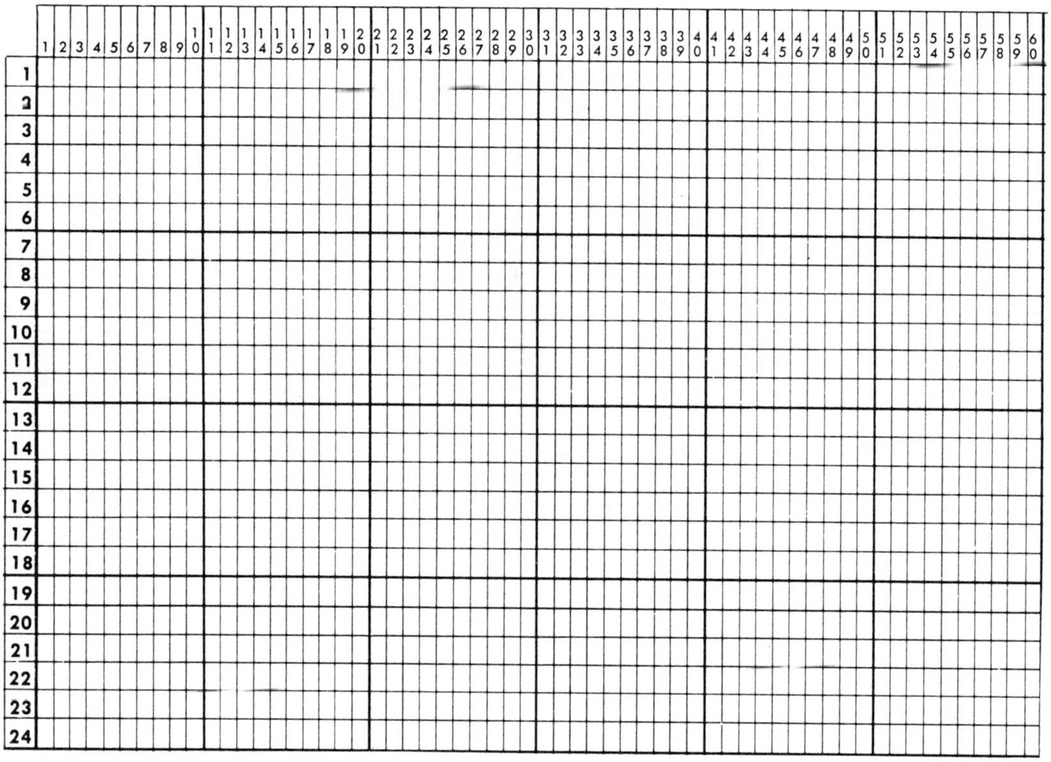

ASSIGNMENTS

Use a flowchart to develop program logic, and a printer spacing chart to plan the spacing of output for one of the following problems. Then write the FORTRAN program, using at least one arithmetic IF statement.

1. *Input Records*

Fields	Card Columns	
Employee number	23-26	(I4)
Employee name	1-20	(5A4)
Hours worked	29-31	(F3.1)
Rate of pay	34-36	(F3.2)
Bonus payment	62-66	(F5.2)

Calculations. For each record, PAY equals hours worked times rate of pay. A bonus is given only to employees who worked more than 40 hours. Total the amount of the earned bonus payments. Count the number of employees who receive the bonus payment. After all records are processed, test whether total bonus payment is greater than $1,000.00.

Output. Print name of company and then column headings. For each employee, print employee name, employee number, hours worked, rate of pay, pay before bonus, bonus if paid, and final pay. (Allow extra position for decimal point.) After the last data card has been processed, print the number of employees receiving bonus payments and the total amount of bonuses paid. If total amount of bonus is greater than $1,000.00, print that fact also at the end of the program.

2. Expand problem 1 by finding the averages of bonuses paid, pay before bonuses, and pay with bonuses included.

3. Expand problem 1 by calculating withholding tax and FICA (as of 1974, 5.8% of the first $13,200). Additional input fields:

Fields	Card Columns	
FICA paid to date	38-42	(F5.2)
Withholding tax rate (%)	44-45	(F2.2)

4. *Input records*

Fields	Card Columns	
Student's name	1-20	(5A4)
Student's identification number	21-26	(I6)
Grade point average to date	38-40	(F3.2)

(Place one data card out of its usual order before processing.)

Calculations. Test every record to see if the grade point average is greater than 4.0. Create an integer "save area" containing 0 at beginning of program. At the *end* of each data card processing, place identification number into "save area." *During* card processing, compare student identification number with number in "save area." If saved number is larger, new identification number is out of sequence.

Printed Report. Print headings with name and location of college. Double space before printing detail lines. For each record, print student's name, identification number, and grade point average. (Allow an extra position for the decimal points.) If the grade point average is greater than 4.0, print an error message to the right of the other data. If the identification number is out of sequence, print an asterisk (*) immediately in front of the printed number.

5. *Input Records*

Fields	Card Columns	
Customer name	1-20	(5A4)
Account name	23-26	(I4)
Beginning account balance	38-44	(F7.2)
Withdrawals	51-57	(F7.2)
Deposits	62-68	(F7.2)

Calculations. Bring accounts up to date and show all accounts with ending balance of $10,000.00 or more. Obtain new balance forward by subtracting withdrawals from beginning account balance and adding deposits to account. Test whether new balance is $10,000.00 or more. Total new balances.

Printed Report. Print company name, double space, print column headings, and double space. For every detail line, print all input fields and new balance. If new balance is greater than $10,000.00, print an asterisk (*) to the right of new balance. After last card is processed, double space and print total balance forward in balance forward column.

6. *Input Records*

Fields	Card Columns	
Pupil's name	1-20	(5A4)
Growth in inches	38-40	(F3.2)
Sex (1 = male; 2 = female)	47	(I1)

Calculations. To study pupils' yearly physical growth, first determine whether a pupil is male or female. Total the growth for boys and for girls. Count the number of boys and the number of girls. After processing the last card, find the average growth for boys and for girls. Determine which group had the larger average.

Printed Report. Print school name and city in headings. Double space. Print column headings. Double space. Detail lines contain student name, M for male or F for female, and the growth in inches (F4.2). After processing the last card, print both averages with explanatory literals. Print an asterisk (*) immediately after the larger average.

7. *Input Records*

Fields	Card Columns	
Student name	1-20	(5A4)
Student identification number	23-27	(I5)
Raw score on 500 question test	38-40	(I3)

Calculations. To check the validity of test results, first count all students and total their scores. Count all students with odd-numbered identification numbers and total their scores. After last card is processed, find the average for each group.

Printed Report. Headings include name of school and school location. Double space before and after column headings. Detail lines contain three input fields and an asterisk (*) after odd-numbered identification numbers. After processing the last card, print both averages with identifying literals.

8. Do problem 7, but convert to percentages rather than raw scores.

Trendata 1000 computer terminal. FORTRAN can now be an interactive language.

Chapter Objectives

1. Be able to explain the meanings of the six relational operators.
2. Be able to write logical IF statements with relational operators.
3. Be able to explain the meaning of the three logical operators.
4. Be able to write logical IF statements with logical operators.

9

Logical IF Statement: Relational and Logical Operators; Logical Expressions

The arithmetic IF statement tests whether an arithmetic expression equals a positive, a negative, or a zero quantity. Sometimes a programmer does not need a numeric quantitative answer. Instead he wants to test the "truth" of an expression. That is, he wants to know whether a condition is true or false. Therefore, instead of testing an *arithmetic* expression with a three-way branch, the logical IF statement tests whether a *logical* expression is true or false with a two-way option.

For example, a logical IF statement can ask if it is true or false that USAGE is greater than 200.0.

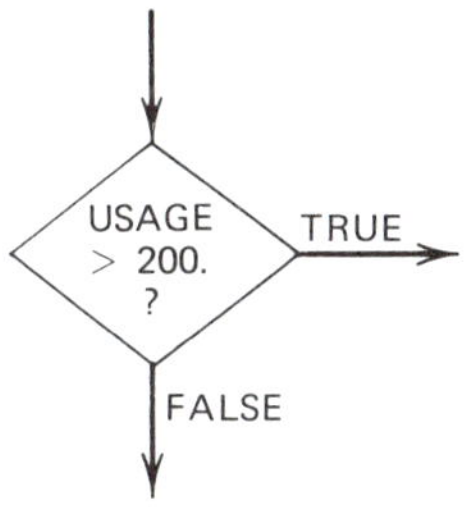

This question can be answered by the arithmetic IF statement, but sometimes testing is accomplished more easily with logical expressions in a logical IF statement. The logical IF statement is especially valuable when the branch of the "true" condition consists of only one extra instruction. Although logical expressions and the logical IF statement are not included in Basic FORTRAN IV, the logical IF statement with relational operators is available with many FORTRAN IV compilers.

In a logical IF statement, the program tests the "truth" of a logical expression; is the condition true or false. Thus, the expression does not have a value that is positive, negative, or zero but has a value of true or false.

The most common type of logical expression uses a relational operator with two arithmetic values to express a condition that can be either true or false. The arithmetic values used in expressing this logical condition can be real or integer fields of either standard or optional length.

Six relational operators can be used within the parentheses of logical IF statements. They require periods both before and after their alphabetic characters. Since they are all on the same level in the logical hierarchy of operations, their order is unimportant in the following list:

.LT. means "is less than"
.LE. means "is less than or equal to"
.EQ. means "is equal to"
.GT. means "is greater than"
.GE. means "is greater than or equal to"
.NE. means "is not equal to"

A logical expression is used in logical IF statements when one of these relational operators is combined with two arithmetic values. The relational operator tests the relationship of the two values. For example: USAGE .GT. 200.0. This is a logical expression with a value of true or false. Its value depends upon whether the current stored value of USAGE is or is not greater than 200.0.

Other examples and explanations follow:

(CREDIT .LT. 100.0)	Is CREDIT less than 100.0?
(CREAD .LE. PREAD)	Is CREAD less than or equal to PREAD?
(DEPTNO .EQ. OLDDPT)	Is DEPTNO equal to OLDDPT?
(IDNUM .GT. SEQCHK)	Is IDNUM greater than SEQCHK?
(BONUS .GE. 500.0)	Is BONUS greater than or equal to 500.0?
(TOTAL .NE. CROSFT)	Is TOTAL not equal to CROSFT?

Like the arithmetic IF, the logical IF statement begins with the word IF.

The logical expression is used in the parentheses of a logical IF statement just as an arithmetic expression is placed in the parentheses of an arithmetic IF statement. Other aspects of the two IF statements are not similar, however. Instead of three *statement numbers* following the parentheses, the logical IF statement has a FORTRAN executable *statement*. For example, TUSAGE is the total of USAGE fields for all customers. After all records are processed, the logical IF statement tests whether or not TUSAGE is greater than 1,000.

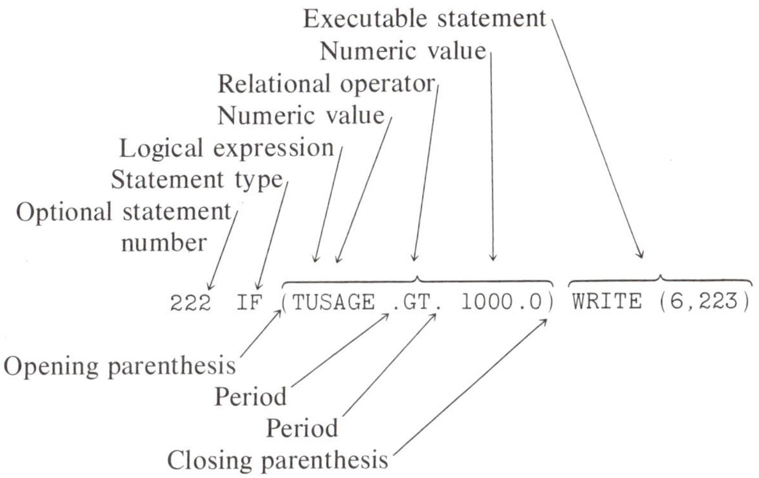

If TUSAGE is greater than 1000.0, the logical expression in the parentheses is true. When this occurs, the statement following the parentheses is executed. Then, unless that statement is a GOTO statement, processing continues with the next executable statement following the logical IF statement. When TUSAGE is not greater than 1000.0, the expression is false and the WRITE statement following the parentheses is ignored. Instead, the next executable statement is processed immediately.

When the logical expression is true, and a GOTO statement follows the parentheses, the program branches to the statement listed in the GOTO and proceeds from that point. Any executable statement except a DO statement or another logical IF statement can follow the parentheses.

Program Logical Usage adds statements 222 and 223 to program USAGE–IF:

```
222 IF (TUSAGE .GT. 1000.0) WRITE (6,223)
223 FORMAT ('+',T76,'SEND OUT NEW BROCHURES')
```

The following printed report is produced when the Logical IF statement is true:

```
                              RENTA COMPUTER, INC.
                                   JUNE, 1974

ACCOUNT          ACCOUNT          CURRENT     PREVIOUS       USAGE        MONTHLY
NUMBER            NAME            READING     READING                     CHARGE

 12548    ANDERSON JOSEPH         2247.36     2138.57       108.79        126.15
 24573    BROWN GORDON            3344.55     3245.67        98.88        119.22
 45342    BUTLER RANDOLPH         3687.52     3572.46       115.06        130.54
 55343    CATALETA PAULINE        1568.97     1154.86       414.11        305.89
 75342    LEVY SAMUEL             3189.54     2483.46       706.08        489.83

                                              TOTAL USAGE:   1442.92 SEND OUT NEW BROCHURES
                                              AVERAGE USAGE: 288.58
 2 WITH 10% DISCOUNT;     0 WITH 5% DISCOUNT
```

The special message appears as an additional comment on the same line with the total usage amount.

REVIEW QUESTIONS

1. How many branching possibilities are offered by a logical IF statement?
2. What are the six relational operators, and what does each mean?
3. If the logical expression is true, what statement is executed immediately?
4. If the logical expression is false, what statement is executed immediately?
5. What kind of statement can follow the parentheses in a logical IF statement?

Logical Operators with Relational Operators

Three logical operators may be used with logical expressions to create more complicated logical expressions:

.AND. means that when the two logical expressions before and after .AND. *both* have true values, this combined expression has a value of .TRUE.. If either one or both of the logical expressions have false values, this expression is .FALSE..

.OR. means that when *either* or *both* of the logical expressions before and after .OR. have true values, this expression has the value .TRUE.. If both are false, then this expression has the value .FALSE..

.NOT. means the truth value is the opposite of the value of the logical expression that *follows*. An expression is not required before .NOT..

Examples illustrate uses of the logical operators with logical expressions containing relational operators. The first example uses logical operator .AND. to test a customer's credit and region:

```
CREDIT.GT. 200.0 .AND. IREGN .NE. 1
```

This logical expression has a value of .TRUE. when CREDIT is greater than 200.0 *and* IREGN is not equal to 1. When CREDIT is less than 200.0, or when IREGN is equal to 1, or when both of these conditions exit, the logical expression has a value of .FALSE.. The entire expression can be used in a logical IF statement:

```
15 IF (CREDIT .GT. 200.0 .AND. IREGN .NE. 1) WRITE (3,17) CREDIT
```

When both expressions with relational operators have a value of .TRUE., the WRITE statement and then the next sequential executable statement will be processed. When either or both of the expressions has a value of .FALSE., the entire logical expression in parentheses has a value of .FALSE.. Then the WRITE statement is ignored, and the next executable statement is processed.

The second example uses the same arithmetic values and relational operators to illustrate logical operator .OR.:

```
CREDIT .GT. 200.0 .OR. IREGN .NE. 1
```

This logical expression has a value of .TRUE. when *either* CREDIT is greater than 200.0, or when IREGN is not equal to 1, or when both expressions have values of .TRUE.. For this logical expression to have a value of .FALSE., *both* expressions with relational operators must be false. This expression also can be used in a logical IF statement:

```
25 IF (CREDIT .GT. 200.0 .OR. IREGN .NE. 1) WRITE (3, 30)CREDIT
```

By using inner sets of parentheses, a logical expression can combine even more groups of .AND. and .OR. logical expressions. For example, a customer must have a credit rating greater than 200.0 and be in a region other than 1, or have a credit rating greater than 150.0 and be in region 8. Two logical expressions, each with logical and relational operators, are combined into one logical expression:

```
35 IF ((CREDIT .GT. 200.0 .AND. IREGN .NE. 1) .OR. (CREDIT
  / .GT. 150.0 .AND. IREGN .EQ. 8)) WRITE (3, 37) CREDIT
```

When statement 35 is executed, a value of the complete expression is true when (1) CREDIT is greater than 200.0 and IREGN is not equal to 1, (2) CREDIT is greater than 150.0 and IREGN equals 8, or (3) both pairs of conditions are true. When any of these three conditions occurs, the WRITE statement is executed before the program proceeds to the next sequential instruction. If none of the conditions is true, the WRITE statement is ignored.

The third logical operator is .NOT.. It is the only one of the logical operators that can be used without a logical expression in front of it. When it does not have a logical expression before it, it establishes the *opposite* of a logical expression following it as .TRUE.. For example, the expression CREDIT .GT. 200. has a value of .TRUE. when CREDIT is greater than 200.0. The opposite is true when logical operator .NOT. comes before the earlier expression: .NOT. CREDIT .GT. 200.0. Now the expression has a value of .TRUE. when CREDIT IS *not* greater than 200.0.

The only time two logical operators can be next to each other is when the second one is .NOT.. The first operator can be either .AND. or .OR.. For example, for a value of .TRUE., CREDIT must be greater than 200.0 and IREGN must have a value not greater than 4:

```
23 IF (CREDIT .GT. 200.0 .AND. .NOT. IREGN .GT. 4) GO TO 10
```

The program will branch to statement 10 only with a value of .TRUE..

The .NOT. can also follow .OR.:

```
24 IF (CREDIT .GT. 200.0 .OR. .NOT. IREGN .GT. 4) GO TO 10
```

The program will now branch to statement 10 with a value of .TRUE. either when CREDIT is greater than 200.0 or when IREGN is not greater than 4, or when both conditions are true.

REVIEW QUESTIONS

6. What is the meaning of each of the three logical operators?
7. Which is the only logical operator permitted to follow immediately after another logical operator?

The logical IF statement can also use logical primaries with or without logical or relational operators. Logical primaries (fields) are not commonly used, however, and are not included in many FORTRAN IV compilers that contain the logical IF statement. Therefore, logical constants are explained and demonstrated later, in Chapter 23.

OBJECTIVES REVIEW

Study the objectives at the beginning of this chapter. Check each one to be certain you have achieved it. Restudy the chapter sections related to any objective you cannot perform.

REVIEW TEST

Study the following FORTRAN program carefully. Using the "data cards" that are given, "process" the program just as the FORTRAN compiler does. On scratch paper, keep a record of what is in storage for every field as the program proceeds. On a printer spacing chart or in the space below, print the output of the test program as it would appear on a printer. Watch both the contents and placement of fields and headings.

Data Cards

```
                      1         2         3         4         5
Columns:   12345678901234567890123456789012345678901234567890
Card 1:    ARMSTRONG CAROL        02  04
Card 2:    BERNAT CHARLES         03  01
Card 3:    DONATTO ALFRED         02  00
Card 4:    FRANKLIN KARI          02  01
Card 5:    HUNT PHILLIP           02  05
Card 6:    /*
```

Program

```
 1 LARGE = 0
 2 KOUNT = 0
 3 KTHREE = 0
 4 KPLUS = 0
 5 LESS = 0
 6 WRITE (6,7)
 7 FORMAT (T29,'ADULTS',T38,'CHILDREN')
 8 READ (5,9,END= 22)G1,G2,G3,G4,G5,NADULT,KIDS
 9 FORMAT (5A4,2X,I2,2X,I2)
10 KOUNT = KOUNT + 1
11 IGROUP = NADULT + KIDS
12 IF (IGROUP .GT. 6) LARGE = LARGE + 1
13 IF (IGROUP - 3) 14, 16, 18
14 LESS = LESS + 1
15 GO TO 19
16 KTHREE = KTHREE + 1
17 GO TO 19
18 KPLUS = KPLUS + 1
19 WRITE (6,20)G1,G2,G3,G4,G5,NADULT,KIDS
20 FORMAT (T6,5A4,T31,I3,T41,I3)
21 GO TO 8
22 WRITE (6,23) KOUNT
23 FORMAT ('0',T6,I3,1X,'GROUPS COUNTED')
24 WRITE (6,25)LESS, KTHREE, KPLUS, LARGE
25 FORMAT ('0',T6,I3,1X,'WITH FEWER THAN 3 MEMBERS'/T6,I3,1X,
  1 'WITH 3 MEMBERS'/T6,I3,1X,'WITH MORE THAN 3 MEMBERS, OF ',
  2 'WHICH',1X,I3,1X,'WERE LARGE GROUPS.')
26 STOP
   END
```

Printout

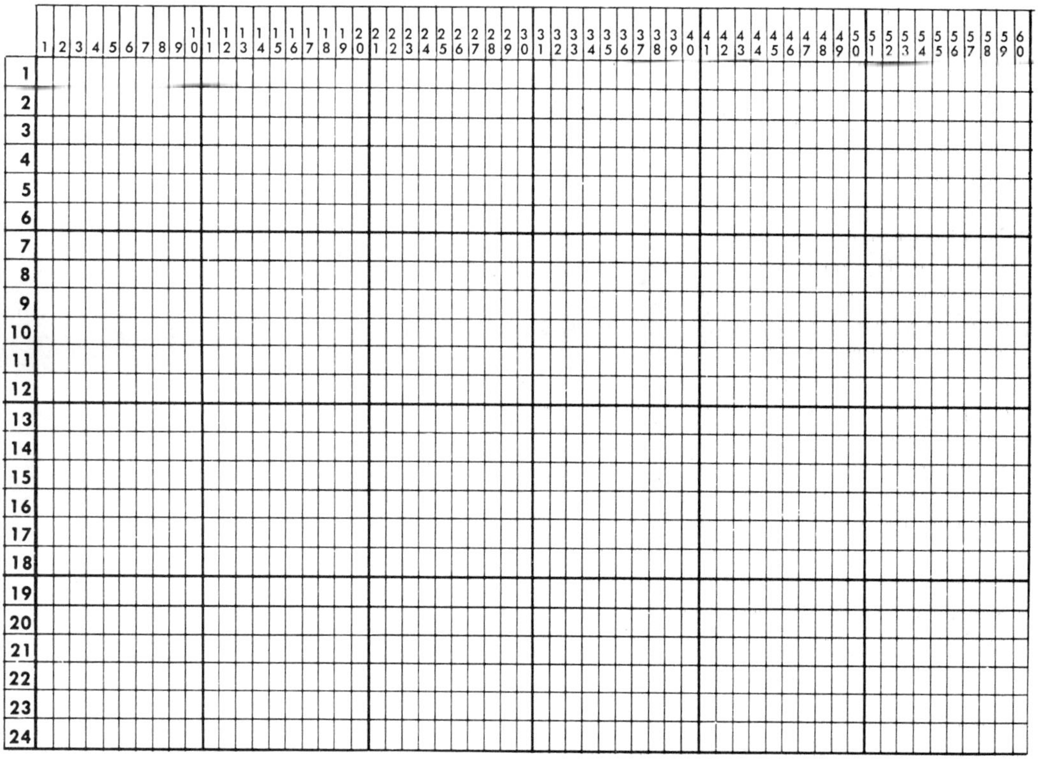

ASSIGNMENTS

Complete a flowchart, printer spacing chart, and FORTRAN instructions that *include the logical IF statement* for one of the following programs.

1. A manufacturer updates his records daily. For each manufactured item, number on hand and new orders are recorded. New orders are subtracted from number on hand for updated number on hand. The updated amount is tested. If it is negative, a special message is printed to tell the number of items required immediately. If the updated amount is less than 1000, an asterisk is printed to the right of the amount.

Input Records

Fields	Card Columns	
Manufactured item	23-27	(I5)
Number on hand	42-45	(I4)
Number on order	52-56	(I4)

After company and column headings, detail lines print input fields, updated number on hand and special messages. After the last card is processed, a message explains that the *—marked orders are for items to be restocked immediately.

2. A business firm has an advancement opportunity for its employees. To be eligible for the new position, an employee must have at least 15 units of accounting, be willing to travel, and have passed the Typist II or Typist III test. Count the eligible employees.

Input Records

Fields	Card Columns	
Employee name	1-20	5A4
Employee number	23-27	I5
Department number	21-22	I2
Accounting units	44-45	I2
Willing to travel (1 = yes; 0 = no)	71	I1
Highest level typing test passed (1 = lowest; 3 = highest)	50	I1

After printing company name, print "OPPORTUNITY ELIGIBILITY LIST." Print column headings. Detail lines contain department number, employee name and number of all eligible workers. If Typist III test was passed, print an asterisk (*) in a special column. After the last record is processed, print a message giving the total number of eligible employees.

3. A large boutique store pays for work by the piece. Therefore pay equals the rate per piece multiplied by the number of pieces. A $25.00 bonus is given if the employee produces more than 100 items. Calculate each employee's pay and the total pay. Count the employees receiving bonuses.

Input Records

Fields	Card Columns	
Employee's name	1-20	5A4
Item produced	23-27	I5
Number of items produced	52-54	I3
Rate per item	71-74	F4.2

Print company name and column headings. Detail lines contain all input fields, bonus (if present) and pay. After the last record is processed, print a message telling the number of employees that are receiving bonuses.

4. Do assignment 3, but also calculate the average pay for men, average pay for women, and average pay for all workers. Additional input field: Sex (1 = male; 2 = female); column 47 (I1). Print the three averages after the bonus message.

5. A manufacturer gives a 5% discount to certain customers. This discount is given before the 3% state sales tax and ½% city sales tax are calculated. Neither tax is calculated if the purchaser is ordering from out of state. Totals are accumulated for the amount of sales, state sales tax, and city tax. Customers within the state receiving a discount, and out of state customers receiving a discount are counted.

Input Records

Fields	Card Columns	
Customer name	1-20	(5A4)
Customer account number	23-27	(I5)
Item number	32-35	(I4)
Number of units sold	43-45	(I3)
Price per unit	52-55	(F4.2)
Discount code (1 = 5% discount)	50	(I1)
Out of state code (5 = out of state)	36	(I1)

After company and column headings, detail lines contain customer name and account number, item number, number of units sold, price per unit, total cost, amounts of state and city taxes. A "D" is printed to the right of total cost if a discount was given. After the last record is processed, the three totals and the two counts are printed with explanatory notes.

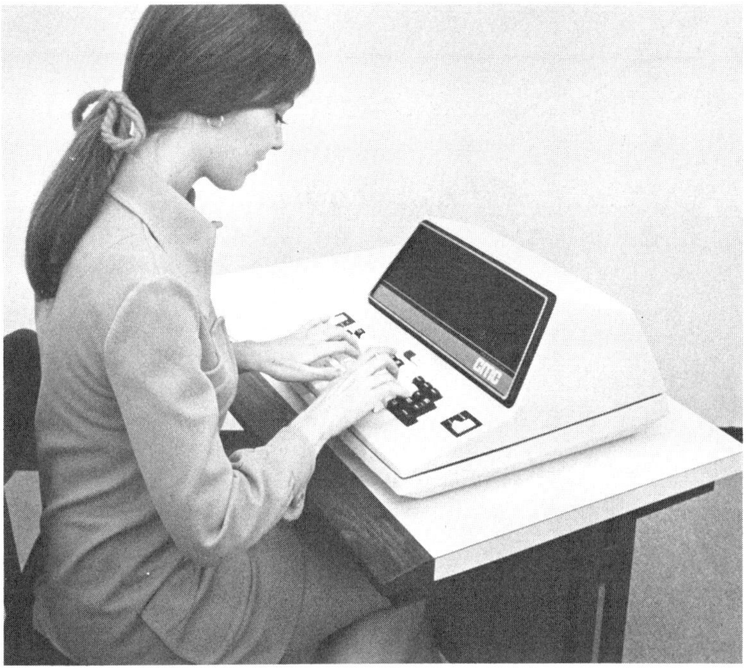

CMC5, key-to-disk data entry system. Entering data for disk at supervisor's console.

Chapter Objectives

1. Be able to use a DO statement to establish a specific number of instruction cycles.
2. Be able to increment the index of a DO loop by more than 1 per cycle.
3. Be able to use a CONTINUE statement as the last statement of a DO loop.
4. Be able to use a DO loop index in calculations and output.
5. Be able to nest DO loops correctly.
6. Be able to use either numeric constants or integer field names to establish beginning, ending, and incrementing values of a DO loop index.

10

DO and CONTINUE Statements

Chapter 8 demonstrated the use of the IF statement in counting, and sometimes in limiting the number of times an instruction or series of instructions is executed. FORTRAN has another technique, however, for establishing a specific number of cycles. Usually called a DO loop, it begins with a DO statement. Frequently, it ends with a CONTINUE statement.

DO and IF statements are the two most powerful FORTRAN statements. Although the two statements can sometimes accomplish the same action, as in terminating cycles, each statement has its own advantages and special uses. The programmer who really studies their actions finds many programming capabilities available to him.

DO and CONTINUE

A prospective customer wants to know how much money will be in his account at the end of a year if he deposits $25.00 a month and the bank pays 6% interest compounded monthly. A flowchart illustrates the program logic on page 156.

The amount of the deposit and the annual interest rate can be established by assignment statements:

```
20 DEPSIT = 25.00
21 PERCNT = .06
```

Or the data can be input as with a data card containing the following format:

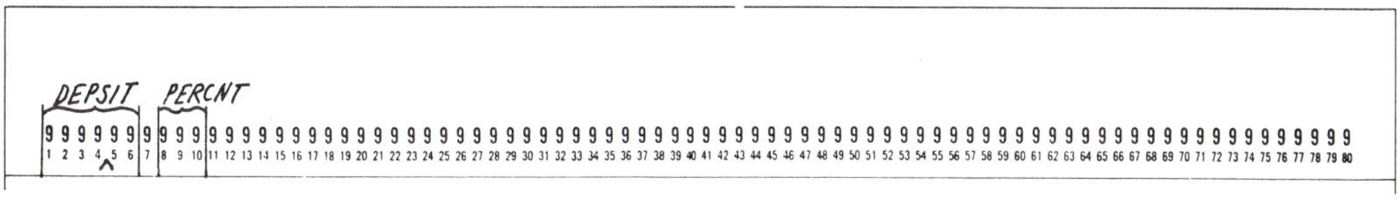

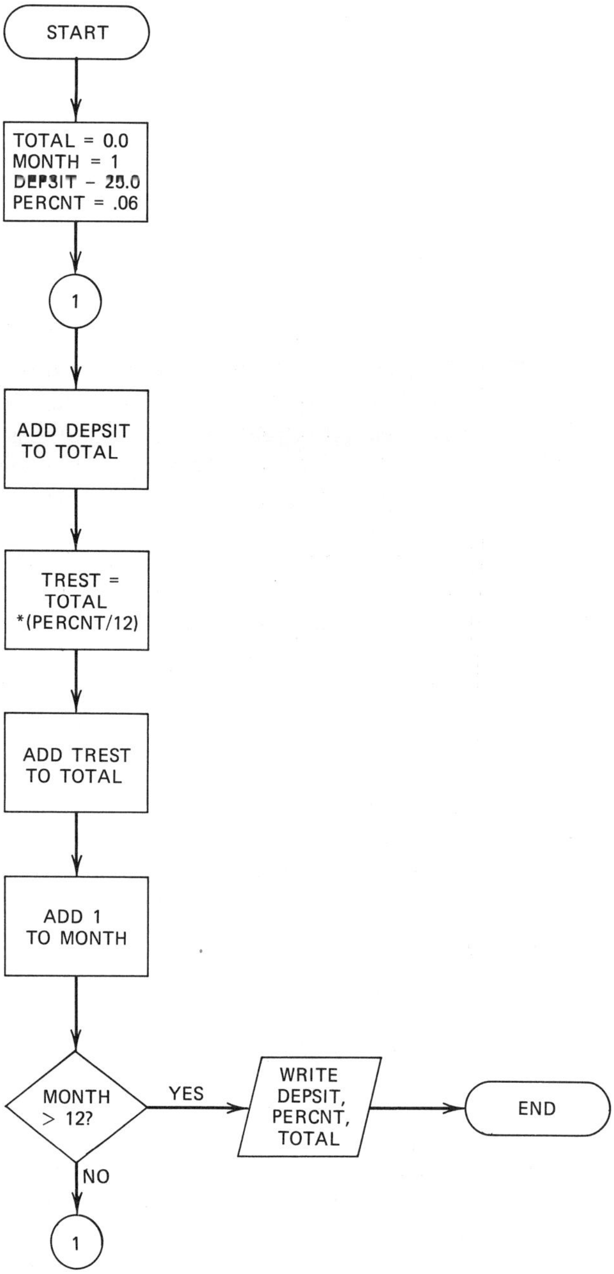
START
TOTAL = 0.0
MONTH = 1
DEPSIT = 25.0
PERCNT = .06
1
ADD DEPSIT TO TOTAL
TREST = TOTAL *(PERCNT/12)
ADD TREST TO TOTAL
ADD 1 TO MONTH
MONTH > 12?
YES
WRITE DEPSIT, PERCNT, TOTAL
END
NO
1

With interactive FORTRAN, the data could of course be input on the terminal.

Output is only one line:

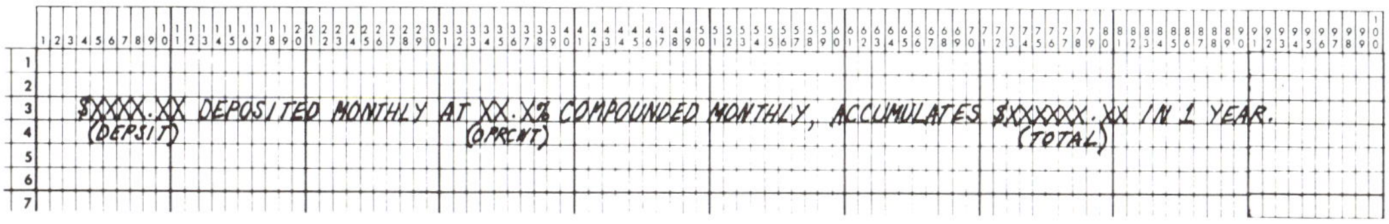

This program is executed most efficiently with a DO loop. It illustrates both the DO and CONTINUE statements. The incrementing integer INDEX represents the flowchart field MONTHS:

```
C PROGRAM INTEREST CALCULATES TOTAL AMOUNT ACCUMULATED IN
C 1 YEAR WHEN A SPECIFIED AMOUNT IS DEPOSITED MONTHLY AND
C INTEREST IS COMPOUNDED MONTHLY. A DO LOOP IS USED.
    1 TOTAL = 0.
    2 READ (5,3) DEPSIT, PERCNT
    3 FORMAT (F6.2,1X,F3.3)
    4 DO 7 INDEX = 1,12
    5 TREST = (TOTAL+DEPSIT) * (PERCNT / 12)
    6 TOTAL = TOTAL + TREST + DEPSIT
    7 CONTINUE
    8 OPRCNT = PERCNT * 100
    9 WRITE (6,10) DEPSIT, OPRCNT, TOTAL
   10 FORMAT(T5, '$', F7.2, 'DEPOSITED MONTHLY AT ',F4.1,
     1'% COMPOUNDED MONTHLY, ACCUMULATES $',F9.2,' IN 1 YEAR.')
   11 CALL EXIT
      END
```

DO statement 4, which does not require a statement number, must begin with the word DO:

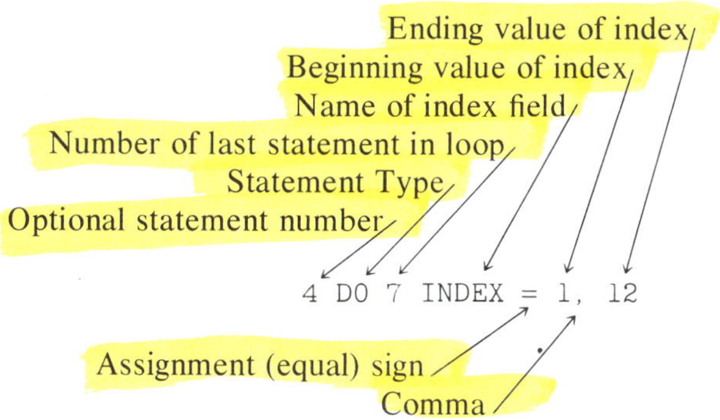

The statement number of the last instruction in the DO loop (7) immediately follows the word DO. Therefore, although the DO statement does not require a number, the last statement of the DO loop must be numbered.

The name of an integer field (INDEX) follows the statement number. This field counts (indexes) the cycles of the DO loop. Care must be taken not to use a field name currently utilized for other purposes in the program. The DO statement indexing alters the field's stored value.

An equal or assignment sign (=) is required immediately after the name of the indexing field. Following the assignment sign are two or three integer numbers, separated by commas.

The first integer (1) after the indexing field name is the value assigned to INDEX the first time the DO loop is executed. The second integer (12) is the value of INDEX the last time the DO loop is performed. To be more exact, the value of INDEX can never be *greater* than the second value in the DO statement. A later example shows why this distinction is made. A third integer (if present) gives the amount by which the indexing field is incremented (increased) each execution of the loop. If, as in statement 4, the third number is omitted, it is assumed to be 1.

The first time statement 4 is executed, INDEX has the value of 1. Each time, just before the loop is reentered, the indexing integer is increasd by the third integer when present or by the value 1 if the third integer is missing. That is, just before the program branches back to begin the DO loop again, the value of the indexing integer (1 during the first loop) is increased by the third value (the implied 1) of the DO statement. Automatically the compiler tests this increased value to see if it is *greater than* the second integer (12). If the indexing integer is less than or equal to the second value, the loop is executed again. If the index value is greater than the second integer, the program automatically "falls through" to the first executable instruction *following* the DO loop. Thus, the program will cycle from statement 4 through statement 7 twelve times.

CONTINUE Statement

Statement 7, CONTINUE, is the simplest of all FORTRAN statements. It is essentially a "do-nothing" executable statement that supplies a required statement number. For example, it provides a "safe" instruction for the end of a DO loop. IF, GOTO, or STOP statements cannot end a DO loop. Neither can nonexecutable instructions, such as FORMAT statements. Using CONTINUE as the last statement of a DO loop assures the programmer that he has a correct loop ending. A CONTINUE statement is, however, a recommended rather than a required end of a DO loop.

When program INTEREST inputs $25.00 for amount and .060 for percent of interest, the following line is output:

```
$  25.00 DEPOSITED MONTHLY AT   6.0% COMPOUNDED MONTHLY, ACCUMULATES $    309.93 IN ONE YEAR.
```

REVIEW QUESTIONS

1. What are generally considered to be the two most powerful FORTRAN statements?
2. What statement is recommended to end a DO loop?
3. What does the first number after the assignment sign in the DO statement represent?
4. What does the second number represent?
5. What does the third number (if present) represent?

Index in Calculations and Output

The indexing integer of a DO statement can be used by the programmer in many ways. Besides being a DO loop counter, it can also be a field in calculations and output. As a simple example of this, program STORE inputs data cards with item number and price per item:

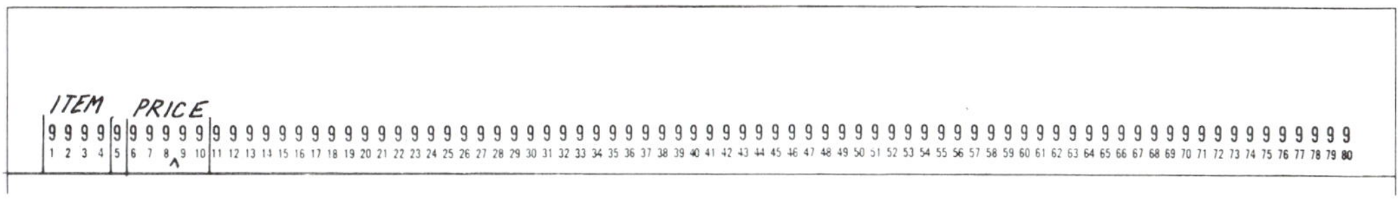

Then a list is printed of prices for one, two, and three units of each of its items. A flowchart documents the program logic on page 160.

A printer spacing chart illustrates the printed report:

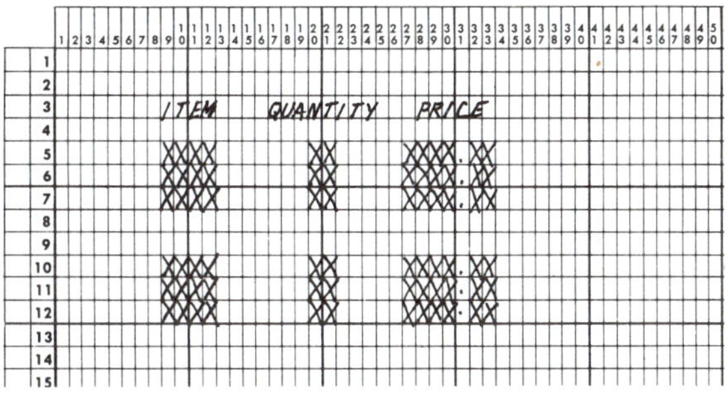

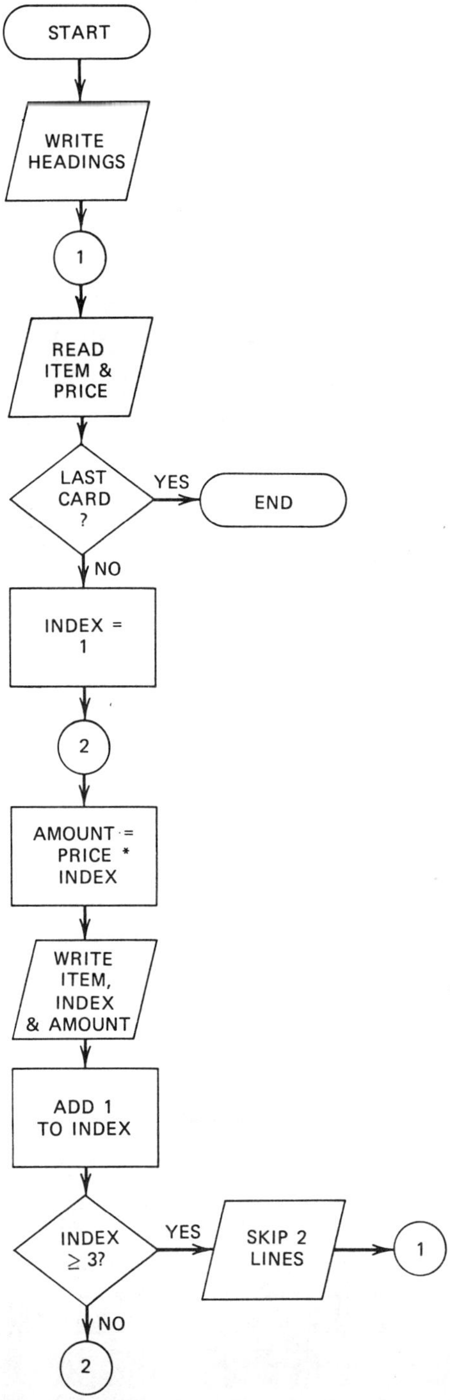
START
WRITE HEADINGS
1
READ ITEM & PRICE
LAST CARD ?
YES
END
NO
INDEX = 1
2
AMOUNT = PRICE * INDEX
WRITE ITEM, INDEX & AMOUNT
ADD 1 TO INDEX
INDEX ≥ 3?
YES
SKIP 2 LINES
1
NO
2

To produce the report, program STORE utilizes a DO loop for calculations and output. Comments and instructions within the DO loop are indented for quick recognition, a practice followed by some programmers.

```
C WRITE HEADINGS AND SPACE
    1 WRITE (6,2)
    2 FORMAT (T10,'ITEM',T18,'QUANTITY',T29,'PRICE'/)
C READ ITEM NUMBER AND PRICE
    3 READ (5,4,END=13) ITEM, PRICE
    4 FORMAT (I4,1X,F5.2)
C DO LOOP THROUGH STATEMENT 9 FOR 3 CYCLES
    5 DO 9 I = 1,3
C           MULTIPLY PRICE TIMES INDEX FOR AMOUNT
    6           AMT = PRICE * I
C           OUTPUT ITEM NUMBER, INDEX, AND AMOUNT
    7           WRITE (6,8) ITEM, I, AMT
    8           FORMAT(T10,I4,T21,I2,T28,F7.2)
    9           CONTINUE
C AFTER COMPLETING DO LOOP, SKIP 2 LINES
   10 WRITE (6,11)
   11 FORMAT ('0')
C BRANCH BACK TO READ NEXT CARD
   12 GO TO 3
   13 CALL EXIT
      END
```

In statements 5– 9 of program STORE, I equals 1 during execution of the first cycle; 2 during the second cycle, and 3 during the third cycle. These three cycles are executed for each data card. During each DO loop cycle, price equals amount times indexing integer I. WRITE statement 7 is also in the DO loop. Item number, index value, and prices are printed for one, two, and three units. To separate the prices of the different items, the printer double spaces immediately after each DO loop "falls through" to the next instruction. The program branches back to read another card and then DO statement 5 begins its loop again. A report is printed with the sample data:

```
ITEM     QUANTITY    PRICE

1254        1        213.85
1254        2        427.70
1254        3        641.55


2457        1        324.56
2457        2        649.12
2457        3        973.68


4534        1        357.24
4534        2        714.48
4534        3       1071.72
```

5534	1	115.48
5534	2	230.96
5534	3	346.44
7534	1	248.34
7534	2	496.68
7534	3	745.02

Incrementing by More Than 1

Further versatility of the DO statement is illustrated by assuming that the store now wants prices for one, three, and five units of each item. Only DO statement 5 changes.

```
5 DO 9 I = 1, 5, 2
```

Although the DO loop again has three cycles, indexing integer I has a different set of three values. During the first cycle, I again equals 1. Just before the second cycle of the DO loop begins, index I is increased by the third value (2). Therefore, during the second cycle, I equals 3. For the third cycle, it is incremented by 2 again and is equal to the second value 5.

The same output results if the middle integer of statement 5 changes from 5 to 6:

```
5 DO 9 I = 1, 6,2
```

Indexing field I has the same values during 3 cycles that it had when the second number was 5. Another cycle cannot be executed because, as was mentioned earlier, the incremented integer cannot *exceed* the value of the second number. Thus, when I tries to increment 5 by the third value 2, the DO statement will not accept 7. Therefore, there still can be only three cycles.

Nested DO Loops

Sometimes DO loops occur within other DO loops. This condition, called nested DO loops, is acceptable with one basic rule: the inner loop can never extend beyond the outer loop. As long as this rule is followed, the number of nested DO loops is unlimited. During the time DO loops are being executed, *each* DO statement must have a *unique name* for its indexing integer. The programmer can use this value, but he cannot alter it in any instruction within the DO loop.

Picturing such loops often helps. A CONTINUE statement concludes each DO loop illustration, but it is an optional ending.

163
NESTED
DO
LOOPS

ACCEPTABLE SINGLE AND NESTED DO LOOPS:

```
  DO 1 I = 1, 5
  (other statements)
          .
          .
1 CONTINUE

  DO 2 I = 1, 6
  DO 3 J = 1, 5
  (other statements)
          .
          .
3 CONTINUE
  (other statements)
          .
2 CONTINUE

  DO 4 I = 1, 3
  DO 4 J = 1, 4
  (other statements)
          .
          .
4 CONTINUE

  DO 5 I = 1, 3
  (other statements)
          .
          .
  DO 5 J = 1, 5
  (other statements)
          .
5 CONTINUE

  DO 7 I = 1, 4
  (other statements)
          .
          .
  DO 6 K = 1, 10
  (other statements)
6 CONTINUE
7 CONTINUE
```

UNACCEPTABLE NESTED DO LOOPS:

```
 8 DO 18 I = 1, 5
 9 DO 19 J = 1, 5
   (other statements)
          .
          .
18 CONTINUE
19 CONTINUE
```

Other statements can be any place in the diagram, but the extension of an inner DO loop beyond the outer DO loop makes the last nesting illegal. Because statement 8 is the first DO statement, it should be the outer loop. Its last statement (18) should be the same as, or come after, the last statement (19) of the DO loop that begins with statement 9. Instead, statement 19 comes *after* statement 18. Thus, the DO loop from statements 9 through 19 is not a valid inner or nested DO loop. The program will be canceled.

Fields as Index Limit Integers

FORTRAN flexibility allows a DO loop even if the number of cycles to be executed changes each time the program is run. For example, each time the program is executed, the limiting number can be established at the beginning of the program by an assignment statement:

```
1 NUMBER = 25
```

This integer field name can be used in place of a numeric constant in the DO statement:

```
65 DO 14 J = 1,NUMBER
```

When statement 65 begins its loop, index J equals 1. J increases by 1 during each loop until J is greater than the stored value (25) of integer field NUMBER.

In another technique for storing the value in a field, the number is read from a special data card placed ahead of other data cards. To accomplish this, two statements are inserted at the beginning of the program:

```
1 READ (5,2) NUMBER
2 FORMAT (I4)
```

Even greater versatility can be seen in a variation of the interest problem. Instead of being limited to calculating interest for only one year, the program can be modified to calculate interest for any number of years. This is accomplished by inputting the top limit of the DO loop (or a field from which the top limit can be calculated) in each transaction card. READ statement 2 now contains a new integer field, IYEARS:

```
2 READ (5,3) DEPSIT, PERCNT, IYEARS
```

Field IYEARS is converted into months for compounding interest:

```
33 MONTHS = IYEARS * 12
```

The complete program follows:

```
 1 TOTAL = 0.
 2 READ (5,3) DEPSIT, PERCNT, IYEARS
 3 FORMAT (F6.2, 1X, F3.3, 1X, I2)
33 MONTHS = IYEARS * 12
 4 DO 7 INDEX = 1,MONTHS
 5 TREST = (TOTAL + DEPSIT) * (PERCNT / 12)
 6 TOTAL = TOTAL + TREST + DEPSIT
 7 CONTINUE
 8 OPRCNT = PERCNT * 100
 9 WRITE (6,10) DEPSIT,OPRCNT,TOTAL,IYEARS
10 FORMAT (T5,'$',F7.2,1X,'DEPOSITED MONTHLY AT ',F4.1,
  1 '% INTEREST COMPOUNDED MONTHLY, '/T5, 'ACCUMULATES $',
  2 F9.2, 1X,'IN ',I2,' YEARS.')
11 CALL EXIT
   END
```

Output reflects this greater versatility:

```
$  25.00 DEPOSITED MONTHLY AT  6.5% INTEREST COMPOUNDED MONTHLY,
ACCUMULATES $   2664.68 IN  7 YEARS.
```

This ability to use either a field name or a numeric constant is valuable in complex programs, especially when the number of times a loop is to be executed depends upon either an input field or a calculated value. Any or all of the 3 values in a DO statement can be an integer field name instead of a number. For example:

```
75 DO 80 INDEX = KOUNT, NUMBER, MORE
```

Statement 75 begins a loop that ends with statement 80. Indexing integer INDEX is equal to KOUNT during the first loop. It is incremented by the value of MORE just before starting each new loop, and continues until INDEX is greater than the value of NUMBER.

Irregular Entrance To or Exit From a DO Loop

A program can branch out of a DO loop, but it cannot reenter the DO loop unless it starts the index again at its first value. If a program branches to an instruction in a DO loop *after* the DO statement, the DO loop is not even started and the program "falls through" as though no loop existed.

REVIEW QUESTIONS

6. Which statement in a DO loop is required to have a label (statement number)?

7. How is the incrementing value of an index established?
8. What basic rule must nested DO loops follow?
9. Can a programmer utilize the indexing integer? If so, how?
10. Can a programmer change the indexing integer? If so, how?

OBJECTIVES REVIEW

Study the objectives at the beginning of this chapter. Check each one to be certain you have achieved it. Restudy the chapter sections relating to any objective you cannot perform.

REVIEW TEST

Study the following FORTRAN program carefully. Using the "data cards" given, "process" the program as the FORTRAN compiler does. On scratch paper, keep a record of what is in storage for every field as the program proceeds. On a printer spacing chart or in the space below, print the output of the test program as it would appear on a printer.

Data Cards

```
                   1         2         3         4
Columns:  1234567890123456789012345678901234567890
Card 1:   356 TRES JOLIE    0700
Card 2:   429 LAVENDER      1200
Card 3:   512 HONEYSUCKLE   0800
Card 4:   /*
```

Program

```
 1 WRITE (6,2)
 2 FORMAT ('1',T20,'LOCAL PERFUMERIES INC.'/)
 3 READ (5,4,END = 25) IDNUM, I1, I2, I3, COST
 4 FORMAT (I3,1X,3A4,1X,F4.2)
 5 PRICE = COST * 1.50
 6 WRITE (6,7) IDNUM, I1,I2,I3,COST
 7 FORMAT ('0',T10,I3,3X,3A4,T34,F5.2)
 8 IF (PRICE-12.0) 9,15,20
 9 DO 13 I= 1,3
10 XPRICE = PRICE * I
11 WRITE (6,12) I, IDNUM, XPRICE
12 FORMAT (T5, I2, T10, I3, T44, F6.2)
13 CONTINUE
14 GO TO 3
15 DO 18 I = 1,4
16 XPRICE = PRICE * I
17 WRITE (6,12) I, IDNUM, XPRICE
18 CONTINUE
19 GO TO 3
20 DO 23 I = 1,2
21 XPRICE = PRICE * I
22 WRITE (6,12) I, IDNUM, XPRICE
23 CONTINUE
```

```
24 GO TO 3
25 CALL EXIT
   END
```

Printout

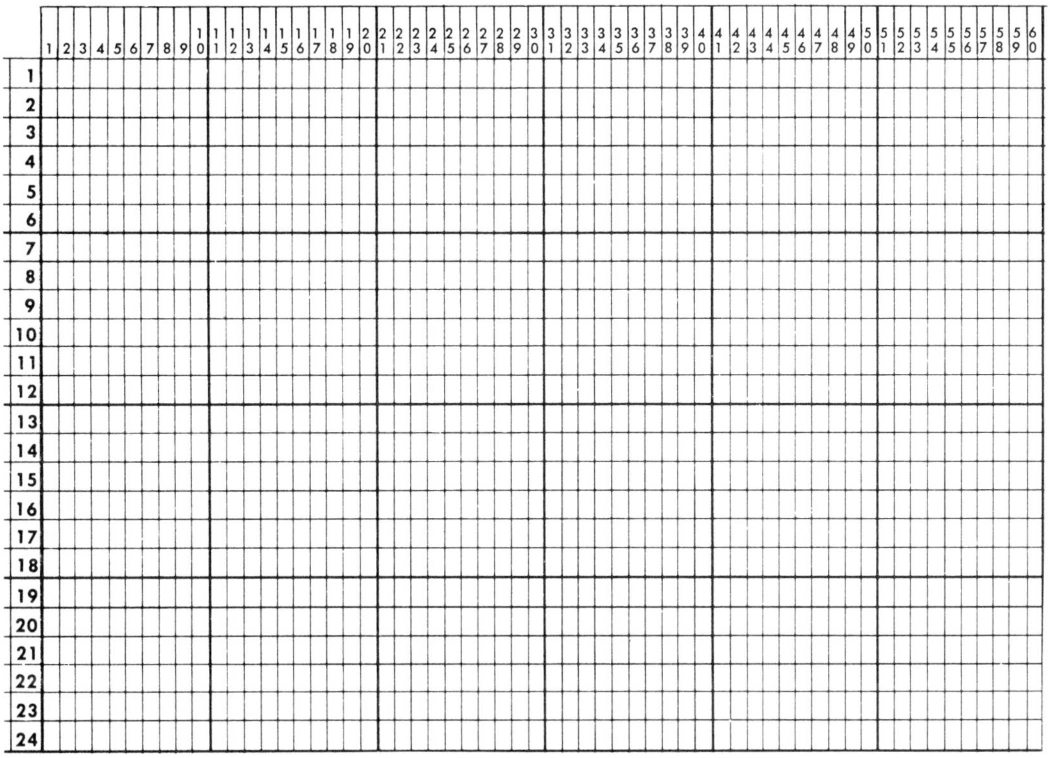

ASSIGNMENTS

Complete a flowchart and printer spacing chart before writing one of the following programs.

1. Write a deposit accumulation plan for a bank or other savings institution:

Input Records

Fields	Card Columns	
Customer number	23-27	(I5)
Customer name	1-20	(5A4)
Monthly deposit amount	40-45	(F6.2)

Calculations. Using a DO loop, calculate the money accumulated at the end of two years if the amount is deposited every month. For 24 months the deposited money earns an annual interest rate of 6% (.005 per month) compounded monthly.

Printed Report. Print savings institution name. Double space before and after printing column headings. For each data card, print customer name and number, monthly amount of deposit, and the total amount accumulated.

2. Write a program to print student records in groups.

Input Records

Fields	Card Columns	
Student name	1-20	(5A4)
Student identification number	23-27	(I5)
Units completed	33-36	(F4.1)
Units in progress	71-73	(F3.1)
Grade point average	38-40	(F3.2)

Calculations. A school prepares a report with five counseling groups of six students each. Use DO loops to number the groups from 1-5, and the students within each group from 1-6.Test for grade point averages equal to or greater than 3.90 (honors), grade point averages greater than 4.00 (error), and those equal to or less than 1.50 (scholastic warning). After the 30 records are processed, write instructions to read any data cards that might be unread.

Printed Report. Print the name of the school, then double space and print COUNSELORS' REPORT. Double space, print column headings, then triple space. Before printing each counseling group, print the group number (by outer DO loop index) and an explanatory literal. On each detail line, number the students from 1-6 (by the inner DO loop index) and print all input fields. If grade point average is 3.90-4.00, print the word HONORS in message area to the right of other fields. If grade point average is less than 1.50, print PROBATION in message area. If grade point average is greater than 4.00, print ERROR in message area.

3. A real estate developer studies a 22-acre land parcel for future building sites. Although the land is sold in acres, the land usage rules are expressed in square feet. The developer can purchase any number of acres from one acre to the entire parcel. After printing company and column headings, use a DO loop to print a report with lines numbered from 1 to 22. These numbers represent possible acre purchases (first line 1 acre, second line 2 acres, etc.) Each line also gives the square footage of the possible purchase (43,560 square feet in 1 acre), and the purchase price if he offers \$265.00, \$283.00, or \$299.00 per acre.

4. A gasoline company requires two tables that convert United States miles to kilometers (1 mile = 1.8532 kilometers). The first table converts every mile from 1 to 20 miles. The second table lists from 5 to 100 miles in increments of 5 miles.

After printing company and column headings, use DO loops to calculate and print the two tables.

5. To stimulate purchases, a store offers lower unit prices if special multiple orders are given. A report is required that shows, for each item, the regular unit price, special unit price, the lowest number of orders, the highest number possible for the special, and the incrementing value for the next special quantity.

Input Records

Fields	Card Columns	
Item number	23-27	I5
Regular price	52-56	F5.2
Percent of discount on special quantities	71-72	F2.2
Beginning special quantity	32	I1
Highest possible quantity for special	21-22	I2
Increment for next special quantity	34	I1

Calculate the special discount price per unit. Using a DO loop, calculate the prices for the special quantity orders.

Print company name and column headings. Then print all specials for each item. The first line for each item contains all input fields. Following lines contain number ordered and special price for that quantity.

Chapter Objectives

1. Be able to establish single and multidimensional arrays in DIMENSION statements.
2. Be able to input and output elements of arrays.
3. Be able to calculate and store elements of arrays.
4. Be able to use both integers and integer field names as array subscripts.
5. Be able to clear an array to zeros with a DO loop.
6. Be able to input, output, or calculate array elements with a DO loop index name as the array subscript.
7. Be able to update array elements that are not arranged sequentially.
8. Be able to input and output arrays without subscripts.

11

The DIMENSION Statement and Arrays

Program USAGE-IF, in Chapter 8, calculates the usage charge for customers of a computer rental company. As each customer record is read, the new input field values replace those from the previously processed customer. Field totals are accumulated and printed. At the end of processing, only data from the last customer record and the last calculations remain in the computer memory.

Although this technique is acceptable for many programs, sometimes a programmer must keep data from *all* input records and calculations available in computer storage. For example, information about charges made to various customers may be required in a later part of the program. Or perhaps a statistical analysis at the end of the program needs information about every fourth salesman. Neither of these problems could be resolved because each new data record wiped out the previous one.

Arrays

FORTRAN solves these situations, however, by utilizing the DIMENSION statement and arrays. When a group of fields share a name, it is called an array. Fields of the array are often called "elements" of the array. The obvious difficulty is to know where each element in the array is located. That is, there must be an order in the arrangement of elements in an array so that the programmer can store or retrieve the element he wants. This is accomplished by referring to the elements according to their position in the array.

The method of referencing elements is called subscripting. In FORTRAN it is accomplished by first giving the array name and then following it by an integer value enclosed in a pair of parentheses. The integer value, which represents the position of the element in the array, can be a field name (such as INTEGR), a number (21), or an arithmetic expression (I + 1). For instance, assume that Renta Computer Company has 100 customers. Their customer identification numbers comprise the 100-element array KUSTMR. The first field in array KUSTMR is referred to as KUSTMR (1). The second element is stored as KUSTMR (2). The one-hundredth is called KUSTMR (100). Storage for this array can be pictured as a long string of 100 adjoining fields:

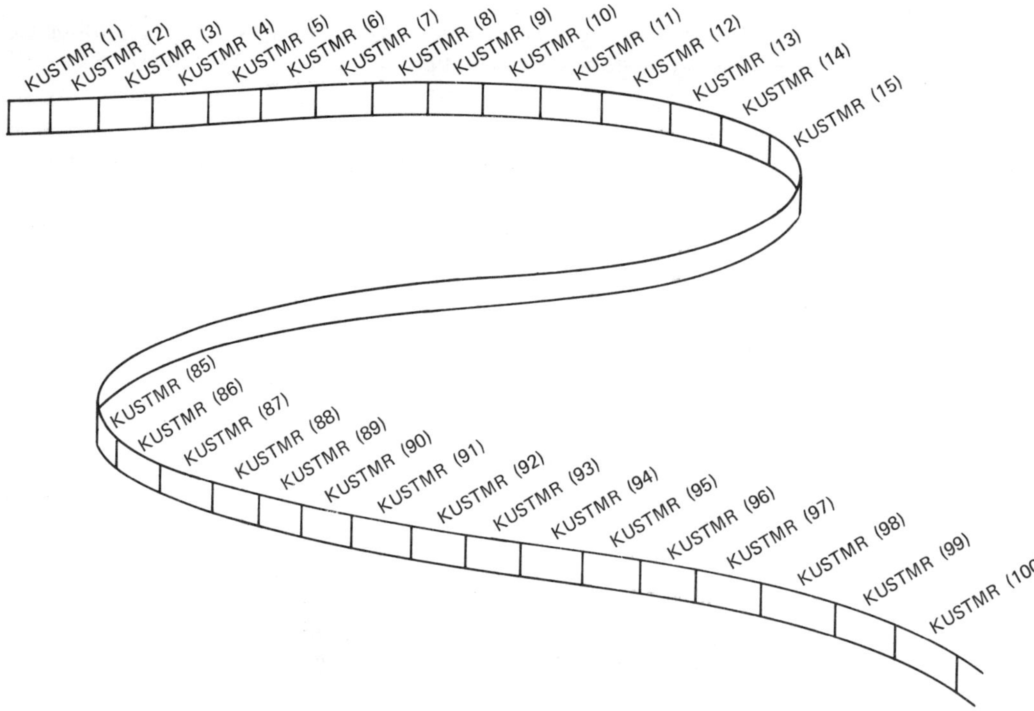

Each element in the array has exactly as much storage space as if it were a separate field.

The DIMENSION Statement

Before arrays can be stored, the computer must be instructed to reserve enough storage area for all the necessary data. This is accomplished by the DIMENSION statement, which *cannot* be numbered. It is a nonexecutable (descriptive) instruction that must come *before any executable statements* in the program. This frequently makes it the first statement in a program.

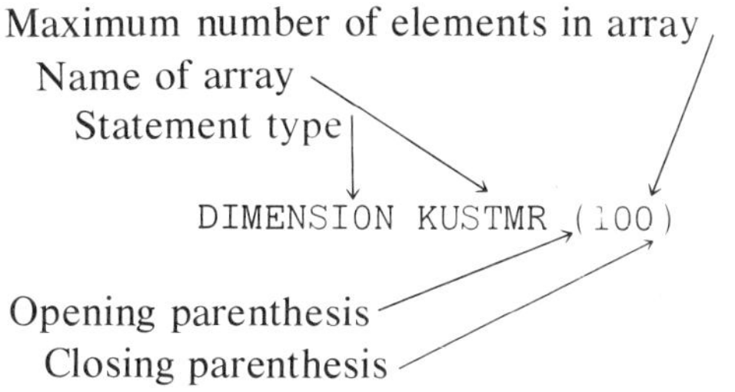

A DIMENSION statement begins with the word DIMENSION. Then an array name is listed, followed by a pair of parentheses containing the *maximum* number of elements in the array. Notice that in the DIMENSION statement the number in parentheses does not refer to a specific element in the array but instead establishes the total number of elements in the array. In the example, the DIMENSION statement reserves 100 adjoining integer field locations in storage, all with the array name KUSTMR.

An unlimited (except by the size of computer memory) number of arrays can be listed in a DIMENSION statement. Commas must be inserted between the number in parentheses and the *next* array name.

```
DIMENSION KUSTMR (100), USAGE (100), CHARGE (100)
```

Arrays of real and integer fields can be listed in the same statement, as demonstrated in the above example. This DIMENSION statement reserves space in computer storage for three arrays, each with 100 elements. One hundred storage locations are reserved for array KUSTMR, 100 locations are reserved for array USAGE, and 100 are reserved for array CHARGE:

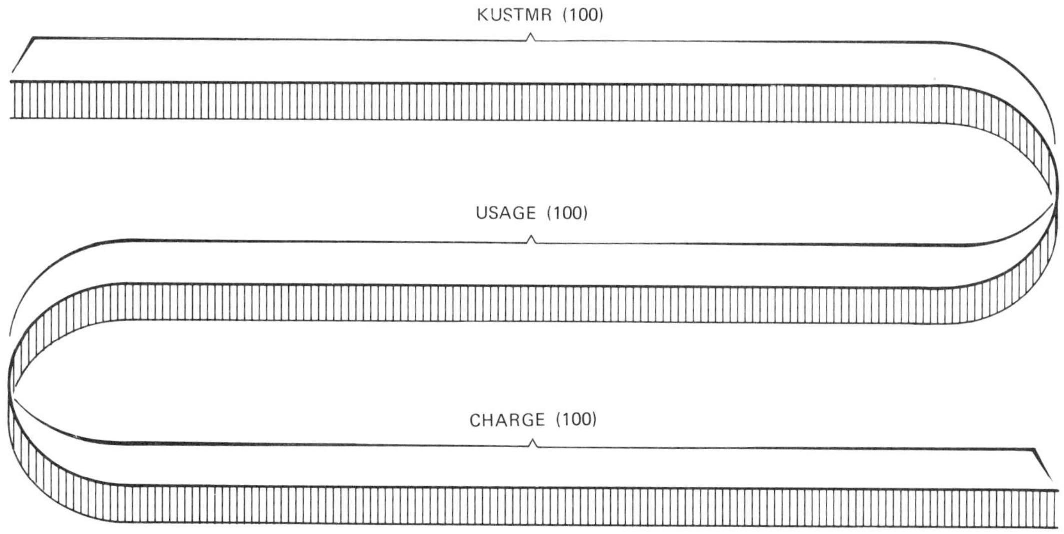

All the data processed as fields PREAD and CREAD could also be in arrays if the program required this information in retained storage. More than one DIMENSION statement can be in a program, but all DIMENSION statements must be placed before any executable statements. DIMENSION statements can also be continued by using a nonzero character in column 6.

```
DIMENSION RATES (15), KUSTMR (250), CHARGE (250), ID (250),
/ REGION (8), DEPTS (34)
```

In DIMENSION statements, arrays need not be listed in any order, such as alphabetic, type, size, etc.

A DIMENSION statement only reserves the requested space. It instructs the compiler to set aside the maximum amount of storage that might be needed for the arrays listed. It does not clear the reserved area to blanks or zeros. If the array elements are not filled by the program, or if they are not cleared by special instruction of the programmer, errors can result from the data still remaining in storage from a previous program. Techniques for clearing arrays are demonstrated in this chapter.

Every array element has as much space as if it were an individual field. The program may require array elements to be in a special order, such as largest to smallest, alphabetically or numerically sequenced, etc., but the compiler has no requirement of this sort. Elements in an array need only be the same type (such as real or integer) as all other fields in the array. Alphameric and numeric data can be in the same array.

DIMENSION statements reserve the maximum number of spaces an array might need. Sometimes the exact number of array elements cannot be predicted precisely. Leaving some array elements unused does not violate any FORTRAN rules. If this practice is overdone, however, the computer may be unable to execute a program because too much storage is reserved for arrays. Special care must also be used to avoid calling for information from an array element that has not yet been given a value.

REVIEW QUESTIONS

1. Which FORTRAN statement instructs the computer to set aside necessary computer storage space for an array?
2. How many arrays can be established in one such statement?
3. Where must such statements be placed in a program?
4. How are elements in an array addressed?
5. How many locations must be reserved in computer memory for an array?
6. In what special sequence, if any, does the FORTRAN compiler require elements of an array to be stored?

Arrays and DO loops

In a new program, USAGE-SUMMARY, the basic input and output formats are unchanged from program USAGE-IF, but there is a summary report after the main part of the program as the flowchart illustrates:

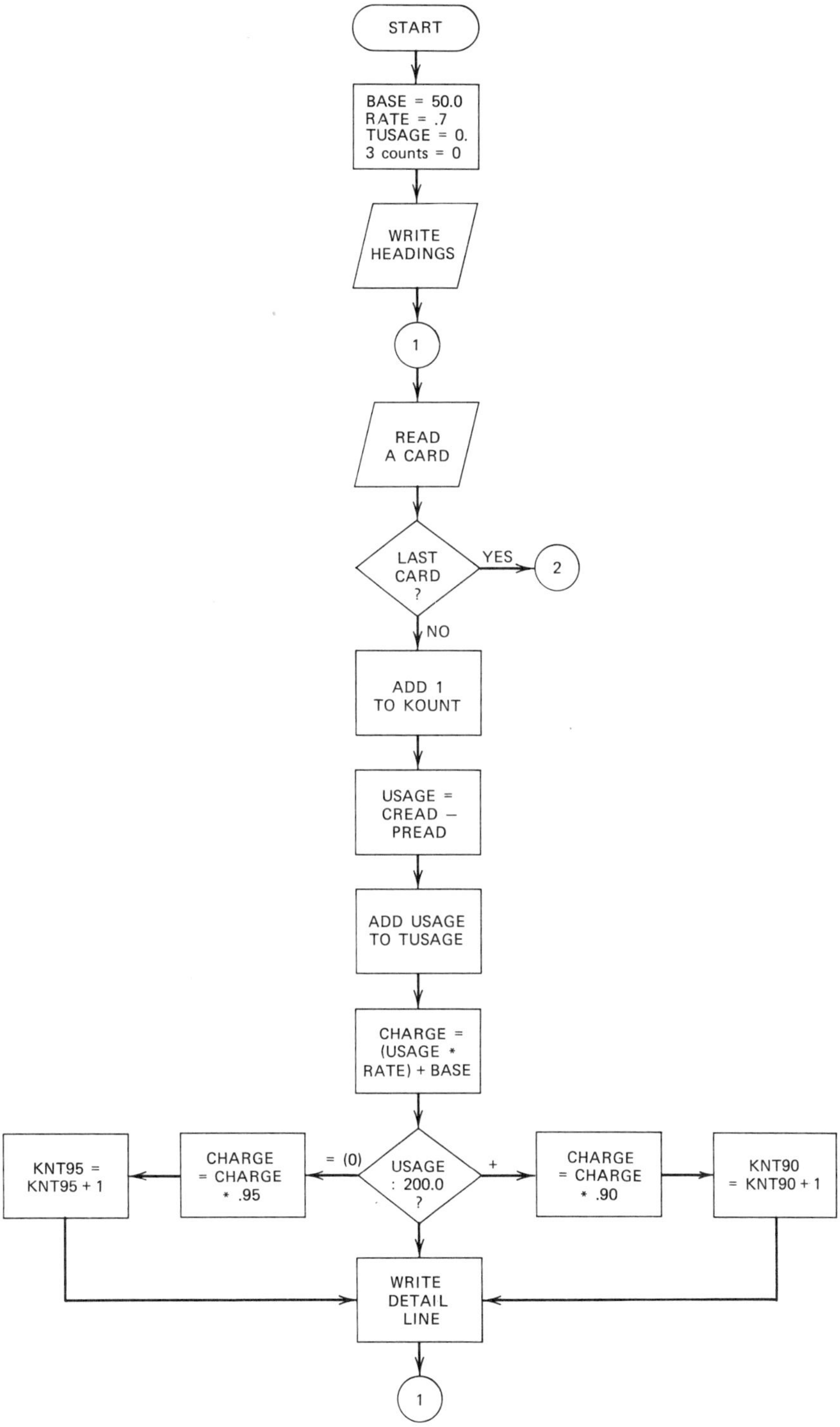
START
BASE = 50.0
RATE = .7
TUSAGE = 0.
3 counts = 0
WRITE HEADINGS
1
READ A CARD
LAST CARD ?
YES
2
NO
ADD 1 TO KOUNT
USAGE = CREAD − PREAD
ADD USAGE TO TUSAGE
CHARGE = (USAGE * RATE) + BASE
USAGE : 200.0 ?
= (0)
+
CHARGE = CHARGE * .95
KNT95 = KNT95 + 1
CHARGE = CHARGE * .90
KNT90 = KNT90 + 1
WRITE DETAIL LINE
1

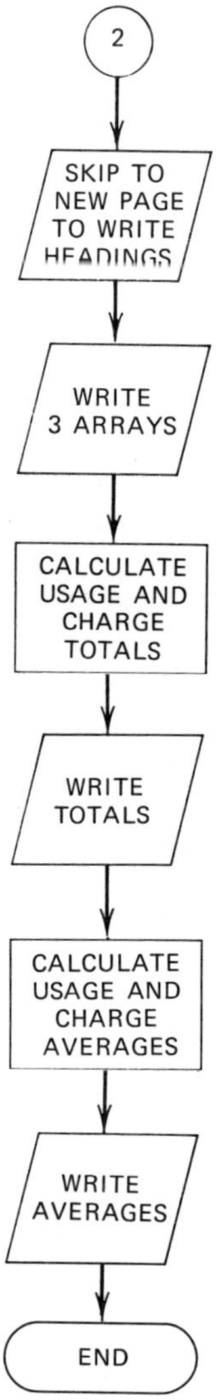
2
SKIP TO NEW PAGE TO WRITE HEADINGS
WRITE 3 ARRAYS
CALCULATE USAGE AND CHARGE TOTALS
WRITE TOTALS
CALCULATE USAGE AND CHARGE AVERAGES
WRITE AVERAGES
END

A printer spacing chart shows the form of the summary report that begins after completion of the detail processing.

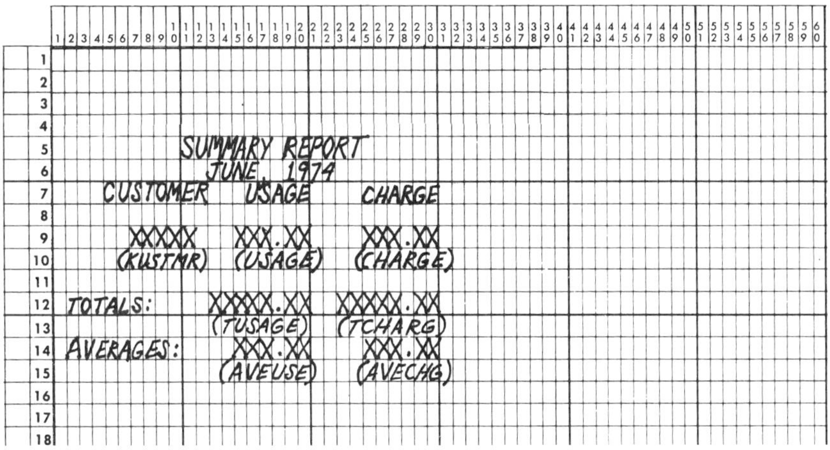

In order to create this extra summary report, customer number, amount of usage, and usage charge are stored in arrays. To accomplish this, a DIMENSION statement creates three 5-element arrays. (Only five customers are used in the demonstration programs.) Then a DO loop is used, with the index ranging from 1 to 5:

```
    DIMENSION KUSTMR (5), USAGE (5), CHARGE(5)
    .
    .
111 DO 120 I = 1,5
112 READ (5,13) KUSTMR(I),N1,N2,N3,N4,N5,CREAD,PREAD
    .
    .
    .
115 USAGE (I) = CREAD - PREAD
116 CHARGE(I) = BASE + (USAGE(I) * RATE)
    .
    .
    .
118 WRITE (6,19) KUSTMR(I),N1,N2,N3,N4,N5,CREAD,PREAD,
   1 USAGE(I), CHARGE (I)
120 CONTINUE
```

When the first data card is read, the index of the DO statement and all the subscripts using that index are equal to 1. When the second data card is read, the index and subscripts equal 2. Whenever the compiler encounters a subscripted array element, it finds the current value of the index field and inserts that value in the subscript. For example, if the value of index I is 5 when the compiler encounters USAGE(I), the array element automatically becomes USAGE(5), the fifth element in array USAGE.

The process of substitution occurs whenever a field name rather than a number is in the subscript. The programmer must be careful of two details: (1) the subscript name must be an integer name, and (2) that integer must have a current value that is a *positive* number not greater than the number of elements established in the DIMENSION statement. In demonstration program USAGE-SUMMARY, subscripts for arrays KUSTMR, USAGE, and CHARGE must fall within the range of 1 to 5. Placing input and calculations within a DO loop guarantees that KUSTMR(1), USAGE(1), and CHARGE(1) all pertain to the first customer processed. KUSTMR(2), USAGE(2), and CHARGE(2) relate to the second customer. This relationship is true for all records processed.

Even after the array elements are printed by WRITE statement 118, they remain in storage. Every time the DO loop is executed, the index is incremented by 1 and another set of array elements is read or calculated. At the completion of all cycles of the DO loop, computer storage contains all the elements of all three arrays. Therefore, a statement within the detail calculations is no longer the only way to accumulate a total. Arrays USAGE and CHARGE can now be printed and/or totaled in DO loops any place in the program after the initialization of the total fields and the completion of the input-calculation DO loop:

```
202 DO 203 I = 1,5
203 WRITE (6,204) KUSTMR (I), USAGE(I), CHARGE (I)
204 FORMAT (T8, I5, 3X, F6.2, 4X, F6.2)
205 DO 208 I = 1,5
206 TCHARG = TCHARG + CHARGE (I)
207 TUSAGE = TUSAGE + USAGE (I)
208 CONTINUE
```

The writing DO loop requires only two statements, although a CONTINUE statement can conclude the loop. The totaling DO loop contains four statements, but the CONTINUE statement is not required. Both writing and calculating could have been combined into one DO loop.

Totals can be accumulated after the main processing because all the array information is retained in computer storage. Each cycle of the short totaling loop adds another element of arrays CHARGE and USAGE to the totals. This type of calculation is frequently used when all information is accessible in an array.

Statements 200-213 demonstrate how the summary report is printed on a separate page following detail transaction records:

```
C SKIP TO NEW PAGE AND WRITE SUMMARY
  200 WRITE (6,201)
  201 FORMAT ('1',T12,'SUMMARY REPORT' /T14,'JUNE, 1974'/T6,
     1'CUSTOMER',3X,'USAGE',4X,'CHARGE'//)
C WRITE 3-FIELD DETAIL LINES
  202 DO 203 I = 1,5
```

```
  203 WRITE(6,204)KUSTMR(I),USAGE(I),CHARGE(I)
  204 FORMAT (T8,I5,3X,F6.2,4X,F6.2)
C CALCULATE TOTAL CHARGE AND TOTAL USAGE FROM ARRAYS
  205 DO 208 I = 1,5
  206 TCHARG = TCHARG + CHARGE(I)
  207 TUSAGE = TUSAGE + USAGE(I)
  208 CONTINUE
C CALCULATE AND WRITE AVERAGE CHARGE AND AVERAGE USAGE
  209 AVECHG = TCHARG / KOUNT
  210 AVEUSE = TUSAGE / KOUNT
  211 WRITE (6,212) TUSAGE, TCHARG, AVEUSE, AVECHG
  212 FORMAT ('0',T3,'TOTALS:',4X,F8.2,2X,F8.2//T3,'AVERAGES:'
     1 ,4X,F6.2,4X,F6.2)
  213 CALL EXIT
      END
```

Program USAGE-SUMMARY is listed on the printer:

```
      DIMENSION KUSTMR(5),USAGE(5),CHARGE(5)
    0 BASE = 50.00
    1 RATE = .7
    2 TUSAGE = 0.0
    3 KOUNT = 0
  102 TCHARG = 0.
    4 WRITE (6,5)
    5 FORMAT ('1',T38,'RENTA COMPUTER, INC.'/T43,'JUNE, 1974')
    6 WRITE (6,7)
    7 FORMAT ('0',3X,'ACCOUNT',11X,'ACCOUNT',11X,'CURRENT',5X,'PREVIOUS'
     1 ,8X,'USAGE',7X, 'MONTHLY')
    8 WRITE (6,9)
    9 FORMAT (4X,'NUMBER',13X,'NAME',13X,'READING',5X,'READING',21X,
     1 'CHARGE')
   10 WRITE (6,11)
   11 FORMAT (' ')
  111 DO 120 I = 1,5
  112 READ (5,13) KUSTMR(I),N1,N2,N3,N4,N5,PREAD,CREAD
   13 FORMAT (I5,5A4,4X,F6.2,2X,F6.2)
   14 KOUNT = KOUNT + 1
  115 USAGE(I) = CREAD - PREAD
  116 CHARGE(I) = BASE + (USAGE(I) * RATE)
  171 IF (USAGE(I) - 200.00) 118,172, 175
  172 CHARGE(I) = CHARGE(I) * .95
  174 GO TO 118
  175 CHARGE(I) = CHARGE (I) * .9
  118 WRITE(6,19)KUSTMR(I),N1,N2,N3,N4,N5,CREAD,PREAD,USAGE(I),CHARGE(I)
   19 FORMAT (5X,I5,5X,5A4,5X,F7.2,6X,F7.2,8X,F6.2,7X,F6.2)
  120 CONTINUE
  200 WRITE (6,201)
  201 FORMAT('1',T12,'SUMMARY REPORT'/T14,'JUNE, 1974'/T6,'CUSTOMER',3X,
     1'USAGE',4X,'CHARGE'//)
  202 DO 203 I = 1,5
  203 WRITE(6,204)KUSTMR (I), USAGE(I), CHARGE(I)
  204 FORMAT(T8,I5,3X,F6.2,4X,F6.2)
  205 DO 208 I = 1,5
  206 TCHARG = TCHARG + CHARGE(I)
  207 TUSAGE = TUSAGE + USAGE(I)
  208 CONTINUE
  209 AVECHG = TCHARG / KOUNT
  210 AVEUSE = TUSAGE / KOUNT
  211 WRITE(6,212) TUSAGE,TCHARG,AVEUSE,AVECHG
  212 FORMAT ('0',T3,'TOTALS:',4X,F8.2,2X,F8.2//T3,'AVERAGES:',4X,F6.2,
     14X,F6.2)
  213 CALL EXIT
      END
```

The output of program USAGE-SUMMARY is the following two page report:

RENTA COMPUTER, INC.
JUNE, 1974

ACCOUNT NUMBER	ACCOUNT NAME	CURRENT READING	PREVIOUS READING	USAGE	MONTHLY CHARGE
12548	ANDERSCN JOSEPH	2247.36	2138.57	108.79	126.15
24573	BROWN GORDON	3344.55	3245.67	98.88	119.22
45342	BUTLER RANDOLPH	3687.52	3572.46	115.06	130.54
55343	CATALETA PAULINE	1568.97	1154.86	414.11	305.89
75342	LEVY SAMUEL	3189.54	2483.46	706.08	489.83

SUMMARY REPORT
JUNE, 1974

	CUSTOMER	USAGE	CHARGE
	12548	108.79	126.15
	24573	98.88	119.22
	45342	115.06	130.54
	55343	414.11	305.89
	75342	706.08	489.83
TOTALS:		1442.92	1171.63
AVERAGES:		288.58	234.33

Another technique that is both space saving and versatile is preplanning the customer identification number to fit an array. For example, if there are 100 customers numbered from 001 to 100, the arrays contain 100 elements, DO statements index from 1 to 100, and customer cards are arranged by customer number. If there are only five customers, as in the demonstration program, they are numbered from 1 to 5, arrays contain 5 elements, DO loop indexes range from 1 to 5, and customer cards are arranged in sequence from 1 through 5. The sequence number now replaces the customer identification number formerly used.

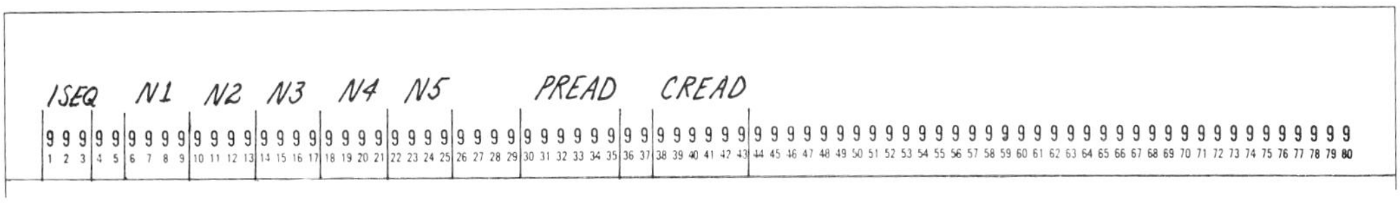

Because customer numbers are planned to coincide with index I, the current value of I matches the number of the customer whose record currently is being processed. Using this technique, array KUSTMR can be eliminated. Whenever an element in an array is called, the current value of the index is inserted by the compiler into the subscript. Since the values for index and customer number are identical, arrays are needed only for amounts of usage and charges. In careful programming, however, the customer number is compared to the indexing value to guarantee that the data cards are in correct sequence.

Matching the customer identification number and subscripts increases versatility because the program may require the retrieval of data about a specific customer. In order to obtain the information, only the customer number is required. This is especially handy when input and output are on tape, disk, typewriter, or a visual image terminal connected to the Central Processing Unit of the computer. For example, when only the customer number is input, both amount of usage and charge for the customer can be output:

```
  DIMENSION USAGE(100), CHARGE (100)
1 READ(8,2) KUSTMR
2 FORMAT (I3)
3 WRITE (9,4) KUSTMR, USAGE(KUSTMR), CHARGE(KUSTMR)
4 FORMAT (T2, I3, 2X, F6.2, 3X, F6.2)
```

The input value of KUSTMR is substituted for the subscript field name when statement 3 is executed. If KUSTMR is 5, the compiler inserts the value 5 for each use of KUSTMR as a subscript:

```
3 WRITE(9,4)KUSTMR,USAGE(5),CHARGE(5)
```

By this technique, an identification number can call out all items pertaining to that number, a valuable aid in information retrieval.

The programmer can also call for array elements by using a numeric constant as a subscript. For example, information about customer 35 can be printed by the following instruction:

```
33 WRITE (9,4) KUSTMR, USAGE(35), CHARGE(35)
```

Although less flexible than techniques demonstrated earlier, this type of subscript is sometimes required by program logic.

REVIEW QUESTIONS

7. Whether a number or a field name, which numeric type must be used in subscripting an array element?
8. What determine the least and the greatest values that can be used as subscripts in referencing array elements?
9. How can an array be totaled when the entire array is stored in the computer memory?
10. How does matching an identification number with the position in an array of data regarding that identification facilitate retrieval of that information?

Updating Arrays

Arrays are not always used with DO loops. Further versatility of arrays, used without a DO loop index, is demonstrated by a program calculating and updating sales commissions. Unlike arrays USAGE and CHARGE that are calculated from summary data cards at the end of each month, the array for sales commission is updated whenever a sale is made.

The input data card for the program contains the sales person's number (from 001 to 100), the amount of sale, and the commission rate:

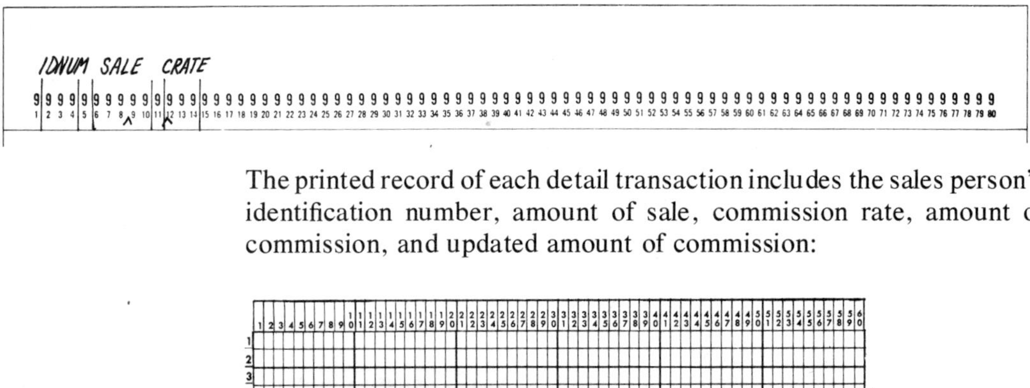

The printed record of each detail transaction includes the sales person's identification number, amount of sale, commission rate, amount of commission, and updated amount of commission:

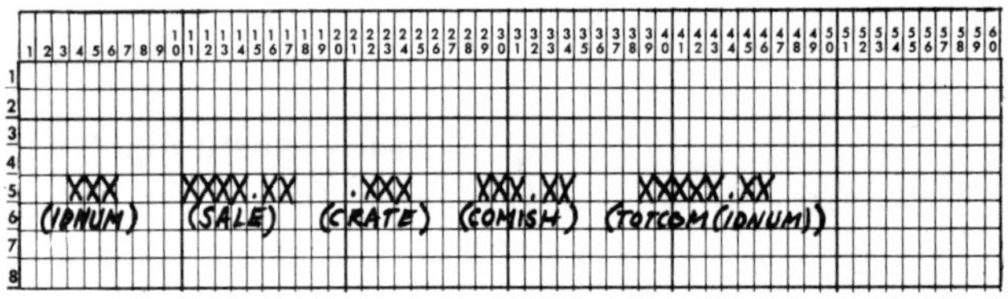

Upon the completion of all transaction details, identification numbers and the updated total amount of commission for all sales people are output:

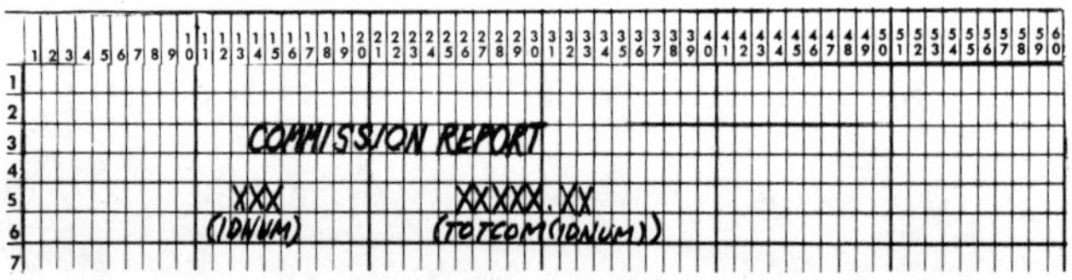

A flowchart illustrates the process by which this report is developed:

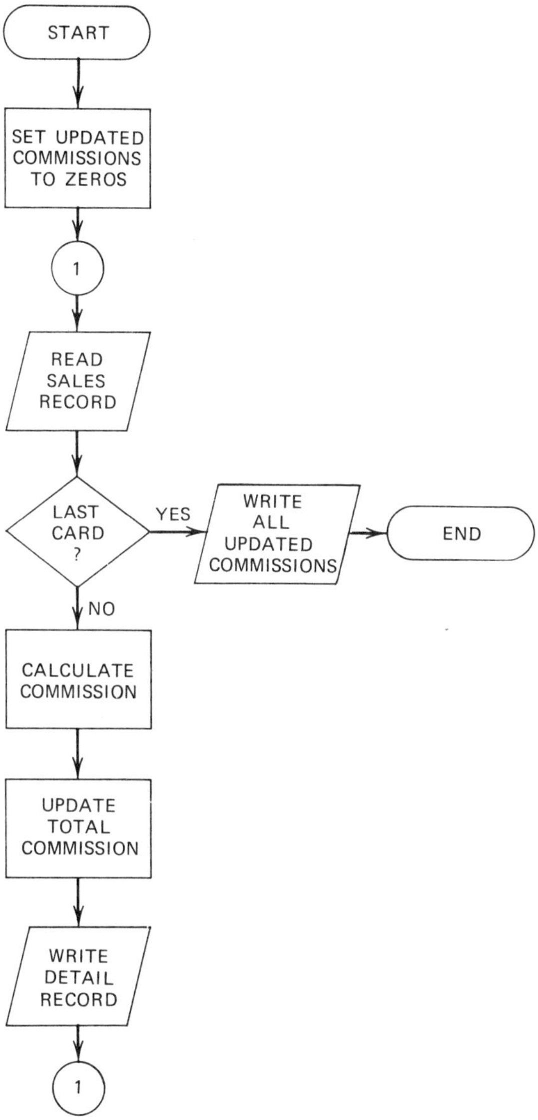

Array TOTCOM (for total amount of commission) is established. Every element in the array is cleared to zero for the beginning of the month. These steps are accomplished by a DIMENSION statement and a small DO loop:[1]

[1]FORTRAN compilers with the DATA statement can clear the array storage area more simply, as demonstrated in Chapter 16.

```
C ESTABLISH AND CLEAR ARRAY OF UPDATED COMMISSIONS
      DIMENSION TOTCOM (100)
    1 DO 3 I = 1,100
    2 TOTCOM(I) = 0.0
    3 CONTINUE
```

For each transaction, the sales person's number, amount of sale, and commission rate are input. From this data, the commission is calculated.

```
    4 READ (5,5,END=11) IDNUM, SALE, CRATE
    5 FORMAT (I3, 1X, F5.2, 1X, F3.3)
    6 COMISH = CRATE * SALE
```

After the commission is calculated, it is added to the appropriate element of array TOTCOM by using the sales person's identification number as the subscript field name. The detail transaction is printed, and the program branches back to read the next record.

```
    7 TOTCOM(IDNUM) = TOTCOM(IDNUM) + COMISH
    8 WRITE (6,9) IDNUM,SALE,CRATE,COMISH,TOTCOM(IDNUM)
    9 FORMAT(T5,I3,T12,F7.2,T22,F4.3,T30,F6.2,T40,F8.2)
   10 GO TO 4
```

Because the integer field IDNUM is input, it is available as the subscript for array elements. Thus, the computer keeps an accurate record no matter how many transactions are recorded. This method, called "random" processing, has the advantage that input data need not be sorted into numeric sequence before program execution.

After all input records have been processed, array TOTCOM is output with the sales persons' identification numbers. This is accomplished with a DO loop that uses the index for the identification number.

```
C SKIP TO NEW PAGE AND WRITE ALL UPDATED COMMISSIONS
   11 WRITE (6,12)
   12 FORMAT ('1',T15,'COMMISSION REPORT'//)
   13 DO 16 I = 1,100
   14 WRITE (6,15) I, TOTCOM(I)
   15 FORMAT ('0',T14, I3, T27, F8.2)
   16 CONTINUE
   17 CALL EXIT
      END
```

Thus array TOTCOM can be output by individual elements, as in the detail transactions, or in its entirety as the final program step.

Sometimes the indexing integers (or other fields) are not printed with array elements. If an entire array is to be input or output consecutively, the DO loop and array subscript can be eliminated. FORMAT statements can be varied, with literals and/or blank spaces, but no other fields can interrupt the array elements. For example, the updated commissions could be listed by statements 111-114.

```
111 WRITE (6,112)
112 FORMAT ('1', T15, 'COMMISSION REPORT'//)
113 WRITE (6,114) TOTCOM
114 FORMAT ('0',T21,F8.2)
```

Each element of array TOTCOM will be on a separate line because FORMAT statement 114 is repeated until the entire array is output.

The FORMAT statement can be altered, for example, so that five elements of the array are printed on each line:

```
114 FORMAT ('0', T21, 5(F8.2, 6X))
```

Especially when working with large arrays, the programmer must remember that listing an array without a subscript causes all elements of the array to be printed even if some are blank or were never cleared.

Alphameric fields can be stored in arrays also. Because they normally are input and output by "implied" DO loops, discussion of alphameric fields in arrays is postponed until the next chapter.

REVIEW QUESTIONS

11. What is the function of a DIMENSION statement?
12. How can elements of an array be updated with random processing?
13. Why are DO loops often used with arrays?
14. What is input or output when an array is listed without a subscript in a READ or WRITE statement?

Multidimensional Arrays

Arrays like USAGE, CHARGE, and TOTCOM are often called lists, strings, single arrays, or one-dimension arrays. Many arrays are two- or three-dimensional arrays. In fact, depending upon the computer model, FORTRAN IV compilers can handle up to either three- or nine-dimensional arrays.

An extension of the commission problem demonstrates the usefulness of multidimensional arrays. The 100 sales people now comprise Department 5 of a large sales organization. This organization has eight departments. None of the departments has more than 100 sales people. Thus, when processing is done simultaneously for all departments, storage must be reserved for eight departments with a possible maximum of 100 sales people in each department. The DIMENSION statement must reflect this enlargement:

```
DIMENSION TOTCOM (8,100)
```

Array TOTCOM is now a two-dimensional or double-dimension array. Although the maximum size of department number is listed first in the DIMENSION statement, the salesperson limit could be listed first.

Once the order is established, however, it must be maintained for that array throughout the program.

The DIMENSION statement reserved storage for 800 elements. That is, eight departments times 100 customers. Because the eight departments do not all have 100 sales people, part of this storage area never will be utilized. Since reserved space is required for the largest number possible in each dimension, though, the programmer must allow for 100 sales people in each of the eight departments.

Although computers do not actually store arrays in the following manner, FORTRAN compiler methods of subscripting allow the programmer to visualize a two-dimensional array easily. A schematic drawing illustrates *addresses,* not contents, of 8 × 100 two-dimensional array TOTCOM:

DEPARTMENT (subscript value listed first)

SALESPERSON (subscript value listed second)

	1	2	3	4	5	6	...	99	100
1	TOTCOM (1,1)	TOTCOM (1,2)	TOTCOM (1,3)	TOTCOM (1,4)	TOTCOM (1,5)	TOTCOM (1,6)	...	TOTCOM (1,99)	TOTCOM (1,100)
2	TOTCOM (2,1)	TOTCOM (2,2)	TOTCOM (2,3)	TOTCOM (2,4)	TOTCOM (2,5)	TOTCOM (2,6)	...	TOTCOM (2,99)	TOTCOM (2,100)
3	TOTCOM (3,1)	TOTCOM (3,2)	TOTCOM (3,3)	TOTCOM (3,4)	TOTCOM (3,5)	TOTCOM (3,6)	...	TOTCOM (3,99)	TOTCOM (3,100)
4	TOTCOM (4,1)	TOTCOM (4,2)	TOTCOM (4,3)	TOTCOM (4,4)	TOTCOM (4,5)	TOTCOM (4,6)	...	TOTCOM (4,99)	TOTCOM (4,100)
5	TOTCOM (5,1)	TOTCOM (5,2)	TOTCOM (5,3)	TOTCOM (5,4)	TOTCOM (5,5)	TOTCOM (5,6)	...	TOTCOM (5,99)	TOTCOM (5,100)
6	TOTCOM (6,1)	TOTCOM (6,2)	TOTCOM (6,3)	TOTCOM (6,4)	TOTCOM (6,5)	TOTCOM (6,6)	...	TOTCOM (6,99)	TOTCOM (6,100)
7	TOTCOM (7,1)	TOTCOM (7,2)	TOTCOM (7,3)	TOTCOM (7,4)	TOTCOM (7,5)	TOTCOM (7,6)	...	TOTCOM (7,99)	TOTCOM (7,100)
8	TOTCOM (8,1)	TOTCOM (8,2)	TOTCOM (8,3)	TOTCOM (8,4)	TOTCOM (8,5)	TOTCOM (8,6)	...	TOTCOM (8,99)	TOTCOM (8,100)

The first subscripted value is the row (horizontal). The second subscripted value is the column (vertical). This is the customary way to illustrate two-dimensional FORTRAN arrays.

Now elements of the arrays must be addressed by *both* subscripted values. In order to update array TOTCOM, both department and salesperson's identification number must be input as integers with the transaction card. The input card is unchanged from the layout form previously used except for the fact that department number is now included.

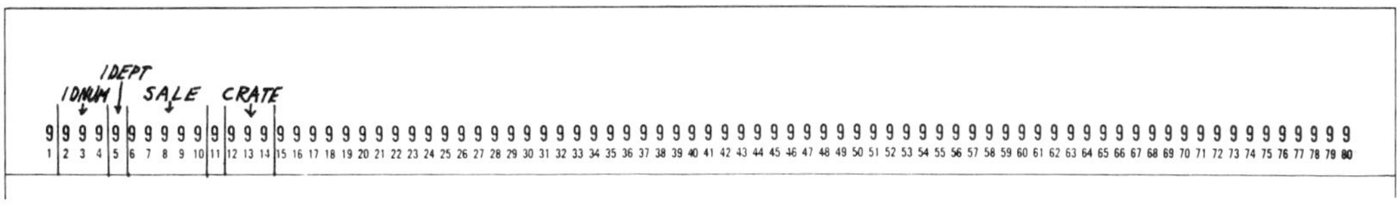

Four fields are now input for each transaction:

```
4 READ (5,5,END = 11) IDNUM, IDEPT, SALES, CRATE
5 FORMAT (1X, I3, I1, F5.2, 1X, F3.3)
```

Assume that a data card contains information that salesperson 63 in department 5 sold an article for $95.50, with a commission rate of .075. The computer reads IDEPT, which is 5, and IDNUM, which is 063, as well as SALE and CRATE. Because values are stored for the two integer fields, the compiler is able to process statement 50 accurately:

```
50 TOTCOM (IDEPT,IDNUM) = TOTCOM (IDEPT,IDNUM) + (SALE * CRATE)
```

The compiler converts each TOTCOM (IDEPT,IDNUM) to TOTCOM (5,63) and then updates the appropriate element of the commission array.

When integers are input in this manner, they may be used to subscript arrays in the same data card. For example, assume that SALE and CRATE are both double-dimension arrays like array TOTCOM. The input card could then be stored with the READ statement 111:

```
      DIMENSION TOTCOM(8,100),SALE(8,100),CRATE(8,100)
      .
      .
      .
111 READ (5,5,END=11)IDNUM,IDEPT,SALE(IDEPT,IDNUM),CRATE(IDEPT,IDNUM)
```

The format and data are unchanged, but the two fields are now elements in arrays. Their position in storage is determined by the integer fields that must be read from the data card first so that they are in storage when needed for the subscript.

Business applications in such areas as investment, financing, or insurance sometimes use arrays with more than three dimensions. Demonstration problems need not involve more than three levels, however, because the same basic principles for multidimensional arrays apply no matter how many dimensions are contained in the array.

Three-dimensional arrays can be demonstrated by assuming further growth in the sales organization. It now consists of four branch stores. The largest branch has eight departments. The largest department employs 100 sales people. Array TOTCOM must now reserve 3200 (4 × 8 × 100) spaces:

```
DIMENSION TOTCOM (4,8,100)
```

The input records now contain a branch identification number as well as all the previous fields:

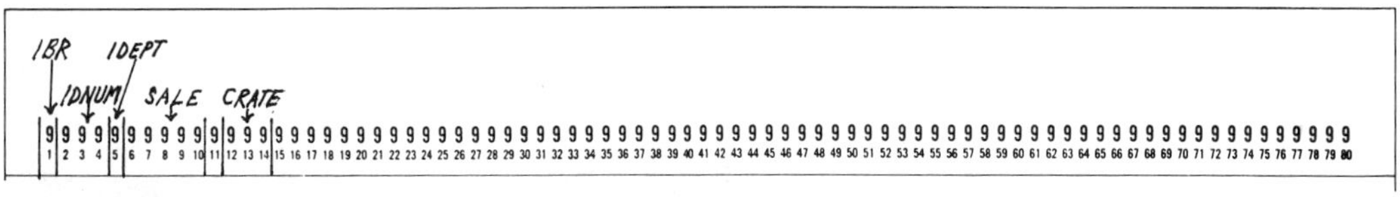

The branch number (IBR) is in the first card column. Thus, the numbers for branch, department, and sales person are read first, followed by amount of sale and commission rate.

```
44 READ (5,45,END=11) IBR, IDNUM, IDEPT, SALE, CRATE
45 FORMAT (I1, I3, I1, F5.2, 1X, F3.3)
```

Commission is calculated and array TOTCOM is updated:

```
46 COMISH = SALE * CRATE
47 TOTCOM (IBR,IDEPT,IDNUM) = TOTCOM (IBR,IDEPT,IDNUM) + COMISH
```

Since the values for branch, department, and salesperson are correctly stored, the updating process is accomplished accurately.

Because each dimension must be large enough for its maximum possible number, the third dimension increases the number of elements in the array to 3200. On most FORTRAN compiler computers, four bytes are allotted to each real or integer element. This great amount of assigned storage is typical of multidimensional array requirements. It means that programmers working with limited storage computers must be particularly careful when creating arrays. Otherwise, the arrays may require more storage than the computer possesses.

Clearing Multidimensional Arrays

Particularly when the DATA statement is not available to a FORTRAN programmer, he may need to clear a multidimensional array before using it. The following program uses a pair of nested DO loops to clear one double-dimension array, ITEMS, with five elements for each of the 100 customers, and three single-dimension arrays (KUSTMR, USAGE, and CHARGE). The same technique can be extended for as many dimensions and arrays as necessary.

```
   DIMENSION ITEMS(5,100),KUSTMR(100),USAGE(100),CHARGE(100)
11 DO 17 I = 1,100
12 KUSTMR(I) = 0
13 USAGE(I) = 0.
14 CHARGE(I) = 0.
15 DO 17 J = 1,5
16 ITEMS (J,I) = 0
17 CONTINUE
```

All the arrays are established in a DIMENSION statement. Then the two DO loops initialize all four arrays to zeroes.

The outer DO loop extends from statements 11 through 17. The nested inner loop consists of statements 15, 16, and 17. Each time the outer loop executes DO statement 15, the inner DO loop is executed five times. Therefore, during the first execution of the outer DO loop, CHARGE(1), USAGE(1), KUSTMR(1), ITEM(1,1), ITEM(1,2), ITEM(1,3), ITEM(1,4), and ITEM(1,5) are all set to zero. The second cycle of the outer DO loop clears CHARGE(2), USAGE(2), KUSTMR(2), ITEM(2,1), ITEM(2,2), ITEM(2,3), ITEM(2,4), and ITEM(2,5). This process continues through 100 outer loops until all 800 reserved areas are equal to zero.

Thus, "garbage" (unknown storage left by previously executed programs) is removed from computer memory. This is particularly important if the current program fails to assign values to any elements in the arrays. The contents from the previous program might be used accidentally during calculations or output. The program would not be reliable then.

REVIEW QUESTIONS

15. Why do arrays sometimes "waste" computer storage space?
16. What is computer "garbage," and what problems can it create, particularly with arrays?
17. How many dimensions can FORTRAN arrays have?

OBJECTIVES REVIEW

Look at the objectives at the beginning of this chapter. Check each one to be certain you have achieved it. Restudy the chapter sections related to any objective you cannot perform.

REVIEW TEST

Study the following FORTRAN program carefully. Using the "data cards" that are given, "process" the program as the FORTRAN compiler does. On scratch paper, keep a record of what is in storage for every field as the program proceeds. On a printer spacing chart or in the space below, print the output of the test program as it would appear on a printer.

Data Cards

```
                    1         2         3         4
Columns:   1234567890123456789012345678901234567890
Card 1:    1246 4000  0350    0700  1
Card 2:    2157 3500  0400    1000  2
Card 3:    3352 4500  0300    0235  1
Card 4:    /*
```

Program

```
      DIMENSION PAY(3)
    1 I = 1
    2 READ (5,3,END= 14) ID, HOURS, RATE, DEDUCT, IDEPT
    3 FORMAT (I4,1X,F4.2,2X,F4.2,3X,F4.2,2X,I1)
    4 IF (HOURS - 40.0) 5, 5, 7
    5 PAY(I) = HOURS * RATE
    6 GO TO 9
    7 OVER = (HOURS - 40.00) * RATE
    8 PAY(I) = (HOURS * RATE) + OVER
    9 CHECK = PAY(I) - DEDUCT
   10 WRITE(6,11)IDEPT,ID,HOURS,RATE,PAY(I),DEDUCT,CHECK
   11 FORMAT(T11,I2,2X,I5,5X,F6.2,5X,F6.2,5X,F7.2,5X,F6.2,5X,F7.2)
   12 I = I + 1
   13 GO TO 2
   14 TPAY = 0.
   15 DO 17 K = 1,3
   16 TPAY = TPAY + PAY(K)
   17 CONTINUE
   18 WRITE (6,19) TPAY
   19 FORMAT ('0',T6,'TOTAL PAY: $',F8.2)
   20 STOP
      END
```

Printout

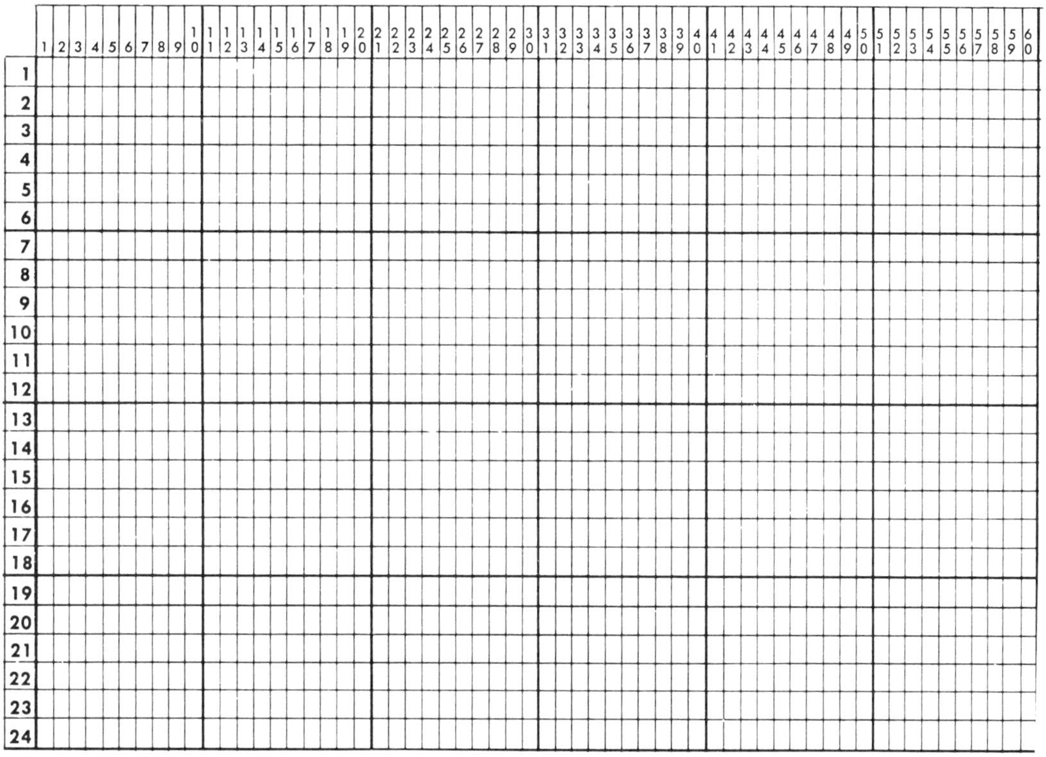

ASSIGNMENTS

1. A bank examiner requires 100 six-digit numbers for a random sampling of savings accounts. Write a program to create these random numbers. One method of creating random numbers uses the Fibonacci number series. This can be found in books on number theory.[2] First print the numbers in the order by which they are generated. Then sort and print the numbers in ascending order for easier use by the bank.

[2]For example, Mario F. Triola, *Mathematics and the Modern World,* Cummings Publication Co., Menlo Park, California, 1973; John R. Durbin, *Mathematics: Its Spirit and Evolution,* Allyn and Bacon, Inc., Boston, 1973.

2. Every time a sale is made, a store inputs data to update its commission calculations. In order to do this, the store first made a table giving each employee's sales to date. Create this table for nine employees by reading into an array the first nine data cards:

Input Record

Fields	Card Columns	
Employee number	49	I1
Amount of sales to date	52-57	F6.2

Print company and column headings, then this table of sales amounts as of the beginning of the period.

To update the records, input cards with employee number and amount of sales.

Input Record

Fields	Card Columns	
Employee number	32	I1
Amount of sale	52-57	F6.2

Every time a transaction card is read, add the amount of sale to the employee's table of sales. After all data cards are read, print the updated table for all employees. (Instructors may also want individual transactions recorded as executed, perhaps on the rightmost side of the paper.)

3. Another store varies the procedure utilized in problem 2. A DO loop index creates the employee array position; two items are stored from the first nine cards.

Input Record

Fields	Card Columns	
Employee name	1-20	5A4
Employee number	23-27	I5

All employees begin with zero amounts in sales to date. After company and column headings, the table is printed in order from left to right: array position, employee number, employee name, amount of sales. The table update utilizes two fields from the remaining data cards:

Input Record

Fields	Card Columns	
Employee array position	32	I1
Amount of sale	52-57	F6.2

After all cards are processed, the updated table is printed.

4. The personnel office of a company needs a printed report listing

employees in the order by which they were hired. Employees must be sorted so that employees are listed from first hired (smallest order of hiring number) to last hired (largest order of hiring number).

Input Record

Fields	Card Columns	
Employee name	1-20	5A4
Employee number	23-27	I5
Order of hiring number	59-60	I2

Printed report has company and column headings, report title, and list in order of hiring.

5. A company manufactures nine different product models. Each data card represents one product order.

Input Record

Fields	Card Columns	
Customer account number	23-27	I5
Item model order number	41	I1
Number of items ordered	29-34	I6

The number of items ordered for each model is totaled in a nine-element array. A count is kept of how many orders are received for each model. Each transaction is recorded on a printed report or on tape.

After all records are processed, the average number ordered for each model is calculated. A summary report is printed with company and column headings and with report date. The total number of items ordered, the number of orders, and the average number per order are given for each product model.

6. A store requires a list of customers with first names before last although the data records contain last names first. This problem can be solved in various ways, but frequently the names are read as a 20-element alphameric array. A special blank first data card is input from which A1 field BLANK or IBLANK is stored. Each character in the name array is compared with the stored blank. Two arrays, for first and last names, are used to count and store letters.

Input Record

Fields	Card Columns	
Names	1-20	20A1

After appropriate headings, print a list with first name followed by last name for each record.

Chapter Objectives

1. Be able to write a READ statement with an implied DO loop to specify alphameric or numeric fields.
2. Be able to write a WRITE statement with an implied DO loop to specify alphameric or numeric fields.
3. Be able to utilize an implied DO loop to print only specified elements of an array.
4. Be able to utilize implied DO loops to input and output only specified elements of multidimensional arrays.

12

Implied DO Loops

The implied DO loop is a special method of storing and retrieving elements of an array. It differs from the ordinary DO loop in three basic ways. First, the implied DO loop does not use the word DO. Second, it loops within only one statement. Third, it is used only in input and output statements.

Implied DO Loop With Alphameric Fields

Because of the common four-character limitation on alphameric fields, an implied DO loop is often used for alphameric fields. For example, the 20 characters comprising a customer's name were stored as five separate fields in READ statements of earlier problems:

```
18 READ (5,19) N1, N2, N3, N4, N5
19 FORMAT (5A4)
```

Some of this repetitious field name listing can be eliminated if the computer stores the five fields as five-element array N.

First, a DIMENSION statement establishes array N:

```
DIMENSION N(5)
```

The computer reserves five storage areas for the elements of array N. Input/output statements can now simply list the name of the array. When the array name is listed without a subscript, all elements of the array are read or written:

```
28 READ (5,29) N
29 FORMAT (5A4)
```

When an input or output statement contains an unsubscripted array name, the computer automatically inputs or outputs the entire array in sequence as it is stored: N(1), N(2), N(3), N(4), and N(5).

Sometimes, however, the programmer does not want to input or output the entire array. This can be true in both single and multi-dimensional arrays. In order to understand these more complex situations, the implied DO loop is first illustrated in a single dimension array that is read in its entirety:

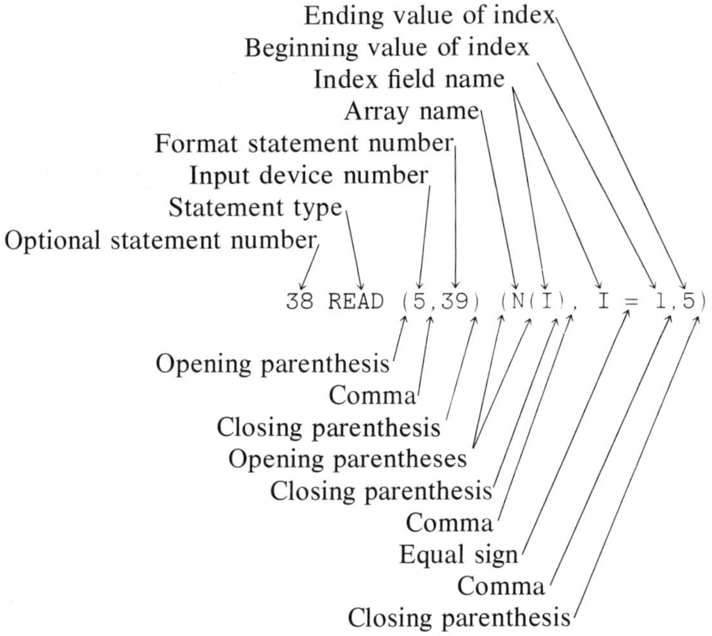

After the word READ and the parentheses with device and FORMAT statement numbers, another pair of parentheses informs the compiler that everything within these parentheses is to be treated as a unit. That is, the outer parentheses mark the beginning and end of an implied DO loop:

```
(N(I), I = 1,5)
```

The inner parentheses enclose the field name (I), which is both the subscript and the indexing integer. A comma is required after the inner parentheses. Then the index name is repeated with its beginning and ending (and sometimes incrementing) values. For example, in (N(I), I = 1,5) I equals 1 during the first cycle of the implied DO loop. Just before each new cycle, I is incremented by 1 because 1 is understood when a third value does not appear after the equal sign. This continues through the last cycle when I equals 5. Thus the compiler reads, in order, N(1), N(2), N(3), N(4), and N(5) each time a card is input.

The five fields from the record are stored as elements of an array, and the array can be output with another implied DO loop:

```
40 WRITE (6,41) (N(I), I = 1,5)
```

The two indexing integer fields need not have the same name for both statements. The WRITE statement could be written:

```
42 WRITE (6,43) (N(J), J = 1,5)
```

Each implied DO loop is complete and independent within its own parentheses.

REVIEW QUESTIONS

1. How many FORTRAN statements can be part of one implied DO loop?
2. In which types of FORTRAN statements are implied DO loops found?
3. Where must the indexing integer be placed in an implied DO loop?
4. What graphic symbol encloses an implied DO loop?

The beginning and ending values of the index need not be digits. They can be integer field names. These field names are particularly useful when the index depends upon input or calculated quantities.

For example, the manager of RENTA COMPUTER, INC. wants a graph to show hourly customer usage. To produce this variation of the USAGE problem, the programmer eliminates the calculations for CHARGE. The output for field USAGE is not numeric but is in the form of a bar graph. In this graph, each asterisk (*) represents 10 hours of customer usage. The program logic is developed in a flowchart on page 198.

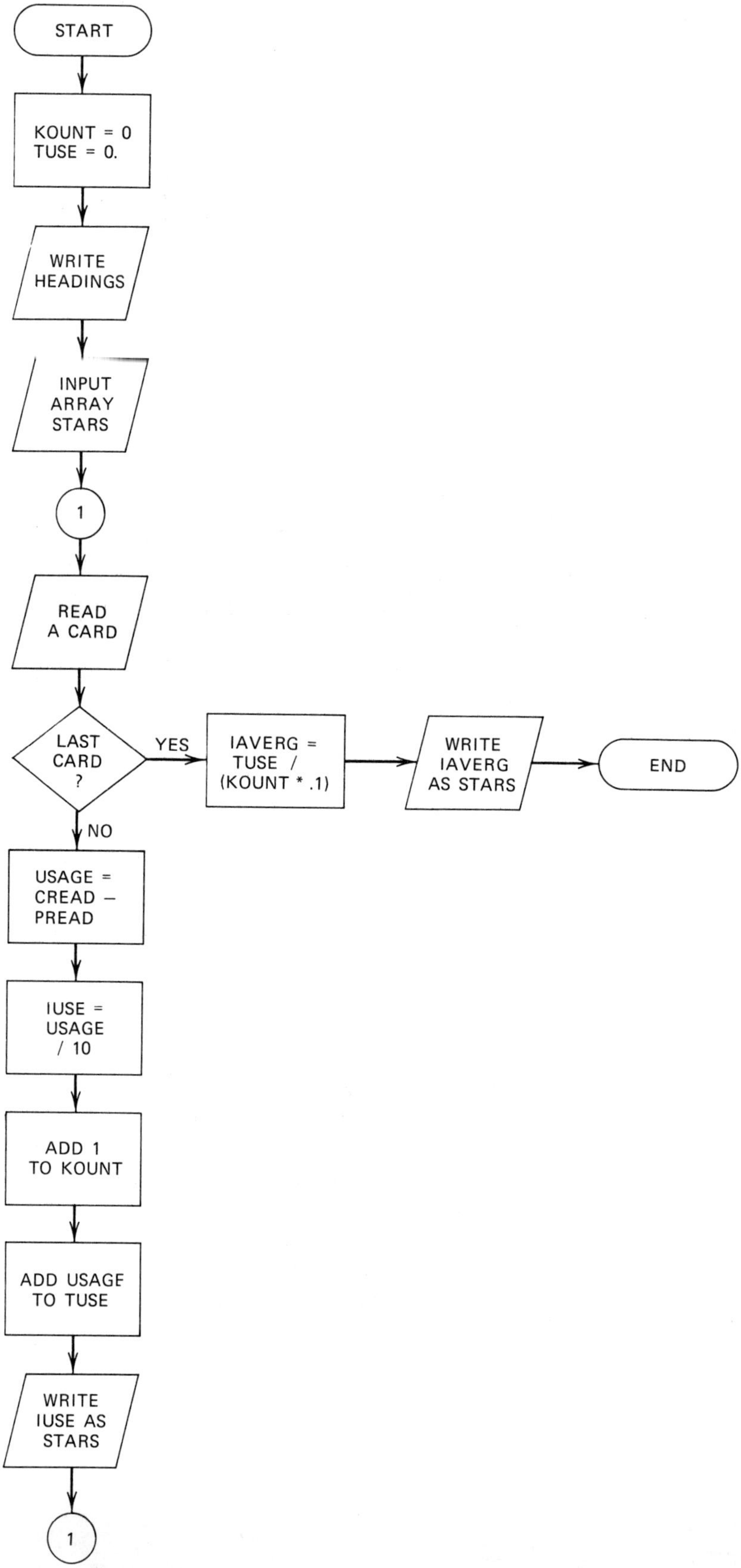
START
KOUNT = 0
TUSE = 0.
WRITE HEADINGS
INPUT ARRAY STARS
1
READ A CARD
LAST CARD ?
YES
IAVERG = TUSE / (KOUNT * .1)
WRITE IAVERG AS STARS
END
NO
USAGE = CREAD − PREAD
IUSE = USAGE / 10
ADD 1 TO KOUNT
ADD USAGE TO TUSE
WRITE IUSE AS STARS
1

199
IMPLIED
DO LOOP
WITH
ALPHAMERIC
FIELDS

The input data cards remain unchanged, but only the customer number, previous meter reading, and current meter reading are read:

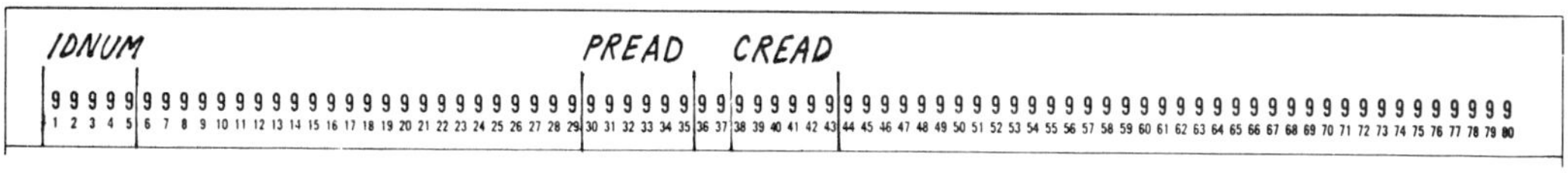

Output is developed on a printer spacing chart:

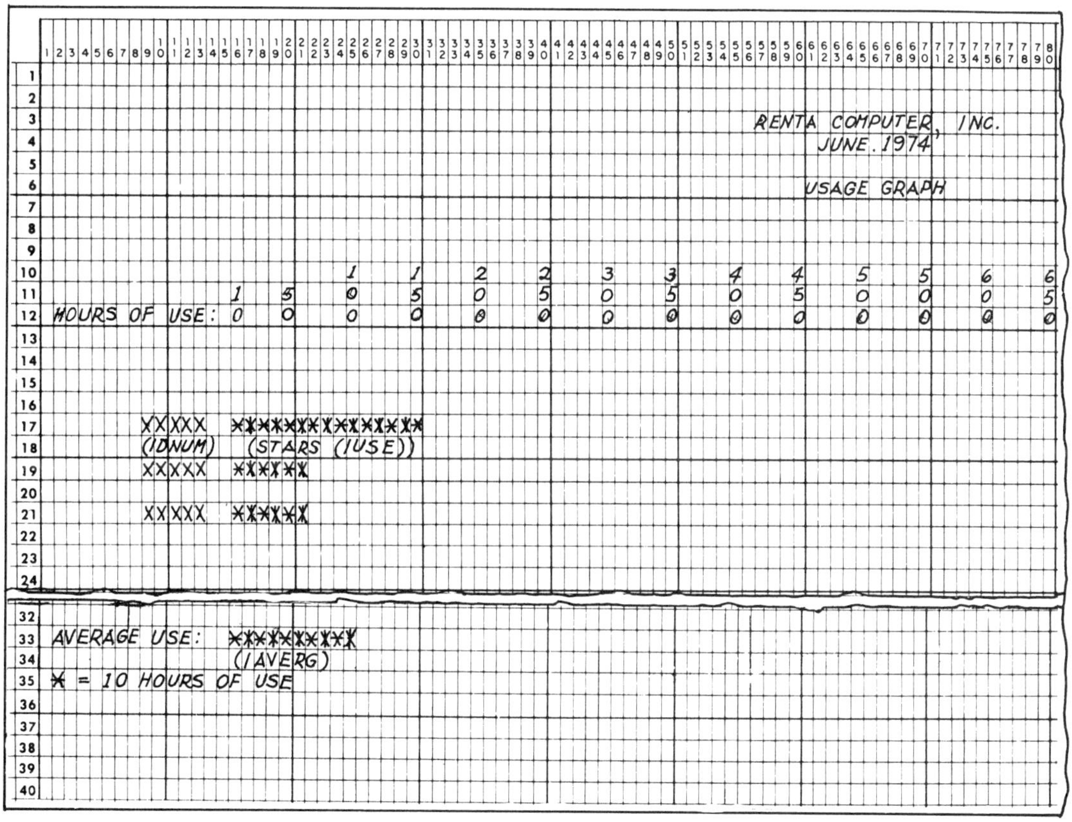

Instead of printing customer usage and average usage as numbers, these fields are now represented by asterisks on a bar graph. Each asterisk represents ten units (hours) of meter usage. The maximum length of a graph line is determined to be 115 asterisks. Therefore STARS is established as a 115-element array:

```
DIMENSION STARS (115)
```

The alphameric character of array STARS is determined when it is input as 115 A1 elements, each an asterisk:[1]

```
5 READ (5,6) STARS
6 FORMAT (80A1)
```

Because the array name is given without subscripts in the READ statement, the entire array of 115 elements will be stored. Then, since only 80 A1 fields can be on one standard size card, statements 5 and 6 cause two cards to be input. Each column of the first card contains an asterisk; the first 35 columns of the second card also contain asterisks:

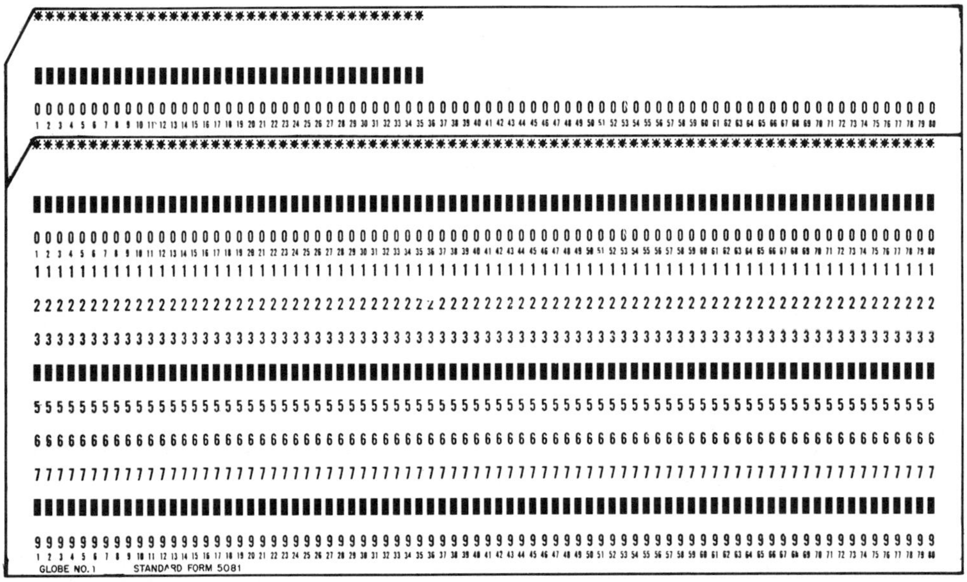

After array STARS is stored, the main input-calculations-output cycle begins. A new calculation divides the usage field by 10 and stores the result as an *integer:*

```
10 IUSE = USAGE / 10
```

This quantity is now expressed in bar graph form. It is output with an implied DO loop that uses field IUSE as the *ending value* of the index:

[1]The alphameric array could also be established by a DATA statement as explained in chapter 16.

```
13 WRITE (6,14) IDNUM, (STARS (I), I = 1, IUSE)
14 FORMAT ('0',T10,I5,T17,115 A1)
```

Even though the format statement lists 115 A1 fields, the implied DO loop calls for printing only those through the current value of IUSE.

After the last card is read, statement 16 is executed. In one statement it calculates the average use, in effect divides by 10 (actually multiplies by .1), and stores the result as integer field IAVERG. Statement 17 utilizes an implied DO loop to print a graph line representing the average use. Now the ending value of the index is IAVERG:

```
16 IAVERG = TUSE / KOUNT * .1
17 WRITE (6,18) (STARS (I), I = 1, IAVERG)
18 FORMAT (///T3, 'AVERAGE USE:', T17, 115A1)
```

In statement 17, the value of IAVERG terminates the implied DO loop.

The program for USAGE-GRAPH is now complete:

```
C PROGRAM BAR GRAPH
C
C ESTABLISH 115-ELEMENT ARRAY STARS
      DIMENSION STARS (115)
C INITIALIZE CUSTOMER COUNTER AND TOTAL USAGE
    1 KOUNT = 0
    2 TUSE = 0.
C PRINT HEADINGS
    3 WRITE (6,4)
    4 FORMAT ('1',T58,'RENTA COMPUTER, INC.'/T63,'JUNE 1974'
     1//T62,'USAGE GRAPH'///T116,'1',3(4X,'1')/T26,2('1',4X),
     22('2',4X),2('3',4X),2('4',4X),2('5',4X),2('6',4X),
     32('7',4X),2('8',4X),2('9',4X),2('0',4X),'1',4X,'1',/
     4T17,'1',T21,'5',11(4X,'0',4X,'5')/T3,'HOURS OF USE: ',
     5'0',3X,22('0',4X),'0'///)
C INPUT ARRAY STARS
    5 READ (5,6) STARS
    6 FORMAT (80A1)
C INPUT CUSTOMER DATA CARDS AND PERFORM CALCUATIONS
    7 READ (5,8,END=16) IDNUM, PREAD, CREAD
    8 FORMAT (I5,24X,F6.2,2X,F6.2)
    9 USAGE = CREAD - PREAD
   10 IUSE = USAGE / 10
   11 KOUNT = KOUNT + 1
   12 TUSE = TUSE + USAGE
C PRINT BAR GRAPH WITH IMPLIED DO LOOP
   13 WRITE (6,14) IDNUM, (STARS (I), I = 1, IUSE)
   14 FORMAT ('0',T10,I5,T17,115A1)
   15 GO TO 7
C CALCULATE AND PRINT AVERAGE USE AFTER LAST CARD IS PROCESSED
   16 IAVERG = TUSE / KOUNT *.1
   17 WRITE (6,18) (STARS (I), I = 1, IAVERG)
   18 FORMAT (///T3,'AVERAGE USE:',T17,115A1)
```

```
19 WRITE (6,20)
20 FORMAT ('0',T3,'* = 10 HOURS OF USE')
21 CALL EXIT
   END
```

Using the same five data cards as the earlier versions of program USAGE, program USAGE–GRAPH prints the following graph:

```
                                                    RENTA COMPUTER, INC.
                                                         JUNE 1974

                                                        USAGE GRAPH


                          1    1    2    2    3    3    4    4    5    5    6    6    7    7    8
                 1    5   0    5    0    5    0    5    0    5    0    5    0    5    0    5    0
HOURS OF USE:    0    0   0    0    0    0    0    0    0    0    0    0    0    0    0    0    0


        12548    **********

        24573    *********

        45342    ***********

        55343    ****************************************

        75342    *************************************************************************


AVERAGE USE:     *****************************

* = 10 HOURS OF USE
```

Just as IUSE and IAVERG were used as the last values of the implied DO loop indexes, so the beginning and incrementing values can be integer field names:

```
50 WRITE (6, 51) (STARS (I), I = ISTART, IUSE, ICOUNT)
```

When statement 50 is executed, I equals the current value of ISTART. The implied loop is incremented by the value of ICOUNT through the current value of IUSE.

Multidimensional Alphameric Arrays

When an implied DO loop is used within a DO loop, two indexing fields usually are needed. For example, when names of 100 customers are all retained in computer memory, array N must be a two-dimensional array:

```
DIMENSION  N ( 100, 5)
```

Array N contains 500 elements to be input and output five at a time in implied DO loops. Because the 5 is the second quantity listed in the DIMENSION statement, the implied DO loop utilizes the second subscripting field, J:

```
40 DO 50 I = 1, 100
41 READ (5, 42) (N (I,J), J = 1,5)
42 FORMAT (5A4)
  .
  .
  .
45 WRITE (6,46) (N (I,J), J = 1,5)
46 FORMAT (T10, 5A4)
50 CONTINUE
```

I is the index for the DO statement that creates a loop from statement 40 through statement 50. I increments from 1 to 100 during the 100 cycles. J is the index for both implied DO loops, although different integer names could have been used. J indexes only the second subscript of array N, incrementing from 1 to 5 during each READ and WRITE statement. These two indexes must have different names because they are used for different counters in the same input or output statement. I counts the cycles of the DO LOOP; J counts each implied DO loop.

Other arrays and fields can be input or output in the same statement with an implied DO loop. For example, the other items in USAGE problems can be input and output within a DO loop:

```
    DIMENSION N(100,5), IDNUM(100), USAGE(100), CHARGE(100)
140 DO 150 I = 1, 100
141 READ (5,142) IDNUM(I) (N(I,J),J=1,5), PREAD,CREAD
```

```
142 FORMAT (I5, 5A4, 4X, F6.2, 2X, F6.2)
     .
     .
     .
145 WRITE (6,146) IDNUM(I),(N(I,J),J=1,5),USAGE(I),CHARGE(I)
146 FORMAT(T5, I5,5X,5A4,5X,F7.2,10X,F8.2)
150 CONTINUE
```

The implied DO loop and its index affect only the items within the loop's parentheses.

REVIEW QUESTIONS

5. What can be used instead of a number for the beginning and ending values of implied DO loops?
6. If a third value is present after the replacement sign, what does it represent?
7. Why must each dimension have a unique index when implied DO loops are used with multidimensional arrays?

Numeric Fields

The implied DO loop can be used for numeric as well as alphameric fields. For instance, amounts sold in eight departments with up to ten salespeople per department can be read as elements of double dimension array SALES:

```
   DIMENSION SALES (8,10)
21 READ (5,22) IDEPT,ISELL,(SALES(IDEPT,I),I=1,ISELL)
22 FORMAT (I2,1X,I2,10F6.2)
```

The DIMENSION statement establishes an array for eight departments, with a maximum of ten employees in any department. Each time the computer inputs a card, the department number and the number of employees in the department are stored. Then the computer reads the sales amounts, with the implied DO loop cycling from 1 through ISELL, the number of employees listed.

In statement 22, all elements of array SALES are input as fields of the same size. This is not required by the computer, however. Even though assigned storage space *in computer memory* is the same for all elements of an array, the lengths for input and/or output need not be identical. When, for example, a payroll array contains gross pay, bonus, deductions for taxes, contributions, dues, and net pay, certain elements of the array are expected to be consistently larger than others. Although they occupy the same space in internal storage, they can be input and output in specifications of differing lengths:

```
   DIMENSION PAYROL (100,6)
26 DO 30 NUMBER=1,100
27 READ (5,28) (PAYROL (NUMBER, I), I = 1,6)
28 FORMAT (F7.2, 1X, F6.2, 1X, 3F5.2, 1X, F7.2)
```

The six elements in each PAYROL set are input as, in order, F7.2, F6.2, F5.2, F5.2, F5.2 and F7.2. Only in *internal* storage must elements of an array be the same length. This same technique of different input/output lengths can be used by integer fields as well.

Sometimes a programmer combines alphameric and numeric fields in the same array. The identification number (now an F5.0 real number), the five fields of the name (five A4 fields), current and previous meter readings (two F6.2 fields), and USAGE are now grouped into an array:

```
   DIMENSION CUSTMR (100,9)
50 DO 60 K=1,100
51 READ (5,52) (CUSTMR (K,I), I = 1,8)
52 FORMAT (F5.0, 5A4, 4X, F6.2, 2X, F6.2)
```

The first eight elements for each customer are stored and manipulated as elements of one array. Later the ninth element, formerly USAGE, is calculated.

Because alphameric field names can be either real or integer, the same mixture of alphameric and numeric data can be grouped within an integer array also.

REVIEW QUESTIONS

8. What are the two main differences between implied DO loops and ordinary DO loops?

9. Why is an implied DO loop frequently used with multidimensional arrays?

OBJECTIVES REVIEW

Look at the objectives at the beginning of this chapter. Check each one to be certain you have achieved it. Restudy the chapter sections related to any you cannot perform.

REVIEW TEST

Study the following FORTRAN program carefully. Using the "data cards" that are given, "process" the program as the FORTRAN compiler does. On scratch paper, keep a record of what is in storage for every field as the program proceeds. On a printer spacing chart or in the space below, print the output of the test program as it would appear on a printer.

Data Cards

```
                   1         2         3         4
Columns:  1234567890123456789012345678901234567890
Card 1:   HAIR BRUSHES        02  02
Card 2:   MANICURE SETS       05  01
Card 3:   MILITARY BRUSH SETS 05  00
Card 4:   RAZORS              02  01
Card 5:   /*
```

Program

```
   DIMENSION ITEMS (4,5), NUMBER (4)
 1 KOUNT = 0
 2 KFIVE = 0
 3 KMORE = 0
 4 KLESS = 0
 5 WRITE (6,6)
 6 FORMAT (T29,'ON HAND',T38,'ORDERED')
 7 DO 21 I = 1,4
 8 READ (5,9) (ITEMS (I,J),J = 1,5), IONHND, IORDER
 9 FORMAT (5A4,I2,2X,I2)
10 KOUNT = KOUNT + 1
11 NUMBER(I) = IONHND + IORDER
12 NUM = NUMBER (I)
13 IF (NUM - 5) 14, 16, 18
14 KLESS = KLESS + 1
15 GO TO 19
16 KFIVE = KFIVE + 1
17 GO TO 19
18 KMORE = KMORE + 1
19 WRITE (6,20) (ITEMS (I,L), L = 1,5), IONHAND, IORDER
20 FORMAT (T6, 5A4, T31, I3, T41, I3)
21 CONTINUE
22 WRITE (6,23)
23 FORMAT ('1')
24 DO 27 I = 1,4
25 WRITE (6,26) (ITEMS (I,M),M = 1,5), NUMBER(I)
26 FORMAT (T10, 5A4, T40, I2)
27 CONTINUE
28 WRITE (6,29) KOUNT
29 FORMAT ('0',T6,I3,1X,'ITEMS COUNTED.')
30 WRITE (6,31) KLESS, KFIVE, KMORE
31 FORMAT ('0',T6,I3,1X,'WITH FEWER THAN 5' / T6,I3,1X,
  1 'WITH 5' / T6,I3,1X,'WITH MORE THAN 5')
32 STOP
   END
```

Printout

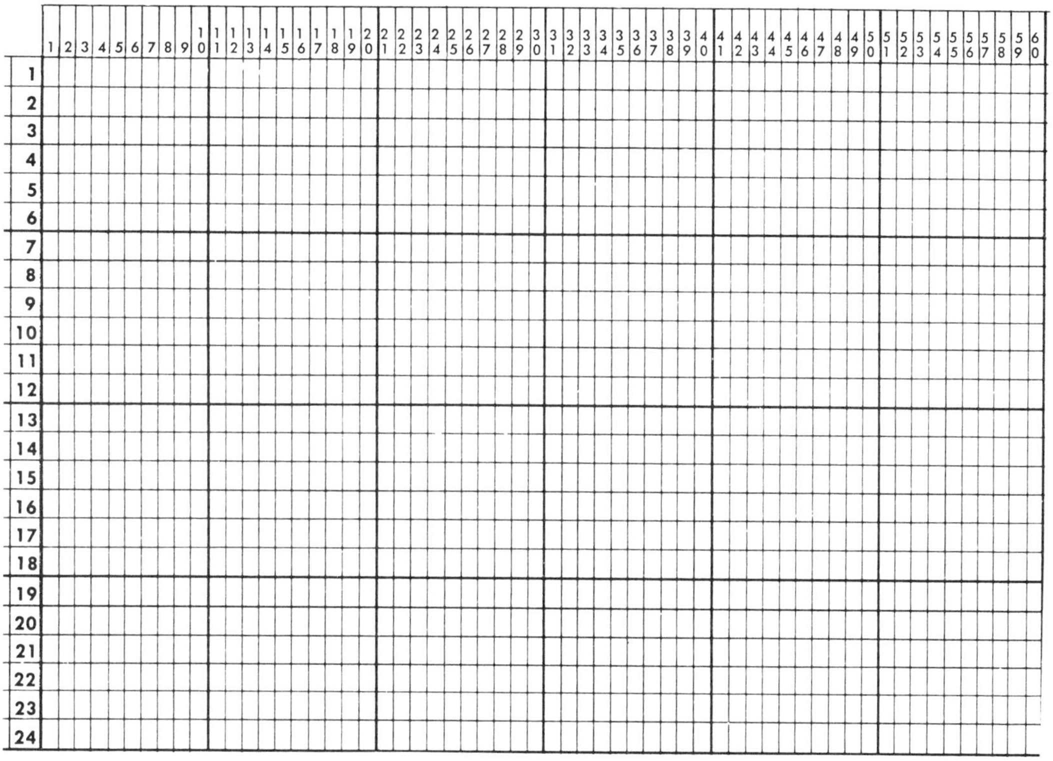

ASSIGNMENTS

Prepare a card layout form, printer spacing chart, and flowchart for one of the following problems. Then write, keypunch, and submit the FORTRAN program.

1. A company sells ten different products. Its records show how many of each product a customer orders.

Input Records

Fields	Card Columns	
Customer name	1-20	(5A4)
(Read in as 5-element array with implied DO loop.)		
Number ordered of:		
Product 1	22-24	(I3)
Product 2	25-27	(I3)
Product 3	30-32	(I3)
Product 4	34-36	(I3)
Product 5	38-40	(I3)

Product 6	43-45	(I3)
Product 7	52-54	(I3)
Product 8	55-57	(I3)
Product 9	62-64	(I3)
Product 10	66-68	(I3)
(Read in as a 10-element array with implied DO loop)		

Another 10-element array totals the number of items ordered for each product. Orders for each item are counted. (Test field for zero condition.) Average number ordered for *each* item and average of these averages are calculated. After company name and column headings, detail lines record each transaction. Use identifying messages.

2. Do all of problem 1. In addition, after all records are processed, print the total number of orders for each product, average order for each product, and average order of all products. Use identifying messages.

3. Provisions of the Mechanics Lien Law require that building materials of each building contract be kept separate from all others. Summary records contain sales invoice of materials supplied directly to the job, sales invoices of materials picked up by contracter, sales of concrete supplied by cement company for which materials supplier is agent, and credit memos for returned materials.

Input Records

Fields	Card Columns	
Contractor's name	1-20	(5A4)
Contractor's account number	21-25	(I5)
Discount code	52	(I1)
Balance forward	30-36	(F7.2)
Amount of sales supplied directly to job	38-44	(F7.2)
Amount of sales picked up by contractor	52-57	(F6.2)
Amount of sales supplied by cement mixer company	62-68	(F7.2)
Amount of credit memos	74-79	(F6.2)

Input the contractor's name with an implied DO loop, and the five monetary fields with another implied DO loop. Update each contractor's account by adding all sales invoice amounts to balance forward amount. Subtract amount of credit memos from balance forward. If 1 is in the discount code, subtract 3% from updated new balance. Count contractors receiving discount. Total amount for each monetary field. Printed report headings contain company name, address, date of report, and column headings. Input fields (except discount code), amount of discount, and updated balance forward are printed for each transaction. After all cards are processed, totals of all monetary fields and count of customers receiving discount are printed.

4. During a sales campaign, a company requires a bar graph to show sales of each employee through both the previous week and the present week.

Input Records

Fields	Card Columns	
Name of sales person	1-20	5A4
Employee number	23-27	I5
Number of items sold by end of previous week	38-41	I4
Number of items sold by end of present week	63-66	I4

Output. Two bar graphs for each sales person show number of items sold. In bar graph for previous week, a period (.) indicates 100 sales items. Immediately below, bar graph for the present week uses an asterisk (*) to represent 100 sales items. Double space between sales people.

5. Do the same problem as assignment 4, but print only one line per sales person. Sales items through the previous week are represented by periods; sales items sold during the present week are represented by asterisks.

In addition, the average number through the previous and present weeks are similarly printed after all employee records are processed.

6. A parcel delivery service calculates the cost of shipping.

Input Records

Fields	Card Columns	
Customer's name (Input as five-element array)	1-20	5A4
Customer account number	21-25	I5
Number of pounds shipped	74-77	I4
Shipping code (1 = regular, 2 = air express, 3 = C.O.D.)	50	I1

If delivery is regular service, charge is 25¢ per pound. Air express is 35¢ per pound. C.O.D. is regular charge plus a $2.00 special charge. Calculate charges for each customer. Count each type of charge. Total number of pounds shipped and charges.

Printed report begins with company name and location, and column headings. Detail lines contain all input fields. Shipping codes are explained on detail line or at end of report. After last card is processed, print counts and totals.

Chapter Objectives

1. Be able to explain how control fields cause control breaks.
2. Be able to explain why a special test is necessary for the first data card in programs with control breaks.
3. Be able to program a "first card test."
4. Be able to test one or more control fields for subtotal control breaks.

13

Subtotals and Control Breaks

Business reports frequently require not only company totals but also departmental or other subtotals. For example, when sales commissions are calculated, the commissions for each sales person are usually required as well as the total amount of the commissions for all salespeople. The sum of each person's commissions is a subtotal.

In another example, sales transactions are accumulated for each customer. A subtotal is gathered for each customer as the company total is being created.

When records are sorted and processed sequentially by salesperson or by customer or by item, these subtotals are often called "control breaks." This name derives from the fact that a "break" in the processing routine occurs when the control field (salesperson's or customer's or item's number or name) changes. This change or "break" requires special instructions.

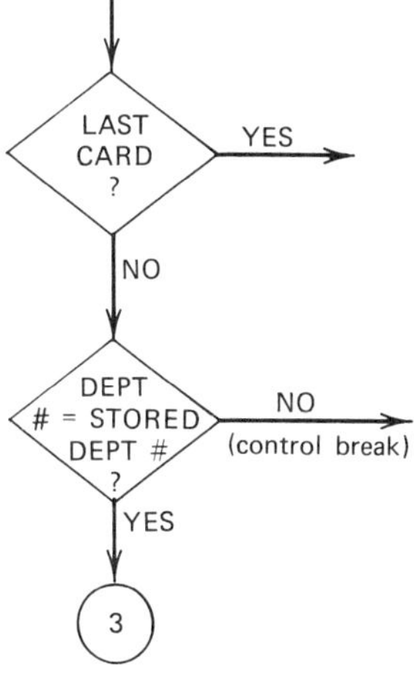

The data record that causes the control break creates complications because the computer does not know it has completed one group of records until it inputs the first record of the next group (department, for example). Therefore it must check the identification or "control" field of each data record before processing other data in that record.

The contents of the control field are compared with the previous control field contents to see if they match. When the field contents are identical, programming proceeds through all detail calculations and detail line printing. After completing these steps, the program ordinarily branches back to read another card:

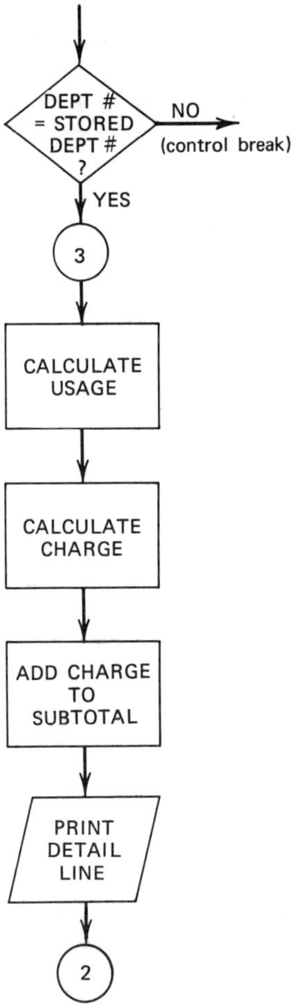

If the control field numbers differ, however, a control break occurs. The subtotal is added to the total. The department subtotal is printed and then the field is cleared to zero. The new department number is stored. A new page can begin with appropriate headings.

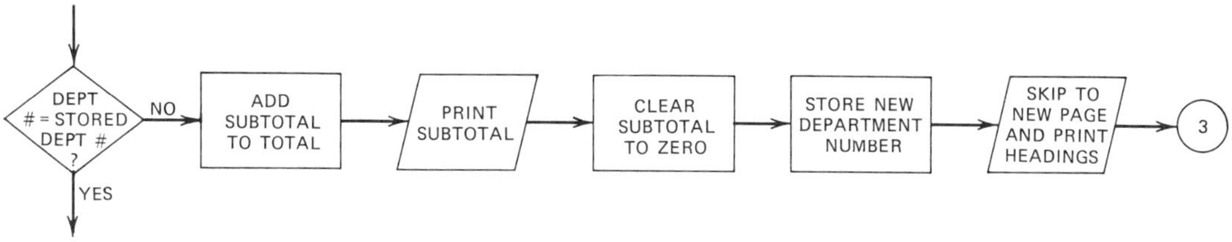

Although charges can be added to the total as well as to subtotal fields during detail processing for each card, the many executions of this addition instruction lengthens the program's execution time. Thus, adding subtotals at control breaktime is an efficient technique.

After the subtotal steps have been processed, detail calculations and output of the card that caused the break are performed. The program then branches back to read a new card.

To illustrate the processing of control breaks, Renta Computer, Inc., program USAGE now subtotals by department. The department number (IDEPT) is part of the altered sample input data cards:

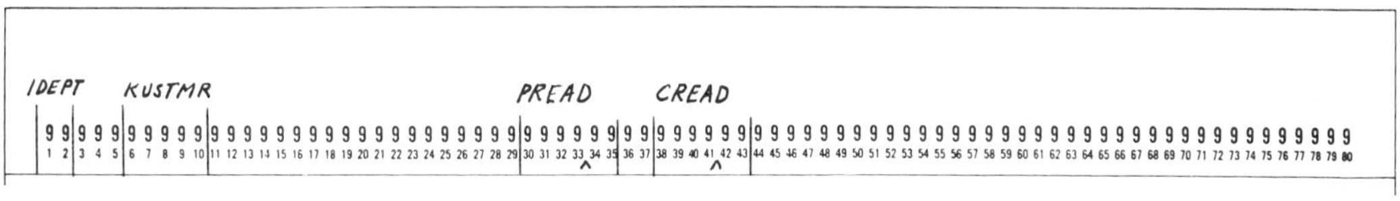

The report of each department is printed on a separate page with charges for the department subtotaled at the end of department detail lines:

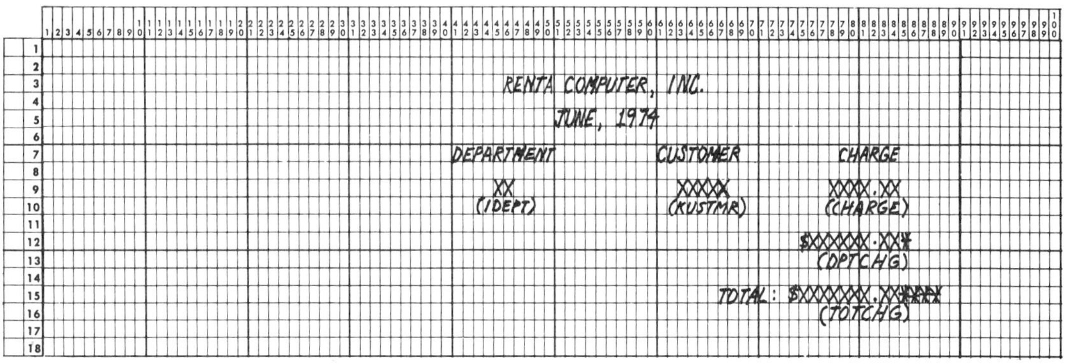

As the flowchart decision symbol illustrates, subtotaling depends upon a test of the control field. In program USAGE 1SUBTOTAL, the department number is compared with the stored department number:

```
9 IF (IDEPT - IDSTOR) 10, 17, 10
```

When the two department numbers are the same, usage and charge are calculated and the charge subtotal is updated. The detail line is printed and the program branches back to read a new record.

```
17 USAGE = CREAD - PREAD
18 CHARGE = (USAGE * .7) + 50.00
19 DPTCHG = DPTCHG + CHARGE
20 WRITE (6,21) IDEPT, KUSTMR, CHARGE
21 FORMAT (T46, I2, T64, I5, T79,F7.2)
22 GO TO 4
```

When the department number has changed, the subtotal is added to the total, printed, and cleared to zero for the next department subtotal:

```
10 TOTCHG = TOTCHG + DPTCHG
11 WRITE (6,12) DPTCHG
12 FORMAT (T76,'$',F9.2,'*')
13 DPTCHG = 0.
```

The new department number is stored for future comparisons:

```
14 IDSTOR = IDEPT
```

Then, so that each department can occupy a separate page of the printed report, the program skips the printer to the top of a new page for headings:

```
15 WRITE (6,16)
16 FORMAT('1',T47,'RENTA COMPUTER, INC.'//T52,'JUNE, 1974'
  1//T42,'DEPARTMENT',T62,'CUSTOMER',T80,'CHARGE'//)
```

After the department headings are printed, the program continues to statement 17 to process the first record of the new department before branching back to read a new card.

REVIEW QUESTIONS

1. What is a control field? Give at least one example.
2. What is a control break and when does it occur?

First Card Test

In programs with subtotals, the first data card requires special handling. Because there is no previous record with which to compare the control field, a special "first card test" must keep subtotals from being printed when the first data card is read. This involves a logical decision:

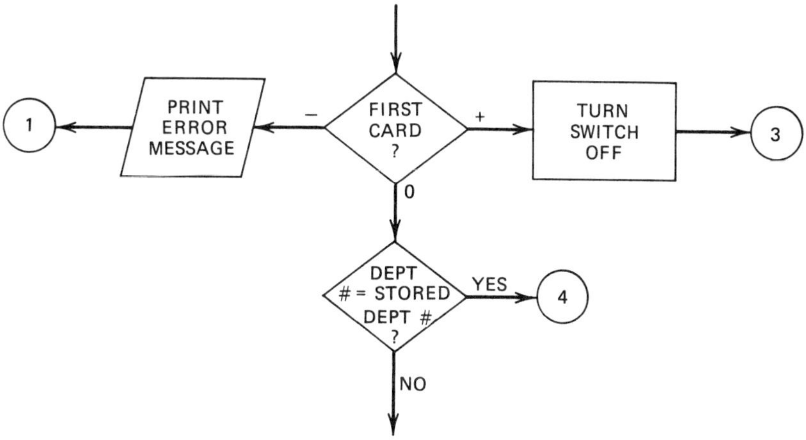

The first card dilemma can be handled in several ways. One of the most common, called a switch, is set "on" or "off" and tested. The first card switch is set on at the opening of the program.

```
1 ISWTCH = 1
```

After each data card is read, the switch field is tested:

```
4 READ ( 5,5,END=26) IDEPT,KUSTMR,PREAD,CREAD
5 FORMAT ( I2,3X,I5,T30,F6.2,2X,F6.2)
6 IF (ISWTCH) 23, 9, 7
```

Since ISWTCH should never be negative, the required branch for a negative quantity is an error message and switch re-setting precautionary routine:

```
23 WRITE (6,24)
24 FORMAT (T12,'ERROR: RESETTING SWITCH')
25 GO TO 1
```

Because the first card switch is on when the first data card is read, the branch for a positive quantity is the special first card routine. The first instruction in this routine turns the switch off for the remainder of the program. The test for matching control field numbers is skipped. Instead, the control department number is stored, headings are printed, and the first card is processed.

```
7 ISWTCH = 0
8 GO TO 14
```

For all cards after the first card, the switch is off. The zero quantity branch immediately tests the department number:

```
9 IF (IDEPT - IDSTOR) 10, 17, 10
```

Thus the setting of the switch reveals whether or not a data card is the first one read so that an appropriate beginning routine can be executed.

Last Card Test

In addition to the first card test, the END= option in the READ statement or a last card test must also be utilized:

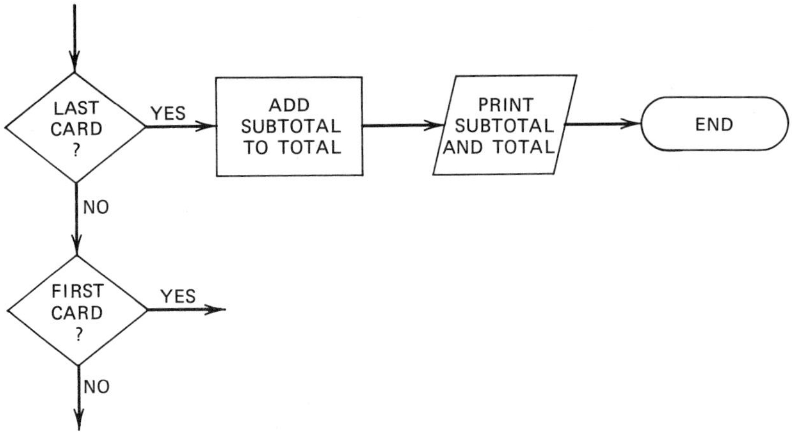

When the last data card is read, the total for customer charges must be updated. Then the last subtotal is printed, usually followed by the total or totals:

```
26 TOTCHG = TOTCHG + DPTCHG
27 WRITE (6,12) DPTCHG
28 WRITE (6,29) TOTCHG
29 FORMAT ('0',T68,'TOTAL:',T75,'$',F10.2,'****')
30 CALL EXIT
```

Five demonstration cards containing the department number as field IDEPT, were processed with program USAGE 1SUBTOTAL:

```
C SET ON FIRST CARD SWITCH
    1 ISWTCH = 1
C INITIALIZE SUBTOTAL AND TOTAL
    2 DPTCHG = 0.
    3 TOTCHG = 0.
C INPUT DEPARTMENT NUMBER, CUSTOMER NUMBER, METER READINGS
    4 READ(5,5,END=26) IDEPT, KUSTMR, PREAD, CREAD
    5 FORMAT (I2,3X,I5,T30,F6.2,2X,F6.2)
C FIRST CARD SWITCH TESTED: TURNED OFF IF ON
```

217
LAST
CARD
TEST

```
    6 IF (ISWTCH) 23, 9, 7
    7 ISWTCH = 0
    8 GO TO 14
C COMPARE DEPARTMENT NUMBERS IF NOT FIRST CARD
    9 IF (IDEPT - IDSTOR) 10, 17, 10
C PROCESS SUBTOTAL CONTROL BREAK
   10 TOTCHG = TOTCHG + DPTCHG
   11 WRITE (6,12) DPTCHG
   12 FORMAT (T76,'$',F9.2,'*')
   13 DPTCHG = 0.
   14 IDSTOR = IDEPT
   15 WRITE (6,16)
   16 FORMAT ('1',T47,'RENTA COMPUTER, INC.'//T52,'JUNE, 1974'
     1//T42,'DEPARTMENT',T62,'CUSTOMER',T80,'CHARGE'//)
C PROCESS DETAIL RECORD
   17 USAGE = CREAD - PREAD
   18 CHARGE = (USAGE * .7) + 50.00
   19 DPTCHG = DPTCHG + CHARGE
   20 WRITE (6,21) IDEPT,KUSTMR,CHARGE
   21 FORMAT (T46,I2,T64,I5,T79,F7.2)
   22 GO TO 4
C PRECAUTIONARY MEASURES IF FIRST CARD SWITCH IS NEGATIVE
   23 WRITE (6,24)
   24 FORMAT (T12,'ERROR: RESETTING SWITCH')
   25 GO TO 1
C BRANCH AFTER READING LAST (/*) CARD
   26 TOTCHG = TOTCHG + DPTCHG
   27 WRITE (6,12) DPTCHG
   28 WRITE (6,29) TOTCHG
   29 FORMAT ('0',T68,'TOTAL:',T75,'$',F10.2,'****')
   30 CALL EXIT
      END
```

The following two-page report was printed:

```
          RENTA COMPUTER, INC.

               JUNE, 1974

DEPARTMENT            CUSTOMER             CHARGE


    10                  12548              126.15
    10                  24573              119.22
    10                  45342              130.54
    10                  55343              339.88
                                       $   715.79*


          RENTA COMPUTER, INC.

               JUNE, 1974

DEPARTMENT            CUSTOMER             CHARGE

    20                  75342              544.26
                                       $   544.26*

                              TOTAL: $    1260.05****
```

REVIEW QUESTIONS

3. Why is a first card test necessary in programs with subtotals?
4. What numeric value is considered "on" for a switch?

Multiple Control Levels

The same basic logic for one subtotal can be used for any number of subtotal levels. Assume, for example, that Renta Computer, Inc. has expanded to become an organization with departments, divisions, and regions. Each of these fields is a control field with subtotals. All three control fields are in the first five columns of each data card:

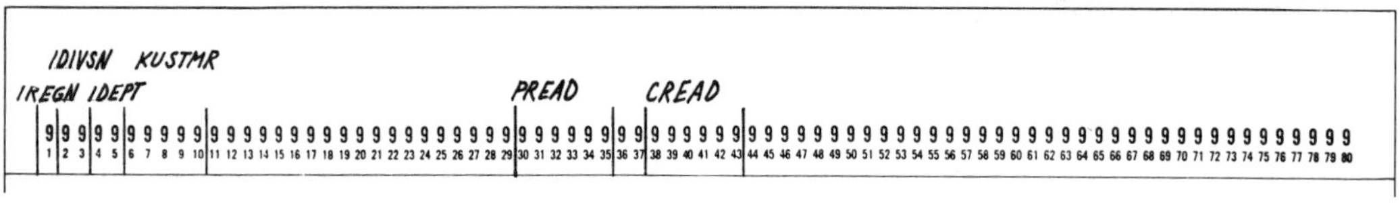

The printed report for program USAGE 3SUBTOTALS uses asterisks (*) to distinguish the different control level breaks. All detail lines are single spaced. Double spaces follow department and divisional subtotals, but regional subtotals are followed by new headings at the top of a new page.

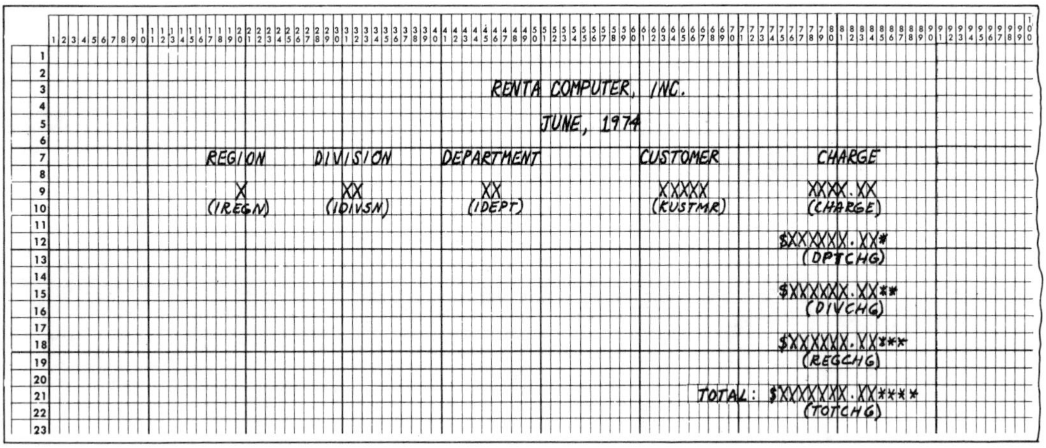

Data records with several levels of subtotals usually are arranged in sequential order within each level. Customers of Renta Computer, Inc., for example, are arranged sequentially by department, by division, and by region. All customers of the first department of the first division of the first region are processed and subtotaled. Then all customers of the next department of the same division and region are processed. This continues until all customers of all departments of the first division are completed. The same procedure is followed for all divisions of the first region. It is used then for all the remaining regions. After all cards are processed, a last card switch is set on. Then the three subtotals are printed. The last card switch is tested, and the "on" (1) position causes the totals to be printed.

Precautions must be taken, however, to insure that region or division number changes are recognized even if the smaller control fields (department or division) happen to be the same. Therefore region, division, and department numbers are tested, in that order, for each record. Switches (ISWREG and ISWDIV) are set as a result of these tests.

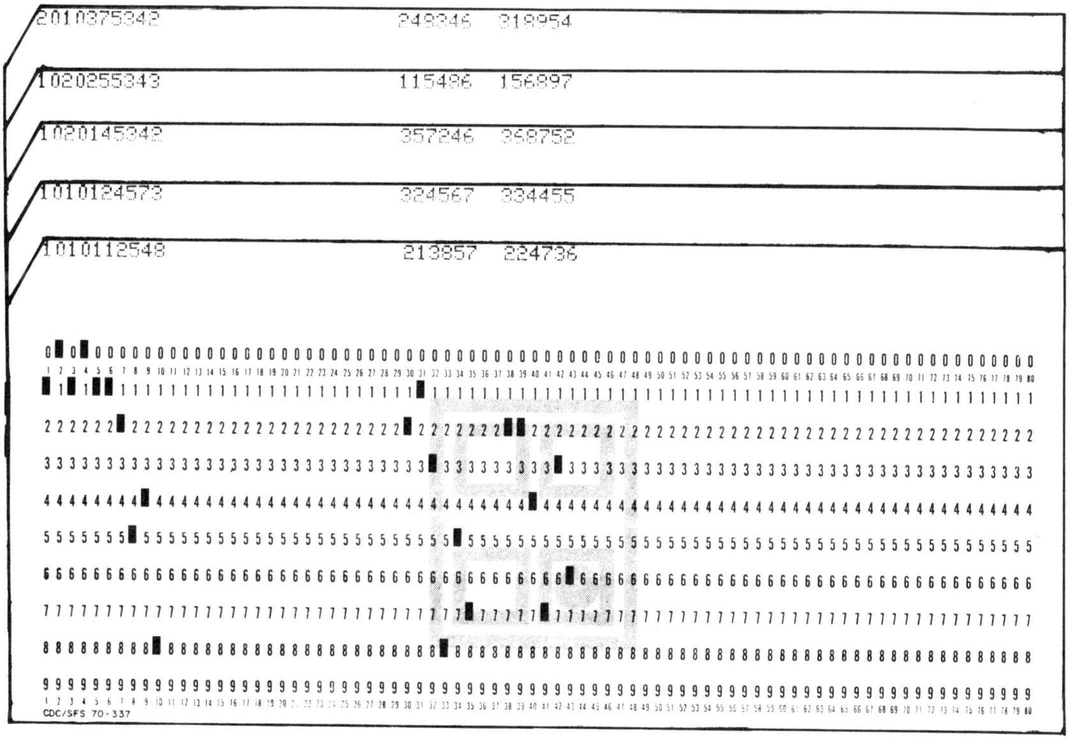

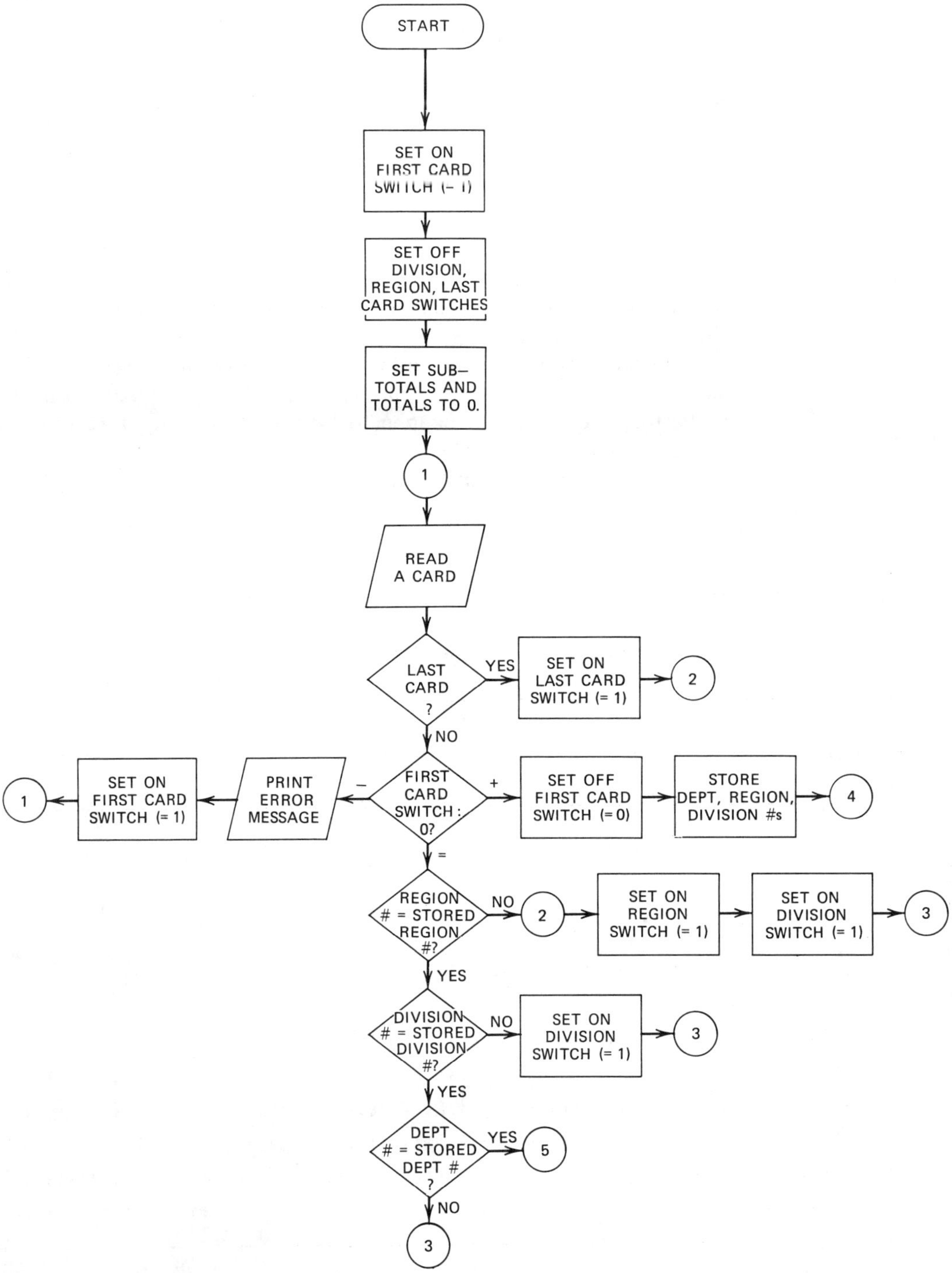
START
SET ON FIRST CARD SWITCH (= 1)
SET OFF DIVISION, REGION, LAST CARD SWITCHES
SET SUB-TOTALS AND TOTALS TO 0.
1
READ A CARD
LAST CARD ?
YES
SET ON LAST CARD SWITCH (= 1)
2
NO
FIRST CARD SWITCH : 0?
−
PRINT ERROR MESSAGE
SET ON FIRST CARD SWITCH (= 1)
1
+
SET OFF FIRST CARD SWITCH (= 0)
STORE DEPT, REGION, DIVISION #s
4
=
REGION # = STORED REGION #?
NO
2
SET ON REGION SWITCH (= 1)
SET ON DIVISION SWITCH (= 1)
3
YES
DIVISION # = STORED DIVISION #?
NO
SET ON DIVISION SWITCH (= 1)
3
YES
DEPT # = STORED DEPT # ?
YES
5
NO
3

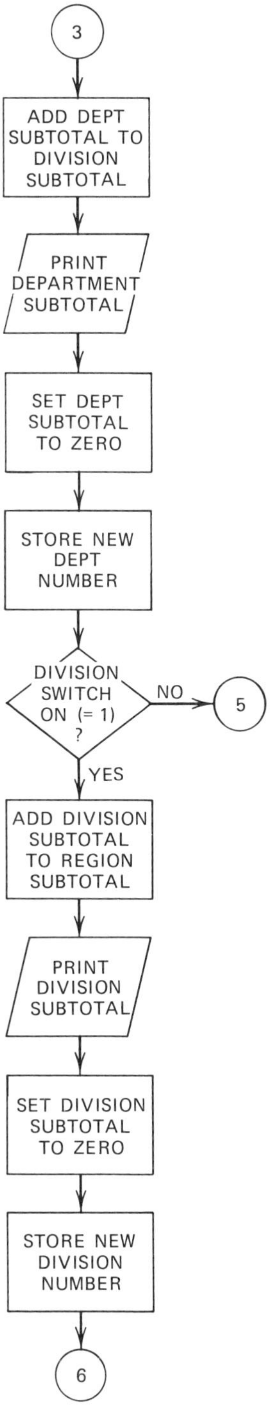
3
ADD DEPT SUBTOTAL TO DIVISION SUBTOTAL
PRINT DEPARTMENT SUBTOTAL
SET DEPT SUBTOTAL TO ZERO
STORE NEW DEPT NUMBER
DIVISION SWITCH ON (= 1) ?
NO
5
YES
ADD DIVISION SUBTOTAL TO REGION SUBTOTAL
PRINT DIVISION SUBTOTAL
SET DIVISION SUBTOTAL TO ZERO
STORE NEW DIVISION NUMBER
6

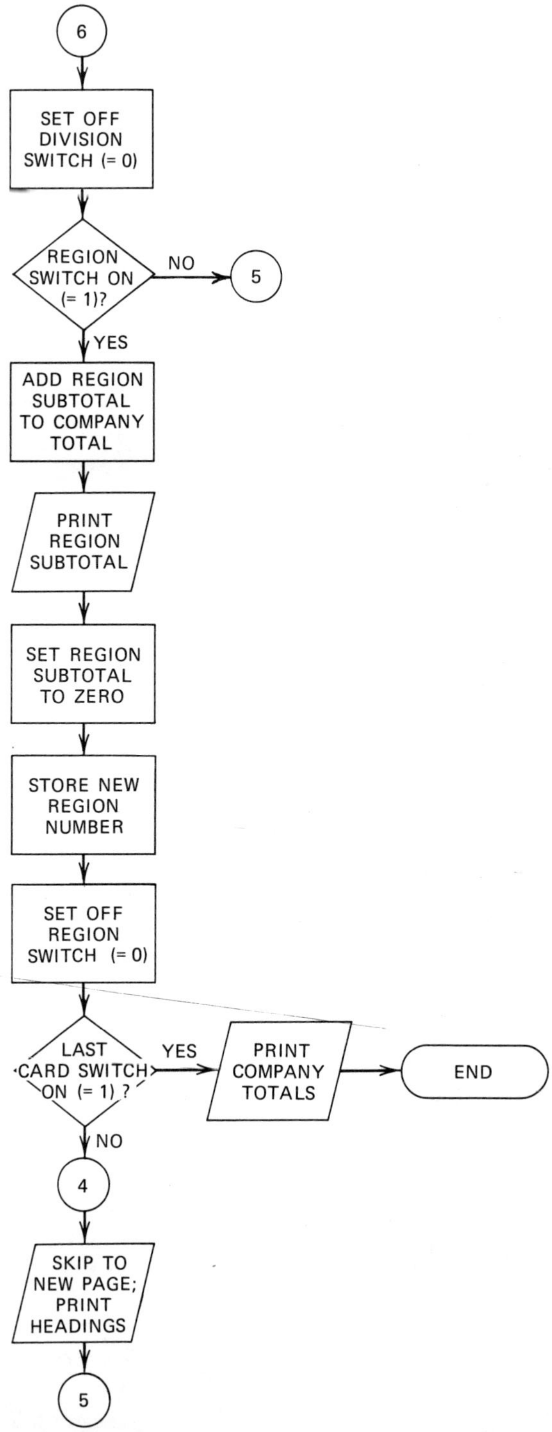
6
SET OFF DIVISION SWITCH (= 0)
REGION SWITCH ON (= 1)?
NO
5
YES
ADD REGION SUBTOTAL TO COMPANY TOTAL
PRINT REGION SUBTOTAL
SET REGION SUBTOTAL TO ZERO
STORE NEW REGION NUMBER
SET OFF REGION SWITCH (= 0)
LAST CARD SWITCH ON (= 1) ?
YES
PRINT COMPANY TOTALS
END
NO
4
SKIP TO NEW PAGE; PRINT HEADINGS
5

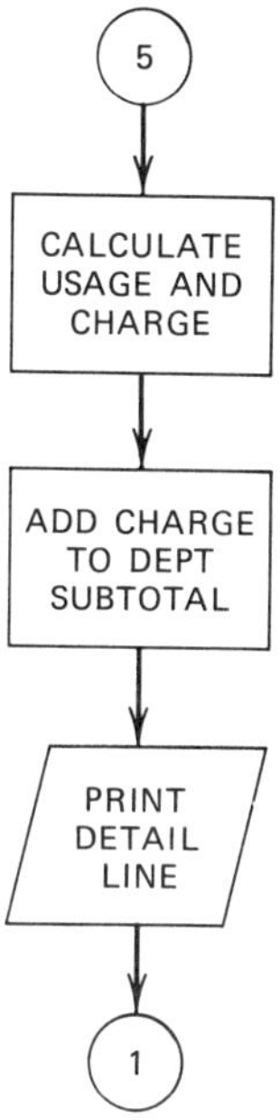

The "first card" switch is set on, and "last card" switch and switches for changes in region and division numbers are set off at the beginning of the program:

```
  1 ISWTCH=1
101 ISWLST=0
201 ISWDIV=0
301 ISWREG=0
```

Subtotals are printed for (1) department, (2) division, and (3) region. Thus all three levels of subtotal fields must be set to zeros at the beginning of the program when the total also is initialized:

```
  2 DPTCHG=0.
102 DIVCHG=0.
202 REGCHG=0.
  3 TOTCHG=0.
```

The main processing cycle begins with the reading of a card. As before, the first card switch must be tested. After the positive branch turns the first card switch off for the rest of the program, all three control field numbers in the first card are stored and the first card processed:

```
  6 IF(ISWTCH)23,109,7
  7 ISWTCH=0
107 IDSTOR=IDEPT
```

```
207 IDVSTR=IDIVSN
307 IREGST=IREGN
108 GO TO 15
```

For all records after the first one, the region, division, and department numbers are compared to the stored numbers. When the region numbers are identical, the program next tests the division number. If division numbers are identical, department numbers are tested:

```
109 IF(IREGN-IREGST)409,209,409
209 IF(IDVSTR-IDIVSN)509,309,509
309 IF(IDEPT-IDSTOR)609,17,609
```

If the region numbers differ, the region and division switches are set on. If the *region* numbers are the same but the *division* numbers differ, the division switch is set on.

```
409 ISWREG=1
509 ISWDIV=1
```

If a control break occurs at any of the three levels, statement 609 is processed next. The department subtotal is added to the second level division subtotals. The department subtotal is printed and cleared to zero, and the new department number is stored:

```
609 DIVCHG=DIVCHG + DPTCHG
 11 WRITE(6,12)DPTCHG
 12 FORMAT (T76,'$',F9.2,'*'//)
 13 DPTCHG=0.
 14 IDSTOR=IDEPT
```

Instead of branching back to read the next card, another test must be made to determine if a change in division occurred with the change in department. An IF statement tests the division switch:

```
114 IF(ISWDIV)214,17,214
```

If the switch is off (equals 0), the program branches to statement 17 to process the detail card that caused the break. If the division switch is on (equals 1), the same basic steps are executed as for a department change. Now, however, division subtotal is added to regional subtotal, division subtotal is printed and cleared to zero, and the new division number is stored. Then the new division switch is turned off:

```
214 REGCHG=REGCHG + DIVCHG
314 WRITE(6,414)DIVCHG
414 FORMAT(T76,'$',F9.2,'**'//)
514 DIVCHG=0.
614 IDVSTR=IDIVSN
714 ISWDIV=0
```

The region switch must be tested next to see if it is on. If the switch equals 0 (is off), the card that caused the break is processed:

```
814 IF(ISWREG)914,17,914
```

If the switch is on, the region (third or highest level) subtotal is added to the company total. Regional subtotal is printed and cleared to zero. The new region number is stored, and the region switch is turned off:

```
 914 TOTCHG=TOTCHG + REGCHG
1014 WRITE (6,1114)REGCHG
1114 FORMAT(T76,'$',F9.2,'***'//)
1214 REGCHG=0.
1314 IREGST=IREGN
1414 ISWREG=0
```

The last card switch must be tested next:

```
1514 IF(ISWLST)15,15,26
```

When this switch is off, the printer skips to a new page and prints the regional headings. Then the record that caused the control break is processed and its detail line printed.

When the last (/*) card is read, the END= option immediately turns on ISWLST:

```
409 ISWLST=1
```

Because all three control break calculations and printings must be executed before the company total is printed, the program sets on region and division switches and continues processing as though region had changed. After all three levels of subtotals are processed and printed, the last card switch branches the program to print company totals and end. The following instructions comprise the completed program:

```
  1 ISWTCH = 1
101 ISWLST = 0
201 ISWDIV = 0
301 ISWREG = 0
  2 DPTCHG = 0.
102 DIVCHG = 0.
202 REGCHG = 0.
  3 TOTCHG = 0.
  4 READ(5,5,END=409)IREGN,IDIVSN,IDEPT,KUSTMR,PREAD,CREAD
  5 FORMAT(I1,I2,I2,I5,19X,F6.2,2X,F6.2)
  6 IF (ISWTCH) 23, 109, 7
  7 ISWTCH = 0
107 IDSTOR = IDEPT
207 IDVSTR = IDIVSN
307 IREGST = IREGN
```

```
 108 GO TO 15
 109 IF (IREGN - IREGST) 509, 209, 509
 209 IF (IDVSTR - IDIVSN) 609, 309, 609
 309 IF (IDEPT - IDSTOR) 709, 17, 709
 409 ISWLST = 1
 509 ISWREG = 1
 609 ISWDIV = 1
 709 DIVCHG = DIVCHG + DPTCHG
  11 WRITE (6,12) DPTCHG
  12 FORMAT (T76,'$',F9.2, '*'//)
  13 DPTCHG = 0.
  14 IDSTOR = IDEPT
 114 IF (ISWDIV) 214, 17, 214
 214 REGCHG = REGCHG + DIVCHG
 314 WRITE (6, 414) DIVCHG
 414 FORMAT (T76, '$', F9.2, '**'//)
 514 DIVCHG = 0.
 614 DIVSTR = IDIVSN
 714 ISWDIV = 0
 814 IF (ISWREG) 914, 17, 914
 914 TOTCHG = TOTCHG + REGCHG
1014 WRITE (6,1114) REGCHG
1114 FORMAT (T76,'$',F9.2, '***'//)
1214 REGCHG = 0.
1314 IREGST = IREGN
1414 ISWREG = 0
1514 IF (ISWLST) 15, 15, 26
  15 WRITE (6,16)
  16 FORMAT('1',T47,'RENTA COMPUTER, INC.'//T52,'JUNE, 1974'//
    1 T18,'REGION',T29,'DIVISION',T42,'DEPARTMENT',T62,'CUSTOMER'
    2 ,T80,'CHARGE'//)
  17 USAGE = CREAD - PREAD
  18 CHARGE = (USAGE * .7) + 50.00
  19 DPTCHG = DPTCHG + CHARGE
  20 WRITE (6,21) IREGN, IDIVSN, IDEPT, KUSTMR, CHARGE
  21 FORMAT (T21,I1,T32,I2,T46,I2,T64,I5,T79,F7.2)
  22 GO TO 4
  23 WRITE (6,24)
  24 FORMAT (T12,'ERROR: RE-SETTING SWITCH')
  25 GO TO 1
  26 WRITE (6,27) TOTCHG
  27 FORMAT ('0',T68,'TOTAL:',T75,'$',F10.2,'****')
  28 CALL EXIT
     END
```

The following report is printed with the demonstration cards:

```
                              RENTA COMPUTER, INC.

                                  JUNE, 1974

REGION      DIVISION      DEPARTMENT          CUSTOMER          CHARGE

   1            1             1                 12548            126.15
   1            1             1                 24573            119.22
                                                          $      245.37*

                                                          $      245.37**

   1            2             1                 45342            130.54
                                                          $      130.54*

                                                          $      130.54**

   1            2             2                 55343            339.88
                                                          $      339.88*

                                                          $      339.88**

                                                          $      715.79***



                              RENTA COMPUTER, INC.

                                  JUNE, 1974

REGION      DIVISION      DEPARTMENT          CUSTOMER          CHARGE

   2            1             3                 75342            544.26
                                                          $      544.26*

                                                          $      544.26**

                                                          $      544.26***

                                                 TOTAL: $      1260.05****
```

If the sequential organization of data cards is difficult to arrange, and if computer storage is large, FORTRAN's capability with arrays and loops enables data records to be processed without such pre-sorting. This can be accomplished in various ways. The simplest is processing all data cards, adding them into the appropriate arrays, then—after all the records are input—printing the stored arrays in subtotal levels.

REVIEW QUESTIONS

5. How many different levels of subtotals can FORTRAN handle?
6. When must subtotals be cleared to zeros?
7. Which subtotals and/or totals are printed when the last card is read?
8. Why is a last card test often required in programs with multiple level subtotals?

OBJECTIVES REVIEW

Study the objectives at the beginning of this chapter. Check each one to be certain you have achieved it. Restudy the chapter sections relating to any objective you cannot perform.

REVIEW TEST

Study the following FORTRAN program carefully. Using the "data cards" that are given, "process" the program as the FORTRAN compiler does. On scratch paper, keep a record of what is in storage for every field as the program proceeds. On a printer spacing chart or in the space below, print the output of the test program as it would appear on a printer.

Data Cards

```
                   1         2         3         4
Columns:  1234567890123456789012345678901234567890
Card 1:   1248 SLACKS             011 2200
Card 2:   2695 TIES               200 0350
Card 3:   2695 TIES               150 0400
Card 4:   3362 SHIRTS             025 1225
Card 5:   /*
```

Program

```
   DIMENSION NAME (4)
 1 SUBTOT = 0.0
 2 IDSTOR = 0
 3 TOTVAL = 0.0
 4 WRITE (6,5)
 5 FORMAT ('1', T31, 'RVS INDUSTRIES'//)
 6 READ (5,7,END = 19) ITEM, NAME, NUMBER, COST
 7 FORMAT (I4, 1X, 4A4, I3, 1X, F4.2)
 8 IF (IDSTOR) 13, 13, 9
 9 IF (IDSTOR - ITEM) 10, 14, 10
10 WRITE (6,11) SUBTOT
11 FORMAT (T58, '$',F8.2/)
```

```
 12 TOTVAL = TOTVAL + SUBTOT
112 SUBTOT = 0.
 13 IDSTOR = ITEM
 14 VALUE = NUMBER * COST
 15 SUBTOT = SUBTOT + VALUE
 16 WRITE (6,17) ITEM, NAME, NUMBER, COST, VALUE
 17 FORMAT (T10,I4,T20,4A4,T40,I3,T46,F5.2,T60,F7.2)
 18 GO TO 6
 19 TOTVAL=TOTVAL+SUBTOT
 20 WRITE (6,11) SUBTOT
 21 WRITE (6,11) TOTVAL
 22 STOP
    END
```

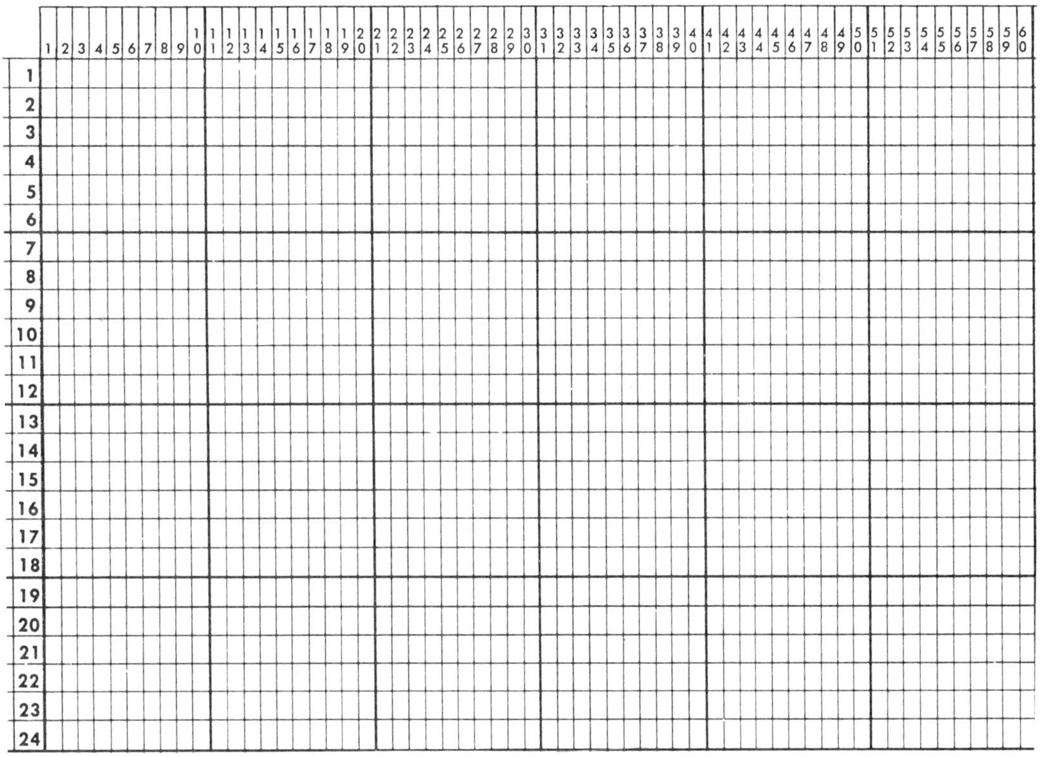

ASSIGNMENTS

Prepare a card layout form, printer spacing chart, and flowchart for one of the following problems. Then write, keypunch, and submit the FORTRAN program with data.

1. A manufacturer requires a cost report analyzed by departments.

Input Records

Fields	Card Columns	
Department number	21-22	(I2)
Job number	23-26	(I4)
Job cost	52-56	(F5.2)
Number of units in job	59-60	(I2)

Calculate unit cost of each job. Count number of jobs in each department and in company. Total job costs and unit costs per job. Calculate average unit cost of all jobs by department and by company. Printed report begins with company name and column headings. Detail lines print input fields and average unit cost. At department break, total job cost and average unit cost are printed, followed by one asterisk (*). After all records are processed, company total and average are printed, followed by two asterisks.

2. A fund-raising organization requires a report of amounts solicited.

Input Records

Fields	Card Columns	
Contributor's name	1-20	(5A4)
Division number	21-22	(I2)
Contributor's number	23-27	(I5)
Code (1 = cash, 2 = pledge)	47	(I1)
Amount of contribution	30-35	(F6.2)

Calculate total amounts pledged and amount collected by division and for the entire organization. Count the number of pledges and the number of cash donors. After last card is processed, find the average amount contributed of each type.

Printed report begins with organization name and location, and column headings. Detail lines print all input fields except code. Division subtotal prints both subtotals followed by one asterisk (*). After last record is processed, organization totals and averages are printed.

3. A store studies the effect of advertising on daily sales volume of three selected items. The report consists only of headings, daily subtotals, and totals.

Input Records

Fields	Card Columns	
Day of week	21	(I1)
Item code number	50	(I1)
Number of items sold	52-55	(I4)

Calculations. For each item, subtotal the number of items sold each day. Total the same fields for the five days. After all records are processed, calculate the percentage of sales for each day. (Place subtotals in one or more arrays.)

Output. Print company and column headings. After the sales for each day are processed, print the day code (1-5) or the name of the day, each item code number (1-3), and the quantity of each item sold that day. After all cards are processed, print totals for the week. Double space and print daily percentages for each item.

4. A company report lists sales by various vendors. There are two control breaks: (1) subtotals are printed after the orders of each customer are processed and (2) after the records of each vendor are processed. Totals are printed after all records are processed.

Input Records

Fields	Card Columns	
Vendor's number	21	(I1)
Customer's number	22-23	(I2)
Item number	34-36	(I3)
Quantity sold	52-54	(I3)
Price per item	62-65	(F4.2)

Calculations. Extension equals quantity times price per item. Subtotal quantity and extension fields by customer and by vendor, and total the same fields for the company.

Output. Print company and column headings. Detail lines contain all input fields and extension. Customer subtotal lines contain vendor and customer numbers and the two subtotals. Vendor subtotal lines contain vendor number and the two subtotals. The total line contains the two total fields.

5. A building contractor is considering the use of floor tiles that are 64¢ a piece in a new development. Each record gives the number of tiles required for the length and width of a room. The contractor wants a report of the number of tiles required for each room and their cost, with subtotals for each building, and totals for the entire development.

Input Records

Fields	Card Columns	
Building code number	21-22	(I2)
Room code number	48-49	(I2)
Number of tiles for side 1	71-72	(I2)
Number of tiles for side 2	44-45	(I2)

Calculations. To obtain the number of tiles required for each room, multiply the number of tiles for side 1 by the number required for side 2. The cost equals the number of tiles times $.64. For each building, subtotal the required number of tiles and their cost. Total the same fields for the entire development. Count the number of rooms for each building and for the development. Calculate the average cost per room for each building. After all records are processed, calculate the average cost per room and per building for the development.

Output. Print the company name and location and column headings. Detail lines contain the four input fields, the number of tiles required, and the cost. Subtotal lines contain the building code number, the number of rooms, and the two subtotals and average with explanatory messages. The total line contains the totals and averages for the development.

CMC5, key-to-disk data entry system. Loading the disk at supervisor's console.

Chapter Objectives

1. Be able to write a computed GOTO statement that branches to any of several different statements.
2. Be able to explain how integer or real numbers can be converted into integer variables tested by a computed GOTO statement.
3. Be able to establish category codes so that the code can be used as the tested variable of a computed GOTO statement.

14

The Computed GO TO Statement

Many times a programmer would like to have several branches from which to choose. A store with ten departments, for instance, might want different calculations for various departments. Although IF statements could be used in such situations, several would be required to determine the correct department. The computed GO TO statement enables multiple choices to be determined with only one FORTRAN instruction.

As an example of the computed GO TO instruction, assume that Renta Computer, Inc. serves eight different geographic regions. The usage rate for customers differs according to region. Regional usage rates are given in the following table:

Region	Usage Rate
1	$.70
2	.90
3	.85
4	.80
5	.85
6	.80
7	.75
8	.85

Customers in regions 4 and 6 are charged 80¢ per unit of usage. Customers in regions 3, 5, and 8 are charged $.85. Regions 1, 2, 4, and 7 each have unique rates. The program must branch to the instruction that multiplies customer usage by the correct charge.

In order to accomplish this, regional numbers are read from data cards as integer field IREGN.

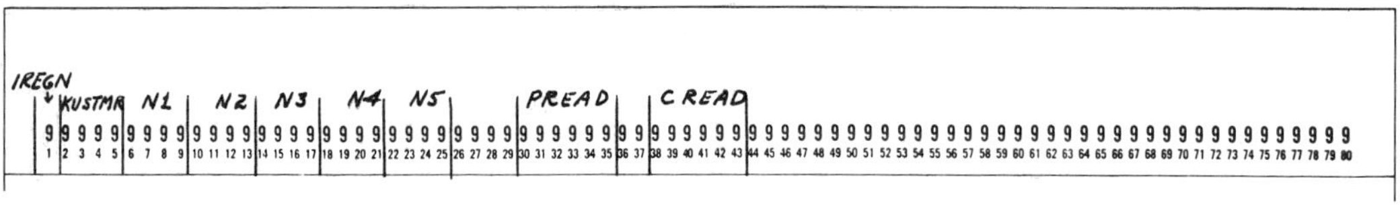

Using IREGN as the determining field, the computed GO TO branches the program to the appropriate instruction.

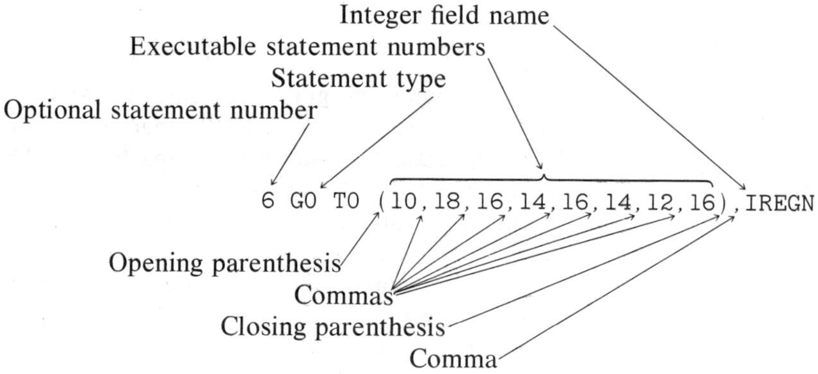

The computed GO TO may be a numbered statement. Like the GO TO and IF statements, the computed GO TO requires the first executable statement following it to be numbered. GO TO begins the computed GO TO instruction, followed by parentheses enclosing a series of executable statement numbers. This list of statement numbers can be as long as the programmer needs. After the closing parenthesis are a comma and a nonsubscripted integer variable. (Omitting the final comma in a computed GO TO statement is a careless but frequent cause of program failure.)

The value of the integer variable determines program branching by *position* in the list. For example:

```
 6 GO TO (10,18,16,14,16,14,12,16), IREGN
 7 WRITE (6,8)
 8 FORMAT (' ',T5,'ERROR')
 9 GO TO 1
10 CHARGE = USAGE * .70
11 GO TO 19
12 CHARGE = USAGE * .75
13 GO TO 19
14 CHARGE = USAGE * .80
15 GO TO 19
16 CHARGE = USAGE * .85
17 GO TO 19
18 CHARGE = USAGE * .90
19 CONTINUE
```

If IREGN contains the value 1, the program will branch to statement 10 because statement number 10 is listed in the *first position*. When IREGN contains 2, the program branches to *second position* statement 18. The process continues until there are as many positions as the largest possible value of the integer. Thus, statement 6 has a list of eight statement numbers because the company has regions numbered from 1 through 8.

Statement numbers listed within the parentheses can be anywhere in the program. They can, in turn, proceed anywhere in the program without regard (except for program logic) for other branches of the computed GO TO. This flexibility enables the computed GO TO to be used in many types of analyses, including alphabetic. (See Program LETTER in Appendix C.)

Statement numbers rarely are in numerical order. Any of the statement numbers can be repeated, as 16 is repeated in the third, fifth, and eighth positions.

Statements 7-9 are precautionary measures. In case an integer larger than 8 or less than 1 is erroneously punched into the region field of a data card, most FORTRAN compilers will automatically "fall through" to the next executable statement. After WRITE instruction 7 prints an error message, statement 9 branches the program back to the READ statement. Program logic requires some such instructions to prevent "falling through" to statement 10 when that is inappropriate.

REVIEW QUESTIONS

1. What kind of field is tested in a computed GO TO statement?
2. How many branches can be in a computed GO TO statement?
3. What determines to which statement the GO TO statement branches?
4. Can a branching statement number be listed more than once in a GO TO statement?
5. What kind of statement must the branching statements be?
6. Where in the program can the branching statements be?

The tested integer field can be read, or calculated, or created in a replacement statement. The fact that it must be an integer rarely hinders the programmer because he can move the contents from a real to an integer field before a computed GOTO statement:

```
100 ISCORE = SCORE
101 GO TO (1,2,3,4,5), ISCORE
```

This same conversion technique can be extended to include other manipulations. For example, the digits immediately to the right and left of the decimal point are essential in a program analyzing item prices from 1¢-$1.99. Various calculations are to be performed, determined by the cost of items in 10-cent groupings.

The obvious difficulty lies in the fact that converting money into an integer field ordinarily causes the fractional part of the dollar to be dropped. This, and other similarly required adjustments, can be handled by arithmetic statements performed before the computed GO TO statement. (Standard flowchart techniques are not yet established for multiple decision making.)

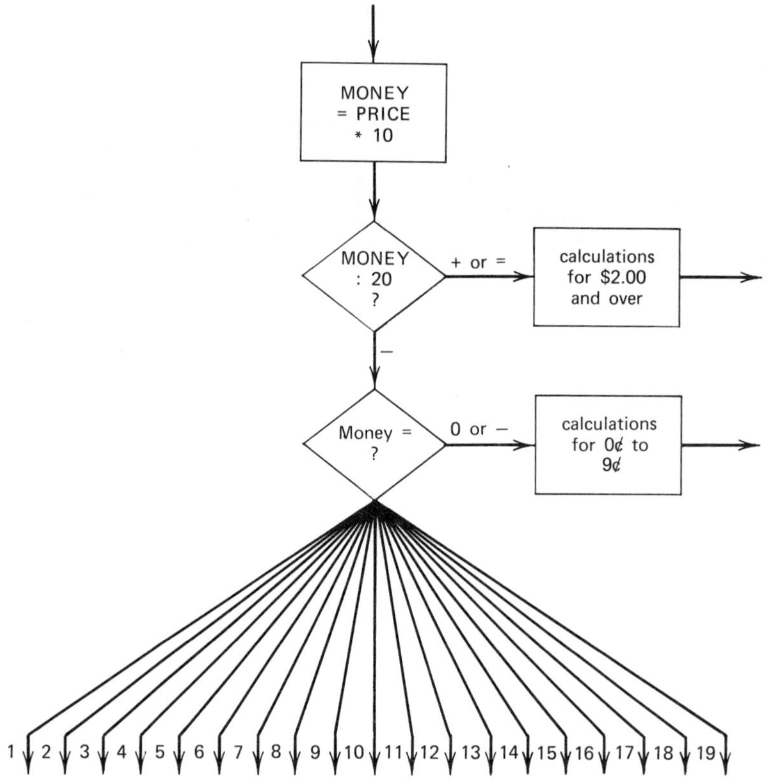

First the item price must be converted into a positive integer by multiplying PRICE times 10 and storing the result in integer field MONEY:

```
100 MONEY = PRICE * 10
```

Thus, for example, if an item costs $.25 (real field PRICE equals .25), integer field MONEY equals 2. If the item price is $1.37 (real field PRICE equals 1.37), integer field MONEY equals 13.

Then, as a precautionary step, statement 101 tests MONEY minus 20:

```
101 IF (MONEY - 20) 102, 103, 103
```

All items equal to or greater than $2.00 give a zero or positive value. These items are branched to special calculations. Thus IF statement 101 keeps prices greater than $1.99 from computed GO TO statement 102 by branching them to statement 103.

When MONEY minus 20 is a negative value, statement 101 branches the program to computed GO TO statement 102:

```
102 GO TO (2,3,4,5,6,7,8,9,10,11,12,13,14,15,16,17,18,19,20),MONEY
  1 K1T09 = K1T09 + 1
200 GO TO 21
```

Items from $.01-$.09 "fall through" the computed GO TO statement to statement 1, the next executable instruction, because MONEY is less than 1. Therefore statement 102 provides branches for all items between $.10 and $1.99.

When, for example, item price is from $.20-$.29, MONEY has a value of 2. This value of 2 causes the program to branch to statement 3, the *second position* within the computed GO TO parentheses. When the item price is $1.45, MONEY equals 14 and the program branches to statement 15, in the *fourteenth position* within the parentheses.

Values less than 1 (items costing from 1-9¢) are deliberately planned to "fall through" to statement 1 for appropriate calculations. Therefore, statement 1 is placed immediately after the computed GO TO statement so that the appropriate calculations can be processed. If statement 101 did not divert item prices greater then $1.99, they also would branch to statement 1 by default.

Manipulating numeric fields by multiplication, division, etc. makes many more fields usable as the integer tested in computed GO TO statements.

The computed GO TO is also valuable with certain types of codes. In a survey, for example, families can be analyzed for various characteristics, depending on establishing coded numeric categories. When each category is represented by a different integer code, the computed GO TO can direct the branching by testing the category code number.

REVIEW QUESTIONS

7. When the tested integer field equals zero, to which statement does it branch?

8. When the tested integer field equals a negative quantity, to which statement does it branch?

9. To which statement does a program branch when the tested value equals 5?

OBJECTIVES REVIEW

Look at the objectives at the beginning of this chapter. Check each one to be certain you have achieved it. Restudy the chapter sections related to any you cannot perform.

REVIEW TEST

Study the following FORTRAN program carefully. Using the "data cards" that are given, "process" the program as the FORTRAN compiler does. On scratch paper, keep a record of what is in storage for every field as the program proceeds. On a printer spacing chart or in the space below, print the output of the test program as it would appear on a printer.

Data Cards

```
                   1         2         3         4
Columns:  1234567890123456789012345678901234567890
Card 1:   JANICE MUIR     0 02000
Card 2:   TAMI GREGORY    3 40000
Card 3:   LORI STEINBERG  1  4000
Card 4:   LAURIE WINTER   2 60000
Card 5:   THEO LASST      0 20000   99
Card 6:   /*
```

Program

```
      DIMENSION NAME(4)
    1 READ (5,2) NAME,NVIO,OLD,IEND
    2 FORMAT (4A4,I1,T19,F5.2,T27,I2)
    3 IF (IEND - 99) 4, 54, 54
    4 IF (NVIO .GT. 2) GO TO 40
    5 INDEX = NVIO + 1
    6 GO TO (10, 20, 30), INDEX
   10 ADJUST = .10
   11 GO TO 50
   20 ADJUST = .25
   21 GO TO 50
   30 ADJUST = .50
   31 GO TO 50
   40 WRITE (6,41) NAME
   41 FORMAT (' ', 4A4, T22, 'CANCEL')
   42 GO TO 1
   50 PREM = OLD + OLD * ADJUST
   51 WRITE (6,52) NAME, PREM
   52 FORMAT (1X, 4A4, T21, F7.2)
   53 GO TO 1
   54 WRITE (6,55)
   55 FORMAT ('0', 'END OF REPORT')
   56 STOP
      END
```

Printout

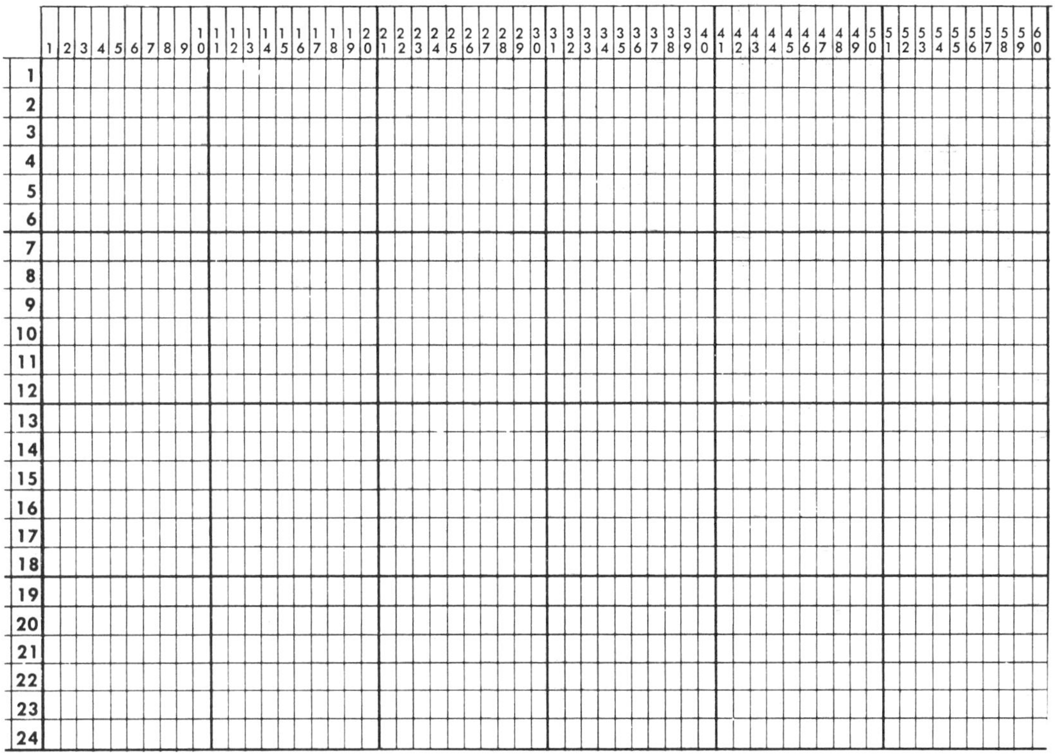

ASSIGNMENTS

Prepare a card layout form, printer spacing chart, and flowchart for one of the following problems. Then write, keypunch, and submit the FORTRAN program.

1. A department store updates its charge accounts sequentially each month. Transactions are coded so that appropriate calculations can be made. Detail lines show each transaction. When the account number changes, subtotals show the updated amount due.

Input Records

Fields	Card Columns	
Customer account number	21-22	I2
Department number	56	I1

Amount of transaction	62-66	F5.2
Day of month of transaction	76-77	I2
(Type 1 cards assume first day of month)		
Transaction code	34	I1
1 = beginning balance		
2 = payment		
3 = purchase		
4 = adjustment credit		
5 = adjustment debit		
Customer name (type 1 only)	1-20	5A4

Calculations. Use the computed GO TO to determine transaction procedure. If code equals 1, store amount of transaction for customer. If code equals 2, subtract amount from stored field. If code equals 3, add amount to stored field. If code equals 4, subtract amount from stored field. If code equals 5, add amount to stored field. Create five total fields: payments, purchases, adjustment credit, adjustment debit, and new balance.

Printed Report. Headings include company name, date of report, column headings. Detail lines: Type 1 lines include customer's name and account number, date of first of month, amount of transaction, and 'BALANCE FORWARD.' Type 2 lines contain date and amount of transaction, followed by 'CR' and 'PAYMENT.' Type 3 lines contain department number, date and amount of transaction, and 'PURCHASE.' Type 4 lines contain department number, date, amount of transaction followed by 'CR,' and 'ADJUSTMENT.' Type 5 lines contain department, date, amount of transaction, and 'ADJUSTMENT.' After all records of a customer are processed, the new balance forward is printed. If the amount is negative, print 'CR' after the amount. After all records are processed, skip to a new page and print headings and the five totals with identifying messages.

2. The headquarters of a national organization assesses its local offices according to a special formula for membership in each local. A report is required to show each local, its membership, its assessment per member, and its total assessed dues.

Input Records

Fields	Card Columns	
Local branch number	23-27	I5
Number of paid members	52-55	I4
Table of assessments		

Number of Members	Amount Due per Member
1-49	$3.00
50-99	2.75
100-149	2.55

150-199	2.50
200-249	2.40
250-299	2.35
300-399	2.20
400-599	2.15
600-749	2.05
750-999	2.00
Over 1000	1.75

Calculations. Use a computed GOTO to determine the correct rate of assessment; then multiply the rate times the number of members to find the total amount of the assessment. Total the membership and the amount due from all local branches. Count the number of locals reporting. After all locals are processed, calculate the average number of members and average amount of assessment.

Printed Report. Headings include organization name and location of headquarters, and column headings. Detail lines contain the local branch number, the number of members, assessment per member, and total local assessment. After all records are processed, print the two totals, the two averages, and the count, with appropriate messages for each.

3. Print net income for each branch office of a nationwide company.

Input Records

Fields	Card Columns	
State code	21-22	I2
Net sales	40-45	F6.2
Selling expenses	63-67	F5.2
General expenses	71-76	F6.2

Calculate the net income for each branch office by subtracting both types of expense from net sales. Create arrays to total net sales, selling expenses, general expenses, and net income for the state and the company. If the net income for a state is less than $2,000, print a special message, 'UNDER CONSIDERATION FOR DISCONTINUANCE' to the right of the net income amount; if between $2,000 and $2,999, print 'NEEDS HELP FROM HOME OFFICE;' if between $3,000 and $3,999, print 'MARGINAL OPERATION;' if $4,000 or more, but less than $6,000, no special message; if $6,000 or more, print 'BONUS.' Determine the message by a computed GOTO statement.

Printed Report. Headings include company name, home office location, date, and column headings. Detail lines include all input fields and net income. After each state is processed, the subtotals are printed. Totals are printed after all records are processed.

4. The speed with which the average merchandise is sold is a standard commonly used by retailers to determine operation efficiency. A service bureau processes the same stock turnover program for several companies. Create individual WRITE and FORMAT statements for each of six companies. Keypunch a special leading card with company number (from 1 to 6) in column 1.

Input Records

Fields	Card Columns	
Item number	23-27	I5
Sum of quantity in all inventories	51-57	I7
Number of inventories taken	71-72	I2
Total number sold	48-52	I5

Calculations. After reading the first data card containing the company number, use a computed GO TO to branch to the appropriate WRITE and FORMAT statements for the company heading. To calculate the average number of inventories required, divide the sum of all the inventories by the number of inventories taken. To get the stock turnover, divide the total number sold by the average number of inventories required. Count the number of items. After the last record is processed, find the average stock turnover for all items.

Output. Print company headings, location, and date. Print column headings. Detail lines contain the input fields and stock turnover. After the last record is processed, print the number of items counted and the stock turnover average with appropriate messages.

5. A research company requires a report of nine products being tested on a rating scale from 01 (low) to 99 (high).

Input Records

Fields	Card Columns	
Person testing product	1-20	5A4
Test number	23-27	I5
Product cost	33-35	F3.2
Product number	32	I1
Rating points given	72-73	I2
Number of times utilized	53	I1

Calculations. Using arrays, total the points received by each product and count the number of tests conducted for each product. After all records are processed, find the average number of points per product. Use a computed GOTO to branch for special product information: for products 1 and 5, total the number of times the product was utilized. After all records are processed, calculate the average number of utilization times for these products. For products 2 and 9, total the product cost. After all records are processed, calculate the average cost of these products. For products 3, 4, and 7, calculate the average cost per utilization by dividing the product cost by number of times utilized. Products 6 and 8 require no special information.

Output. Headings include research company name and location, report date, and column headings. Detail lines include all input fields and special calculated fields when appropriate. (Special fields require extra care in preliminary printer spacing chart planning.) After all records are processed, print all totals and averages.

Chapter Objectives

1. Be able to use an INTEGER specification statement to override FORTRAN name conventions for fields and arrays *not* beginning with I, J, K, L, M, or N.
2. Be able to use a REAL specification statement to override FORTRAN name conventions for fields and arrays beginning with I, J, K, L, M, or N.
3. Be able to establish integers stored in only two bytes of computer memory.
4. Be able to create real fields with eight bytes of computer storage.
5. Be able to use integer and real optional lengths with alphameric fields.
6. Be able to explain why a complex number requires two fields in FORMAT specifications.
7. Be able to use the optional length of complex numbers for long alphameric fields.
8. Be able to override FORTRAN name conventions with the IMPLICIT type specification.

15

Type Specification Statements

Integer and real numbers are the most common types of numeric constants and variables, but FORTRAN has other kinds of numeric fields. When a programmer wants to establish another kind of numeric field, when he wants to break the FORTRAN name conventions for integer or real field, or when he wants to alter the number of bytes ordinarily used by the computer in storing a field, he uses a type specification statement. Specification statements can list variables, arrays, or functions (discussed in Chapter 20).

Although FORMAT statements inform the compiler of field size for *input* and *output,* the length of a field and its form in computer *storage* are determined by its designated type. Each field type is stored in a predetermined form, and each has a standard length and (except for one type, DOUBLE PRECISION) an optional length in most computers.

Knowledge of the different lengths of fields is particularly important when the programmer is working with exceedingly large or exceptionally small numbers, or if he has great quantities of data that must all be stored at the same time. This knowledge is also valuable in storing and manipulating alphameric data.

Type specification statements must come before any executable statements, and they cannot be numbered. If fields listed in a type specification statement are used in any other nonexecutable statement (such as a DIMENSION statement), the type statement must come first in the program.

REVIEW QUESTIONS

1. In what two ways can field types be established in FORTRAN?
2. Where must type specification statements be placed in a FORTRAN program?

INTEGER Specification Statement

When a programmer wants to use a field name not permitted by FORTRAN name conventions, he can override the convention by using either an explicit or IMPLICIT type specification statement. For example, field names beginning with the letters I, J, K, L, M, or N normally are reserved for integer fields. All other letters and the dollar sign (regarded as the last letter of the FORTRAN alphabet) are reserved for the first letter of real fields. If the programmer wants an integer field to begin with a letter other than I-N, he must use a type specification statement to inform the compiler of this change from the normal field name convention. For example, the following INTEGER specification statement establishes REGION and AMOUNT as integers:

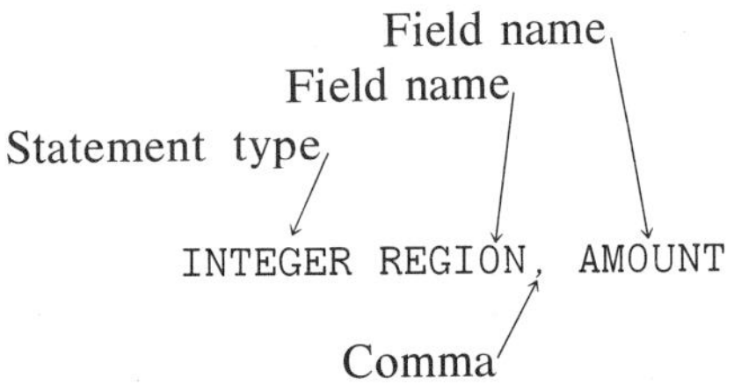

The unnumbered type specification begins with the type name INTEGER in or after column 7. Names of the fields are listed after the field type. Field names, which cannot exceed the six-character field name limit and which cannot contain any special characters, are separated by commas. The example INTEGER statement establishes REGION and AMOUNT as integer fields even though their first letters are R and A. Just like other integer fields, REGION and AMOUNT must be input and output with I (or A) format specifications throughout the program.

In another program, the programmer not only wants REGION and AMOUNT to be integers, but he also wants TOTALS to be a 5 × 5 integer array. Because arrays can be established in specification statements, the DIMENSION statement need not be used. Instead, both the fields and the array can be established in the INTEGER specification:

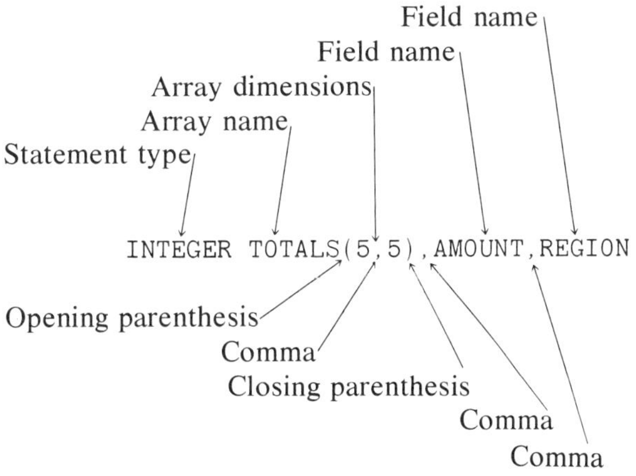

If the programmer wants to reserve space for an integer array that follows field name conventions, he can include that array also in the INTEGER specification:

```
INTEGER TOTALS(5,5),AMOUNT,REGION,NUMBER(50)
```

By including array NUMBER in the INTEGER specification statement, the programmer has eliminated the need for a DIMENSION statement in the program.

REVIEW QUESTIONS

3. Fields require the INTEGER statement when they begin with which letters?
4. Which FORTRAN statement becomes unnecessary when an INTEGER statement establishes an array?

REAL Specification Statement

In the same way that the INTEGER specification establishes fields and arrays (and functions) without conventional integer names as integers, so the REAL specification statement permits fields and arrays (and functions) with expressed or understood decimal points to have names usually reserved for integers. For example:

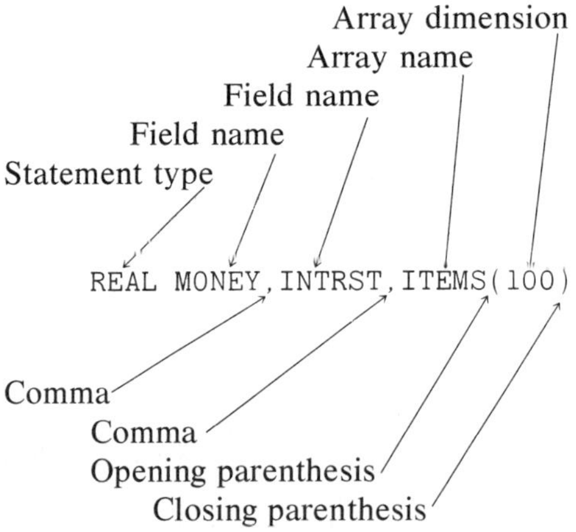

Field type REAL is listed first, in or after column 7. Field names follow, separated from each other by commas. The example establishes MONEY and INTRST as real fields, and ITEMS as a 100-element real array. In FORMAT statements, both the fields and the array elements are input or output with F, E, D, or A format specifications.

REVIEW QUESTIONS

5. Which type specification statement establishes fields without decimal fractions when field names do not begin with I,J,K,L,M, or N?
6. Which type specification statement establishes fields with expressed or understood decimal points when field names begin with I,J,K,L, M, or N?

Every real or integer field and each element in a real or integer array normally occupies four bytes in IBM S/360 and S/370 storage. This space is allotted by the compiler regardless of the contents of the field. Like field name conventions, however, standard field lengths for integer and real fields can be altered. The programmer can call for the optional length of the field type. The optional length for integers is two bytes, and the optional length for real fields is eight bytes.

Variable Type	Standard Length	Optional Length
Integer	4 bytes	2 bytes (except constants)
Real	4 bytes	8 bytes

Integer Field Lengths

Sometimes programs require many variables or a very large array in main storage at the same time so that calculations and manipulations, such as updating tables, can be performed on any of the fields. If these variables are integers, the programmer can conserve space by shortening the allotted storage length from four to two bytes. Of course, the programmer must be certain that his data will not exceed the two-byte size. To figure the maximum quantity allowed requires some knowledge about the way in which the FORTRAN compiler utilizes integer storage.

Every byte in the IBM S/360 or S/370 computer is composed of 8 bits (binary digits). Four bytes, the standard length for integers, thus contain 32 bits. For example, the decimal integer value 75 is stored in binary or base 2 form (separated here into bytes only for reading convenience) as 00000000 00000000 00000000 01001011. The decimal value 12,822,000 is stored as binary number 00000000 11000011 10100101 11110000. The integer decimal value 32,767 is stored as 00000000 00000000 01111111 11111111 in binary form. This last number is important because an integer field with contents *not exceeding* the decimal value 32,767 (2^{15}-1) contains only zeros in the two leftmost bytes of its normal 4-byte storage location. Thus, all integers with four or fewer decimal digits, and some (10,000 to 32,767 and negative 10,000 to negative 32,766) with five decimal digits can be *stored* as 2-byte integers, with the leftmost bit acting as the sign.

The usefulness of this knowledge can be illustrated by a program requiring a large array of 4-digit employee numbers. The programmer can save half the normal storage allotment if he eliminates the two leftmost bytes containing only 0's in standard 4-byte locations. CUSTMR is established as an array of 2-byte integer elements:

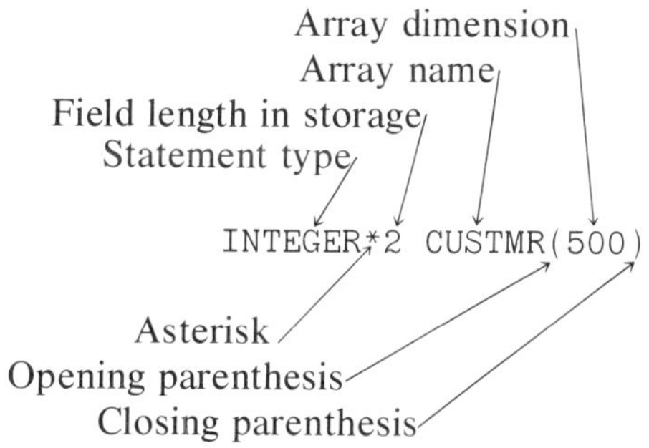

Each element still requires an I4 format specification in input and output FORMAT specifications. The asterisk and optional length (2) following the specification type, however, change every element in array CUSTMR from 4 bytes to 2 bytes in *storage*. The INTEGER*2 specification saves 1000 bytes of computer storage (500 elements times 2 eliminated bytes = 1000).

More then one field or array can be listed when specification type, asterisk, and optional length are all at the beginning of the specification statement. Field or array names in the list must be separated by commas. Each field or array element is stored in a 2-byte location. For example:

```
INTEGER*2 CUSTMR(500),TOTALS(50,5),INDEX
```

The INTEGER*2 specification establishes arrays CUSTMR and TOTALS and field INDEX in 2-byte integer locations. These same specifications can be written:

```
INTEGER CUSTMR (500)*2,TOTALS (50,5)*2, INDEX*2
```

This flexibility allows length change in the same specification with field type name change but standard field length:

```
INTEGER COUNT,REGION(500)*2,TOTALS(50,5)*2,AMOUNT,INDEX*2
```

Elements in arrays REGION and TOTALS are stored in 2-byte locations; field INDEX has a 2-byte location; fields AMOUNT and COUNT are stored in standard 4-byte locations.

REVIEW QUESTIONS

7. What is the standard storage length of an integer field?
8. What is the standard storage length of a real field?
9. What are the optional lengths of integer and real fields?
10. What is the largest decimal number that fits into an optional integer field length?
11. How are standard and optional integer field lengths designated in the same type specification statement?

Alphameric Uses of Optional INTEGER Length

The ability to shorten integer storage space provides unexpected advantages when dealing with large quantities of 1 and 2 character alphameric fields.[1] Such situations occur when storing alphabetic codes, analyzing answers to multiple choice questions, studying age or IQ data, or analyzing alphameric responses. With the integer 2-byte storage option, half as much space is required in main storage. A section of a program with 80 1-character answers per card illustrates how such an array can be stored:

```
  INTEGER*2 ANSWER(1200)
1 READ (5,2) ANSWER
2 FORMAT (80 A1)
```

Normally the 1200 elements of array ANSWER require 4 bytes each. Utilizing the optional integer length of 2, array ANSWER requires only 2400 bytes instead of 4800 bytes required with the standard length allocation. Such savings often determine whether a program will or will not execute.

[1]See Chapter 23, Logical Primaries, for optional 1-byte fields available on some FORTRAN compilers.

Real and Double Precision Field Lengths

Instead of being diminished, computer storage for real fields and array elements (and functions) can be enlarged from standard 4 bytes to optional 8 bytes. Most FORTRAN compilers store a real field of fewer than eight decimal digits (ignoring the decimal point) in four bytes of storage. If the field is eight digits or larger, most FORTRAN compilers automatically assign it eight storage bytes. If the programmer wants to be certain that eight bytes of storage are reserved for his real field, he cannot depend upon the name convention. Instead, he must use a specification statement. Both the REAL*8 specification and the DOUBLE PRECISION specification create real fields with eight bytes per field in storage. (A 4-byte real field is sometimes called a "single precision" field.) Double precision fields are stored only in 8-byte locations and have no optional length.

Two type specification statements create identical storage allocations. The first uses the REAL*8 specification:

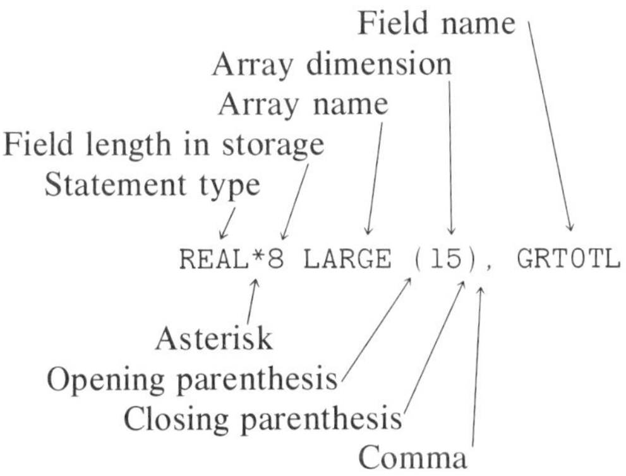

The second uses the DOUBLE PRECISION specification:

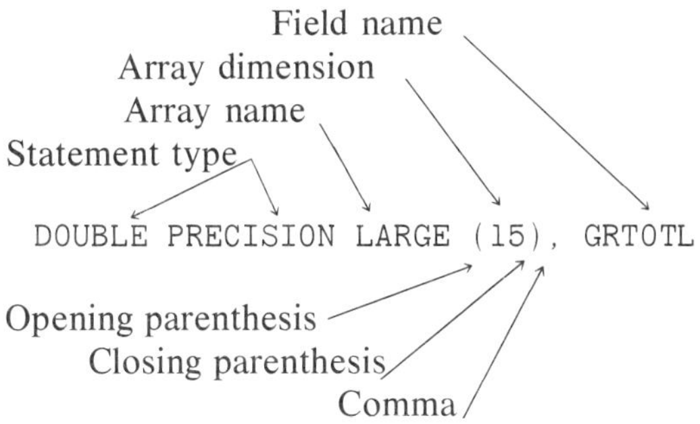

Both the REAL*8 and the DOUBLE PRECISION type specifications establish real array LARGE with 15 8-byte locations and real field GRTOTL with eight bytes of storage.

Statistical studies and scientific calculations frequently use numbers that are either very large or exceedingly small. The use of the

REAL *8 or the DOUBLE PRECISION statement enables these studies to achieve greater accuracy. Both statements can utilize either the F format or the D format in input/output specifications:

```
  DOUBLE PRECISION TINY, HUGE
1 READ (5,2) TINY, HUGE
2 FORMAT (F17.10, D17.4)
```

Both TINY and HUGE require 17 card columns. For TINY, the rightmost 16 positions are digits to the right of the decimal point. HUGE is stored in exponential form, with the D format.

Alphameric Uses of Optional Real and Double Precision Length

Alphameric fields were shown earlier to utilize space best in multiples of 4. This results from the fact that four bytes is the standard *storage* length of both integer and real fields. Just as the shortened form of the INTEGER specification aids certain types of alphameric storage problems, however, so the REAL * 8 and DOUBLE PRECISION specifications are useful in alphameric work.

If a series of words or names is to be manipulated, the alphameric fields can be eight characters long instead of four. Storage space is not saved by the change to double precision length fields, but the programmer's coding can be easier.

For example, a program requires eight alphameric characters for each item in a 100-item list. Using standard field lengths, each item is stored as two 4-byte elements. The 100 items require a two-dimensional 100 × 2 array. The array can be stored by the following instructions:

```
   DIMENSION ITEMS (100,2)
 5 ISTART = 1
 6 DO 11 I = 1,10
 7 IEND = ISTART + 9
 8 READ (5,9) ((ITEMS(K,L),K = ISTART,IEND), L = 1,2)
 9 FORMAT (20 A4)
10 ISTART = ISTART + 10
11 CONTINUE
```

ITEMS will be stored as ITEMS (1,1), ITEMS (1,2), ITEMS (2,1), ITEMS (2,2), ITEMS (3,1)...ITEMS (100,2). Eight hundred bytes will be required to store the 100 by 2 array.

Using a REAL*8 or DOUBLE PRECISION statement, the same data can be stored in 8-byte locations with simpler instructions:

```
   DOUBLE PRECISION ITEMS (100)
18 READ (5,19) ITEMS
19 FORMAT (10 A8)
```

The array still requires 800 bytes of storage even though it is now a 100-element single dimension array. The 8-byte division of storage, however, makes input and output much simpler.

If alphameric fields can be kept to eight characters by abbreviations or other coding techniques, single fields and single dimension arrays can be used instead of more involved double dimension arrays. Not only the coding for input and output, but all manipulating instructions are easier with fewer dimensions. Sorting, for example, becomes both faster and easier to code.

REVIEW QUESTIONS

12. Which type specification does not have an optional length?
13. When are REAL*8 and DOUBLE PRECISION useful for alphameric data?
14. For what kinds of numeric data are REAL*8 and DOUBLE PRECISION valuable?
15. When is INTEGER*2 useful for alphameric data?

COMPLEX Specification Statement

The COMPLEX specification, like the other explicit specification statements, must come at the beginning of a program before any executable statements. It cannot be a numbered statement.

```
        Field name
Statement type
   COMPLEX POINT
```

Complex numbers are rarely used in business data processing except in linear programming or numerical analysis. Complex numbers are a *pair* of numbers separated by a comma. When established in an arithmetic assignment statement, the pair must be enclosed in parentheses.

```
  COMPLEX POINT
1 POINT = (6.0,-1.0)
```

The first number in parentheses represents the real part of the complex number; the number following the comma represents the imaginary part of the complex number. Each part is stored as a real, standard length, 4-byte field with "real" in a meaning different from the mathematical reference to "real" in complex numbers.

If the pair of numbers is input, both F and E formats are acceptable. For example:

```
  COMPLEX VECTOR
1 READ (5,2) VECTOR
2 FORMAT (F10.3,E17.3)
```

Two real fields comprising the complex number VECTOR are stored in 8 bytes of storage (4 bytes each). Therefore, every time a complex number is referenced, two fields must be listed in the appropriate FORMAT statement.

Complex numbers have certain FORTRAN limitations: they cannot be used in ordinary arithmetic operations but require special subroutines. Also, since they cannot be used in IF statements, they cannot be sorted into ascending or descending order.

COMPLEX Field Lengths

If either the real or imaginary part of a complex number requires more than 4 bytes, *both numbers* must be enlarged to the double dimension 8-byte size. In such cases, the complex number requires 16 bytes of storage. The DOUBLE PRECISION or REAL*8 specifications cannot be used. Instead, the COMPLEX*16 type specification statement allots 8 bytes to each of the pair of numbers:[2]

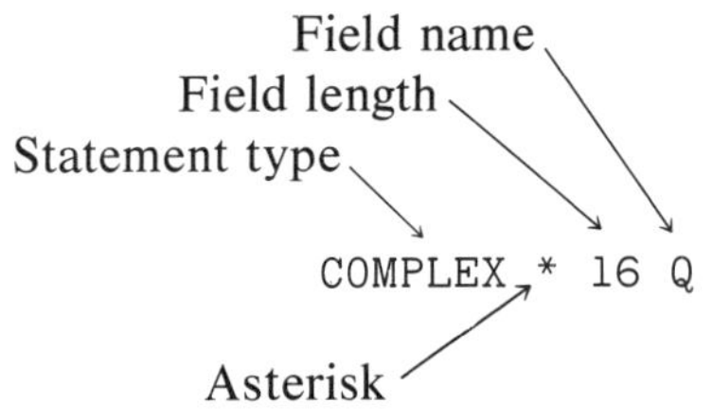

Complex number Q is read from the data card as two fields, each established by the COMPLEX*16 statement as 8 bytes.

```
11 READ (5,12) Q
12 FORMAT (2D15.2)
```

The example uses the D format. E or F formats can be used without altering the length, however, because the COMPLEX specification assigns 16 bytes of storage for Q.

Alphameric Uses of Complex*16 Type Specification

Even though complex numbers are rarely used in more customary business operations, the COMPLEX*16 specification has an unex-

[2]A few large FORTRAN compilers now have a COMPLEX*32 specification. It has all characteristics of the COMPLEX*16 specification except that each field has twice as much assigned storage space.

pected value for nonmathematical programming: more alphameric characters can be called by one complex field name than by any other type specification. The COMPLEX*16 alphameric field is especially valuable for data that is only input and output, not sorted or otherwise manipulated. This limitation exists because complex fields are two separate numbers to the compiler and complex numbers cannot be compared in IF statements. As a result, data in complex fields cannot be sorted into ascending or descending order.

Each COMPLEX field requires the listing of two fields in FORMAT statements, but only one field name is given in READ and WRITE statements:

```
    COMPLEX * 16 MESSAG
  4 READ (5,5) MESSAG
  5 FORMAT (2A8)
    .
    .
    .
 16 WRITE (6,17) MESSAG
 17 FORMAT (T53,2A8)
```

The COMPLEX*16 specification establishes 16-byte complex field MESSAG. Statements 4 and 5 input a data card with MESSAG in the first columns:

```
         11111111112
12345678901234567890
JUDY'S BOUTIQUE
```

Statements 16 and 17 instruct the computer to print MESSAG centered on the page for a heading:

```
                    JUDY'S BOUTIQUE
```

Notice that printing an apostrophe or single quotation mark does not require two apostrophes in this construction since the phrase is not enclosed in apostrophes.

Storing 16 characters with one field name is even more useful when different messages are to be output under various conditions. For example, by the logic of a program, an integer field called IVALUE can contain the integers 1, 2, or 3. After each data card containing IVALUE is read, one of three phrases is printed, depending upon the contents of field IVALUE. A flowchart illustrates the program logic on page 258.

First the COMPLEX*16 specification establishes array NOTE with three elements, each stored in 16 bytes:

```
COMPLEX * 16 NOTE(3)
```

The three values of NOTE are read by statements 1 and 2.

```
1 READ (5,2) NOTE
2 FORMAT (6A8)
```

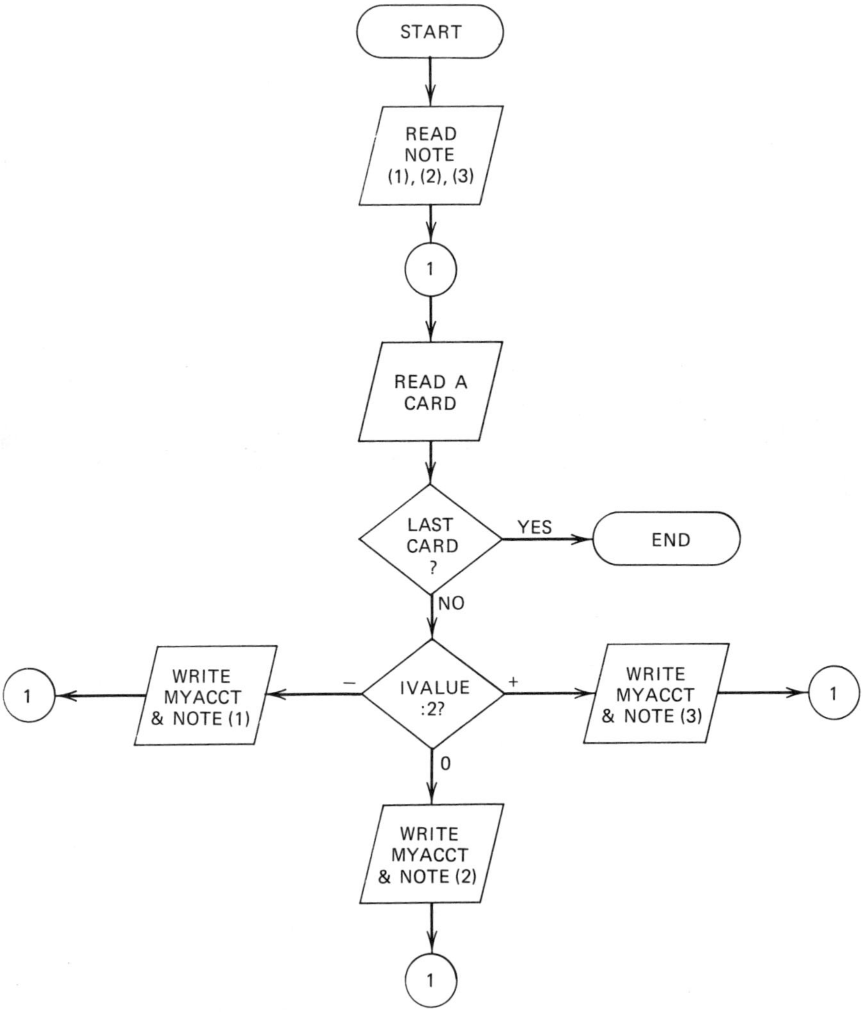

An array of three complex fields is listed in the READ statement. Because each complex number is stored as two fields, six A8 fields are listed in the FORMAT statement. The single data card contains three separate messages.

```
         11111111112222222222333333333344444444445
12345678901234567890123456789012345678901234567890
SELL IMMEDIATELYWAIT TWO DAYS   BUY 100 SHARES
```

With array NOTE input, the main part of the program reads the remaining data cards. Among the fields input is integer field IVALUE:

```
3 READ(5,4) MYACCT,AMOUNT, OLDBAL, IVALUE
4 FORMAT (I5,2F6.2,I2)
```

A line is printed using IVALUE as a subscripting value of complex number NOTE:

```
16 WRITE (6,17)MYACCT,NOTE (IVALUE)
17 FORMAT (T10, I5, 3X, 2A8)
```

When IVALUE contains 1, the first element of array NOTE is printed. For example, the following line might be output:

```
23750    SELL IMMEDIATELY
```

When IVALUE contains 2, the second element is output, and when IVALUE contains 3, the third element is printed.

This ability to output various messages, each containing up to 16 characters (or 32 characters when COMPLEX*32 is available), gives the programmer considerable flexibility. The subscripting integer can be either input or the result of calculations, Many lists, such as departments of a store or branches of a company, can be stored and output in this way.

REVIEW QUESTIONS

16. How many fields comprise each complex number?
17. How are complex numbers useful with alphameric data?

Length Specification Variations

The length assignment feature can be overridden within type specification statements. For example:

```
REAL * 8 TOTAL1, TOTAL2, ITEMS * 4, CNT (5,10)
```

The above statement established TOTAL1 and TOTAL2 as 8-byte real fields, ITEMS as a 4-byte real field, and CNT as an array with each of its 50 (5 × 10) elements in 8-byte locations. Although CNT follows ITEMS, the 4-byte specification applies only to ITEMS. The original (REAL * 8) length specification applies to every variable or array listed unless the name is followed by an asterisk and the overriding length (ITEMS * 4). This capability is available for all field types with both optional and standard lengths.

SUMMARY OF FORTRAN FIELD TYPES
AND LENGTHS IN STORAGE

Field Type	Standard Length (in bytes)	Optional Length (in bytes)
INTEGER	4	2
REAL	4	8
DOUBLE PRECISION	8	—
COMPLEX	8	16 or 32
(LOGICAL	4	1)[2]

IMPLICIT Specification Statement

IMPLICIT is a comparatively new FORTRAN statement not included in all FORTRAN compilers. It does not change the field type of *individual* fields and arrays as do INTEGER, REAL, DOUBLE PRECISION, and COMPLEX specifications. Instead the IMPLICIT specification changes *all* fields or arrays with first letters of their field names included in an IMPLICIT statement. For example:

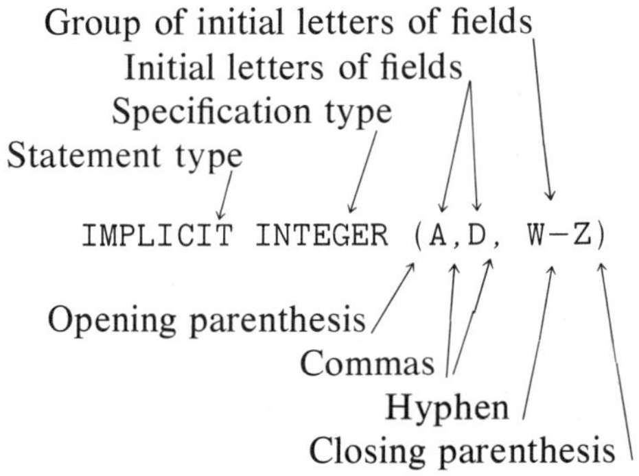

This IMPLICIT statement changes the name convention so that not only field and array names beginning with I-N but also those beginning with A, D, W, X, Y, or Z will be stored as integers and input and output with I formats.

Implicit specification statements, which cannot be numbered, begin with the word IMPLICIT, followed immediately by the specification type. The initial letters for which the FORTRAN name conventions are changed are then listed in parentheses. As the example demonstrates, single letters can be listed or a group of letters can be written with a hyphen (minus sign; 11 punch) between the first and last letters of the

[2]Logical constants are discussed in chapter 23.

group. If more than one letter or group of letters is listed, they must be separated by commas. Any letter of the alphabet or the dollar sign (the last "letter" of the FORTRAN alphabet) may be listed in an IMPLICIT statement. Letters need not be listed in their alphabetic order except that group letters include not only the letters listed but all those between in the alphabet.

The IMPLICIT specification can also be utilized in length change:

```
IMPLICIT INTEGER * 2 (I)
```

All fields and elements of arrays with I as the first letter of their name are now stored in 2-byte storage locations.

This ability to establish field types with either standard or optional field lengths is also followed when IMPLICIT specifications establish the other field types. The only exception is DOUBLE PRECISION which cannot be used in IMPLICIT statements. The following are examples of IMPLICIT statements:

```
IMPLICIT REAL (L-N, I)
IMPLICIT REAL *8 (D)
IMPLICIT COMPLEX (P,K,C)
IMPLICIT COMPLEX *16 (A, E-H)
```

Only one IMPLICIT type specification is permitted in a program. Therefore, more than one field type can be specified in a single IMPLICIT specification statement. For example:

```
IMPLICIT INTEGER (W-$), REAL *8 (L,B), COMPLEX (T)
```

Commas are required between field types when more than one type is listed in a single statement.

IMPLICIT statements *cannot* establish arrays. DIMENSION capability statements must be used for arrays affected by IMPLICIT statements. Since field type must be set for arrays before storage is reserved, the IMPLICIT specification must be the first statement in a program. The following IMPLICIT and DIMENSION statements illustrate the use of a DIMENSION statement with the IMPLICIT specification when establishing an array:

```
IMPLICIT REAL * 8 (N)
DIMENSION NUMBRS (10,10)
```

All fields and array elements with names beginning with N are stored as 8-byte real fields. Arrays like NUMBRS, however, must be established in a DIMENSION-like statement following the IMPLICIT statement.

If an IMPLICIT statement establishes all fields beginning with a certain letter as a particular field type, the programmer can override this rule for specific fields. He does this by using an explicit type specification *after* the IMPLICIT statement, overriding the IMPLICIT specification in the same way the IMPLICIT statement overrides standard name conventions. For example:

```
IMPLICIT INTEGER (A-D)
REAL BONDS, CHANGE
```

The IMPLICIT statement specifies all field names beginning with the letters A, B, C, or D as integers. The explicit REAL type specification overrides the IMPLICIT specification for fields BONDS and CHANGE so that, despite their initial letters, BONDS and CHANGE are real fields.

REVIEW QUESTIONS

18. When are DIMENSION statements required with IMPLICIT statements?
19. How many IMPLICIT statements can be in a program?
20. How can a programmer override an IMPLICIT statement?

OBJECTIVES REVIEW

Look at the objectives at the beginning of this chapter. Check each one to be certain you have achieved it. Restudy the chapter sections related to any objective you cannot perform.

ASSIGNMENTS

Prepare a card layout form, printer spacing chart, and flowchart for one of the following problems. Then write, keypunch, and submit the FORTRAN program.

1. Print stockholders; equity for branch offices of a nationwide company.

Input Records

Fields	Card Columns	
Branch number	59-60	I2
Partnership code	2	A1
Number of common stocks (in hundreds)	51-56	F6.0
Number of preferred stocks (in hundreds)	61-65	F5.0

Calculations. Create 2-byte integer fields for branch number and for partnership code. When an "A" is the partnership code, no calculations are executed, but the word "Partnership" is printed in a special rightmost column. For all other entries (including blank), equity is determined by adding common stock to preferred stock. These two fields are then added to the total number of each type of stock and to the stockholder's equity for the entire company. The number of nonpartnership branches is counted; after the last record is processed, the average amount of stockholders' equity is calculated.

The printed report begins with company name and location and column headings. Nonpartnership detail lines contain all input fields and the stockholders' equity for each branch. After the last record is processed, the company totals and averages are printed.

2. A boutique pays for some of its sales items by a piece rate plan, that is, the rate per piece is multiplied by the number of pieces produced. A bonus is paid to all employees producing more than 500 pieces.

Input Records

Fields	Card Columns	
Name of seller	1-20	(A)
Seller's number	23-26	(I4)
Rate per piece	52-54	(F3.2)
Number of pieces	32-34	(I3)

Calculations. Store seller's number and number of pieces as 2-byte integer fields. Calculate payment by multiplying rate per piece times number of pieces produced. If number produced is greater than 500, a 5% bonus is earned. Calculate the bonus and add it to payment. Count the sellers receiving a bonus, and total the bonuses. Total all payments.

Output. Headings contain boutique shop name, date of report, and column headings. Detail lines contain all input fields, piece rate payment, bonus if paid, and combined payment. After all records are processed, print total bonus, total payment, and the number of sellers receiving a bonus.

3. Sales records are arranged sequentially for daily totals.

Input Records

Fields	Card Columns	
Stock item number	21-22	(I2)
Clerk identification number	26-27	(I2)
Quantity sold	33-36	(I4)
Unit price	52-55	(F4.2)

Calculations. Calculate amount of sale by multiplying quantity sold times the unit price. Total the quantity sold and the amount of sale. Count all sales with quantities greater than 2000. Store stock item number and clerk identification number as 2-byte integer fields. Store the totals as double precision fields.

Output. Headings include company name and location and column headings. Detail lines contain all input fields and amount of sale. If quantity is greater than 2000, print as asterisk (*) after quantity field.

After all records are processed, print total quantity, total amount of sale, and number of sales greater than 2000.

4. A store requires a report showing the operating profits for each of its departments, and for the entire store.

Input Records

Fields	Card Columns	
Department number	48-49	(I2)
Gross sales and allowances	38-45	(F8.2)
Cost of merchandise	71-77	(F7.2)
Sales returns	52-57	(F6.2)
Expenses	31-36	(F6.2)

Calculations. Store department numbers as 2-byte integer fields. Store all money fields as double precision fields. Calculate net sales, gross margin, and operating profit for each department. Total all money fields for the entire store. Net sales equal gross sales minus sales returns and allowances. Gross margin equals net sales minus the cost of merchandise. Operating profit equals gross margin minus expenses.

Output. Headings include store name and location, and column headings. Detail lines contain all input fields, net sales, gross margin, and operating profit. After all records are processed, print all totals.

5. A company being liquidated is selling all its usable assets.

Input Records

Fields	Card Columns	
Asset identification number	23-27	I5
Book value	31-36	F6.2
Sale price	52-57	F6.2
Department number	21	I1

Create a COMPLEX*16 array with five elements for a special data card to be input before other data. In this data card, keypunch names of five store departments, 16 columns per name. Determine whether the sale was a profit or a loss and by how much above or below book value the sale price was. Total book values, sale prices, sales profits, and losses. After all records are processed, determine whether the sale of assets yielded a profit or loss for the company.

Headings include company name, date of report, and column headings. Detail lines contain name of the department (called out by subscripting the array), asset identification number, book value, sale price, and profit-or-loss designation. A minus sign is printed immediately after any loss amount. After all records are processed, print all totals and a statement of profit or loss with the final amount.

Xerox 530 with magnetic tape and printer.

Chapter Objectives

1. Be able to use the DATA specification statement to establish initial values for numeric fields.
2. Be able to use the DATA specification to establish fields containing literals.
3. Be able to use the DATA specification to initialize arrays and individual array elements with numeric values or literals.
4. Be able to explain the order by which multidimensional arrays are stored.
5. Be able to use implied DO loops to initialize arrays in DATA specifications.
6. Be able to use the DATA specification capability with type specification statements.

16

DATA Specification Statement

Many FORTRAN compilers contain the DATA specification statement. It initializes values *before* a program begins execution. The DATA statement can initialize any field or array element, whether numeric or alphameric, in integer, real, or complex form, of either standard or optional length. Usually logical fields (discussed in chapter 23) and hexadecimal data forms are also permitted.

Like other specification statements, the DATA statement is nonexecutable. That is, it establishes its information during the compilation cycle when FORTRAN source language statements are translated into machine language instructions. Since FORTRAN compilation time is much faster than its execution time, DATA statement initialization saves program time. Initializing during compilation time also saves main storage space because instructions for execution-time initializing are not stored with other program instructions.

Data specifications must *follow* any specification statement (such as DIMENSION or type specification) that refers to variables or arrays in the DATA statement. Except for this restriction, however, DATA statements can occur anywhere within a program. Unlike other specification statements, they need not come before executable statements. The programmer must remember, however, that no matter where in the program such statements occur, the listed values are established during compilation time, *before* execution time begins. Thus, regardless of whether they were established earlier by DATA statements or by input or calculations, values *cannot be reestablished* by DATA specifications during the execution of a program.

Initializing Variables

The DATA specification statement, which cannot be numbered, has a simple form although variations give it great flexibility. For example, fields can be established separately:

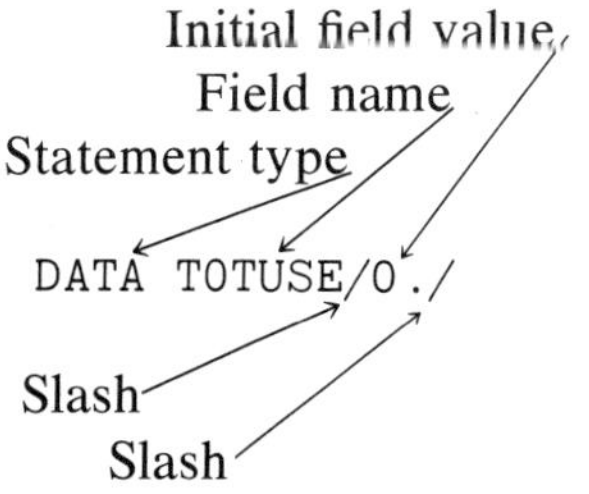

The DATA statement always begins with the word DATA in column 7 or later. The name of a field to be initialized (TOTUSE) is listed immediately following the word DATA. The value of the field when the program begins (0.) is then given between a pair of slashes.

If other fields are initialized, a comma must separate each closing slash from the name of the next field:

```
DATA TOTUSE/0./, RATE/.7/, KOUNT/0/
```

In the statement above, one integer and two real fields are initialized. TOTUSE is established as 0.; RATE is set at .7; KOUNT is equal to 0. The DATA list can contain an unlimited number of fields of any or all types.

A variation of this most basic form of the DATA specification establishes the same three values in a somewhat different way:

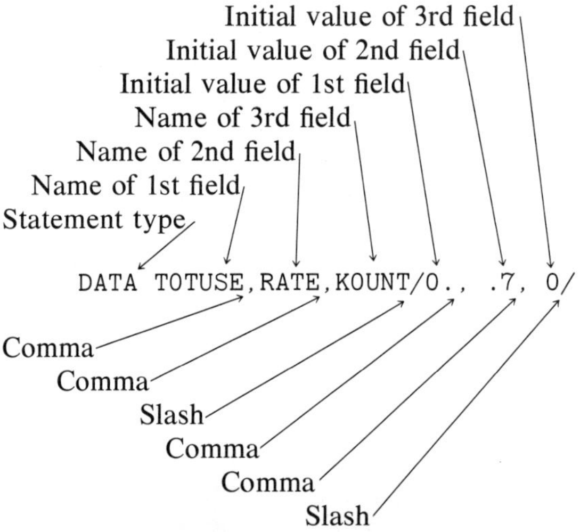

The three fields being initialized (TOTUSE,RATE,KOUNT) are listed together. The last field name is followed by a pair of slashes enclosing the three initializing values (0., .7, and 0). Both the field names and the initializing values are separated by commas. Fields and values are matched in the order by which they are listed. Thus, in this form also, TOTUSE equals 0., RATE equals .7, and KOUNT equals 0.

The data between the slashes must be either numeric as in the DATA statements establishing TOTUSE, RATE, and KOUNT, or a literal enclosed in single quotation marks. The following DATA specification includes a literal:

```
REAL*8 CO
DATA TOTUSE/0./, RATE/ .7/, KOUNT/0/,CO/'COMPANY:'/
```

The REAL type specification statement establishes CO as an 8-byte (double precision) real field. Therefore, it can contain the 8-character alphameric literal COMPANY:. To output field CO during the program requires an A8 format:

```
1 WRITE(6,2)CO
2 FORMAT(T10,A8)
```

The literal COMPANY: will print without the enclosing apostrophes. This ability to establish alphameric literals with field names is very useful.

The DATA specification statement accepts real numbers not only in decimal digit form but in the exponential D and E formats as well. For example:

```
DOUBLE PRECISION Z
DATA X,Y,Z/31.25,2.1E2,1.82D3/
```

X is input in decimal digit form, Y in single precision E format, and Z in double precision D format. All are acceptable forms.

When complex numbers are established in arithmetic assignment statements, the two fields comprising the complex number must be enclosed in a pair of parentheses:

```
  COMPLEX G
3 G = (1.0, 2.3)
```

In a DATA specification (and when reading data from punched cards) parentheses are not present:

```
COMPLEX G2
DATA G2/1.0,2.3/
```

At the beginning of execution, complex variable G2 contains the same values that complex variable G will contain after the execution of assignment statement 3: 1.0 and 2.3.

REVIEW QUESTIONS

1. Where can DATA specifications be placed in a program?
2. When does DATA statement initialization occur?
3. How are fields with literals established in DATA specifications?

Hexadecimal Representation

The most frequently encountered combinations of the 8 bits in a byte are listed in both binary and hexadecimal (base 16) form in Appendix E. Hexadecimal representation of numerals and characters is used most frequently in Assembly Language, but it can also be utilized in many versions of FORTRAN IV. In a DATA specification, any type of field or array element can be initialized in hexadecimal representation if Z is the first character between the slashes. For example:

```
DATA ONETWO/ZF1F2/
```

Real field ONETWO contains the *input/output* form of the numbers 1 and 2. In other computer manipulations, however, the same combination of bits represents the decimal value 61,938. Thus, numeric hexadecimal representation is tricky because the computer utilizes numbers in one form for input and output, and in other forms for calculations and manipulations.

Alphabetic data can also be input with hexadecimal representation. For example:

```
REAL*8 ALPHA
DATA ALPHA/ZC1D3D7C8C1C2C5E3/
```

Eight-character field ALPHA contains the hexadecimal representation of the letters ALPHABET. Of course the computer is unaware of the fact that this is alphameric data. No apostrophes are required. Numeric manipulations with field ALPHA would reveal it as an astronomically large but negative number.

Initializing Arrays

The chapter on the DO statement discussed the value of DO loops in initializing arrays. For instance, if a 50-element array should begin the program with all zeros, elements of the array are initialized in a DO loop by the following two statements:

```
6 DO 7 I = 1,50
7 ARRAY(I) =0.
```

A 100 × 50 two-dimensional array is initialized by three statements:

```
16 DO 18 I=1,100
17 DO 18 J=1,50
18 ARRAY2(I,J)=0.
```

This procedure can be extended for as many dimensions as the array contains. It consumes considerable execution time, however, because ARRAY requires 50 executions of statement 7 to clear all 50 elements, and ARRAY2 requires 5000 executions of statement 18 to clear its 100 × 50 elements.

If values must be reset *during* a program, this technique still must be followed. A large percentage of the time, though, such value-setting is required only at the *beginning* of a program. Then a DATA statement can save both execution time and main storage space for instructions.

First a DIMENSION statement establishes the array:

```
DIMENSION ITEMS (25)
```

After the DIMENSION statement reserves space for the 25 elements of array ITEMS, then the DATA statement initializes the entire array to the same value by a replication factor:

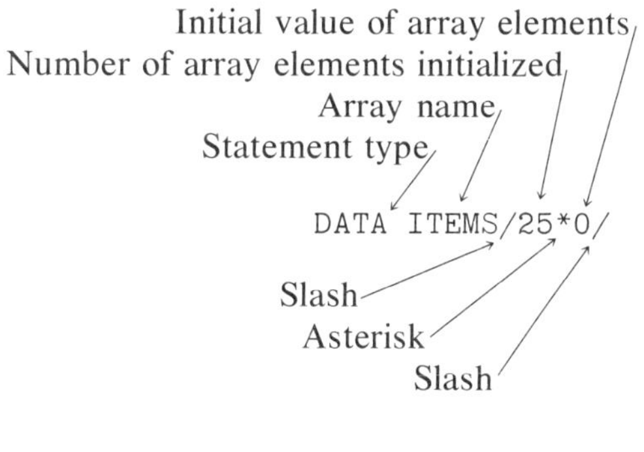

The array name is listed immediately after the word DATA. Because the array name is given without a subscript, the compiler assumes that the entire array is being initialized. Within the pair of slashes, integer 25 (the replication factor), the asterisk, and 0 establish the 25 elements of array ITEMS with the value of 0 before the program begins execution.

The replication form can be used even when all elements of an array will not contain the same value. For example, ASCEND is a one-dimensional array with 30 elements. At the beginning of the program, the first five elements of the array must equal 0.; the second five elements, 1.; the next five elements, 2.; elements 16-19, 3.; elements 20-25,

4.; elements 26-30, 5. After a DIMENSION statement, values are established by this form of the DATA specification:

```
DATA ASCEND/5*0.,5*1.,5*2.,4*3.,6*4.,5*5./
```

The compiler follows the order of entries and establishes the values for all 30 elements of array ASCEND.

All elements in an array need not be initialized. Separate elements can be initialized by using a subscripting numeral. Variable names are not permitted as subscripts in DATA specifications.

```
DIMENSION DEFINS (25)
DATA DEFINS(10)/2.0/, DEFINS(20)/3.0/
```

Elements 10 and 20 of array DEFINS are initialized to 2.0 and 3.0, respectively. The other 23 elements are not defined; therefore, their contents are unknown at the beginning of program execution.

The programmer must watch the order of field and array names and the order of their listed contents because the computer stores data in the order by which the variables are listed. The programmer also must see that the number of field names or array elements equals the number of values.

A special caution must be used in establishing two- or three- (or larger) dimension arrays. If elements are subscripted, their contents are stored in the order by which the elements are listed. Most frequently, however, the entire array is initialized by listing only the array name. If all elements are initialized to the same value, there is no problem. For example:

```
DIMENSION ARRAY(5,6)
DATA ARRAY /30*0./
```

All 30 elements of the 6 × 5 array are set to 0.

When array elements are initialized to different values, however, knowledge of the order by which the computer stores arrays is essential to correct placement of constants. For example, ARRAY1 is to be established as a 5 × 6 array with the following values:

I ↓ J→	1	2	3	4	5	6
1	0.	0.	0.	0.	0.	0.
2	1.	1.	1.	1.	1.	1.
3	1.	1.	1.	1.	1.	1.
4	2.	2.	2.	2.	2.	2.
5	2.	2.	2.	2.	2.	2.

The first array subscript (I) is considered the row counter; the second subscript (J) is the column counter. The entire first row is to be filled with 0's; the second and third rows with 1's; the fourth and fifth rows with 2's. If the programmer wrote the DATA statement that seems so obvious, values would be stored differently from what he wants:

```
DIMENSION ARRAY1 (5,6)
DATA ARRAY1 /6*0., 12*1., 12*2./
```

This DATA statement stores ARRAY1 in the following way:

I ↓ J→	1	2	3	4	5	6
1	0	0	1	1	2	2
2	0	1	1	1	2	2
3	0	1	1	1	2	2
4	0	1	1	2	2	2
5	0	1	1	2	2	2

This results from the FORTRAN compiler rule that the first subscripting value changes fastest, then each succeeding subscripted value. Thus ARRAY1 is stored in this order: 1,1; 2,1; 3,1; 4,1; 5,1; 1,2; 2,2; 3,2; 4,2; 5,2; 1,3; 2,3; 3,3; 4,3; 5,3; 1,4; 2,4; 3,4; 4,4; 5,4; 1,5; 2,5; 3,5; 4,5; 5,5; 1,6;2,6; 3,6; 4,6; 5,6. 0's are stored in the first 6 elements, 1's in the next 12 elements, and 2's in the last 12 elements of ARRAY1.

This formula is utilized by all multidimensional arrays. A $3\times4\times5$ three-dimensional array is stored from a DATA specification in the following manner:1,1,1; 2,1,1; 3,1,1; 1,2,1; 2,2,1; 3,2,1; 1,3,1; 2,3,1; 3,3,1; 1,4,1; 2,4,1; 3,4,1; 1,1,2; 2,1,2; 3,1,2; 1,2,2; 2,2,2; 3,2,2; 1,3,2; 2,3,2; 3,3,2; 1,4,2; 2,4,2; 3,4,2; 1,1,3; 2,1,3; 3,1,3; 1,2,3; 2,2,3; 3,2,3; 1,3,3; 2,3,3; 3,3,3; 1,4,3; 2,4,3; 3,4,3; 1,1,4; 2,1,4; 3,1,4; 1,2,4; 2,2,4; 3,2,4; 1,3,4; 2,3,4; 3,3,4; 1,4,4; 2,4,4; 3,4,4; 1,1,5; 2,1,5; 3,1,5; 1,2,5; 2,2,5; 3,2,5; 1,3,5; 2,3,5; 3,3,5; 1,4,5; 2,4,5; 3,4,5.

Sometimes the problem of row initialization can be solved simply by turning the array on its side. Then the rows become columns, and the columns become rows. For example:

```
DIMENSION ARRAY2 (6,5)
DATA ARRAY2 / 6*0., 12*1., 12*2./
```

Then the field array looks like this:

J ↓ I→	1	2	3	4	5
1	0	1	1	2	2
2	0	1	1	2	2
3	0	1	1	2	2
4	0	1	1	2	2
5	0	1	1	2	2
6	0	1	1	2	2

Of course, the programmer must then alter the subscripting order of the array wherever it appears in the program.

At other times, especially with multidimensioned arrays, the simplest solution is to read in the data as constants:

```
DIMENSION IARRAY (5,6)
DATA IARRAY/0,1,1,2,2,0,1,1,2,2,0,1,1,2,2,0,1,1,2,2,0,1,1,2,2,0,1,1,2,2/
```

The array is stored as the programmer wants: 0's in the first row; 1's in the second and third rows; 2's in the fourth and fifth rows.

The replication form is not reserved exclusively for arrays. For example, when several fields are to be set to 0's and others to 1's, the following statements could be used:

```
DIMENSION TABLE (4,10)
DATA A,TOTAL1,TOTAL2, ACCUM, QUANT, TABLE, ONE, COM, VALUE/45*0.,3*1./
```

Fields A, TOTAL1, TOTAL2, ACCUM, and QUANT, and all elements of array TABLE, are set to 0. Fields ONE, COM, and VALUE are established as 1.

Literals in Arrays

The array-initializing aspect of the DATA statement is valuable in working with literals, which are enclosed by apostrophes. For example, several company names are used in a report. Appropriate company names must be retrieved from an input identification number. Although the possibilities are virtually limitless, let us assume that five company names are required: ABC ENTERPRISES, J WILLS: AZALEAS, DATA HANDLERS, PAUL MARTIN INC., SICILIA & PAYNE. Each company has an assigned identification number, ranging in order from 1 to 5.

First, the programmer establishes array NAMES as a 5-element array, with each element assigned 16 bytes with a COMPLEX * 16 specification. Then company names are initialized into the array:

```
 COMPLEX * 16 NAMES (5)
 DATA NAMES/'ABC ENTERPRISES','J WILLS: AZALEAS', 'DATA HANDLERS'
1,'PAUL MARTIN INC.','SICILIA & PAYNE'/
```

When the program begins execution, the 16-byte complex field NAMES(1) contains ABC ENTERPRISES; NAMES(2) contains J WILLS: AZALEAS; NAMES(3) contains DATA HANDLERS; NAMES(4) contains PAUL MARTIN INC.; and NAMES(5) contains SICILIA & PAYNE. (If 16 alphameric characters are not enclosed in a literal, blanks "pad" the remaining rightmost positions.)

Because these literals are stored as complex fields, they cannot be used in sorting or other comparison operations, but they are valuable for printed reports. For example, a column in the data record is designated KODE. It contains the assigned integer identification number 1,2,3,4, or 5. After the data record is read, the company name can be printed with the following:

```
   WRITE (6,21) NAMES (KODE)
21 FORMAT ('1',T50, 2A8)
```

If KODE equals 2, J WILLS: AZALEAS is printed at the top of a new page. (Note that complex numbers have one name but two format fields.)

A different kind of heading can appear if the variable CO is also included as a DATA specification literal:

```
   COMPLEX * 16 NAMES (5)
   REAL * 8 CO
   DATA NAMES/'ABC ENTERPRISES', 'J WILLS: AZALEAS',
  1'DATA HANDLERS', 'PAUL MARTIN INC.', 'SICILIA & PAYNE'
  2/, CO/'COMPANY:'/
22 READ (5,23)...KODE
23 FORMAT (...I1)
24 WRITE (6,25) CO, NAMES(KODE)
25 FORMAT (26X, A8, 2X, 2A8)
```

If KODE equals 4, the top line of the page now reads:

```
COMPANY:  PAUL MARTIN INC.
```

Thus, the initializing characteristics of the DATA specification increase the flexibility of FORTRAN.

REVIEW QUESTIONS

4. What must be the first character in a hexadecimal constant?
5. In what order are multidimension arrays stored?
6. In a DATA statement, what kind of data is enclosed by apostrophes?

In program USAGE-DATA, array MESSAG contains three alphameric elements. They are established in the DATA statement:

```
DIMENSION MESSAG(3),N(5)
DATA MESSAG/' 5%','10%','   '/
```

Including the blank spaces, each element of the array is three characters long.

The program compares USAGE with 200.00. Each branch of the IF statement leads to a different value for K, the integer that is used to subscript array MESSAG in the printed detail line:

```
  271 IF (USAGE - 200.00) 218, 172, 175
C BRANCH WHEN USAGE EQUALS 200.00
  172 CHARGE = CHARGE * .95
  173 KNT95 = KNT95 + 1
  273 K = 1
  174 GO TO 18
C BRANCH WHEN USAGE IS GREATER THAN 200.00
  175 CHARGE = CHARGE * .9
  176 KNT90 = KNT90 + 1
  276 K = 2
  277 GO TO 18
C BRANCH WHEN USAGE IS LESS THAN 200.00
  218 K = 3
C DETAIL LINE
   18 WRITE (6,19) IDNUM, N, CREAD,PREAD,USAGE,CHARGE, MESSAG(K)
   19 FORMAT (5X,I5,5X,5A4,5X,F7.2,6X,F7.2,8X,F6.2,7X,F6.2,1X,A3)
```

The three elements of MESSAG must be the same length so that each will fit the A3 specification in FORMAT statement 19.

The demonstration data cards printed the following report with the special messages appearing on some detail lines:

```
                                   RENTA COMPUTER, INC.
                                       JUNE, 1974

ACCOUNT          ACCOUNT              CURRENT     PREVIOUS         USAGE        MONTHLY
NUMBER            NAME                READING     READING                       CHARGE

 12548    ANDERSCN JOSEPH             2247.36      2138.57        108.79        126.15
 24573    BROWN GORDON                3344.55      3245.67         98.88        119.22
 45342    BUTLER RANDOLPH             3687.52      3572.46        115.06        130.54
 55343    CATALETA PAULINE            1568.97      1154.86        414.11        305.89 10%
 75342    LEVY SAMUEL                 3189.54      2483.46        706.08        489.83 10%

                                                   TOTAL USAGE:  1442.92
                                                   AVERAGE USAGE: 288.58

 2 WITH 10% DISCOUNT;      0 WITH 5% DISCOUNT
```

Implied DO Loops

Some compilers permit the use of implied DO loops within DATA specification statements. This is particularly helpful when only sections of arrays are to be initialized. For example, array WORKRS contains 20 elements. The middle 10 elements do not require initialization. The first five and the last five elements must be initialized to 0's. This initialization is accomplished with implied DO loops in the DATA statement:

```
DIMENSION WORKRS(20)
DATA (WORKRS(I),I=1,5),(WORKRS(I),I=16,20)/10*0./
```

Elements 1-5 and 16-20 of array WORKS are initialized to 0 by the two implied DO loops. Elements 6-15 are established by the DIMENSION statement, but their contents are unknown.

When implied DO loops are used in DATA specifications, only numeric values can be used as parameters for the subscripting values. Variables (such as I = 1,KOUNT or I = BEGIN,KOUNT) are not permitted.

DATA Capability in Field Specification Statements

If a FORTRAN compiler contains the DATA statement, it ordinarily also contains the DATA specification capability for type specification statements (except DOUBLE PRECISION and IMPLICIT). This extra feature is illustrated by examples of explicit field specification statements:

```
INTEGER COUNT, TOTAL /0,0/
```

COUNT and TOTAL are established as integers, each with a value of 0 at the beginning of program execution.

```
INTEGER * 2 DATA(100)/100*0/
```

DATA is established as an array of 100 2-byte elements, each with the value of 0. This statement combines the capabilities of the INTEGER field specification, the DIMENSION, and the DATA specification statements.

If array elements are to contain one or two alphameric characters rather than digits, the following statement clears all elements of the array to blanks:

```
INTEGER * 2 LETTRS(100)/100*' '/
```

The blank between the single quotation marks is stored as an alphameric character in each of the 100 elements of LETTRS. Because literals that do not completely fill a field are "padded" with blanks to the rightmost end of the field, either one or two blanks between the quotation marks produce identical fields.

```
REAL * 8 CASH(5)/5*100.0/
```

The REAL field specification establishes all five elements of array CASH with values of 100.0. Each of the five elements is in an 8-byte storage location.

```
REAL PAYRAT(4)/1.52,2.43,3.3,4.25/,L,A,S,T/'THIS', 'IS','THE','END.'/
```

In this example, the four elements of real array PAYRAT are numeric variables. They can be used in calculations, and output with either F or E formats. Real fields L,A,S, and T are literals. Surprisingly, perhaps, they also can be used in some calculations. Their output (in meaningful form) requires the A format:

```
26 WRITE (6,27) L,A,S,T
27 FORMAT (1X,4(A4,1X))
```

Statements 26 and 27 print the following:

```
THIS IS     THE    END.
```

For more evenly spaced printing, fields L,A,S, and T should be established as:

```
REAL L,A,S,T/'THIS',' IS ','THE ','END.'/
```

Then a format specification with 1X, 4A4 prints:

```
THIS IS THE END.
```

The DOUBLE PRECISION specification is the only explicit type specification that cannot contain the data initialization capability. Therefore, its fields and arrays must be initialized in a separate DATA specification.

```
DOUBLE PRECISION MONEY(5), OVHEAD
DATA MONEY/5*100.0/,OVHEAD/0./
```

At the beginning of execution time, each of the five elements of array MONEY is equal to 100.0, and OVHEAD equals 0.

Because complex numbers consist of 2 fields (in mathematics the first is termed "real" and the second is termed "imaginary"), six constants are needed to satisfy the listing of three complex field names.

```
COMPLEX P,Q,R/1.1,2.1,2.7,3.2,1.2,3.5/
```

P is 1.1 and 2.1; Q is 2.7 and 3.2; R is 1.2 and 3.5.

The D format for double precision real fields is also acceptable. Each part of complex field TIME is 8 bytes in storage.

```
COMPLEX * 16 TIME/1.84D2,3.1D3/,ENERGY(6)12 * 0./
```

Twelve fields are set to 0 to initialize the six complex elements of array ENERGY.

REVIEW QUESTIONS

7. When are implied DO loops used in DATA statements?
8. If the FORTRAN compiler contains the DATA specification, which field specifications can utilize this capability?
9. If a literal does not have enough characters to fill the designated length, with what character does the compiler fill the field?

OBJECTIVES REVIEW

Study the objectives at the beginning of this chapter. Check each one to be certain you have achieved it. Restudy the chapter sections relating to any objective you cannot perform.

ASSIGNMENTS

Prepare a card layout form, printer spacing chart, and flowchart for one of the following problems. Then write, keypunch, and submit the FORTRAN program.

1. The speed with which the average merchandise is sold is a standard commonly used by retailers to determine operation efficiency. A service bureau processes the same stock turnover program for several companies. Using the DATA capability of the COMPLEX*16 specification, create a heading for each of the six companies in a 6-element array. Keypunch a special leading card with company number (from 1 to 6) in column 1.

Input Records

Fields	Card Columns	
Item number	23-27	I5
Sum of quantity in all inventories	51-57	F7.0
Number of inventories taken	71-72	I2
Total number sold	74-78	I5

Calculations. After reading the first data card containing the company number, call out the appropriate heading array element. To calculate the average number of inventories required, divide the sum of all the inventories by the number of inventories taken. To get the stock turnover, divide the total number sold by the average number of inventories required. Count the number of items. After the last record is processed, find the average stock turnover for all items.

Output. Print company headings, location, and date. Print column headings. Detail lines contain the input fields and stock turnover. After the last record is processed, print the number of items counted and the stock turnover average with appropriate messages.

2. A manager requires a modified purchaser's journal.

Input Records

Fields	Card Columns	
Department number	21	I1
Invoice number	23-27	I5
Purchaser's discount code	52	I1
Price	30-34	F5.2

Create a 2-element COMPLEX*16 array, with the messages '10% DISCOUNT' and '5% PENALTY.' Create 5-element array for department names.

Calculations. Determine invoice price by discount code. If the code is 1, 10% is deducted from price. If the code is 2, the price is increased 5% for late payment. If the code is 0 or 3-9, the invoice price is the same as the price. Total the prices and invoice prices. Total the purchasers' discounts. Count customers receiving discounts and customers with late penalties.

Output. Headings include company name and location, report date, and column headings. Detail lines contain department name, invoice number, price, and invoice price with messages when appropriate. After all records are processed, print three totals and two counts.

3. A radio station conducts a popularity contest in which listeners vote for the "top 10" musicians.

Input Records

Fields	Card Columns	
Listener's name	1-20	A
Listener call number	23-27	I5
Vote for musician	43	I1

Calculations. Create a 10-element COMPLEX*16 array containing the names of 10 different singers or musical groups. Create a 10-element INTEGER*2 array for counting votes, each element initialized to 0. Test vote for 0; if present, convert to 10 when subscripting name array. Total votes for each musician.

Output. Headings include radio station call letters and location, and date of the contest. Detail lines contain listener's name and call number, and the name of the musician for whom the listener voted. After all records are processed, print the list of 10 musicians with the total number of votes cast for each.

4. Print out net income for each branch office of a nationwide company.

Input Records

Fields	Card Columns	
District in which branch is located	54-55	I2
Branch office number	23-25	I3
Net sales	40-45	F6.2
Selling expenses	63-67	F5.2
General expenses	71-76	F6.2

Calculate the net income for each branch office by subtracting both types of expense from net sales. Create arrays to total net sales, selling expenses, general expenses, and net income for the district and the company. If the net income for a state is less than $2,000, print a special message, "Under consideration for discontinuance", to the right of the net income amount. If between $2,000 and $2,999, print "Needs help from Home Office"; if between $3,000 and $3,999, print "Marginal Operation"; if more than $4,000 but less than $6,000, no special message. If more than $6,000, print 'BONUS'. Determine message by computed GO TO.

Output. Headings include company name and address (established in DATA statement) and report date. First page also has column headings for detail lines. Detail lines contain input and calculated fields related to each office as its record is processed. (If tape output is available, these detail records could be output to the tape rather than printed.) When all records are processed, skip to a new page to print column headings for district subtotals and messages. (A test for 0 can be used to eliminate unreferenced array elements.) After all district information is printed, print company totals below the appropriate district columns.

5. Print a report of cash received from customers.

Input Records

Fields	Card Columns	
Customer number	23-27	I5
Customer name	1-20	A
Old balance	51-56	F6.2
Amount of payment	32-35	F4.2

Calculation. The amount of payment is subtracted from the old balance to obtain new balance. Total the amounts paid.

Output. Headings include name of loan company, location, date, and column headings. All except column headings are established in DATA statements. Detail lines contain all input fields and new balance. After all cards are processed, print total amounts paid.

Chapter Objectives

1. Be able to equivalence fields in order to conserve computer storage space.
2. Be able to equivalence individual field names with elements of arrays.
3. Be able to create subfields by the EQUIVALENCE statement.
4. Be able to equivalence a field that unintentionally has two or more names.
5. Be able to convert multidimensional subscripts into single dimension subscripts when single subscripts are required for an EQUIVALENCE statement.

17

The EQUIVALENCE Statement

The primary purpose of the EQUIVALENCE statement is to conserve computer storage space within a single program. It accomplishes this by enabling two or more quantities to share the same location in computer storage. This ability also permits the creation of subfields within an array. It has another, less formal use: it frequently eliminates the need to rewrite statements that are incorrect because of inaccurate keypunching of field names or from forgetfulness or lack of coordination between programmers working on different parts of the same program.

Like other specification statements, the EQUIVALENCE statement cannot be numbered. It must come before any executable statement. Individual fields, arrays, and array elements can be equivalenced.

EQUIVALENCE To Correct Errors

The use of the EQUIVALENCE statement to correct errors probably is an unintentional bonus rather than a planned effort by creators of the FORTRAN compiler. For instance, when two programmers work on different parts of the same problem, they may accidentally use different names for the same field or array. One programmer calls employee number EMPNUM, and the other calls it EMPLOY. One refers to ITEM and the other to ITEMS. These differences are important because the computer does not recognize that the same data fields are being referenced. Ordinarily, statements would need re-writing so that each field has only one name. The EQUIVALENCE statement, however, makes such rewriting unnecessary by giving more than one name to the same storage location. Two pairs of field names are equivalenced:

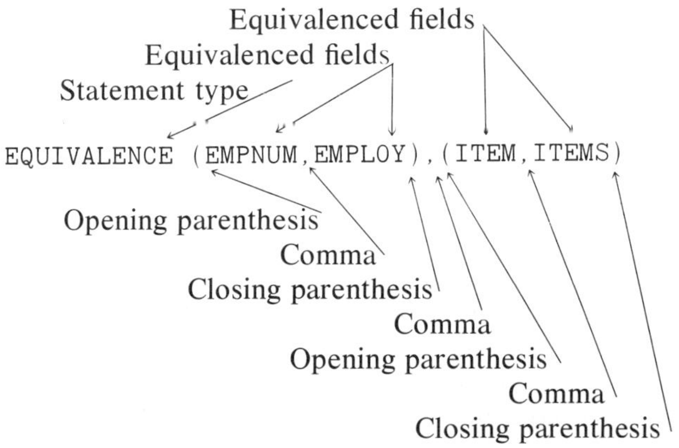

The word EQUIVALENCE must be the first word of the specification, beginning in column 7 or later. Names of variables being made equivalent to each other are enclosed in a pair of parentheses. Commas separate items listed within the parentheses. When the statement contains more than one set of parentheses, a comma separates the pairs of parentheses.

The EQUIVALENCE specification above establishes the fact that the first bytes of fields EMPNUM and EMPLOY are the same byte in storage, and that the first bytes of fields ITEM and ITEMS are the same. Since the fields are the same length and type in both cases, fields EMPLOY and EMPNUM now share the same bytes in storage. This means that they share the same storage contents. ITEMS and ITEM also share both location and contents. Therefore, statements using either field name are acceptable and need not be rewritten and keypunched.

Although it probably is not a practice to be encouraged, the EQUIVALENCE statement can serve essentially the same purpose if a keypunching error frequently occurs. For example, if the field name is TOPIC2, but several statements contain keypunching errors of TOPICZ or TOPICS, the three names can be equivalenced:

```
EQUIVALENCE (TOPICZ,TOPICS,TOPIC2)
```

All three names are recognized now as the same address location in storage.

REVIEW QUESTIONS

1. How can a field be referenced by two or more different names?
2. Where are EQUIVALENCE statements placed in a program?

The EQUIVALENCE Statement to Create Subfields

Sometimes the programmer finds his logic easier to develop if he can address specific data by more than one name. During part of the program, he wants an overall array name that will call out several fields easily. At other times, he wants to refer to a specific field or array within the larger array.

For example, a company compares prices of six competitive products. Each data card contains the item number, then the current prices of product A, product B, product C, etc. After the six prices are input, the average price is calculated. Although item number usually is an integer, there is no harm in listing it as a real number with no digits to the right of the decimal point. As a real number, it can be an element in an array consisting of item number, six prices, and average price.

A data card inputs the first seven elements of 8-element array COMPAR:

```
  DIMENSION COMPAR(8)
1 READ (5,2) (COMPAR(I),I=1,7)
2 FORMAT (F5.0, 6F7.2)
```

All elements in an array need not be the same *input* or *output* length. Only in *storage* are they required to be the same length, as the standard four bytes are for elements of COMPAR.

The average of the six products is calculated and stored as the eighth element of COMPAR:

```
3 TOT = 0.
4 DO 6 I = 2,7
5 TOT = TOT + COMPAR(I)
6 CONTINUE
7 COMPAR(8) = TOT / 6
```

After the six cycles of the DO loop, the average of the six prices is calculated and stored as COMPAR(8).

Later in the program, the programmer finds that logic is more apparent and coding is easier when he can use the terms ITEM and AVERAG instead of COMPAR(1) and COMPAR(8). He adds REAL and EQUIVALENCE statements to the beginning of his program:

```
REAL ITEM
DIMENSION COMPAR(8)
EQUIVALENCE (COMPAR(1),ITEM), (COMPAR(8),AVERAG)
```

The item number can now be called either COMPAR(1) or ITEM. The price average is either COMPAR(8) or AVERAG.

If the programmer wants to create more equivalences, each product price can be equivalenced with its product name, pairing COMPAR(2) with A, COMPAR(3) with B, etc.

A somewhat different use of subfield names is demonstrated by a store making a 10-week study of its sales records to see if a predictable pattern of buying exists on certain items. Each data card contains the test week number, the item number, and the number of items sold each of the six weekdays the store is open. The two-dimensional array *addresses* are pictured in matrix form in Table ARRAY 1.

For input and part of the output, all 80 array elements are needed. For certain calculations and for other output, however, the programmer needs to manipulate single days of the week. He wants to be able to refer to them by name and by week number. Therefore, in addition to two-dimensional array SALES, he also creates six 10-element arrays for the various days. All arrays are of the same numeric type:

```
INTEGER SALES(10,8),MON(10),TUES(10),WED(10),THUR(10),FRI(10),SAT(10)
```

The computer stores arrays continuously in storage, with the first subscripting number changing fastest. That is, the storing order of a two-dimensional array is *down* columns rather than *across* rows. Therefore, the arrays for each day can be equivalenced to the first SALES element for that day:

```
 EQUIVALENCE(SALES(1,3),MON(1)),(SALES(1,4),TUES(1)),(SALES(1,5),
/WED(1)),(SALES(1,6),THUR(1)),(SALES(1,7),FRI(1)),(SALES(1,8),SAT(1))
```

As Table ARRAY 2 shows, the address locations of SALES elements (1,3), (2,3), (3,3), (4,3), (5,3), (6,3), (7,3), (8,3), (9,3), and (10,3) are now also the locations of elements 1-10 of array MON. The same is true for each column representing a day of the week.

Calculations and output can utilize whichever array name is most appropriate.

This type of equivalence also demonstrates the importance of knowing exactly how the computer stores multidimensional arrays.

REVIEW QUESTIONS

3. Why is the storage pattern of multidimensional arrays important for the user of the EQUIVALENCE statement to know?
4. Can individual elements of an array be equivalenced? If so, how?

Conserving Storage Locations by Equivalence

The main purpose of the EQUIVALENCE statement is to conserve storage. This can also be its most complicated use. A simple illustration introduces the concept.

An employee's tax rate is input from a data card and stored. After the tax rate is used in calculating the employee's tax, the tax rate field

TABLE ARRAY 1

Week Number	Item Number	Monday	Tuesday	Wednesday	Thursday	Friday	Saturday
SALES(1,1)	SALES(1,2)	SALES(1,3)	SALES(1,4)	SALES(1,5)	SALES(1,6)	SALES(1,7)	SALES(1,8)
SALES(2,1)	SALES(2,2)	SALES(2,3)	SALES(2,4)	SALES(2,5)	SALES(2,6)	SALES(2,7)	SALES(2,8)
SALES(3,1)	SALES(3,2)	SALES(3,3)	SALES(3,4)	SALES(3,5)	SALES(3,6)	SALES(3,7)	SALES(3,8)
SALES(4,1)	SALES(4,2)	SALES(4,3)	SALES(4,4)	SALES(4,5)	SALES(4,6)	SALES(4,7)	SALES(4,8)
SALES(5,1)	SALES(5,2)	SALES(5,3)	SALES(5,4)	SALES(5,5)	SALES(5,6)	SALES(5,7)	SALES(5,8)
SALES(6,1)	SALES(6,2)	SALES(6,3)	SALES(6,4)	SALES(6,5)	SALES(6,6)	SALES(6,7)	SALES(6,8)
SALES(7,1)	SALES(7,2)	SALES(7,3)	SALES(7,4)	SALES(7,5)	SALES(7,6)	SALES(7,7)	SALES(7,8)
SALES(8,1)	SALES(8,2)	SALES(8,3)	SALES(8,4)	SALES(8,5)	SALES(8,6)	SALES(8,7)	SALES(8,8)
SALES(9,1)	SALES(9,2)	SALES(9,3)	SALES(9,4)	SALES(9,5)	SALES(9,6)	SALES(9,7)	SALES(9,8)
SALES(10,1)	SALES(10,2)	SALES(10,3)	SALES(10,4)	SALES(10,5)	SALES(10,6)	SALES(10,7)	SALES(10,8)

TABLE ARRAY 2

SALES(1,1)	SALES(1,2)	SALES(1,3) MON(1)	SALES(1,4) TUES(1)	SALES(1,5) WED(1)	SALES(1,6) THUR(1)	SALES(1,7) FRI(1)	SALES(1,8) SAT(1)
SALES(2,1)	SALES(2,2)	SALES(2,3) MON(2)	SALES(2,4) TUES(2)	SALES(2,5) WED(2)	SALES(2,6) THUR(2)	SALES(2,7) FRI(2)	SALES(2,8) SAT(2)
SALES(3,1)	SALES(3,2)	SALES(3,3) MON(3)	SALES(3,4) TUES(3)	SALES(3,5) WED(3)	SALES(3,6) THUR(3)	SALES(3,7) FRI(3)	SALES(3,8) SAT(3)
SALES(4,1)	SALES(4,2)	SALES(4,3) MON(4)	SALES(4,4) TUES(4)	SALES(4,5) WED(4)	SALES(4,6) THUR(4)	SALES(4.7) FRI(4)	SALES(4,8) SAT(4)
SALES(5,1)	SALES(5,2)	SALES(5,3) MON(5)	SALES(5,4) TUES(5)	SALES(5,5) WED(5)	SALES(5,6) THUR(5)	SALES(5,7) FRI(5)	SALES(5.8) SAT(5)
SALES(6,1)	SALES(6,2)	SALES(6,3) MON(6)	SALES(6,4) TUES(6)	SALES(6,5) WED(6)	SALES(6,6) THUR(6)	SALES(6,7) FRI(6)	SALES(6,8) SAT(6)
SALES(7,1)	SALES(7,2)	SALES(7,3) MON(7)	SALES(7,4) TUES(7)	SALES(7,5) WED(7)	SALES(7,6) THUR(7)	SALES(7,7) FRI(7)	SALES(7,8) SAT(7)
SALES(8,1)	SALES(8,2)	SALES(8,3) MON(8)	SALES(8,4) TUES(8)	SALES(8,5) WED(8)	SALES(8,6) THUR(8)	SALES(8,7) FRI(8)	SALES(8,8) SAT(8)
SALES(9,1)	SALES(9,2)	SALES(9,3) MON(9)	SALES(9,4) TUES(9)	SALES(9,5) WED(9)	SALES(9,6) THUR(9)	SALES(9,7) FRI(9)	SALES(9,8) SAT(9)
SALES(10,1)	SALES(10,2)	SALES(10,3) MON(10)	SALES(10,4) TUES(10)	SALES(10,5) WED(10)	SALES(10,6) THUR(10)	SALES(10,7) FRI(10)	SALES(10,8) SAT(10)

contents are no longer necessary in the program. In a later part of the program, however, a field containing the employee's calculated bonus is created and must be stored until printing. Information about this bonus has been fully utilized and is no further value by the time the next data card with another employee's tax rate is read. Therefore, because tax rate and bonus data never are needed simultaneously in the program, they can be assigned the same storage location without creating errors.

If the two fields are of the same length (see Chapter 15, Type Specification Statements), they share the entire storage location. Assuming that BONUS and TAXRAT are both standard 4-byte real fields, the two fields occupy the same 4 bytes of storage at different times in program execution. They can also share the full storage location if one is an integer and one is real, so long as both are standard 4-byte fields. If one is a 2-byte integer field, an 8-byte double precision or complex field, or a 16-byte complex field, first bytes are aligned.

This difference in lengths is especially important when arrays or array elements are equivalenced. Because arrays involve many storage locations, great quantities of computer storage can be saved when arrays are equivalenced. In one program, for example, a table (array) of pay rates is required in the early part of the program. After this use, the information is not necessary. Later in the program, however, a table (array) of subtotals is created and stored. Because the need for information from the first array is completely satisfied before the other array is created, the two arrays can occupy the same storage locations. Since each table contains 30 4-byte elements, equivalencing the first elements of the arrays enables them to share storage for the entire length of both arrays:

```
DIMENSION PAYRAT (30), SUBTOT(30)
EQUIVALENCE (PAYRAT(1),SUBTOT(1))
```

Because the computer stores arrays continuously in storage, and all elements of both arrays share storage locations, the EQUIVALENCE statement uses subscript (1) for both PAYRAT and SUBTOT. PAYRAT (2) and SUBTOT (2) share the 4-byte location immediately following the 4-byte location of the first element listed in the EQUIVALENCE statement. This pattern continues until both arrays are exhausted. The addresses of these *shared* storage locations can be shown pictorially:

PAYRAT (1) SUBTOT (1)	PAYRAT (2) SUBTOT (2)	PAYRAT (3) SUBTOT (3)	PAYRAT (4) SUBTOT (4)	PAYRAT (5) SUBTOT (5)	PAYRAT (6) SUBTOT (6)	PAYRAT (7) SUBTOT (7)	PAYRAT (8) SUBTOT (8)	⋯	PAYRAT (30) SUBTOT (30)

Any array in an EQUIVALENCE statement must be listed by a subscripted element. The graph demonstrates why elements from the same two arrays cannot be listed together more than once in

EQUIVALENCE statements. Either they duplicate the original alignment or they try to change the arrangement:

```
EQUIVALENCE (PAYRAT(2),SUBTOT(1)),(PAYRAT(1),SUBTOT(5))
```

The EQUIVALENCE statement above tries to establish a contradictory arrangement. Therefore, it is invalid.

Arrays often differ in the number of elements contained. Equivalence need not always start and end together. For example, PAYRAT again has 30 elements, but SUBTOT has only 10 elements. They still can share storage. Although the compiler does not require that both arrays begin with the first element, the following EQUIVALENCE statement establishes them in that order:

```
DIMENSION PAYRAT(30), SUBTOT (10)
EQUIVALENCE (PAYRAT(1), SUBTOT(1))
```

Pictorially, storage is arranged as follows:

PAYRAT (1) SUBTOT (1)	PAYRAT (2) SUBTOT (2)	PAYRAT (3) SUBTOT (3)	PAYRAT (4) SUBTOT (4)	PAYRAT (5) SUBTOT (5)	PAYRAT (6) SUBTOT (6)	PAYRAT (7) SUBTOT (7)

PAYRAT (10) SUBTOT (10)	PAYRAT (11)	PAYRAT (30)

The first 10 elements of PAYRAT share the same storage locations with 10-element array SUBTOT.

REVIEW QUESTIONS

5. Why is the EQUIVALENCE statement most useful with arrays?
6. Why is a knowledge of field length important when using the EQUIVALENCE statement?
7. What is the standard length of both integer and real fields?

A graph demonstrates other possibilities of equivalencing. For instance, PAYRAT contains 30 4-byte elements, and SUBTOT has only 10 elements. A third array, DEPTS, with 10 elements is also in the program now. Like SUBTOT, DEPTS is created and utilized only in the later part of the program. Therefore, the two shorter arrays can both utilize space occupied by PAYRAT during the first part of the program. In order not to overlay SUBTOT and DEPTS, however, all three arrays cannot begin with subscript (1). To begin DEPTS in storage immediately following SUBTOT requires the following specifications:

```
DIMENSION PAYRAT(30), SUBTOT(10), DEPTS(10)
EQUIVALENCE (PAYRAT(1), SUBTOT(1)), (PAYRAT(11),DEPTS(1))
```

This pairing of SUBTOT(1) with PAYRAT(1), and DEPTS(1) with PAYRAT(11) is shown graphically:

PAYRAT (1) SUBTOT (1)	PAYRAT (2) SUBTOT (2)	PAYRAT (3) SUBTOT (3)	PAYRAT (4) SUBTOT (4)	PAYRAT (5) SUBTOT (5)

PAYRAT (10) SUBTOT (10)	PAYRAT (11) DEPTS (1)	PAYRAT (12) DEPTS (2)	PAYRAT (13) DEPTS (3)	PAYRAT (14) DEPTS (4)	PAYRAT (20) DEPTS (10)

Because arrays are stored consecutively, only the first elements of SUBTOT and DEPTS need be listed. It is the programmer's responsibility to see that no unintentional overlap occurs.

Multidimension Array Subscripts

Multidimensioned arrays require special care in subscripting because *only the first variable listed* in an EQUIVALENCE parenthetical grouping can contain more than a single number as its subscript. To demonstrate, PAYRAT contains 30 elements but now it is a two-dimensional 5 × 6 array. If PAYRAT continues to be the first element listed in EQUIVALENCE parentheses, it may be listed with the double subscript used in other statements of the program. If it is not the first element listed, however, it must be specified by only one subscript number. Since computers really store multidimensional arrays as single arrays, single subscript specifications are available. This requires the programmer to be aware of how arrays are stored.

As pointed out earlier, in storing arrays, the FORTRAN compiler changes the first subscript most rapidly. The 5 × 6 array PAYRAT is stored in the following order:

R ↓ C→	1	2	3	4	5	6
1	1	6	11	16	21	26
2	2	7	12	17	22	27
3	3	8	13	18	23	28
4	4	9	14	19	24	29
5	5	10	15	20	25	30

Thus, if the programmer lists PAYRAT first, he can use either the single number subscript for PAYRAT:

```
EQUIVALENCE (PAYRAT(1),SUBTOT(1)),(PAYRAT(11),DEPTS(1))
```

or the double form used in other FORTRAN statements:

```
EQUIVALENCE (PAYRAT (1,1),SUBTOT(1)),(PAYRAT(1,3),DEPTS(1))
```

Because the PAYRAT element is listed first in both groupings, the double subscript can be used. If SUBTOT or DEPTS is listed first, however, only the single subscript can be used for PAYRAT:

```
EQUIVALENCE (SUBTOT(1),PAYRAT(1)), (DEPTS(1),PAYRAT(11))
```

Because PAYRAT is not the first element named in either group, it cannot use the double subscript form.

When two or more multidimensioned arrays are equivalenced, only the first one can utilize the multidimensional subscript. For instance, two tables can share storage because they are created and used in different sections of the program, with no danger of overlapping. TABLE1 is a 5 × 7 array; TABLE2 is a 6 × 6 array. MAJOR is a variable sharing storage with the last element of TABLE2. These equivalences can be created with different EQUIVALENCE statements:

```
EQUIVALENCE (TABLE1(1,1), TABLE2(1)),(TABLE2(6,6),MAJOR)
```

TABLE1 has a double subscripted number because it is the first element in the first equivalence group. Its equivalenced element of TABLE2 can use only the single subscript, however, because it is not the first item listed in the parentheses. In the second equivalence group, TABLE2 can use the double subscript because it is the first element listed. MAJOR is a variable and has no subscript.

When the listed fields are reversed, the subscripts must change:

```
EQUIVALENCE (TABLE2 (1,1),TABLE1(1)),(MAJOR, TABLE2(36))
```

As the first element of the first group, TABLE2 can use the double subscript. In the second group, however, it can use only the single subscript because it is not the first element listed. So long as the variables and arrays are properly aligned, the FORTRAN compiler permits the groupings to be in any order.

EQUIVALENCE With Length Differences

When equivalenced fields are of different lengths, alignments must be considered. For example, TOTAL is a 5 × 8 array of 40 REAL*8 elements, and ITEMS is a 12 × 15 array of 4-byte integers. The program completes its use of ITEMS before it creates TOTAL, and the two arrays can share storage locations despite their different lengths. The arrays are established and equivalenced in specification statements:

```
REAL*8 TOTAL (5,8)
DIMENSION ITEMS (12,15)
EQUIVALENCE (TOTAL (1,1),ITEMS(1))
```

Storage can be pictured in this way:

TOTAL (1,1)		TOTAL (2,1)		...
ITEMS (1,1)	ITEMS (2,1)	ITEMS (3,1)	ITEMS (4,1)	...

TOTAL (5,1)		TOTAL (1,2)		TOTAL (2,2)		...	TOTAL (5,8)		
ITEMS (9,1)	ITEMS (10,1)	ITEMS (11,1)	ITEMS (12,1)	ITEMS (1,2)	ITEMS (2,2)	...	ITEMS (7,7)	ITEMS (8,7)	...

Two elements of array ITEMS occupy the 8-byte locations reserved for *one* element of array TOTAL. Additionally, ITEMS has 100 4-byte elements stored beyond the equivalenced area that ITEMS and TOTAL share. This condition is completely acceptable to the FORTRAN compiler.

When arrays do not start their mutual storage locations with the first element of both arrays, programmers must be especially careful about alignment. The first element in each EQUIVALENCE group automatically begins at an 8-byte (Doubleword) storage alignment. Double precision or REAL * 8 fields also must begin on an 8-byte alignment. If EQUIVALENCE statements attempt to establish variables that break these rules of alignment, the specification is invalid. For example, TOTAL remains an array of REAL*8 elements. ITEMS and SUBTOT are arrays of 4-byte elements. An *invalid* condition arises if the following specifications are given:

```
READ * 8 TOTAL (5,8)
DIMENSION ITEMS (12,15),SUBTOT(4)
EQUIVALENCE (ITEMS(1,1),(SUBTOT(1)),(ITEMS(6,1),TOTAL(1))
```

The first equivalence group establishes ITEMS(1,1) and SUBTOT(1) on an 8-byte boundary. The second group tries to assign the first byte of TOTAL (1) to the same storage location as the first byte of ITEMS (6,1).

ITEMS (1,1)	ITEMS (2,1)	ITEMS (3,1)	ITEMS (4,1)	ITEMS (5,1)	ITEMS (6,1)	ITEMS (7,1)	ITEMS (8,1)	ITEMS (9,1)	ITEMS (10,1)
SUBTOT (1)	SUBTOT (2)	SUBTOT (3)	SUBTOT (4)		TOTAL (1,1)		TOTAL (2,1)		TOTAL (3,1)

ITEMS (11,1)	ITEMS (12,1)	ITEMS (1,2)	ITEMS (2,2)	ITEMS (3,2)	ITEMS (4,2)	ITEMS (5,2)	ITEMS (6,2)
	TOTAL (4,1)		TOTAL (5,1)		TOTAL (1,2)		TOTAL (2,2)

Because ITEMS (6,1) occupies the *second half* of an 8-byte location, REAL * 8 array TOTAL cannot begin with the proper alignment. Therefore, the EQUIVALENCE statement is invalid.

REVIEW QUESTIONS

8. How are multidimensioned arrays arranged in computer storage?
9. When must multidimension array elements be listed with a single subscript?
10. Why is alignment important with variables of different lengths?

OBJECTIVES REVIEW

Look at the objectives at the beginning of this chapter. Check each one to be certain you have achieved it. Restudy the chapter sections related to any you cannot perform.

ASSIGNMENTS

Prepare a card layout form, printer spacing chart, and flowchart for one of the following problems. Then write, keypunch, and submit the FORTRAN program.

1. An instructor gives five tests during a school term. A list of all students is required, with scores for each test, total score, and average test score for each student.

Input Records

Fields	Card Columns
Student name	1-20 (A)
Test 1 score	32-33 (I2)
Test 2 score	35-36 (I2)
Test 3 score	41-42 (I2)
Test 4 score	53-54 (I2)
Test 5 score	65-66 (I2)

Calculations. Create an array for the five test scores, final score, and average score. Make each element of the array equivalent to the appropriate test score name. Add the test scores for each student and then calculate the average test score. Total the scores for each test. Count the tested students. After all records are processed, calculate the average score for each test and for the sum of the tests.

Output. Headings include school name and location and column headings. Detail lines contain all input fields, student total score and average tested students. After all records are processed, calculate the average with explanatory messages.

2. A car dealer in a state with a 4% sales tax prints a report showing car price, sales tax, and combined amount for each sale and the totals for all sales.

Input Records

Fields	Card Columns	
Sales number	21-26	(I6)
Car price	40-45	(F6.2)

Calculations. For the car price field, use field names CPRICE for input, PRICE for calculations, and AMOUNT for output, but equivalence them. Convert the car price to an integer and multiply the integer by .04. Subtract the integer from car price to obtain the fraction of a dollar not yet taxed. Using IF statements, find the appropriate amount for the following scale: 0 - 14¢, nothing; 15¢ - 28¢, 1¢; 29¢ - 54¢, 2¢; 55¢ - 80¢, 3¢; 81¢ - 99¢, 4¢. Add the two tax amounts to obtain the correct sales tax. Add car price and sales tax for combined amount. Total car prices, sales tax, and combined amount, using double precision fields.

Output. Headings contain name and location of car dealer, date of report, and column headings. Detail lines contain sales number, car price, sales tax, and combined amount. After all records are processed, print the three totals.

3. A large company requires a report showing the percent that gross profit is of net sales for all its branch stores. The ratio of gross profit to net sales is of major importance because all expenses must be paid out of gross profit before the net profit can be realized.

Input Records

Fields	Card Columns	
Branch store number	23-27	(I5)
Gross profit	32-36	(F5.0)
Net sales	41-45	(F5.0)

Calculations. Gross profit is input as GROSSP, used in calculations as GPROFT, and output as GRPRFT. Net sales field is equivalenced as SALESN (for input) and SALNET (for calculations and output.) To calculate the ratio in percentage form, divide gross profit by net sales and then multiply the quotient by 100. Total all percentages. Count branch stores. After all records are processed, calculate average percentage.

Output. Headings include company name and head office location, date of report, and column headings. Detail lines contain all input fields and calculated percentage. After all records are processed, print average percent for all branch stores.

4. A class report shows the percentage of correct answers by each student for a 95 question test.

Input Records

Fields	Card Columns	
Student name	1-20	(A)
Student identification number	23-27	(I5)
Number of correct answers	32-33	(I2)

Calculations. Number of correct answers field is equivalenced so that NUMBER is used for input and output, and NANSER is used for calculations. The percentage of answers correct is calculated by dividing the number of correct answers by the number of questions in the test, then multiplying the quotient by 100. Total the percentages. Count the number of students. After all records are processed, calculate the average percentage.

Output. Headings include names of school and teacher, and column headings. Detail lines contain all input fields and percentage of answers correct. After all records are processed, print the average percentage for the class.

18

Subprograms: Introduction

A programmer frequently finds that he is repeating the same algorithm or series of calculations at various points in his program. Sometimes it is with the same quantities whenever it appears. For instance, a decision point in the program has three different paths that can be taken. Along each of these paths, the same specific computation or series of computations must be made. A flowchart illustrates a simplified example:

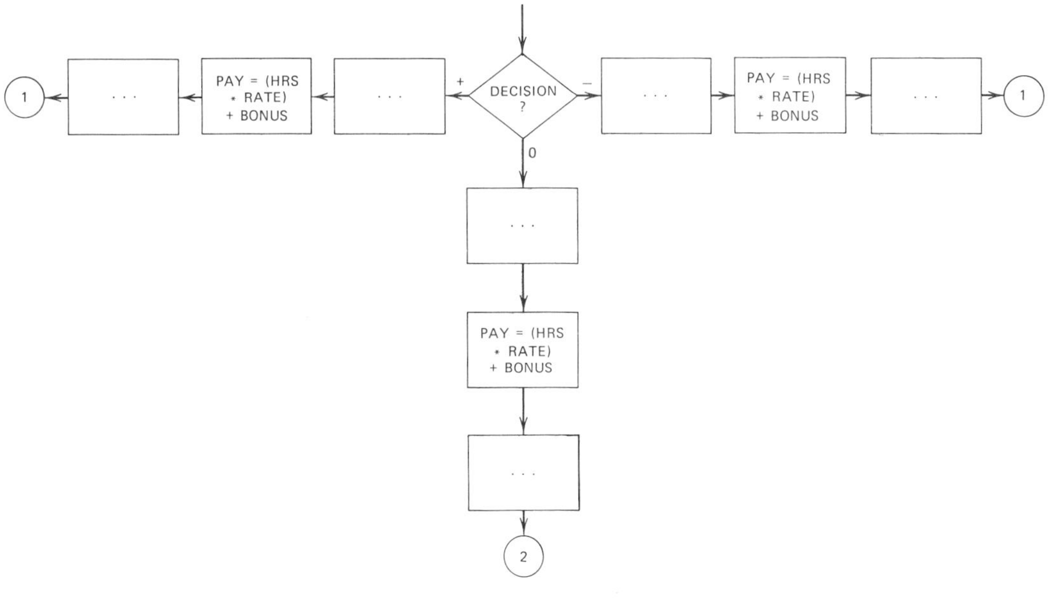

Sometimes the same calculations are needed at various points in the program but each time with different variables. For example, in the following flowchart, each of the detailed calculations requires subtraction, then multiplication:

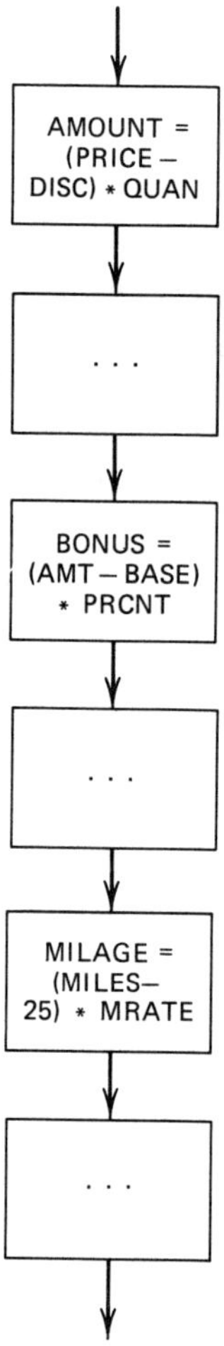

In both cases, coding the arithmetic processes only once simplifies the programming. This can be accomplished by statement functions, subprogram functions, and subprogram subroutines. Each has special uses and capabilities, but they also share many characteristics.

If all the required calculations can be included in one FORTRAN statement, the statement function can be used. Sometimes called the "internal function," it is not a true subprogram separate from the main program. It is a statement in the program executed only when "called" by another statement within the program.

If the repeated computation requires more than one FORTRAN statement but only one "answer" is required, either the function subprogram (sometimes called "external function") or the subroutine subprogram can be utilized. If more than one returning variable is changed in the calculations, the subroutine subprogram ordinarily is used. In some instances of this type, however, the function subprogram can be used.

A subroutine can also be utilized when no values change but certain "services," such as complicated input or output routines, are performed.

Two aspects of subprograms simplify programming. First, because subprograms are compiled separately and are less complex than full programs, they make the debugging task easier by breaking the program into clearly defined segments. Second, some utility services and mathematical functions that are used in many programs are provided as function or subroutine subprograms by the computer manufacturer. These enable the programmer to use routines already written and debugged.

The statement function, function subprogram, and subroutine subprogram share several characteristics. They all have names; they are executed when that name is "called" by another statement; they all can transfer or change values; all can use arguments. Yet each of the three forms is unique, even in its way of achieving their shared characteristics. Therefore, although the three will be compared and contrasted to show their separate abilities and advantages, each will be discussed separately.

Because they are used only with subprograms, the COMMON statement, the BLOCK DATA subprogram, and the EXTERNAL statement are also included in the subprograms discussions.

Chapter Objectives

1. Be able to write and use correctly the statement function to store a value in a field.
2. Be able to write and use correctly the statement function as part of another calculation.
3. Be able to write a statement calling a statement function.
4. Be able to explain why the statement function is not a true subprogram.

19

Subprograms: Statement Functions

The statement function is not a true subprogram. It shares so many characteristics of the function subprogram, however, that it usually is included in discussions of subprograms.

A function is a statement of the relationship between two or more variables. For example, CHARGE is the function of (that is, its value depends on) the variables CREAD, PREAD, and RATE. Thus the value of CHARGE is the value of CREAD minus PREAD, with the answer multiplied by RATE.

The statement function is not a true subprogram because the same FORTRAN program contains both (1) the definition of the relationship between variables and (2) the variables themselves. This is different from function and subroutine subprograms, which are independently written programs utilized by other programs.

The statement function is most useful when (1) there are several variables, (2) the relationships among the variables are complicated, and (3) the function is required at different points in the program. The *technique* of the statement function can be demonstrated by simple examples, however. Assume, for instance, that several times within a program, values for various fields are obtained by subtracting one variable from another variable, then multiplying the difference times a third variable. CHARGE, as shown earlier, meets these requirements.

The program also calculates such values as sales commission by subtracting the base requirement from the amount sold, then multiplying the answer by the commission percentage rate.

In order to generalize these relationships so that the function can be used whenever needed, a statement function is specified.

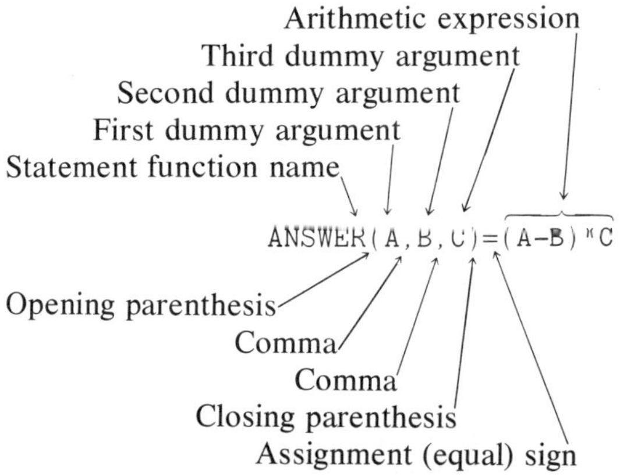

ANSWER is the name of the statement function. A, B, and C are false or "dummy" arguments of statement function ANSWER. These dummy arguments represent the variables (actual arguments) upon which the value of the function depends. Using the dummy arguments, the arithmetic expression follows the assignment (equal) sign.

The statement function, which cannot be numbered, must come before the first executable statement of the program. It is executed, however, only when it is "called." This occurs when the name of the function, followed by a list of actual arguments, appears in a FORTRAN statement. The form of the *calling* statement determines in which of two ways the value of the statement function name can be used. First, the value of the name can be returned so that it can be used in other calculations and/or output. This requires that only the function name and its arguments be listed to the right of the assignment sign:

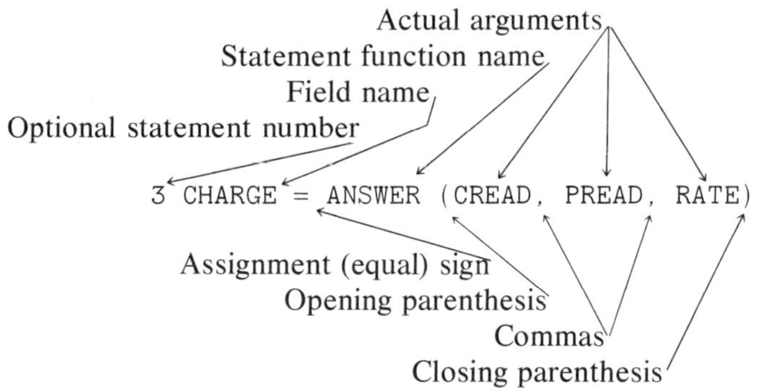

Statement 3 is read: "CHARGE is assigned the value of (or is equal to) the ANSWER of CREAD, PREAD, and RATE."

When statement 3 "calls" statement function ANSWER, the variables listed as actual arguments in statement 3 replace, in order, the dummy arguments of the statement function. These actual arguments must be the same type as the corresponding dummy arguments.

Because CREAD is the first argument in the calling statement list and A is the first argument in the statement function list, the FORTRAN compiler automatically inserts the current value of CREAD wherever A appears in the arithmetic expression of the statement function. The current value of second-listed PREAD is substituted for B, and third-listed RATE replaces C when these dummy arguments appear. The arithmetic expression is executed when it is referenced or called, and the result is stored in CHARGE as if statement 3 had been CHARGE = (CREAD − PREAD) * RATE. As CHARGE, the value can be used in calculations or in output.

The same process of substitution and execution is followed when statement 9 calls the same statement function:

```
9 COMISH = ANSWER(AMTSLD,BASE,PERCNT)
```

AMTSLD, BASE, and PERCNT replace A, B, and C, and the executed value is stored in COMISH.

The second type of calling statement returns the value of the statement function name as part of a calculation. It is not stored as a separate field. Statement 4 illustrates:

```
4 GRPAY = PAY + ANSWER(AMOUNT,BASE,PERCNT)
```

In statement 4, the calculated value of statement function ANSWER is added to PAY to obtain the value of GRPAY. Because the value of the statement function is only *part* of variable GRPAY, the function value cannot be a separate field in output or in other calculations unless it is called again in another statement.

REVIEW QUESTIONS

1. Where is a statement function placed in a program?
2. When is a statement function executed?
3. When can the value of a statement function be output as a separate value?
4. What is a dummy argument and where is it listed?
5. What is an actual argument and where is it listed?

Statement Function Name

The statement function name begins no earlier than column 7 in the function statement. The name must be unique; it cannot be used as the name of any other function, subprogram, or variable in the program. Function names follow FORTRAN name conventions. They must be from one to six alphabetic or numeric characters in length, with the first character alphabetic. The first character determines the numeric type of variable that is returned as the function name.

Field specifications can override the name convention for statement function names as they override other FORTRAN names. The name convention establishes ANSWER as a real field. When the program requires 8 bytes for the contents of ANSWER, this can be accomplished by a REAL*8 or a DOUBLE PRECISION specification statement, or by an IMPLICIT REAL*8 statement if it is available to the compiler:

```
REAL*8 ANSWER
DOUBLE PRECISION ANSWER
IMPLICIT REAL*8 (A)
```

Whichever of these type specifications is used, it must be placed *before* the statement function.

When they are appropriate, INTEGER, INTEGER * 2, and COMPLEX type specifications can also be declared for statement functions. They also must be placed before the statement function.

Statement Function Arguments

At least one argument must be listed in a statement function. As many as 15 arguments can be listed, if each is used in the arithmetic or logical expression of the statement. Each of the arguments must appear only once in the argument list.

Arguments need not be listed in the order by which they appear on the right side of the replacement sign. The variables listed as dummy arguments can be actual argument names also, or they can be used as variables elsewhere in the program. Although it can cause confusion and therefore is not a good programming technique, A, B, and C of the statement function can be dummy arguments, with a different A, B, and/or C in the program. The two A's, B's, and C's are then completely unrelated and stored in separate storage locations.

The arguments for statement functions are always enclosed in parentheses immediately following the statement function name. When the statement function is called, the actual arguments are listed in parentheses in the calling statement. The statement function and the calling statement must both contain the same number of arguments. The order of the arguments is important, as shown earlier, since replacements are made as the arguments are listed.

Arguments in the statement function must be nonsubscripted variables. They cannot be numeric constants or subscripted elements of an array. Arguments in the calling statement, however, can be any expression of the same numeric type as the corresponding dummy argument. For example, a constant can be an argument in the calling statement:

```
11 $MILES = ANSWER(TMILES,250.0, $RATE)
```

TMILES replaces A; the numeric constant 250.0 replaces B; $RATE replaces C. Then the statement function is executed and the value returned as variable $MILES.

A previously defined statement function[1] can be an argument in a calling statement. For example:

```
12 SUBTOT = ANSWER(A,SIZES(E,F,G),RATE)
```

When statement 12 calls statement function ANSWER, the second argument is the value of previously defined statement function SIZES, with program variables E, F, and G as the actual arguments of function SIZES.

If both the arithmetic expression of the statement function and the rest of the program use the same variables, those variables need not be listed as arguments. Statement function DEPTOT illustrates:

```
DEPTOT(Q,R) = R + PAY + BONUS + Q
```

Because PAY and BONUS are variables used in the program, their names need not be listed as arguments. These fields must have a stored value whenever statement function DEPTOT is called. Q and R can be either dummy arguments or actual variable names from the program.

A statement calls statement function DEPTOT:

```
13 DTOTAL=DEPTOT(COMISH,EXPENS) - RETRNS
```

Only the two arguments that replace dummy arguments Q and R are listed. They and the current values of PAY and BONUS are automatically inserted when the statement function is called for execution.

REVIEW QUESTIONS

6. How can the programmer alter the amount of computer storage allotted for a statement function field?
7. How many actual arguments must be listed in a calling statement?
8. Why is the order of the argument listing important?

Statement Function Expression

The expression to the right of the assignment or equal sign in the statement function defines the operations performed when the function is called. In FORTRAN IV, any arithmetic or logical expression that does not contain subscripted variables is valid. In Basic FORTRAN IV,

[1]Or a function subprogram, discussed in the next chapter.

any arithmetic expression that does not contain subscripted variables is acceptable.

If a statement function name appears in the expression, it must be defined earlier. For example, statement function ANSWER is defined, followed by statement function DIFF:

```
ANSWER(A,B,C)=(A - B) * C
DIFF(D,E,F,S)=ANSWER(D,E,F) - S
```

Statement 11 calls for statement function DIFF:

```
11 PROFIT=DIFF(CREAD,PREAD,RATE,COST)
```

When statement 11 is executed, it calls for statement function DIFF. Function DIFF calls for statement function ANSWER. Therefore, both statement functions are executed whenever statement 11 is executed.

A statement function being defined cannot be included in the expression of the *same* statement function. For example, statement function TOPIC is invalid:

```
TOPIC(E,F,G) = E-TOPIC(F,G)
```

TOPIC appears in its own arithmetic expression; therefore, it is not valid.

Since a statement function expression can contain as many as 15 different variables, it can be a quite complicated expression. This is particularly helpful when the complications are required several places in the program. Then the programmer really appreciates the ability to call the statement by arguments rather than repeating the intricacies of the expression each time.

REVIEW QUESTIONS

9. What rules do statement function names follow?
10. When is a statement function most useful?
11. When can a statement function be part of the arithmetic expression in a statement function?

OBJECTIVES REVIEW

Look over the objectives at the beginning of this chapter. Be sure that you can accomplish each of them. If there are any you cannot perform, study the section of the chapter related to the objective.

ASSIGNMENTS

Prepare a card layout form, printer spacing chart, and flowchart for one of the following problems. Then write, keypunch, and submit the FORTRAN program.

1. To get a typical cross-section, a school analyzes the grade distribution of each 10:00 a.m. class.

Input Records

Fields	Card Columns	
Instructor's name	1-20	(A)
Department code	21-22	(I2)
Class section number	23-27	(I5)
Number of students receiving A's	33-34	(I2)
Number of students receiving B's	44-45	(I2)
Number of students receiving C's	38-39	(I2)
Number of students receiving D's	52-53	(I2)
Number of students receiving F or W	74-75	(I2)

Calculations. Add students in the five categories to find the total number of students in each class. Using a statement function, calculate the percentage receiving each grade in every class. Total the number of students in each grade category. Count the number of class sections processed. Calculate the school total of the number in each category. After all records are processed, use the statement function to calculate percentages for the school.

Output. Print the name and location of the school, date of the report, and column headings. For each detail line, print all input fields, the number of students in the class, and the calculated percentages. After all records are processed, print total number of students and percentage for each of the five categories.

2. A report is required by a loan company in a state with a maximum annual interest of 18%.

Input Records

Fields	Card Columns	
Loan number	21-25	(I5)
Amount of loan	52-57	(F6.2)
Number of days of loan	38-40	(I3)
Annual interest rate	71-73	(F3.1)

Calculations. Time of the loan is the number of days divided by 360 (a bank year is 360 days). With a statement function, calculate the amount of interest: it equals the amount loaned (principal) multiplied by the interest rate, multiplied by the time. Maturity value equals the principal plus the interest. Total amount of loan and amount of interest for all customers. Total the number of days for each loan. Count the number of loans. After all records are processed, calculate the average loan time.

Output. Print company name, report date, and column headings. Each detail line contains all input fields, amount of interest, and maturity value. After all records are processed, print totals and average.

3. After an earthquake, an insurance company requires a report of property it insures.

Input Records

Fields	Card Columns	
Name of insured	1-20	(A)
Policy number	21-27	(I7)
Amount of insurance	61-66	(F6.0)
Amount of estimated damage	51-56	(F6.0)

Calculations. Add the assessed land and improvements values to find the the amount of damage covered by insurance. After value is returned, test to avoid percentage greater than 100%. Count all policy holders with amount of damage 100% insured. Total amount of damage. Total percentage of damage insured. Count policy holders. After all records are processed, calculate average percentage of damage insured.

Output. Headings include insurance company name, date of report, and column headings. Detail lines contain all input fields and calculated percentage of damage insured. After all records are processed, print total amount of damage and average percentage of damage insured.

4. The unincorporated sections of a county require a printed report of their property taxes. Tax rates are expressed per $100 of assessed valuation of both land and improvements.

Input Data. Use a DATA statement to establish the following tax rates: county tax, $2.79; county school tax, $5.26; special district tax, $0.48.

Input Records

Fields	Card Columns	
Property owner's name	1-20	A
Property tax book number	23-27	I5
Assessed land value	52-56	F5.0
Assessed improvements value	62-66	F5.0

Calculations. Add the assessed land and improvements values to find the total assessed valuation. For each tax, use a statement function to calculate 1/100 the assessment value and multiply that quantity by the appropriate tax rate. Add the three tax amounts to obtain the total tax for each property owner. Total each of the three types of taxes for all property owners. Count the property owners. After all records are processed, calculate the average amount paid for each type of tax.

Printed Report. Headings include county name and state, date of report, title of tax report, and column headings. Detail lines include property owner's name, tax book number, assessed land value, assessed improvements value, three taxes and total tax for the property. After all records are processed, three totals and three averages are printed with explanatory messages.

5. A report of student class grades is required.

Input Records

Fields	Card Columns	
Student identification number	23-27	I5
Student name	1-20	A
Number of points earned	72-74	I3

Calculations. The highest possible number of points earned is 999. When a student receives 90% or more of the points possible, the grade is A; between 80% and 89%, the grade is B; between 60% and 79%, the grade is C; between 50% and 59%, the grade is D. Below 50%, the grade is F. Use a statement function to calculate the percentages. Count the number of students receiving each letter grade.

Output. Headings include name and location of school, date the semester ends, and column headings. Detail lines include all input fields and the letter grade. After all records are processed, print the number of students receiving each letter grade.

Chapter Objectives

1. Be able to explain the differences between a statement function and a subprogram function.
2. Be able to write and use a FUNCTION statement correctly.
3. Be able to write and use a RETURN statement correctly.
4. Be able to write statements that assign a value to the function name.
5. Be able to write a statement calling a function so that the returned value can be stored as a separate field.
6. Be able to write a statement calling a function so that the returned value can be used in calculations of the calling arithmetic statement.
7. Be able to override the FORTRAN name conventions for a function subprogram name.
8. Be able to use an object-time DIMENSION statement with arguments that are arrays.
9. Be able to use more than one RETURN statement in a function subprogram.
10. Be able to use the ENTRY statement in a function subprogram.
11. Be able to explain the three different ways in which subprograms can be called.
12. Be able to write and use the EXTERNAL statement when it is required.

20

Subprograms: Functions

A subprogram is a program that is executed only when it is called (referenced) by another program. It can either be stored already in the computer—by the manufacturer or by a programmer—or it can follow the main calling program, ahead of data cards.

FORTRAN has two kinds of subprograms: subroutines and functions. Although a function subprogram is not part of the calling program as the statement function is, it has many other characteristics in common with the statement function. With both, the term "function" means a statement of the relationship between two or more variables. In both, the function is defined by specifying arithmetic operations (and/or logical operations with larger compilers) to be performed. Either type of function is executed when its name is referenced in a program. Each needs at least one nonsubscripted argument, and each requires a function name that is not used for any other variable or subprogram. Each returns a value for this name when it is called.

Like the statement function, the subprogram function is most valuable when it is somewhat lengthy and when it is called from several points in a program. Its value also increases when it can be used by various programs.

Like virtually all computer capabilities, the subprogram function becomes more complicated as it displays more flexibility and maneuverability. The number of options and extra statements within it are increased. The least frequently used of these extra capabilities will only be mentioned so that the programmer knows of them but is not overwhelmed by the many examples and explanations necessary to detail the possibilities.

The function subprogram is more complicated than the statement function. Unlike the single-instruction statement function, the subprogram can use several expressions to determine the value of the function name.

The function subprogram requires a minimum of four statements: (1) the FUNCTION statement, (2) a statement establishing a value for the function name, (3) a RETURN statement, and (4) an END statement. The subprogram can contain any FORTRAN statement except SUBROUTINE, BLOCK DATA, or another FUNCTION statement. It can, however, call any subprogram except itself.

A realistic but simple illustration of a function subprogram and its uses is provided by a program that requires the total amount of interest paid for a loan over a specified number of months. Instead of calculating the amount, the main program calls function TOTINT to give the amount when it is needed.

A flowchart illustrates the subprogram logic (see page 313).

TOTINT, which follows the flowchart logic, is a function subprogram:

```
  FUNCTION TOTINT (PR,PA,R,M)
1 TOTINT = 0.
2 DO 7 I = 1,M
3 TREST = (PR * (R/ 12)
4 AMOUNT = PA - TREST
5 PR = PR - AMOUNT
6 TOTINT = TOTINT + TREST
7 CONTINUE
8 RETURN
  END
```

At the end of execution, the variable TOTINT contains the value to be returned to the main program. TOTINT is the total amount of interest paid during the length of the loan. Its value depends on the relationships of four dummy arguments: the principal amount to be borrowed (PR), the monthly payment amount (PA), the annual interest rate (R), and the number of months necessary to repay the loan (M). The actual arguments are transferred when the function subprogram is called.

The function name and dummy arguments are listed in the FUNCTION statement, which must be the first statement in a function subprogram.

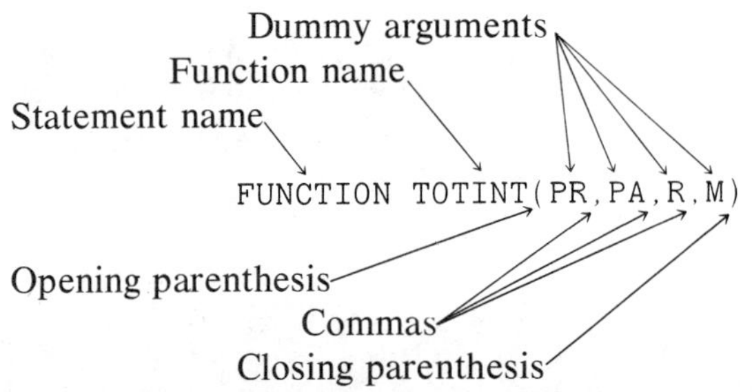

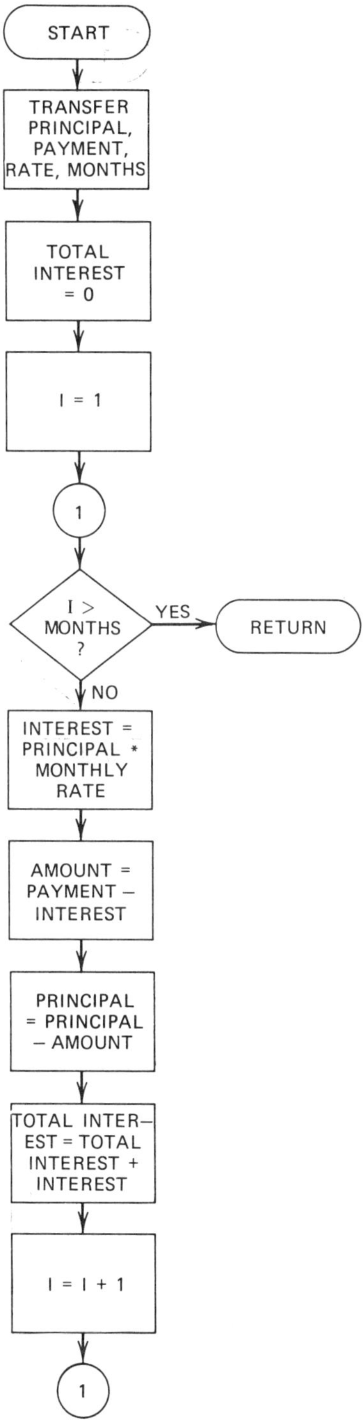
START
TRANSFER PRINCIPAL, PAYMENT, RATE, MONTHS
TOTAL INTEREST = 0
I = 1
1
I > MONTHS ?
YES
RETURN
NO
INTEREST = PRINCIPAL * MONTHLY RATE
AMOUNT = PAYMENT – INTEREST
PRINCIPAL = PRINCIPAL – AMOUNT
TOTAL INTER– EST = TOTAL INTEREST + INTEREST
I = I + 1
1

The FUNCTION statement cannot be numbered. It requires at least three elements: (1) the word FUNCTION, (2) the name of the subprogram, and (3) the "dummy" or false arguments enclosed in parentheses.

The Function Name

The name of a function subprogram, like the name of a statement function, follows the general rules for variables. That is, the name must be unique. It cannot be used for any other purpose within either the function or the calling programs. It must be from one to six alphabetic or numeric characters in length, with the first character alphabetic. Using standard FORTRAN name conventions, the first letter determines the type of variable returned to the main program as the value of the function name.

The name of the function must be assigned a value at least once during the subprogram. Most frequently, the function name receives a value when it is on the left side of an equal sign in an assignment statement. For example, statement 6 in function TOTINT assigns a value to TOTINT:

```
6 TOTINT = TOTINT + TREST
```

After statement 6 is executed in the last cycle of the DO loop, TOTINT contains the value to be returned to the main program.

The function name can also receive a value by an input statement within the subprogram. For example, function SUM receives the value for SUM when a READ statement is executed:

```
  FUNCTION SUM(N,Q)
1 READ (5,2) N, Q, SUM
2 FORMAT (I5, 2F6.2)
3 RETURN
  END
```

Function name SUM is equal to the value input by the READ statement. Incidentally, values were also acquired for arguments N and Q. These values will be returned also.

The third method of acquiring a value for the function name is rarely used. The function name receives its value as an argument in a statement calling another function or subroutine subprogram.

REVIEW QUESTIONS

1. How does a function subprogram differ from a statement function?
2. Which statements are required in a function subprogram?
3. What is the most common way for a function name to receive a value?

Function Arguments

At least one argument must be listed in the FUNCTION statement. The arguments listed are dummy or false arguments used in the function. These arguments can be in the form of a nonsubscripted variable, an array, or a dummy name of a subroutine or another function subprogram. Actual arguments must be the same numeric type as the dummy arguments they replace, but they can also be numeric constants or arithmetic expressions.[1] They are transferred by the calling statement of the main program. For example, the main program inputs the amount of a loan, the monthly payment, rate of interest, and length of the loan in months, as well as variables A and R:

```
2 READ(5,3) AMT, PAY, RATE, MONTHS, A, R
```

Perhaps other calculations are performed. Then the program requires the total amount of interest paid. Instead of coding the calculations to find this value, the program calls for function TOTINT:

```
5 TOTAL=TOTINT(AMT, PAY, RATE, MONTHS)
```

The values of the actual arguments in statement 5 replace, in order, the dummy arguments in the FUNCTION statement. Thus, when statement 5 references function TOTINT, the subprogram stores the current value of AMT for dummy argument PR, the value of PAY for dummy argument PA, the value of RATE for R, and the value of MONTHS for M. Then the subprogram is executed and the value for the function returned to the main program.

Because numeric constants can be arguments in the calling program, the calling statement could be:

```
55 TOTAL=TOTINT(AMT,PAY,.07,MONTHS)
```

An arithmetic expression can also be an argument:

```
555 TOTAL=TOTINT(AVAIL-REQIRE,PAY,RATE,MONTHS)
```

Another subprogram value can be an argument:

```
515 TOTAL=TOTINT($LOANS(CASH,CREDIT),PAY,RATE,MONTHS)
```

Subprogram function $LOANS, with arguments CASH and CREDIT, is executed to provide the value of the first argument.

Each calling statement stores the value of function TOTINT as the

[1]The five kinds of actual arguments allowed are discussed in detail in Chapter 21, Subprograms: Subroutines.

variable TOTAL. As TOTAL, it can be used in calculations or it can be output. If the value of the function name is needed only within a calculation, it need not be stored as a separate variable but can simply be part of an arithmetic statement:

```
6 XMONEY = RENTS + TOTINT(AMT,PAY,RATE,MONTHS)
```

Because the value of function TOTINT is only part of variable XMONEY, the value of the function cannot be a separate quantity in output or in other calculations without being called again.

Both the calling and the called programs have statements numbered 2 and 5. They both have variables named R. This seeming duplication of names and statement numbers is completely acceptable because statement numbers and field names in a subprogram do not relate to statement numbers or variable names in the calling program. This differs from the statement function where variable names are assumed to be the same unless argument names declare otherwise. The compiler regards names and statement numbers in one program as completely independent of those from another program. The programmer, however, may have difficulty keeping the identical variable names separate in *his* memory.

REVIEW QUESTIONS

4. What replaces the dummy arguments in the function statement?
5. What kind of calling statement allows the value of a function name to be stored as a separate field?
6. What kind of calling statement does not allow the value of the function name to be output as a separate field?

The RETURN Statement

A function program must contain at least one RETURN statement to transfer computed values and control back to the calling program. Some function subprograms are more flexible, however, if the return can be made from various points in the program. This situation often occurs when the function subprogram contains an IF statement. For example, the USAGE program gives a discount under certain conditions; see flowchart on page 317.

No discount is given if USAGE is less than 200.0. A 5% discount is given when USAGE equals 200.0. When USAGE is greater than 200.0, a 10% discount is given. In program USAGE FUNCTION, statement 15 calls for function CHRG:

```
15 CHARGE = CHRG(CREAD,PREAD,RATE)
```

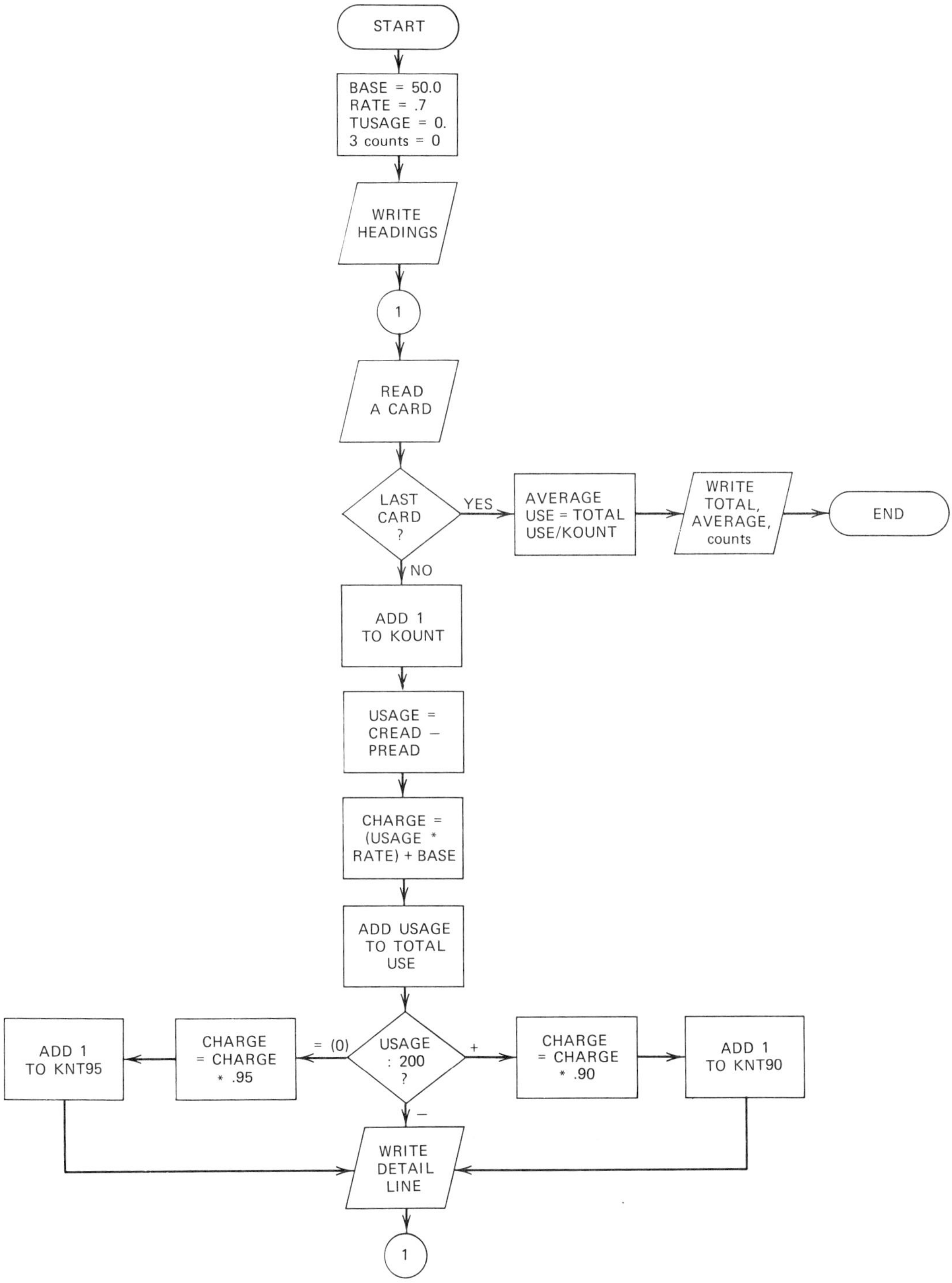
START
BASE = 50.0
RATE = .7
TUSAGE = 0.
3 counts = 0
WRITE HEADINGS
1
READ A CARD
LAST CARD ?
YES
AVERAGE USE = TOTAL USE/KOUNT
WRITE TOTAL, AVERAGE, counts
END
NO
ADD 1 TO KOUNT
USAGE = CREAD − PREAD
CHARGE = (USAGE * RATE) + BASE
ADD USAGE TO TOTAL USE
USAGE : 200 ?
= (0)
CHARGE = CHARGE * .95
ADD 1 TO KNT95
+
CHARGE = CHARGE * .90
ADD 1 TO KNT90
−
WRITE DETAIL LINE
1

The function subprogram tests to see if a discount should be given, and then calculates the correct amount of the charge:

```
  FUNCTION CHRG(C,P,R)
1 U = C - P
2 IF (U - 200.0) 3, 5, 7
3 CHRG = U * R
4 RETURN
5 CHRG = (U * R) * .95
6 RETURN
7 CHRG = (U * R) * .9
8 RETURN
  END
```

The IF statement tests the value of USAGE, called U in the function. The result causes a branch to statements 3, 5, or 7. Each branch establishes a different value for CHRG, then encounters a RETURN statement which transfers the value (and control) back to the main program. Thus, three separate RETURN statements create three separate points of exit from the subprogram.

The END Statement

The last statement of every FORTRAN program is END. Even though more than one RETURN statement can be in a subprogram, only one END statement is permitted.

REVIEW QUESTIONS

7. What is the minimum number of RETURN statements required in a function subprogram?

8. What is the maximum number of END statements allowed in a function subprogram?

Manufacturer-Supplied Function Subprograms

Some mathematical functions are used so often that computer manufacturers include these subprograms in their FORTRAN compilers. One of the most frequently called functions is SQRT, the square root function for standard length real numbers. It is called in the same manner as any other function subprogram:

```
8 SQ = SQRT(F)
```

Field SQ will be assigned the value of the square root of F.

A manufacturer-supplied function is referenced just as an individually written function subprogram is, but the manufacturer-supplied program already is in the compiler. Some of these functions are called "open" and others are called "closed," but the technical differences are rarely important to a FORTRAN programmer. If such information is essential, it can be found in the manufacturer's manuals.

Manufacturers' manuals list function requirements for argument type, length, etc. The most commonly supplied functions are given in appendix D.

Function Name Type Override

For the function name the programmer can override the predefined conventions of letters I-N for integers, and all other letters plus the dollar sign for real numbers. If he does, however, he must be certain to declare the change in *both* the calling program and the called subprogram.

The *called* subprogram can declare the change in the FUNCTION statement. This requires another element in the FUNCTION statement, a first word that establishes the function name type. For example, function COUNT must return COUNT as an integer value:

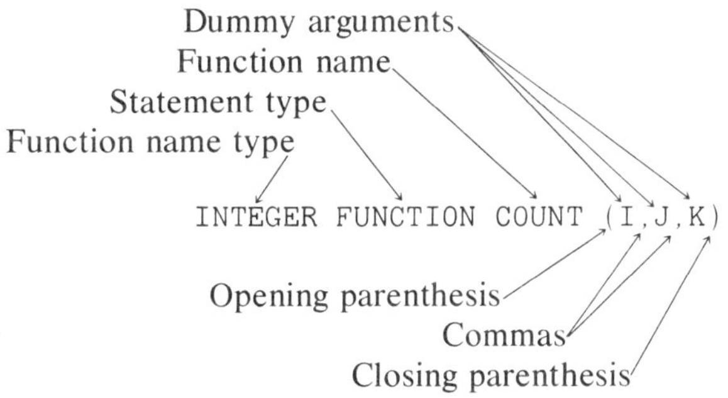

The word INTEGER specifies that the value for function name COUNT is an integer, even though COUNT begins with the letter C. The same procedure is followed for REAL, COMPLEX, and LOGICAL type changes, but DOUBLE PRECISION cannot be used.

If the stored length of the function name field is to be changed, length specification is the fifth element possible in the FUNCTION statement. When present, it must come between the function name and the arguments in parentheses:

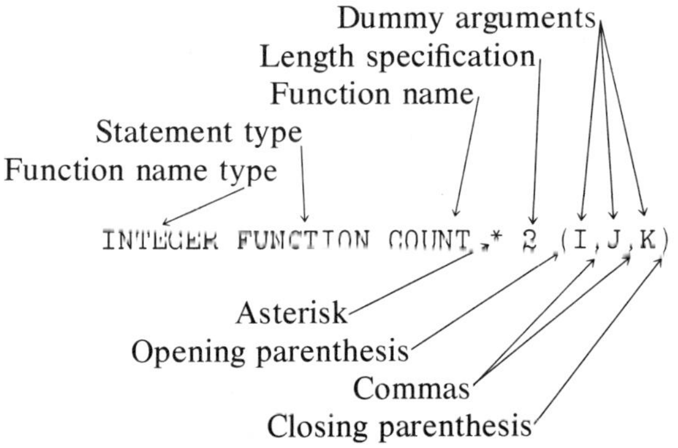

Function name COUNT is now stored as a 2-byte integer field. The same procedure is followed when a function name is declared REAL * 8, COMPLEX * 16, COMPLEX * 32, or LOGICAL * 1, if the FORTRAN compiler contains these possibilities.

If type and length change are not declared in the FUNCTION statement, they can be established within the subprogram. This is accomplished either by the IMPLICIT specification or by an explicit field specification. Whichever specification form is utilized, it must follow immediately after the FUNCTION statement. For example, changes can be declared in an IMPLICIT specification:

```
FUNCTION COUNT (I,J,K)
IMPLICIT INTEGER (C)
```

or

```
FUNCTION COUNT (I,J,K)
IMPLICIT INTEGER * 2 (C)
```

or in an explicit field specification:

```
FUNCTION COUNT (I,J,K)
INTEGER COUNT
```

or

```
FUNCTION COUNT (I,J,K)
INTEGER * 2 COUNT
```

The *calling* program must utilize either an IMPLICIT or an explicit field specification when the function name type changes. The way in which type is declared need not match the way in which it is declared in the subprogram. In fact, if the change is declared in the FUNCTION statement, the calling program cannot do the same.

At the beginning of the calling program (perhaps among other type changes for the program) a field specification establishes the value of function name COUNT as an integer:

```
INTEGER COUNT
```

or

```
IMPLICIT INTEGER (C)
```

If length is changed in the subprogram, the field specification of the calling program must include that change also. The form is the same as for other variables:

```
INTEGER * 2 COUNT
```

or

```
INTEGER COUNT * 2
```

or

```
IMPLICIT INTEGER * 2 (C)
```

REVIEW QUESTIONS

9. Are manufacturer-supplied function subprograms called differently from programmer-supplied function subprograms? If so, how?
10. How can a programmer override FORTRAN name conventions for function names?
11. Which type specification cannot be used to override name conventions for a function name?

Arrays as Arguments

If a FUNCTION statement argument is an array, array elements in both the calling and the called programs must be the same type, stored length, and number. In addition, DIMENSION statements must be included in *both* programs. For example, a calling program transfers 10-element array SUBTOT to function TOT to replace dummy argument array DEPTS. The calling program must dimension array SUBTOT so that the array elements can be used in the calling statement:

```
    DIMENSION SUBTOT (10)
    .
    .
    .
12  TOTALS = TOT (CASH, CREDIT, SUBTOT)
```

Function TOT, which statement 12 calls for, has the following coding:

```
  FUNCTION TOT (A, B, DEPTS)
  DIMENSION DEPTS (10)
1 TOT = 0.
2 DO 4 I = 1, 10
3 TOT = TOT + DEPTS (I)
4 CONTINUE
5 TOT = (TOT + A) - B
6 RETURN
  END
```

The elements in both arrays are standard length real fields. Both arrays are dimensioned for ten elements. When function TOT is called, the ten elements of array SUBTOT are stored as the ten elements of dummy argument array DEPTS. Although function name TOT is on the left side of three assignment statements, its value when the RETURN statement is processed is the value returned to the calling program.

The Object-Time DIMENSION Statement

Sometimes a function subprogram is more useful if the array size of the dummy argument can vary with the size of the array in the calling program. FORTRAN IV, but not Basic FORTRAN IV, allows this flexibility for all arrays except those listed in a COMMON statement. The flexibility is accomplished by an adjustable or object-time DIMENSION statement that permits the use of a variable instead of a constant in the DIMENSION statement of the *called* program.[2] This is the only time a field name is allowed as a DIMENSION delimiter.

To use the object-time DIMENSION statement, the value of the DIMENSION statement variable must be transferred as a 4-byte integer argument. For example, SUBTOT is again a 10-element array. Its values will be transferred to T, a called program:

```
  DIMENSION SUBTOT(10)
1 KOUNT = 10
2 TOTAL = T(CASH, CREDIT, SUBTOT, KOUNT)
```

The DIMENSION statement in the *calling* program declares the actual number of elements in the array. This same number 10 is also established as a 4-byte integer variable, KOUNT, *before the calling statement is executed,* and listed as an argument in the calling statement.

A variation in the calling statement would allow the same result with a constant instead of variable KOUNT as the argument:

[2]Subroutine subprograms also permit object-time DIMENSION statements.

```
  DIMENSION SUBTOT (10)
2 TOTAL = T(CASH, CREDIT, SUBTOT, 10)
```

The called program is unaffected because the fourth argument again establishes the size of the array. Dummy argument N is used in the DIMENSION statement to establish the size of dummy array DEPTS in function subprogram T:

```
  FUNCTION T(A,B,DEPTS,N)
  DIMENSION DEPTS(N)
1 T = 0.
2 DO 4 I = 1, N
3 T = T + DEPTS (I)
4 CONTINUE
5 T = (T + A) - B
6 RETURN
  END
```

Dummy argument N is also used in the DO statement to indicate the number of times the loop is to be executed. Thus, while function TOT can be utilized only with 10-element arrays, function T, with an object-time DIMENSION statement, can be used with arrays of any size. The only restriction is that the dummy argument used in the DIMENSION statement cannot be redefined in the subprogram. That is, the dummy argument giving the array size cannot be on the left side of an assignment statement or input by a READ statement in the function subprogram.

Changing Argument Values

Sometimes values of arguments change in subprograms. If the actual arguments are not used again in the calling program, this is not important. If they are used again, however, the programmer should be aware that a change has occurred. Sometimes he can utilize this situation to return more than one value with a function subprogram. This is shown in function OVRTM, which is utilized for calculating overtime pay for hours greater than 40.0.

The main program inputs hours and rate, and then begins calculations. Overtime pay (OVERPA) equals 0. before the value of hours (HRS) is tested:

```
13 OVERPA = 0.
```

If the value of HRS is greater than 40.0, the IF statement branches the program to statement 15:

```
14 IF (HRS - 40.0) 16, 16, 15
15 OVERPA = OVRTM (RATE, HRS)
```

Statement 15 calls function OVRTM to calculate overtime pay:

```
  FUNCTION OVRTM (R,H)
1 OH = H - 40.0
2 OVT = R * 1.5
3 OVRTM = OH * OVT
4 H = 40.0
5 RETURN
  END
```

After overtime pay (OVRTM) is calculated, H is reestablished as 40.0. As a result, when the subprogram has been executed, actual argument HRS contains the new value of 40.0. This enables the calling program to "fall through" to statement 16 with valid results for all employees:

```
16 GPAY = HRS * RATE + OVERPA
```

Reestablishing and returning the value of 40.0 for HRS is important because the employee would receive two and a half, instead of one and a half, times his regular rate for overtime hours if the value of HRS did not change.

REVIEW QUESTIONS

12. Where must DIMENSION statements be used if a function argument is an array?
13. When can a field name be used as a DIMENSION delimiter?
14. How can a function subprogram return more than one value?

The ENTRY Statement

Just as RETURN can supply multiple exits from a function subprogram, so ENTRY can provide additional entry points when using a FORTRAN IV, but not a Basic FORTRAN IV, compiler. The *unnumbered* ENTRY statement must have its own unique name. It also must list at least one argument just as the FUNCTION statement must. Function ADD, with ENTRY ADD1, illustrates:

```
  FUNCTION ADD(A)
1 B = A**2
  ENTRY ADD1 (A,B)
2 ADD = A + B
3 RETURN
  END
```

If the sum of AMT and AMT^2 is wanted, the program calls function ADD:

```
10 PLUS = ADD (AMT)
```

The ENTRY statement is ignored in calculating function name ADD. Statements 1, 2, and 3 of the function program are executed.

If the sum of *any* two items is required, ENTRY ADD1 is called:

```
11 ADDIT = ADD1 (CASH, CREDIT)
```

The function now executes only statements 2 and 3. Because the compiler stores the entry and function names as equivalents, the returned value is the last value assigned to either the function or entry name.

As function ADD demonstrates, dummy arguments in FUNCTION and ENTRY statements need not be the same. They must agree in type, number, etc., only with the actual arguments in the calling statement. ENTRY and RETURN statements can be utilized to create function subprograms that execute a variety of calculations.

The ENTRY statement is particularly valuable when an array or several variables that do not change values during the program must be transferred to a function subprogram. The function is needed several times during the execution of the main program, and all or part of these elements must be used each time the function is called. Considerable execution time is saved by initializing the array or variables only once, and then always entering the subprogram at an ENTRY statement following the initialization.

For example, TABLE is the 8-element array containing the rate charged customers in each region by the Renta Computer Company. Whenever the charge is calculated, the correct rate must be used. The rate schedule for the eight regions is established and transferred to function RCHRG from the calling program:

```
  DIMENSION TABLE (8)
1 DUMMY = RCHRG (TABLE,8)
```

Function RCHRG receives the transferred array and returns a meaningless value of 0.0 for RCHRG:

```
  FUNCTION RCHRG (T,N)
  DIMENSION T (N)
1 RCHRG = 0.0
2 RETURN
```

The RETURN statement transfers control back to the main program. Throughout the remainder of the main program, whenever the regional charge for the customer is calculated, entry R is called:

```
10 REGN = R (USAGE,IREGN)
```

When ENTRY R is called, the actual calculations of the function occur:

```
  ENTRY R (U, I)
3 RCHRG = U * T(I)
4 RETURN
  END
```

Because the array values are already transferred to the function, only the amount of usage and the region number (IREGN) are listed as arguments. IREGN (called I in the function) is the subscript to the previously stored rate table, and so no execution time is wasted in repeatedly transferring the array values. After the execution of statement 10, REGN contains the calculated value of the function.

Referencing Other Subprograms

Subprograms can be both called and calling programs. Because this type of reference can be quite complicated, the three ways in which it can be done will be only briefly illustrated.

The first method is the most common: an assignment statement in the function subprogram calls for a value from another subprogram. For example, function A1 calls for a value from function NEW:

```
  FUNCTION A1 (B, C, D, E)
1 A1 = E + NEW (B, C, D)
2 RETURN
  END
```

Function NEW is called with arguments brought in from the main program. The value of NEW is calculated and returned as part of variable A1.

In the second method, a subprogram value is referenced as an actual argument. This involves a calling program and at least two subprograms. For example, a program calls for function TRY, with function NEW and its arguments as an argument of function TRY:

```
5 H = 100.0 + TRY (A, NEW(B, C, D))
```

The value of NEW (B,C,D) is calculated first by the FORTRAN compiler so that the value can be transferred as an argument of function TRY.

The third way of referencing a subprogram uses the function (or subroutine) name *without arguments* as an argument in a calling statement. This is used if the subprogram can call different subprograms under different circumstances. For example, either function MULT or function DIVIDE is called from function CALC, depending upon values determined by an IF statement in the main program:

```
3 IF (A − C) 4, 1, 6
4 B = E + CALC(F,C,MULT)
5 GO TO 8
6 B = E + CALC(F,C,DIVIDE)
```

Function CALC receives either function name MULT or DIVIDE as its third argument:

```
      FUNCTION CALC (R, S, T)
    1 CALC = S**2 + T(R)
    2 RETURN
      END
```

Both function MULT and function DIVIDE have one argument, transferred from function CALC as argument R. Function T receives the function name from statements 4 or 6 in the calling program. Therefore function MULT is called from statement 4, and function DIVIDE from statement 6. The appropriate function is called when statement 1 in function CALC is executed.

The EXTERNAL Statement

When the third method of referencing a subprogram is used, there is an additional requirement. In order for the computer to execute calling statements 4 and 6, the names of the programs to be called must first be listed in an EXTERNAL statement of the *main* program. That is, in the program containing the statement calling the subprogram name (without arguments) as an actual argument of a subprogram. EXTERNAL is a non-executable statement that begins in column 7 or later:

```
      EXTERNAL MULT, DIVIDE
```

The EXTERNAL statement must come before any executable statements. It cannot be a numbered statement.

The EXTERNAL statement is required only when the function name is an argument for another subprogram but has no arguments of its own following its name.

REVIEW QUESTIONS

15. What is the purpose of an ENTRY statement?

16. How is the ENTRY statement valuable in function subprograms that contain arrays?

17. In what three ways can function subprograms reference other function subprograms?

18. When must an EXTERNAL statement be used?

OBJECTIVES REVIEW

Look over the objectives at the beginning of this chapter. Be certain that you can accomplish all of them. If there are any you cannot perform, study the section of the chapter related to that objective.

ASSIGNMENTS

Prepare a card layout form, printer spacing chart, and flowchart for one of the following problems. Then write, keypunch, and submit the FORTRAN program.

1. A company requires a weekly report of account purchases by commission "men."

Input Records

Fields	Card Columns	
Name of commission "man"	1-20	(A)
Account number of commission "man"	23-27	(I5)
Item quantity	52-54	(I3)
Item price	61-65	(F5.2)
Freight charge	31-35	(F5.2)
Cartage charge	42-45	(F4.2)
Storage charge	38-41	(F4.2)
Commission rate	71-72	(F2.2)

Calculations. Use a function subprogram to calculate the commission by multiplying item quantity by item price and then multiplying the result by the commission rate. Use a function to total freight, cartage, and storage charges for each account. Total commissions, freight charges, cartage, and storage charges for all accounts.

Output. Headings include company name, report date, and column headings. Detail lines contain name and account number of commission man, item quantity, item price, commission rate, commission, freight, cartage, and storage charges, and the total of the last three charges. After all records are processed, the four company totals are printed.

2. The economic order quantity (EOQ) is used by manufacturers to determine the most economic quantity of a product to produce under variable conditions. A company requires a report of EOQ's for various items with one setup cost and three inventory cost approximations for each item.

Input Records

Fields	Card Columns	
Product number	23-27	(I5)
Required yearly quantity (in 1000's)	31-33	(I3)
Setup cost per order	35-36	(F2.0)
Inventory cost per item (first approximation)	74-76	(F3.3)
Inventory cost per item (second approximation)	71-73	(F3.3)
Inventory cost per item (third approximation)	41-43	(F3.3)

Calculations. For each item, utilize the square root function to find the Economic Order Quantity for every inventory cost approximation. The EOQ equals the square root of (1) the yearly requirement (2) multiplied by the setup cost per order (3) with the result multiplied by 2 and (4) that result divided by the inventory cost per item.

$$\left(Q = \sqrt{\frac{2RS}{I}}\right)$$

Output. Headings include manufacturing company name and location, and column headings. The three detail lines for each item contain product number, required yearly quantity, setup cost per order, inventory cost per item, and the economic order quantity for that inventory cost.

3. Job applicants are given a battery of six aptitude tests, each of which has a maximum of 99 points. The personnel office requires a printed report of all job applicants, their score for each test, and their total score.

Input Records

Fields	Card Columns	
Job applicant name	1-20	(A)
Job applicant number	23-27	(I5)
Test 1 score	32-33	(I2)
Test 2 score	35-36	(I2)
Test 3 score	41-42	(I2)
Test 4 score	53-54	(I2)
Test 5 score	55-56	(I2)
Test 6 score	65-66	(I2)

Calculations. Use a function subprogram to sum the test scores for each applicant. Total the scores for each test and for the sum of the tests. Count job applicants. After all records are processed, calculate the average score for each test and for the total scores.

Output. Headings include company name and location, job test title, date, and column headings. Detail lines contain all input fields and applicant's total score. After all records are processed, print test totals and averages with explanatory messages.

4. Trade discounts are given on catalogue prices by a wholesale merchant. For a group of items, the wholesaler gives chain discounts of 30/15/5. That is, the retail buyer's price is found by deducting 30% from the published price, deducting 15% from the remainder, and deducting 5% from the second remainder. (Note that this is not the same as deducting 50% from the original price.)

Input Records

Fields	Card Columns	
Sales order number	48-49	(I2)
Department number	32	(I1)
Item number	44-45	(I2)
Catalogue price	52 57	(F6.2)

Calculations. Use a function to calculate the trade discount price for each item ordered. Using an array, total discount prices for each department.

Output. Headings include name and location of wholesale company, report date, and column headings. Detail lines include all input fields and the calculated trade price. Total lines include department number and the total of trade discount prices for each department.

5. A teacher gives a three-part examination. A report prints the number of points for each part of the test, the total number of points, and the average number of points per test segment for each student. Class averages are also printed.

Input Records

Fields	Card Columns	
Student name	1-20	(A)
Student identification number	23-27	(I5)
Score for part 1	32-33	(I2)
Score for part 2	41-42	(I2)
Score for part 3	53-54	(I2)

Calculations. Use a function that calculates the average of three items to find the average for each student. Count the students. Total the scores for all students for each part of the test. After all records are processed, find the average for each part of the test. Using a function, find the class average of the averages.

Output. Headings include names of the school, class, and teacher. Column headings are also printed. Detail lines contain all input fields, student total, and student average of the three parts. After all cards are processed, averages for each of the three segments and the average of all segments are printed.

NCR Century 300 with magnetic disks, magnetic tape, and printer.

Chapter Objectives

1. Be able to explain the main differences between function and subroutine subprograms.
2. Be able to write and use correctly a SUBROUTINE statement with arguments.
3. Be able to write and use correctly a SUBROUTINE statement without arguments.
4. Be able to write a statement calling a subroutine subprogram.
5. Be able to write a subroutine with an ENTRY statement.
6. Be able to write a subroutine that can return to various points in the calling program.
7. Be able to call a subroutine so that it can return to various points in the calling program.

21

Subprograms: Subroutines

Subroutine subprograms are the most versatile form of called programs. Like function subprograms and statement functions, subroutine subprograms can return a value to the calling program, but they are not restricted to this use. They can return several values or, instead of returning any value, they can perform a ''service.''

Unlike a function subprogram, a subroutine subprogram does not return values by the subprogram name. Therefore names of subroutines can be from one to six alphabetic or numeric characters, beginning with an alphabetic character, but without regard to name type conventions. Because all subroutine values are both sent and returned by arguments, a subroutine program can use its own name only in the SUBROUTINE statement. The name cannot appear in an assignment or other statement.

CALL Statement

A subroutine subprogram is not called as a function subprogram is called. Instead of calling the subprogram by using its name (or an ENTRY name) and arguments in an assignment statement, a subroutine is referenced by a CALL statement in the calling program:

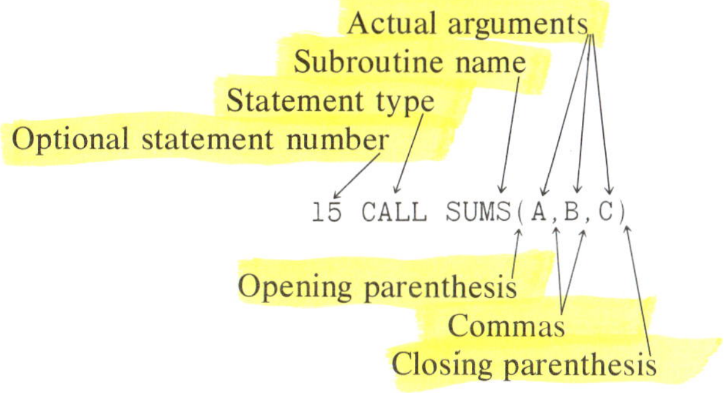

The CALL statement, which can be numbered, has one optional and two required elements. The word CALL and the subroutine or entry name are required. The third and optional element is the argument list enclosed in parentheses.

SUBROUTINE Statement

Although usually there are at least four statements, a subroutine has only two *required* statements. The first is the SUBROUTINE statement:

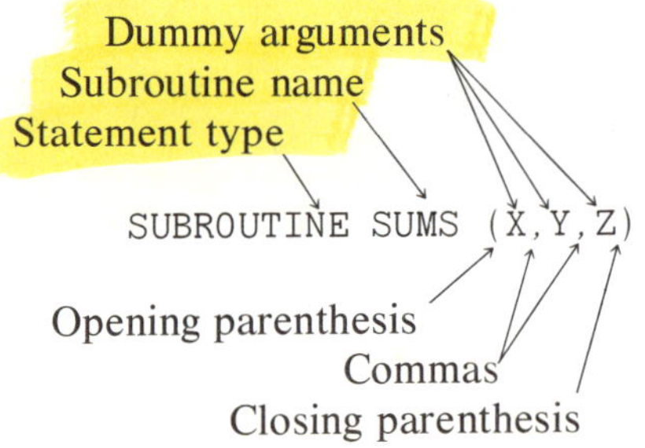

The SUBROUTINE statement *cannot* be numbered, but, like the CALL statement, it has two required words and one optional element. The two required words are SUBROUTINE and the name of the subroutine. The optional element is the argument list enclosed in parentheses.

The second required statement is END, which must be the last statement in all FORTRAN programs.

RETURN is not a compiler requirement of subroutines but it normally is required by program logic. RETURN is omitted only when the *calling* program is to end when the subprogram ends. This is the case in the manufacturer-supplied service subprogram often used to terminate a program:

```
CALL EXIT
```

Subroutine EXIT does not contain RETURN because the calling program is not to continue.

Any FORTRAN statement except FUNCTION, BLOCK DATA, or another SUBROUTINE statement can be in a subroutine program.

REVIEW QUESTIONS

1. What rules must a subroutine name follow?
2. What is the minimum number of arguments in a SUBROUTINE statement?
3. What kind of statement calls a subroutine?
4. What two kinds of statements are required in every subroutine?

ENTRY Statement

The ENTRY statement is an additional point of entry for subroutine subprograms just as it is for function subprograms. For example, a program uses subroutine HEADING, with entry LINES for output:

```
      SUBROUTINE HEADNG (A, B, C)
    1 WRITE (6,2)
    2 FORMAT ('1',T55,'J AND J COMPANY'//T57,'SANTA MONICA'/
     1 T58, 'CALIFORNIA')
C POINT OF ENTRY FOR DETAIL LINES ONLY
      ENTRY LINES (A, B, C)
    3 WRITE (6,4) A, B, C
    4 FORMAT (T10, F6.2, T30, F6.2, T50, F8.2)
```

Statement 1 causes a skip to the top of a new page and then the printing of company headings. Statement 3 prints a detail line. (Note that comment cards are acceptable in subprograms.)

When a line count in the main program indicates that the printer should skip to a new page and print headings before printing detail lines, the program references the subroutine name HEADNG. When just a line of detail printing is needed, the program calls entry LINES:

```
40 IF (LINECT - 45) 43, 41, 41
41 CALL HEADNG (X, Y, Z)
42 GO TO 44
43 CALL LINES (X, Y, Z)
```

If subroutine HEADNG consisted of only statements 1 and 2, it would be a "service" program not requiring any arguments.

Subroutine Arguments

Function arguments are used primarily to send actual arguments from the calling program to replace dummy arguments in the called program, although the value of an argument can be changed by execution of a function subprogram. Ordinarily, a function argument receives an actual value when the subprogram begins execution.

This situation is not true of subroutine arguments. Since they are intended for both *sending* and *receiving* values, some arguments leave the calling program without a predictable value until execution of the subprogram returns a value for that argument. For example, AMT has no assigned value when subroutine TAXES is called:

```
20 CALL TAXES(GROSS,PERCNT,AMT)
```

The calculation of dummy argument A in the SUBROUTINE gives AMT a value when values and control are returned to the main program:

```
      SUBROUTINE TAXES (G, P, A)
    1 A = G * P
    2 RETURN
      END
```

Because values are returned in arguments, the type of value returned (if any) depends upon the type of name in the argument lists. The actual argument and the dummy argument must agree. For example, both AMT and A are, by FORTRAN name convention, real fields of standard length.

If the programmer wants to override name conventions, either explicit or IMPLICIT field specifications can be used. If IMPLICIT is used, it must be the second statement in the program. Explicit field specifications must come before any executable statement.

If any kind of field specification is used, care must be taken to see that the value is assigned the same type and length in both actual and dummy arguments. For instance, QUANT in the next calling program is a REAL*8 field that is the first argument when subroutine CUBE is called:

```
      REAL*8 QUANT
          .
          .
          .
    8 CALL CUBE(QUANT,A)
```

In subroutine CUBE, the first argument, Q, must also be established as a REAL*8 field:

```
      SUBROUTINE CUBE(Q,A)
      REAL * 8  Q
    1 Q = 0.
    2 IF (A) 4,4,3
    3 Q = A**3
    4 RETURN
      END
```

Both the calling and the called program contain REAL*8 specifications. If the arguments did not agree on type and length specifications, the returned value would be inaccurate.

Types of Actual Arguments

Five kinds of actual arguments can be used by either function or subroutine subprograms:

1. Any type of constant except hexadecimal. The third argument in statement 21, calling subroutine MLTPLY, is a standard length constant:

```
21 CALL MLTPLY(PREAD,CREAD,.07)
```

2. Any type of variable except one last defined by an ASSIGN statement.[1] Some small compilers do not accept subscripted variables (elements in arrays), but many FORTRAN IV compilers permit them. A(1), the first argument in statement 22 calling subroutine SUB, is a subscripted variable. B, the second argument, is a nonsubscripted variable:

```
22 CALL SUB(A(1),B)
```

3. An array name. DEPTS is a 15-element array that must first be dimensioned:

```
   DIMENSION DEPTS(15)
18 CALL SUBT(DEPTS,TOTAL)
```

When an array name is an argument, the called program also requires a DIMENSION statement:[2]

```
  SUBROUTINE SUBT (D, T)
  DIMENSION D (15)
1 T = 0.
2 DO 4 I = 1, 15
3 T = T + D (I)
4 CONTINUE
5 RETURN
  END
```

4. An arithmetic or logical (if available) expression. Statement 28 contains both. The first argument, USAGE .GT. 200.0, is a logical expression. The second actual argument, USAGE * RATE, is an arithmetic expression.

```
28 CALL TEST(USAGE .GT. 200.0, USAGE * RATE, .90,CHARG)
```

The logical expression is tested, as dummy argument L, in subroutine statement 1. The arithmetic expression is used in subprogram statements 2 and 4 as dummy argument A:

[1]See Chapter 24 for information about the ASSIGN statement.

[2]See Chapter 20, Subprograms: Functions, for information about object-time DIMENSION statements.

```
  SUBROUTINE TEST (L, A, D, C)
1 IF (L) GO TO 4
2 C = A
3 RETURN
4 C = A * D
5 RETURN
  END
```

Two RETURN statements provide exits for each condition of the logical IF statement.

5. The *name* of a function or subroutine subprogram (except itself). If the name of a subprogram without arguments is an argument, the subprogram name must be listed in an EXTERNAL statement in the original calling program.[3] QMEAN is a function subprogram, and STADEV is a subroutine subprogram. Both are called by subroutine ANALYZ:

```
   EXTERNAL QMEAN, STADEV
   DIMENSION A (100)
   .
   .
   .
48 CALL ANALYZ (A, 100, B, C, QMEAN, STADEV)
```

Subroutine ANALYZ calls the two subprograms as arguments Q and S:

```
  SUBROUTINE ANALYZ (A, N, X, Y, Q, S)
  DIMENSION A (N)
1 TOTA = 0.
2 DO 4 I = 1,N
3 TOTA = TOTA + A(I)
4 CONTINUE
5 X = Q (A, N, TOTA)
6 CALL S (A, N, X, Y)
7 RETURN
  END
```

Dummy argument X returns the function value to actual argument B, and dummy argument Y returns the subroutine calculation to actual argument C.

Multiple RETURN Statements

Sometimes a sixth kind of actual argument can be used when calling subroutine, but not function, subprograms. This argument, available only on large FORTRAN compilers, is a statement number in the *calling* program. It is used as an irregular point of return to the calling program.

[3]The EXTERNAL statement is discussed in Chapter 20.

This statement number must be preceded by an ampersand (&) in the calling statement. For example, the last two arguments in statement 31 are statement numbers in the *calling* program:

```
31 CALL TEST2 (USAGE,USAGE.GT.200.0,USAGE*RATE,.90,
  1 CHARG, &35, &38)
32 WRITE (6,33)
33 FORMAT (' ')
34 GO TO 40
35 WRITE (6,36)
36 FORMAT (T2, 'DISCOUNT')
37 GO TO 40
38 WRITE (6,39)
39 FORMAT (T2,'CHECK FOR SPECIAL RATE')
40 CONTINUE
```

Each statement number in the argument list of the *called* program is represented by an asterisk (*):

```
   SUBROUTINE TEST2 (U, L, A, D, C, *, *)
 1 IF (L) GO TO 4
 2 C = A
 3 RETURN
 4 C = A *D
 5 IF (U .GE. 300.0) GO TO 7
 6 RETURN1
 7 RETURN2
   END
```

When the logical IF in statement 1 has a "false" value, statement 2 is executed. Then RETURN statement 3 transfers control normally to the statement immediately following calling statement 31. When statements 2 and 3 are skipped by a "true" value in statement 1, the comparison in IF statement 5 determines where control shall be returned in the calling program. When USAGE is less than 300.0, the subprogram "falls through" to statement 6. The number 1 after the word RETURN transfers control to the first statement number listed as an argument (35). When USAGE is greater than or equal to 300.0, the subprogram branches to statement 7. RETURN2 transfers control to the second statement number in the argument list (38). Thus, three separate statements in the calling program can be points of return from a subroutine.

REVIEW QUESTIONS

5. How do subroutine arguments differ from function arguments?
6. How can an arithmetic or logical expression be transferred to a subroutine?
7. When a FORTRAN compiler can use a statement number as an argument, how is the number written in the calling statement?
8. How is it written in the SUBROUTINE statement?

OBJECTIVES REVIEW

Study the objectives at the beginning of this chapter. Be certain that you can accomplish all of them. If there are any you cannot perform, study the chapter section pertaining to that objective.

ASSIGNMENTS

Prepare a card layout form, printer spacing chart, and flowchart for one of the following problems. Then write, keypunch, and submit the FORTRAN program.

1. A store requires a list of merchandise to be reordered.

Input Records

Fields	Card Columns	
Inventory number	23-27	(I5)
Number on hand	52-55	(I4)
Reorder level	63-65	(I3)
Minimum reorder quantity	71-73	(I3)
Unit price	74-77	(F4.2)

Calculations. If the amount on hand is equal to or greater than the reorder level, no reorder quantity is necessary. If the amount on hand is less than the reorder level, however, use a subroutine to calculate the number to be reordered and the cost. The number below the reorder level plus the minimum reorder quantity are the reorder quantity. This quantity is multiplied by the unit price to obtain the cost. Total the units to be reordered and their cost.

Output. Headings include company name, location, date of report, and column headings. Detail lines for reordered items include inventory number, number on hand, quantity to be reordered, and the reorder cost. When the item is not reordered, call a subroutine to print the inventory number, the number on hand, followed by the message 'ON HAND.' After the last record is processed, print the total units reordered and the total cost.

2. If a policy holder cancels his automobile insurance, the insurance company is permitted to retain the exact prorated amount of the premium for the number of days the policy has been in force, based on a 365-day year.

Input Records

Fields	Card Columns	
Policy holder	1-20	(5A4)
Policy number	23-27	(I5)
Days policy in force	64-66	(I3)
Amount of premium paid	52-57	(F6.2)

Calculations. Using a subroutine, determine both the amount the insurance company is entitled to keep and the amount refunded to the insured. Total the amount paid and both calculated amounts.

Output. Headings include the insurance company name and location, date of report, and column headings. Detail lines contain all input fields and both calculated amounts. After all records are processed, print the three total amounts.

3. A company requires a printed schedule of straight-line depreciation for its recently acquired assets.

Input Records

Fields	Card Columns	
Department number	21-22	(I2)
Item number	23-27	(I5)
Cost of asset	62-67	(F6.0)
Useful life in years	71-72	(I2)

Calculations. Divide the cost of the asset by its years of useful life to obtain the annual depreciation. For each year of the life of the asset, subtract the annual depreciation from the current book value. The remainder is the next year's book value. Total each year's depreciation to obtain the accumulated depreciation.

Output. Headings include company name, location, and report date. Before printing the schedule for each asset, utilize a subroutine to print the following items with data:

```
DEPARTMENT:
ASSET ACCOUNTING NUMBER:
COST:
LIFE:
```

Detail lines of the depreciation schedule include the year of the schedule (1, 2, 3, etc.), current book value, annual depreciation, and accumulated depreciation.

4. Throughout the school term, an instructor gives six tests, each of which has a maximum of 99 points. A list is required of all students, their scores on each test, their total score, and their average test score.

Input Records

Fields	Card Columns	
Student name	1-20	(A)
1st test score	32-33	(I2)
2nd test score	35-36	(I2)
3rd test score	41-42	(I2)
4th test score	53-54	(I2)
5th test score	55-56	(I2)
6th test score	65-66	(I2)

Calculations. Use a subroutine to sum the test scores for each student and to calculate his average test score. Total the scores for each test. Count the number of students. After all records are processed, calculate the average score for each test and for the sum of the tests.

Output. Headings include school name and location, date, and column headings. Detail lines contain all input fields, student total score and average test score. After all records are processed, print test totals and averages with explanatory messages.

5. A store requires a report showing the operating profits for each of its departments and for the entire store.

Input Record

Fields	Card Columns	
Department number	48-49	(I2)
Gross sales and allowances	38-45	(F8.2)
Cost of merchandise	71-77	(F7.2)
Sales returns	52-57	(F6.2)
Expenses	31-36	(F6.2)

Calculations. Use a subroutine to calculate net sales, gross margin, and operating profit for each department and for the entire store. Net sales equals gross sales minus sales returns and allowances. Gross margin equals net sales minus the cost of merchandise. Operating profit equals gross margin minus expenses. Total all money fields.

Output. Headings include store name and location and column headings. Detail lines contain all input fields, net sales, gross margin, and operating profit. After all departments are processed, print all totals.

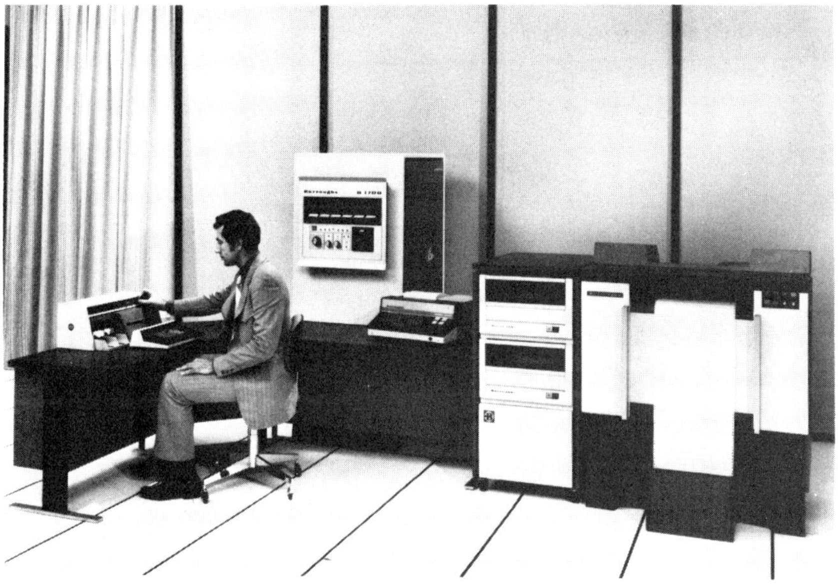

Burroughs B1700.

Chapter Objectives

1. Be able to write and use COMMON statements in a main program and in subprograms to establish storage in the common area.
2. Be able to extend the common area by the EQUIVALENCE statement.
3. Be able to write and use the BLOCK DATA statement to establish fields in labeled blocks of the common area.
4. Be able to write COMMON statements so that fields in labeled blocks of the common area can be used.
5. Be able to explain the value of the common area, especially when more than one subprogram utilize many variables or large arrays.

22

Subprograms: COMMON and BLOCK DATA Statements

When the values of fields are transferred from a program to a subprogram, these values are usually transferred as arguments from the calling statement to the FUNCTION or SUBROUTINE statement. When few variables are involved, only a negligible amount of execution time and computer storage space are needed to transfer these values from the main program to the subprogram and back to the main program. When several variables or large arrays are involved, however, computer storage is saved by storing the elements only once instead of once for each of the two programs. In addition, if the subprogram is called several times during the execution of a program, or if more than one subprogram requires the same values, execution time is cut by sharing the values without transferring them every time a subprogram is called. Storage is also saved by eliminating the FORTRAN instructions required to transfer data.

The COMMON Statement

These advantages are accomplished by using a separate area of storage called common. This area is *outside* the area allotted to any particular program, but it is "common" to all programs. That is, it may be utilized by any or all programs being processed. Unlike an EQUIVALENCE statement that lets more than one field in the same program share a storage location, the COMMON statement enables fields and arrays from more than one program to share storage locations.

Contents of the common area are established by COMMON statements within *each program* using the common area. These statements can appear anywhere in the program before the field is used. When more than one COMMON statement appears in a program, the compiler automatically makes the contents cumulative, adding the new items in order as though continuing the first COMMON statement of that program. This order is most important because the common area is useful only if the programmer stores his values in it carefully. Then programs can share data accurately.

Names used for fields in the common area by each program are entirely independent of names used by the other programs. The order or sequence of the names in the COMMON statement list and the lengths of the fields determine the location of fields in the common area.

To illustrate how the COMMON statement and common area work, the arguments of subroutine CHRG are placed in the common area. The three arguments required of the subroutine are standard 4-byte real fields: PREAD, CREAD, and USAGE. When used before, they had to be listed in the CALL statement:

```
15 CALL CHRG (PREAD, CREAD, USAGE)
```

Now instead of being transferred as arguments, fields PREAD, CREAD, and RATE are established in the common area of the main program:

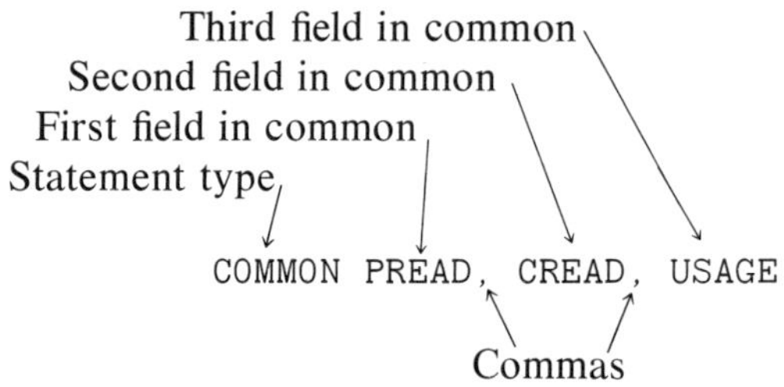

In its simplest form, the COMMON statement consists of the word COMMON, beginning in column 7 or later, followed by the names of variables to be stored, separated by commas. The COMMON statement cannot be numbered.

Fields PREAD, CREAD, and USAGE are now established in the first 12 (3 × 4) bytes of the common area. The same locations must be given names by a COMMON statement within the subroutine.

```
COMMON P, C, U
```

Fields P, C, and U are also 4-byte real fields. Since the COMMON statement for each program begins from the same starting location in the common area, fields P, C, and U also are established in the first 12 bytes of the common area of storage.

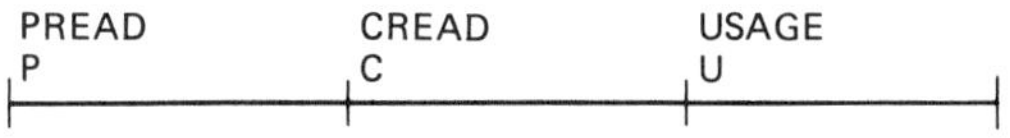

Neither the calling statement in the main program

```
14 CALL CHRG
```

nor the SUBROUTINE statement

```
      SUBROUTINE CHRG
```

contains the argument list. Fields in the common area of a program *cannot* be arguments in the calling statement of the main program or in the subprogram FUNCTION or SUBROUTINE statements.

Accurate use of the common area requires an understanding of field lengths and alignments.[1] A table presents all field types possible in FORTRAN, and their standard and optional lengths:

SUMMARY TABLE OF FORTRAN FIELD TYPES
AND LENGTHS IN STORAGE

Type	Standard Length (in bytes)	Optional Length (in bytes)
INTEGER	4	2
REAL	4	8
DOUBLE PRECISION	8	—
COMPLEX	8	16[2]
LOGICAL	4	1

Field types must begin (be aligned) by byte positions acceptable for their length. Alignments in storage can be diagrammed to illustrate acceptable starting points:

[1]Field lengths and alignments are discussed in Chapter 15, Type Specification Statements.

[2]Some new, very large FORTRAN compilers now contain the capability for an optional 32-byte complex field.

Storage assignments for an area in common always begin on 8 or 16-byte alignment points. All programs share this original starting point.

The correct starting point or alignment for a multibyte field is correct for all fields with fewer bytes. Thus, correct alignment for a 16-byte or 8-byte field correctly aligns 4, 2, or 1-byte fields. Alignment for a 4-byte field is correct for 2 and 1-byte fields; 2-byte field alignment is correct for 1-byte fields.

REVIEW QUESTIONS

1. How does use of the COMMON statement save computer storage?
2. How does use of the COMMON statement save execution time?
3. What is the standard storage length of integer and real fields?

Arrays in Common Area

If PREAD, CREAD, and USAGE are stored for 100 customers, three 100-element arrays instead of three variables are required. In such a program, the common area is even more valuable because eliminating argument lists saves so much transfer time. Since elements listed in a COMMON statement cannot appear in a DIMENSION statement, array dimensions are given in the COMMON statement of both the calling and called programs.

The calling program establishes the arrays in the common area:

```
COMMON PREAD (100), CREAD(100), USAGE(100)
```

Although it could have names of fields not in common, the calling statement contains no arguments:

```
10 CALL CHRG2
```

The COMMON statement establishes the entire first array in the common area, followed by the entire second array, and then the entire third array. The called subroutine also lists three arrays to begin at the same point in the common area:

```
SUBROUTINE CHRG2
COMMON P(100), C(100), U(100)
```

A drawing represents the shared common area address locations:

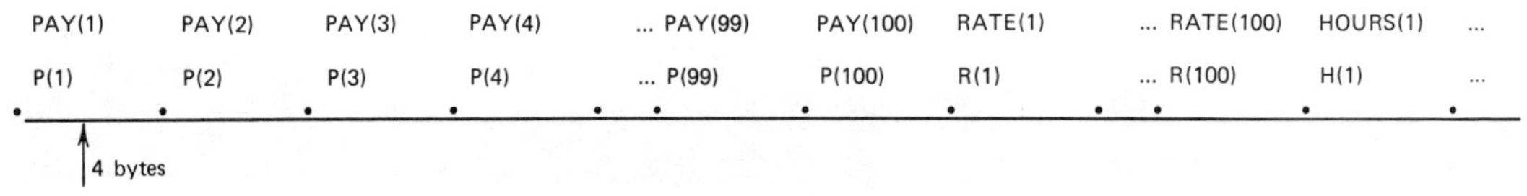

Arrays sharing the same locations in common need not have the same number of array elements. Neither must elements sharing the same area be the same type, if program logic allows the difference. For example, four REAL*8 fields can share the same area with eight 4-byte real or integer fields. Two REAL*8 fields as well as four standard length real or integer fields can occupy the same area as one COMPLEX*16 field. However, the programmer must be aware of the possibilities of incorrect answers when such complications are utilized.

Extending the Common Area by EQUIVALENCE

Two fields in the common area cannot be equivalenced with each other but a field in either a calling program or a subprogram can be made equivalent to an element in the common area. If the equivalenced element is part of an array, the entire array is stored in common. For example, a program stores three variables in common:

```
COMMON PAY,RATE,HOURS
```

Called subroutine WEEKLY has not only a COMMON statement but also an EQUIVALENCE statement:

```
SUBROUTINE WEEKLY
COMMON P, R, H
DIMENSION EMP (3)
EQUIVALENCE (P, EMP(1))
```

The EQUIVALENCE statement in the subprogram pairs variable P with the first element of array EMP. This automatically equivalences EMP(2) with R, and EMP(3) with HOURS. Thus, each of the three locations in storage has three names:

PAY	RATE	HOURS
P	R	H
EMP(1)	EMP(2)	EMP(3)

If array EMP had five rather than three elements, the common area would contain EMP(4) and EMP(5) also:

PAY	RATE	HOURS		
P	R	H		
EMP(1)	EMP(2)	EMP(3)	EMP(4)	EMP(5)

This extension cannot come before the first established field in the common area. For instance, if H and EMP(5) were equivalenced, EMP(1) and EMP(2) would come before P and EMP(3). This type of equivalence is invalid.

When elements of two arrays have been made equivalent, any further equivalence of the two arrays is invalid. For example, the equivalence of A(1) and X(1) automatically places both arrays in common:

```
DIMENSION A(10), B(6)
COMMON X(4),Y(10),Z(10)
EQUIVALENCE (X(1),A(1)),(A(7),Y(1))
```

Sequential order of the arrays does not permit the second part of the EQUIVALENCE statement that attempts to align A(7) and Y(1). Contradiction of the arrangement of arrays in common area creates an invalid equivalence:

A(1)	A(2)	A(3)	A(4)	A(5)	A(6)	A(7)	A(8)	A(9)	A(10)					
X(1)	X(2)	X(3)	X(4)	Y(1)	Y(2)	Y(3)	Y(4)	Y(5)	Y(6)	Y(7)	Y(8)	Y(9)	Y(10)	Z(1) ...

REVIEW QUESTIONS

4. Why is the COMMON statement especially valuable when a large array is used by both a main program and a subprogram?
5. Can two fields in the common area be equivalenced? If yes, how?

Labeled Common

The common storage area for all the preceding examples is called a blank or unlabeled common area. That is, the *area* in common where the fields (with names) are stored has not been given a name. However, the area in common can be divided into various blocks. Each block, except the one called blank or unlabeled common, is given a unique name.

This division of the common area is useful when several subprograms are called, and the calling program shares elements in one common block with one or more subprograms and elements in a different common block with one or more other subprograms. This division into blocks also aids program documentation, for the name of the block can include several variables.

A labeled common block is named in the COMMON statement.

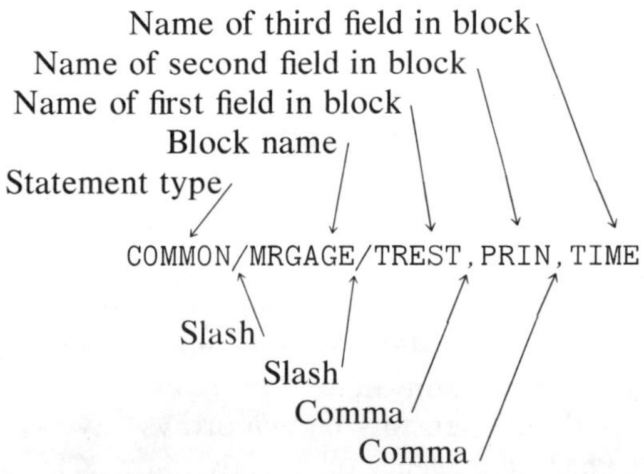

The name of the block in common is from one to six alphabetic or numeric characters. The first character must be alphabetic but has no type significance. The name of the block is always enclosed in slashes. All variables that follow the second slash are included in the labeled block of the common area, without regard to field type. Therefore, variables TREST, PRIN, and TIME are all in common block MRGAGE. Like blank common, elements listed in a labeled common area are cumulative throughout a program. Also like blank common, there cannot be a duplication of fields.

Blank and labeled common fields can be established in the same COMMON statement.

```
COMMON PAY,RATE,HOURS/MRGAGE/TREST,PRIN,TIME
```

PAY, RATE, and HOURS are in blank common; TREST, PRIN, and TIME are in the common block labeled MRGAGE.

If two blocks in common are established in the same COMMON statement, the second block name is also enclosed in slashes and the names of variables within that block follow the second slash:

```
COMMON PAY,RATE,HOURS/MRGAGE/TREST,PRIN,TIME/MAP/XLONG(15),XLAT(15)
```

The second block of common area is labeled MAP. It contains two 15-element arrays, XLONG and XLAT.

A program calling two subprograms illustrates the advantage of block areas in common. In both subprograms, PAY, RATE, and HOURS are needed. Only subroutine ONE needs TREST, PRIN, and TIME; only subroutine TWO requires arrays XLONG and XLAT. The COMMON statement for each program is different, calling only what is needed. The calling program lists all areas of common:

```
COMMON PAY,RATE,HOURS/MRGAGE/TREST,PRIN,TIME/MAP/XLONG(15),XLAT(15)
```

Subroutine ONE lists the fields in unlabeled common and in block MRGAGE:

```
SUBROUTINE ONE
COMMON P,R,H/MRGAGE/E,P,T
```

Subroutine TWO lists the fields in unlabeled common and in block MAP:

```
SUBROUTINE TWO
COMMON PA,R,HRS/MAP/XLO(15),XLA(15)
```

This technique is especially valuable in very large programs utilizing several subprograms. Common lists of subroutines usually are shorter than the main program common area list.

REVIEW QUESTIONS

6. How are divisions of the common area useful?
7. How are labeled areas of the common area established?

BLOCK DATA Statement

Data within the blank or unlabeled common area cannot be initialized, but variables in labeled common can be given values by the DATA statement or by data initializing statements. This initializing is done in a separate BLOCK DATA subprogram with no executable statements. It can contain only the BLOCK DATA statement, and DATA, COMMON, DIMENSION, EQUIVALENCE, type specification, and END statements. The BLOCK DATA, COMMON, and END statements are required.

The BLOCK DATA statement, which must be the first statement in the subprogram, consists of only two words:

Statement type

```
BLOCK DATA
```

If the BLOCK DATA subprogram contains an IMPLICIT statement, it must follow immediately after the BLOCK DATA statement. The COMMON statement must come before any data initialization statements. It must list *all* elements of a common block, in order, even though some elements are not initialized. For example, in the following BLOCK DATA subprogram, TREST and TIME but not PRIN in common block MRGAGE, and XLONG but not XLAT in common block MAP, are initialized:

```
BLOCK DATA
COMMON/MRGAGE/TREST,PRIN,TIME/MAP/XLONG(15),XLAT(15)
REAL TREST/.065/,TIME/24./,XLONG/15*0.0/
END
```

The COMMON statement establishes positions in the common area. Therefore it must list all the elements of each common block that contains a field being initialized. The REAL statement, however, lists only the real fields being initialized.

The COMMON and REAL statements can be changed so that array XLONG is dimensioned in the REAL statement instead of the COMMON statement:

```
COMMON/MRGAGE/TREST,PRIN,TIME/MAP/XLONG,LAT(15)
REAL TREST/.65/,TIME/24./,XLONG(15)/15*0.0/
```

The variables are established with the same result.

Although data may be entered for more than one common block in a BLOCK DATA subprogram, only one BLOCK DATA subprogram can be used to enter data into one particular common block.

If a variable for blank common comes after a common block and its elements, the end of labeled common is signaled by two slashes with no name between:

```
COMMON PAY,RATE,HOURS/MRGAGE/TREST,PRIN,TIME//MILES
```

The common block labeled MRGAGE contains TREST, PRIN, and TIME. Blank common contains, in order, PAY, RATE, HOURS, and MILES.

REVIEW QUESTIONS

8. Where is a BLOCK DATA statement placed in a subprogram?
9. How can areas in a common block be initialized?
10. How many BLOCK DATA statements can initialize one block area of common?

OBJECTIVES REVIEW

Study the objectives listed at the beginning of this chapter. Check each one to be certain that you have achieved it. Restudy the sections of the chapter related to any objectives you have not achieved.

ASSIGNMENTS

Prepare a card layout form, printer spacing chart, and flowchart for one of the following problems. Then write, keypunch, and submit the FORTRAN program.

1. A store totals its sales by departments for a daily report. Transactions are input and calculated randomly. They are totaled by department, with all department totals output after all records are processed.

Input Records

Fields	Card Columns	
Sales order number	48-49	I2
Department number	32	I1
Employee number	27	I1
Item number	44-45	I2
Amount of sale	52-57	F6.2

Calculations. Establish a 9-element array for department totals in the common area of storage. Add the amount of sale to the correct department total. In a subroutine for total output, use either input data or the DATA statement to create nine department names.

Output. Headings include company name and location, date of report, and column headings. Detail lines contain all input fields. Totals are output by a subroutine. Total lines contain department number, department name, total amount of sales for the department.

2. A manufacturer randomly tests 20 items of each product. A report requires the standard deviation for each of the products.

Input Records

Fields	Card Columns
Product number	48-49 I2
Scores for tests 1-20 (all I2 fields)	21-22, 23-24, 25-26, 29-30, 31-32, 33-34, 35-36, 39-40, 41-42, 43-44, 49-50, 51-52, 53-54, 55-56, 59-60, 63-64, 65-66, 67-68, 73-74, 75-76

Calculations. For the scores of each product tested, create a 20-element array in the common area of storage. Write two functions: one to calculate the mean average of the test scores, and one to calculate the standard deviation of the 20 array elements. Standard deviation can be determined in various ways, but the following method is often used. In the first function, sum all the elements in the array. Calculate the mean by dividing the sum by the number of elements in the array. In the second function, subtract the mean from each element in the array. Calculate the square of all the differences, and sum the squared differences. Divide this sum of the differences by the number of elements. The square root of the quotient is the standard deviation. Total the mean averages.

Output. Headings include the name of the manufacturer, test date, and column headings. Detail lines contain all input fields, mean average, and standard deviation for each product. After all records are processed, print the mean average of all products.

3. A company is evaluating several possible store purchases. A report presents the estimated percentage return on several potential investments and then ranks them by percentages.

Input Records

Fields	Card Columns	
Store identification number	23-27	I5
Store sales (in $1000's)	34-36	F3.0
Net merchandise profit (% fraction)	52-53	F2.2
Capital investment (in $1000's)	62-64	F3.0

Calculations. In the common area of storage, create a two-dimension array (or two single-dimension arrays) for the investment identification numbers and the calculated percent return on the investments. The profit (in dollars) is calculated by multiplying sales by percent of net merchandise. To calculate capital turnover, divide store sales by capital investment. Using a function, calculate percentage return on investment by dividing the profit by the capital investment and multiplying the quotient by 100. After all records are processed, use a subroutine to sort the stores into descending sequence by percentage return.

Output. Headings contain company name and location, date of report, and column headings. After each record is processed, all input and calculated fields are printed. After all records are processed, the report skips to a new page, prints company name and 'SUMMARY REPORT'. Then the store identification numbers and percent of return on investment are printed in sorted order.

4. A clothing company requires a retail operating statement from each of its branch stores. Calculations can be made in a single function that returns several values by using the common area of storage.

Input Records

Fields	Card Columns	
Branch store number	23-27	I5
Gross sales	32-36	F5.0
Sales returns and allowances	54-57	F4.0
Cost of goods sold	38-42	F5.0
Expenses	65-68	F4.0

Calculations. In the common area of storage, establish the four input money fields, net sales, and gross margin. Using a function, calculate retail operating profit or loss. Net sales equals gross sales minus sales returns and allowances. Gross margin equals net sales minus cost of goods sold. Operating profit (or loss) equals gross margin minus expenses. Calculate totals for net sales, gross margin, and operating profit.

Output. Headings include company name, home office address, and column headings. Detail lines include all input fields, net sales, gross margin, and operating profit. After all records are processed, the three totals are printed.

5. A delivery service requires a report of costs of shipping various packages.

Input Records

Fields	Card Columns	
Customer's name	1-20	A
Customer account number	21-25	I5
Number of pounds shipped	74-77	I4
Shipping code (1 = regular; 2= air; 3=C.O.D.)	50	I1

Calculations. If delivery is regular service, charge is 25¢ per pound. Air express is 35¢ per pound. C.O.D. is regular charge plus a $2.75 special charge. Using three function subprograms, with customers' names and numbers stored as arrays in the common area, calculate charges for each customer. Count each type of charge. Total the number of pounds shipped and the charges.

Output. Headings include company name and location, and column headings. Detail lines contain all input fields. Shipping codes are explained on detail lines or at the end of the report. After the last record is processed, tallies and totals are printed.

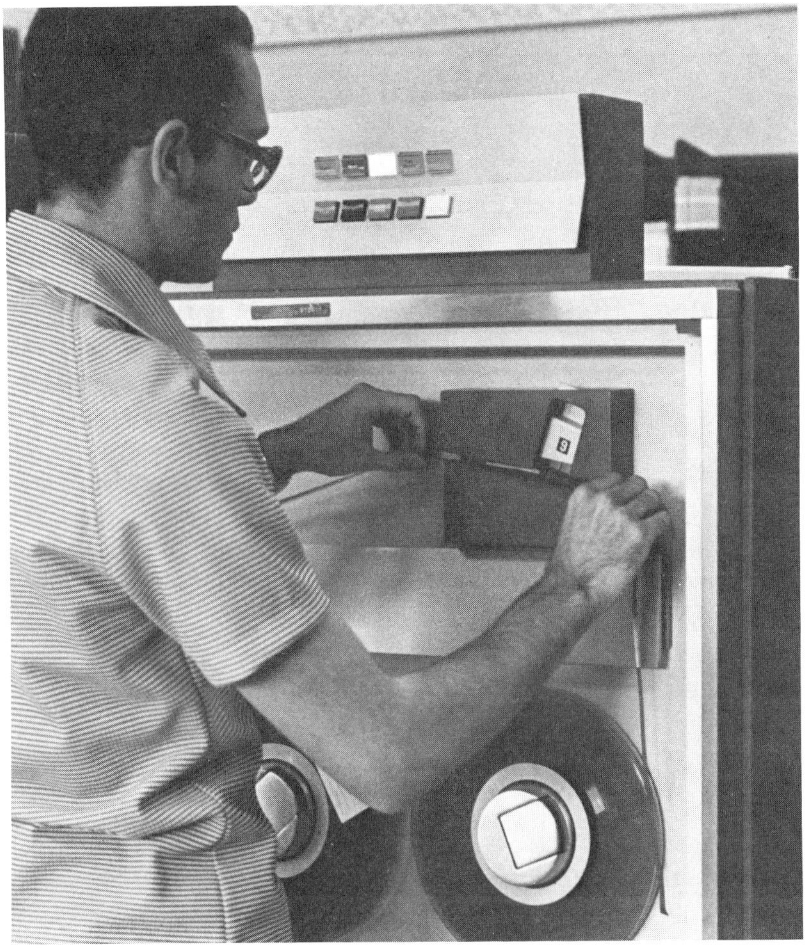

Loading magnetic tape on an IBM 2415 tape unit.

Chapter Objectives

1. Be able to establish standard length logical fields in IMPLICIT or LOGICAL statements.
2. Be able to establish optional length logical fields in IMPLICIT or LOGICAL statements.
3. Be able to initialize logical values in a DATA statement.
4. Be able to write format specifications for input and output of logical constant values.
5. Be able to test logical primaries in logical IF statements.
6. Be able to use .TRUE.,.FALSE.,.T., or .F. to establish a value for a logical primary in an assignment statement.
7. Be able to use other logical primaries to establish a value for a logical primary in an assignment statement.

23

Logical Primaries

In addition to logical expressions created by arithmetic values with relational and logical operators, large FORTRAN compilers also accept logical expressions that are single logical primaries. A logical primary can be a logical constant, a logical variable, a logical element in an array, or a logical function reference. Before it can be used, a logical primary requires an IMPLICIT statement or an explicit specification statement declaring it a logical type. For example, an IMPLICIT statement establishes all fields with names beginning with R as logical fields:

First letter of declared fields
Field type
Statement type

```
IMPLICIT LOGICAL (R)
```

Opening parenthesis
Closing parenthesis

All fields beginning with the letter R now have only logical values of either .TRUE. or .FALSE.. Unless the IMPLICIT statement is overridden, no variable or constant beginning with the letter R can have a stored numeric value.

An explicit field specification establishes three fields as logical rather than numeric variables:

```
LOGICAL TEST, OKAY, LVALUE
```

TEST, OKAY, and LVALUE now can contain only the logical values of .TRUE. or .FALSE.. They cannot hold numeric contents.

Logical primaries can receive their values in three ways: (1) logical assignment statements, (2) DATA statements, and (3) input.

Logical Assignment Statements

After the IMPLICIT or LOGICAL specification statements establish the fields as logical primaries, the fields can receive values in logical assignment statements. For example, LVALUE and OKAY are assigned values:

```
2 LVALUE = .FALSE.
3 OKAY = .TRUE.
```

LVALUE is a 4-byte logical field with the value .FALSE.. OKAY is also a 4-byte logical field, but it has the value .TRUE..

```
4 OLD = .T.
5 NEW = .F.
```

Like OKAY, OLD has a value of true. OLD, however, is stored in a 1-byte field, while OKAY is stored in a 4-byte field. In the same way, LVALUE and NEW both have values of false, but LVALUE has 4-bytes allotted in storage and NEW has only one byte in storage.

The 1-byte storage allotment must be declared in the type specification statement since 1 byte is the optional length for logical fields and 4 bytes is the standard length. The IMPLICIT field specification can be used:

```
IMPLICIT LOGICAL * 1 (S)
```

All fields beginning with the letter S will have 1-byte logical values of .T. or .F..

The LOGICAL explicit field specification can also declare the 1-byte size:

```
LOGICAL * 1 NEW, OLD, LOGIC
```

NEW, OLD, and LOGIC now have 1-byte each in storage.

Both the optional and the standard lengths can be combined into one specification statement:

```
LOGICAL TEST1, TEST2, TEST3 * 1
```

Fields TEST1 and TEST2 are established as 4-byte logical fields, and TEST3 is established as a 1-byte logical field. When assignment statements 2, 3, 4, and 5 are executed, LVALUE and OKAY are assigned the 4-byte .TRUE. and .FALSE. values, and OLD and NEW are assigned .T. and .F. 1-byte values.

Once logical values are established for fields, they can be used in assignment statements with other logical fields:

```
6 TEST1=LVALUE
7 LOGIC=OKAY
```

TEST1 has the value of .FALSE. because LVALUE was assigned the value .FALSE.. LOGIC has the value .T. because OKAY has the value .TRUE..

By using logical operator .NOT., the opposite value can be assigned:

```
11 SUPER = .NOT. TEST1
```

SUPER has the logical value .TRUE. because TEST1 has the value .FALSE.. Since SUPER does *not* have the value of TEST1, it receives the only alternative, the value .TRUE.. In the same way, if TEST1 has the value .TRUE., SUPER has the value .FALSE..

Although a bit more complicated, the logical operators .AND. and .OR. can also be used in assignment statements for logical fields:

```
12 SOLD = OKAY .AND. OLD
13 NUVALU = LVALUE .AND. NEW
14 SOME = LVALUE .AND. LOGIC
```

Utilizing previous assignments, SOLD has the value .TRUE. because both logical primaries OKAY and OLD have true values. NUVALU and SOME both have values of .FALSE.. NUVALU is false because LVALUE and NEW both have .FALSE. values; SOME is false because LOGIC is .TRUE. but LVALUE is .FALSE.. When .AND. is used, *both* logical expressions must be true for the assigned field to be .TRUE..

When the same logical primaries are combined with .OR. instead of .AND., the receiving fields sometimes get different values.

```
22 SOLD2 = OKAY .OR. OLD
23 NUVAL2 = LVALUE .OR. NEW
24 SOME2 = LVALUE .OR. LOGIC
```

With .OR. the logical operator, SOLD2 and SOME2 have true values because both have *at least one* logical expression with the value of .TRUE.. NUVAL2 again has a value of .FALSE. because both of its logical primaries are .FALSE..

.NOT. can also be used in logical assignment statements with two or more logical expressions. For example, STEST is assigned a value when OKAY has a value of .TRUE. and LVALUE is stored as .FALSE.:

```
25 STEST = OKAY .AND. .NOT. LVALUE
```

STEST has a value of .TRUE., because OKAY has a true value and .NOT. LVALUE implies .TRUE. since LVALUE is false.

REVIEW QUESTIONS

1. What are the standard and optional lengths of logical variables?
2. Which statements can establish logical primaries?
3. In what three ways can logical values be established?

Initializing Logical Values in the DATA Statement

Logical fields can receive values from DATA statements. For example, fields A, B, C, and D are established as 4-byte logical fields, and field E is established as a 1-byte logical field in a LOGICAL field specification. Then the DATA specification gives logical values to the fields:

```
LOGICAL A, B, C, D, E*1
DATA A, B, D / 3*.TRUE./, C/ .FALSE./, E/.T./
```

The DATA statement initializes with the value true for fields A, B, D, and E. C is initialized with the value .FALSE..

Logical Format Specification

The logical primary is often tested after it is input. For example, the personnel office of a company is directed to find an employee with the following characteristics: married, able to type, willing to travel, able to speak either or both Spanish and French, and less than or equal to 50 years of age. Employee personnel records contain five logical fields: TYPING, TRAVEL, SINGLE, SPANSH, and FRENCH. These fields are established as logical fields in a type specification:

```
LOGICAL*1 TYPING, TRAVEL, SINGLE, SPANSH, FRENCH
```

A data card is read for each employee:

```
10 READ (6,11) IDNUM,IAGE,TYPING,TRAVEL,SINGLE,SPANSH,FRENCH
```

FORMAT specification 11 establishes the placement of fields on the card, including the five logical fields:

```
                                        Field width
                                        Field type
                                   Number of fields
                                        Field width
                                    Field type
                              Number of fields
                         Field width
                    Field type
11 FORMAT (I5,1X,I2,5X, L1, 2X, 2L1, 1X, 2L1)
```

The letter L establishes a logical field. The 1 following each L indicates that the field occupies one card column. Either a T or an F is punched in the field, representing .TRUE. or .T. or .FALSE. or .F.. If the field is wider than one position, for either input or output, the other positions are blank. In output, the logical value is output in the rightmost position of the field.

After each card in the employee personnel search is input, the fields are combined to test the several conditions in a single statement. The logical IF is constructed to give a value of true when (1) ability to type (TYPING) and (2) willingness to travel (TRAVEL) are both true, (3) SINGLE is false, (4) the ability to speak either or both Spanish or French is shown by SPANSH and/or FRENCH having a value of true, and (5) AGE is less than or equal to 50.0.

```
30 IF (TYPING .AND. TRAVEL .AND. .NOT. SINGLE .AND. (SPANSH
  / .OR. FRENCH) .AND. (IAGE .LE. 50))WRITE (6, 31) IDNUM
```

If all the conditions in statement 30 are met, the WRITE statement is executed. If the final value is .FALSE., the program ignores the WRITE statement and immediately executes the next sequential instruction.

Statement 30 utilizes logical primaries (TYPING, TRAVEL, SINGLE, SPANSH, and FRENCH), a numeric variable (IAGE), a numeric constant (50), a relational operator (.LE.), and all three logical operators (.AND., .OR., and .NOT.).

If the program requires it, the logical value of the same logical expressions can be stored in a logical primary. Assuming that ANSWER is a logical field, statement 32 stores the value of the combined expression.

```
32 ANSWER=TYPING.AND.TRAVEL.AND..NOT.SINGLE.AND.(SPANSH.OR.
  / FRENCH).AND.(IAGE.LE.50)
```

ANSWER can now be tested or used in other logical expressions.

Hierarchy of Operations

When logical expressions have more than one computation, the computer follows its hierarchy or order for computations. The operations, listed with the *first executed* at the top, are performed from left to right in the following order:

1 Parenthetical expressions as nested, innermost first
2 Evaluation of functions
3 Exponentiation
4 Multiplication and division
5 Addition and subtraction
6 Relational operators: .LT., .LE., .EQ., .NE., .GT., .GE.
7 .NOT.
8 .AND.
9 .OR.

When complicated expressions with many arithmetic and logical evaluations are made, knowledge of this hierarchy is essential.

REVIEW QUESTIONS

4. With which format specification is a logical field input?
5. What data contents are input or output in logical field specifications?
6. What is the hierarchy of relational and logical operators?

Alphameric Uses of Logical Primaries

Logical fields can be used to store alphameric information. The standard 4-byte logical field length has no advantages over real or integer fields. The 1-byte logical field, however, offers the most compact storage form for a one-character field element. An example is answers to multiple choice test questions:

```
LOGICAL * 1 ANSERS(35)
```

Only 35 bytes are required to store the 35 alphameric logical fields in array ANSERS.

The DATA statement can also be used with LOGICAL * 1 for alphameric messages:

```
LOGICAL * 1 MESSAG (9)
DATA MESSAG/'A','B','C','D','F','+','-','*',' '/
```

These elements can be called out by calculating subscripts for MESSAG:

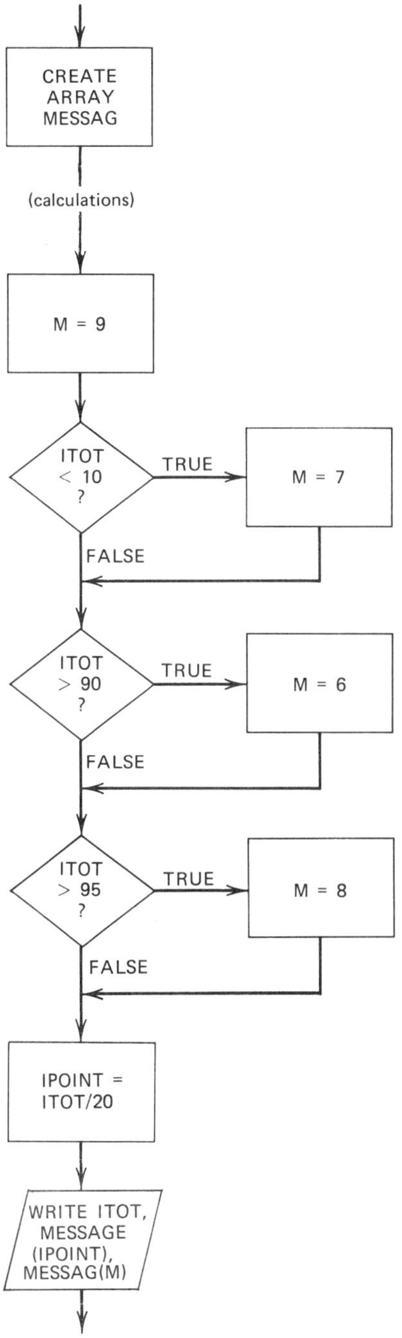

Output is planned on a printer spacing chart:

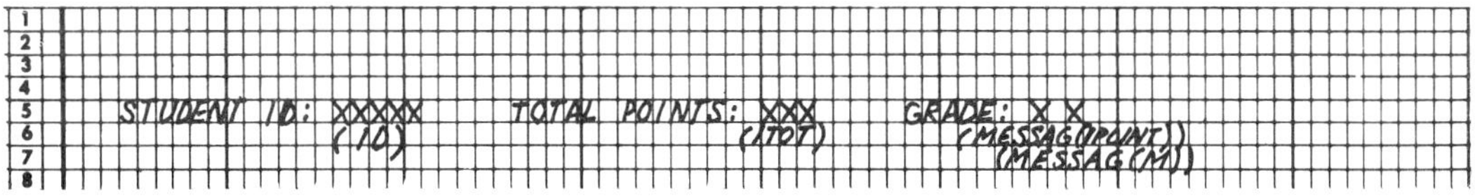

Then the program segment is written:

```
19 M=9
20 IF(ITOT .LT. 10)M=7
21 IF(ITOT .GT. 90)M=6
22 IF(ITOT .GT. 95)M=8
23 IPOINT = ITOT/20
24 WRITE(6,25)ID, ITOT, MESSAG(IPOINT), MESSAG(M)
25 FORMAT(T6,'STUDENT ID:', 1X,I5, 5X,'TOTAL POINTS:',
   11X, I3, 5X, 'GRADE: ', L1, 1X, L1)
```

In this way, two LOGICAL*1 elements of array MESSAG are printed when WRITE statement 24 calls FORMAT statement 25.

REVIEW QUESTIONS

7. Which logical field length is especially useful for alphameric information?

8. What is its chief advantage?

9. What examples of alphameric data can utilize this logical form?

OBJECTIVES REVIEW

Study the objectives at the beginning of this chapter. Check each one to be certain you have achieved it. Restudy the chapter sections relating to any objective you cannot perform.

ASSIGNMENTS

Prepare a card layout form, printer spacing chart, and flowchart for one of the following problems. Then write, keypunch, and submit the FORTRAN program.

1. Print stockholders' equity for subsidiaries of a nationwide company.

Input Records

Fields	Card Columns	
Subsidiary number	59-60	I2
Partnership	46	L1
Number of common stocks (in hundreds)	51-56	F6.0
Number of preferred stocks (in hundreds)	61-65	F5.0

Calculations. Create a 2-byte integer field for subsidiary number, and a 1-byte logical field for partnership. When the subsidiary is a partnership (partnership field is true), no calculations are executed. For all other entries, equity is determined by adding common stock to preferred stock. These two fields are then added to the total number of each type of stock and to the stockholders' equity for the entire company. The number of nonpartnership subsidiaries is counted. After the last record is processed, the average amount of stockholders' equity is calculated.

The printed report begins with company name and location, and column headings. When the subsidiary is a partnership only the word "Partnership" is printed in a special rightmost column. Detail lines for nonpartnerships contain input fields and the stockholders' equity for each subsidiary. After the last record is processed, the company totals and averages are printed.

2. After labor negotiations, some of a company's hourly employees receive a 7% increase in their hourly rate of pay.

Input Records

Fields	Card Columns	
Employee's name	1-20	5A4
Employee's ID number	23-27	I5
Hourly pay rate	39-41	F3.2
Increase code	69	L1

Calculations. Create a LOGICAL*1 field for increase. For each employee, test the increase field. If it is true, calculate the new rate. After printing the company and column headings, the report lists the input fields for all employees. The new hourly pay rate, in dollars, is printed for employees receiving the increase.

3. An insurance company requires a statistical report of policyholders.

Input Records

Fields	Card Columns	
Policyholder's name	1-20	5A4
Policyholder's account number	21-25	I5
Fewer than three traffic violations (in previous year)	46	L1
Sex (1=male; 2=female)	47	I1
Nonsmoker	69	L1
Marital status (1 = single, 2=married, 3=divorced or widowed)	50	I1

Calculations. Create the two LOGICAL*1 input fields. Test if the policyholder has fewer than three traffic tickets in previous year and if he is a nonsmoker. Count the number of women, men, single women, married women, divorced or widowed women, single men, married men, and divorced or widowed men. Count the number in each of these categories who have fewer than three traffic tickets and the number who are nonsmokers. Count all nonsmokers who have fewer than three traffic violations. Print insurance company name and column headings.

For detail lines, print all input fields. If codes are printed, explain the symbols at beginning or end of report. After the last record is processed, print the counted fields with explanatory captions.

4. During a sales campaign, a company requires a bar graph to show sales of each employee through both the previous week and the present week.

Input Records

Fields	Card Columns	
Name of sales person	1-20	5A4
Employee number	23-27	I5
Number of items sold by end of previous week	38-41	I4
Number of items sold by end of present week	63-66	I4

Calculations. Use the LOGICAL*1 specification to create arrays for output periods and asterisks.

Output. Two bar graphs for each sales person show number of items sold. In the bar graph for the previous week, a period indicates 100 sales items. Immediately below, a bar graph for the present week uses an asterisk (*) to represent 100 sales items. Double space between sales people.

FORTRAN IV is now available in an interactive version for computer terminal use.

Chapter Objectives

1. Be able to write an ASSIGN statement that associates an integer field with a FORTRAN statement.
2. Be able to write an assigned GOTO statement to branch a program to the assigned FORTRAN statement.

24

ASSIGN and Assigned GOTO Statements

The assigned GO TO statement has certain unique qualities. It cannot, however, be utilized by all FORTRAN IV compilers. Its use requires a large compiler that contains the ASSIGN statement.

The ASSIGN Statement

Sometimes a program requires branching for which arithmetic or logical testing is either awkward or inappropriate. The branching can be done by "assignment." A variation of the "first card" dilemma discussed in the chapter on control breaks provides a simple demonstration of the usefulness of the assigned GOTO statement. Instead of branching the first data card around subtotal "breaks" by setting and testing switches, branching can be accomplished by ASSIGN and assigned GOTO statements. A flowchart on pages 372 and 373 illustrates the "first card" dilemma.

Two ASSIGN statements and an assigned GOTO statement can determine the branching. The ASSIGN statement associates an executable FORTRAN statement number with a nonsubscripted integer field used only for such assignments. (Compilers accept an integer field used for other purposes in the program, but the results are too unpredictable to be useful.) For example, the value 7, representing the number of executable statement 7, is assigned to integer field J:

Associated integer field name
Assignment word
Assigned statement number
Statement type
Optional statement number

```
1 ASSIGN 7 TO J
```

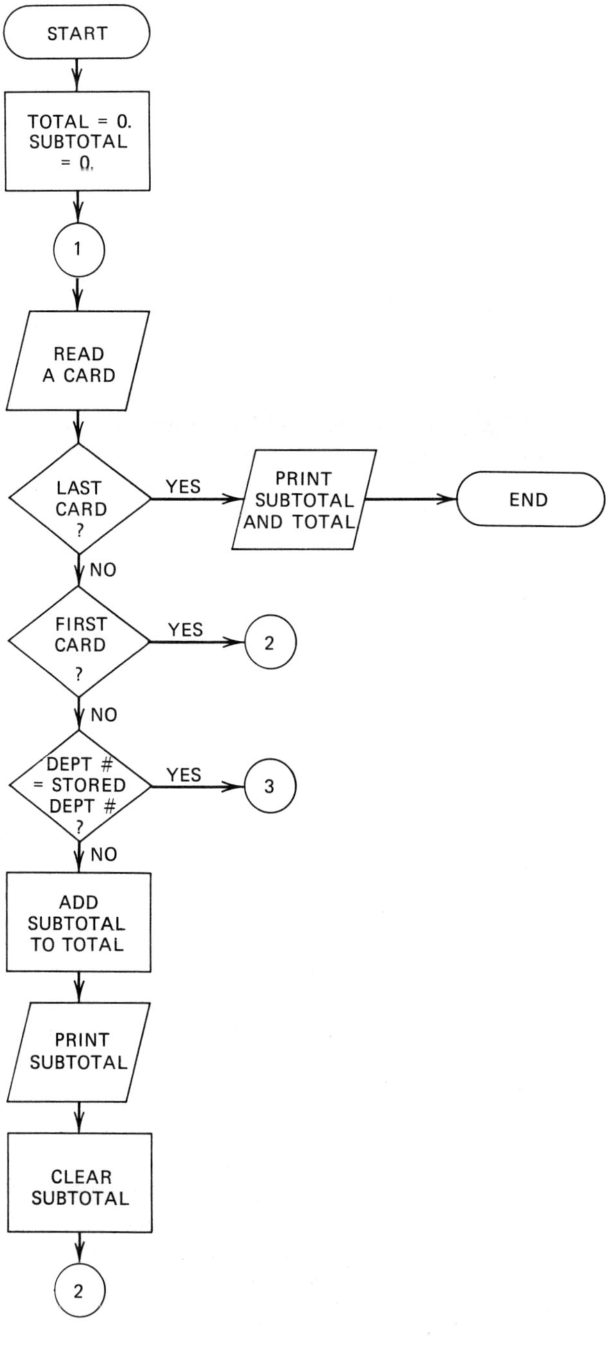
START
TOTAL = 0.
SUBTOTAL
= 0.
1
READ
A CARD
LAST
CARD
?
YES
PRINT
SUBTOTAL
AND TOTAL
END
NO
FIRST
CARD
?
YES
2
NO
DEPT #
= STORED
DEPT #
?
YES
3
NO
ADD
SUBTOTAL
TO TOTAL
PRINT
SUBTOTAL
CLEAR
SUBTOTAL
2

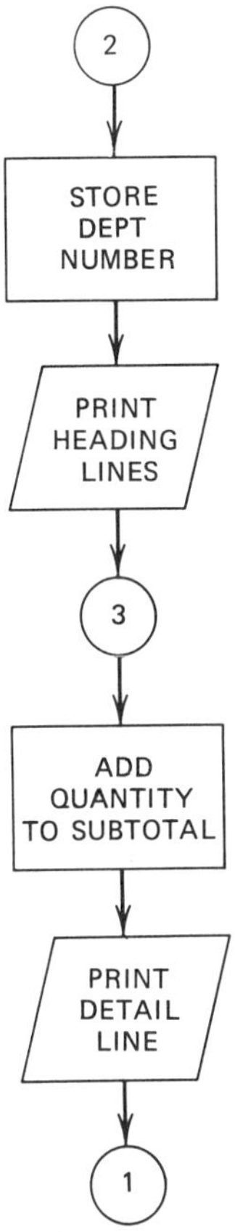

The ASSIGN statement begins in column 7 or later with the word ASSIGN. It is followed by the number of the statement to which the program will branch when as assigned GO TO instruction is executed. After the statement number is the word TO, and then the associated integer field name. No punctuation is used in the statement.

If more than one ASSIGN statement with the same integer name is encountered before an assigned GO TO statement, the program branches to the statement numbered in the ASSIGN statement encountered last. The same statement number can be assigned by more than one ASSIGN statement if program logic requires it.

The Assigned GO TO Statement

The assigned GO TO statement begins like the computed GO TO instruction, but it has essential differences. Statement 6 illustrates an assigned GO TO statement:

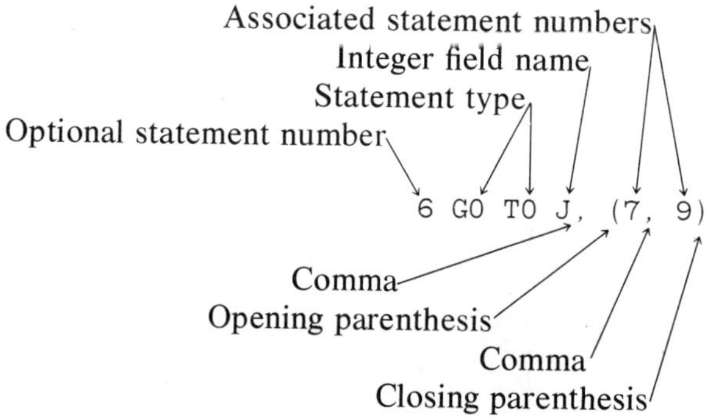

In the assigned GO TO statement, the integer variable name (J) follows the statement type GOTO. Then a comma is required between the variable name and an opening parenthesis. Statement numbers assigned to J in various parts of the program are listed within the parentheses. The numbers need not be in sequence. The program branches to the listed statement number last assigned to the variable. If the number last encountered is not in the parentheses, the program "falls through" to the next instruction. Statement numbers in the list are separated by commas. Nothing can follow the closing parenthesis.

Like the GOTO statement, the assigned GOTO instruction can be numbered, but the first executable instruction after the assigned GO TO statement *must* be a numbered instruction.

REVIEW QUESTIONS

1. With what is an integer field "associated" in the ASSIGN statement?
2. When there are several ASSIGN statements for the same integer, to which statement does the assigned GOTO statement branch?
3. Under what conditions does the program "fall through" to the next sequential instruction after an assigned GOTO statement?

Program SUBTOT2 revises the earlier program SUBTOT so that the "first card" test is solved by ASSIGN and assigned GOTO statements. The logic is flowcharted.

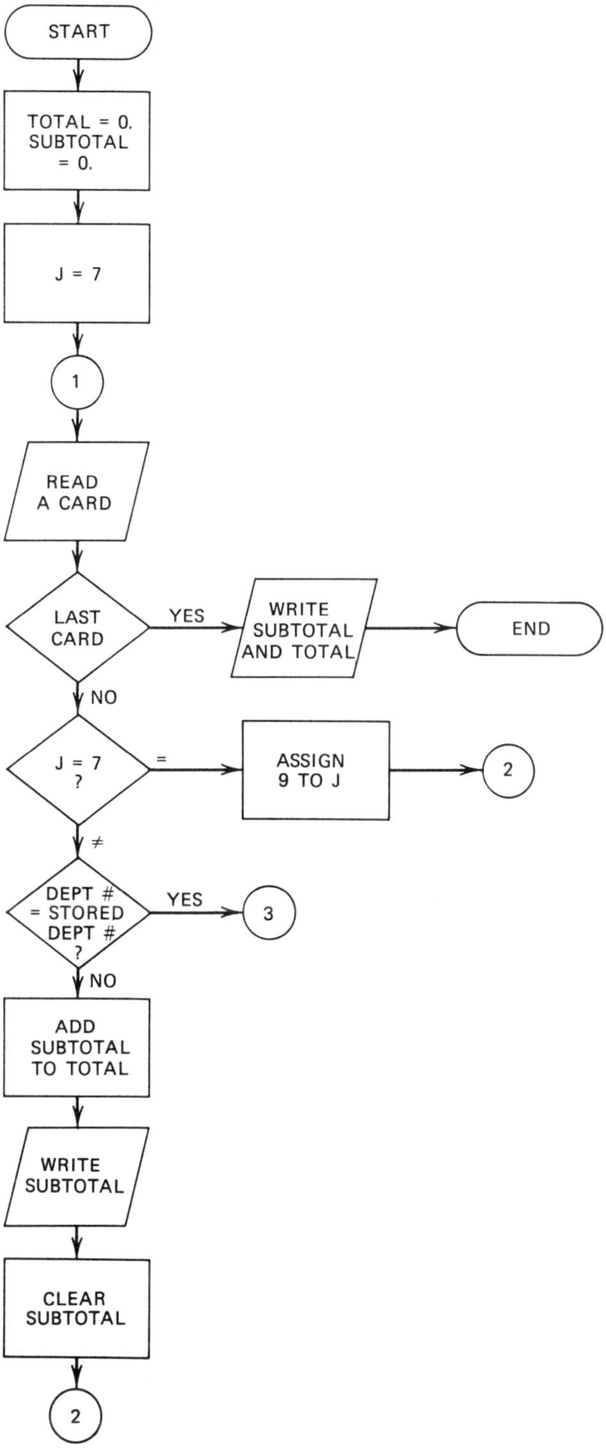
START
TOTAL = 0.
SUBTOTAL
= 0.
J = 7
1
READ
A CARD
LAST
CARD
YES
WRITE
SUBTOTAL
AND TOTAL
END
NO
J = 7
?
=
ASSIGN
9 TO J
2
≠
DEPT #
= STORED
DEPT #
?
YES
3
NO
ADD
SUBTOTAL
TO TOTAL
WRITE
SUBTOTAL
CLEAR
SUBTOTAL
2

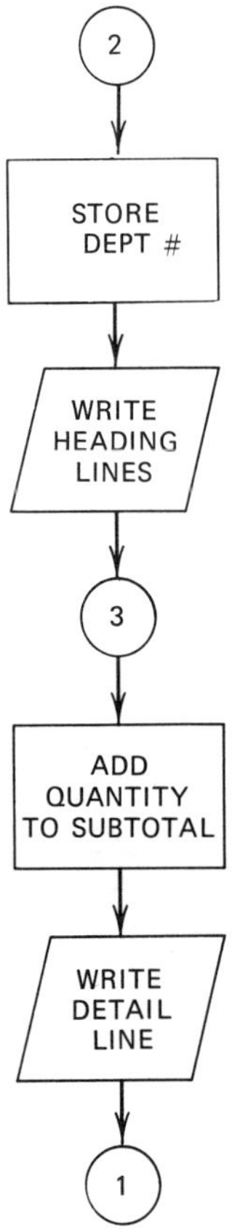

The input format is represented on the card layout form:

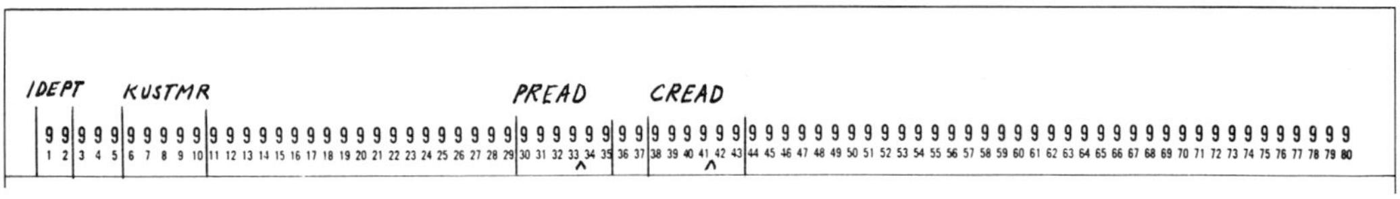

Output is planned on the printer spacing chart:

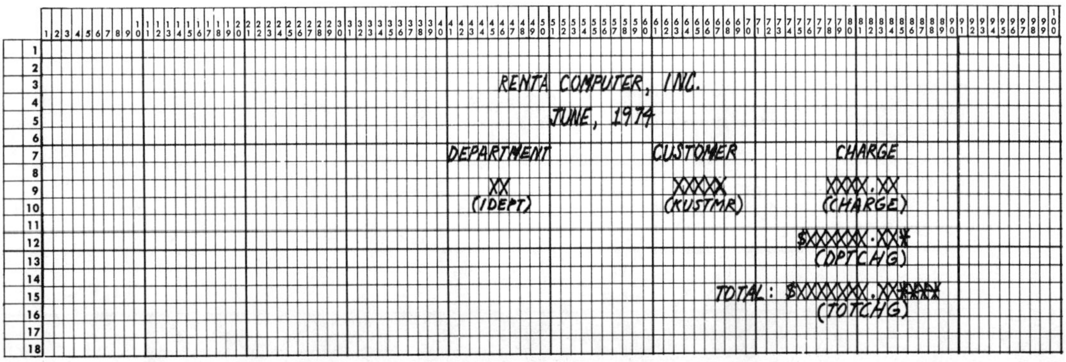

Integer variable J is associated with statements 7 and 9 at two different points in the program. The program begins by assigning statement number 7 to integer J:

```
1 ASSIGN 7 TO J
```

Subtotals and total are cleared to zeros. The first data card is read. Then statement 6, the assigned GO TO, is processed:

```
6 GO TO J, (7,9)
```

Since 7 was assigned to J in statement 1, the program branches to statement 7. In statement 7, J is associated with statement 9:

```
7 ASSIGN 9 TO J
```

The next instruction branches the program to statement 14, where item number is stored. Then headings are printed and detail processing begins.

Because statement 20 branches the program back to READ statement 4 after each data card is processed, statement 1 is not executed again. Statement number 9 remains assigned to J for the rest of the program. Thus, the assigned GO TO solves the problem of unmatched fields in the first data card.

The complete program is coded:

```
C PROBLEM SUBTOT2
C ASSIGN STATEMENT NUMBER 7 TO J TO AVOID FIRST CARD SUBTOTALS
    1 ASSIGN 7 TO J
    2 SUBTOT = 0.
    3 TOTAL = 0.
    4 READ(5,5,END=23) IDEPT,KUSTMR,PREAD,CREAD
    5 FORMAT (I2,3X,I5,T30,F6.2,2X,F6.2)
    6 GO TO J, (7,9)
C IF FIRST DATA CARD, ASSIGN 9 TO J, THEN BRANCH TO ITEM PROCESSING
    7 ASSIGN 9 TO J
    8 GO TO 14
C IF NOT FIRST CARD, COMPARE ITEM NUMBER AND STORED NUMBER
    9 IF (IDEPT-IDSTOR) 10,17,10
   10 TOTAL = TOTAL + SUBTOT
   11 WRITE (6,12) SUBTOT
   12 FORMAT (T76,'$',F9.2,'*')
   13 SUBTOT = 0.
   14 IDEPT = IDNUM
   15 WRITE (6,16)
   16 FORMAT ('1',T47,'RENTA COMPUTER,INC.'//T52,'JUNE, 1974'//
     1 T42,'DEPARTMENT',T62,'CUSTOMER',T80,'CHARGE'//)
```

```
17 USAGE = CREAD - PREAD
18 CHARGE = (USAGE * .7) + 50.00
19 SUBTOT = SUBTOT + CHARGE
20 WRITE (6,21) IDEPT,KUSTMR, CHARGE
21 FORMAT (T46,I2,T64,I3,T79,F7.2)
22 GO TO 4
23 TOTAL = TOTAL + SUBTOT
24 WRITE (6,12) SUBTOT
25 WRITE (6,26) TOTAL
26 FORMAT ('0',T68,'TOTAL:',T75,'$',F10.2,'****')
27 CALL EXIT
   END
```

Using the demonstration data cards of program USAGE-SUBTOTAL, the program printed the following report:

```
        RENTA COMPUTER, INC.

              JUNE, 1974

DEPARTMENT             CUSTOMER               CHARGE


     10                  12548                126.15
     10                  24573                119.22
     10                  45342                130.54
     10                  55343                339.88
                                        $     715.79*

        RENTA COMPUTER, INC.

              JUNE, 1974

DEPARTMENT             CUSTOMER               CHARGE


     20                  75342                544.26
                                        $     544.26*

                              TOTAL: $     1260.05****
```

Assigned GO TO With Multiple Branching

The assigned GO TO is even more useful in complicated programs. For example, a program has several branches determined by a calculated numeric value; in this case, one-tenth of the price of an item from 1¢ to $2.00. All branches eventually merge, but instructions have altered or lost the original values of the differentiating field. Then differentiation is required again on the original basis.

Because calculations after the multiple decision making (computed GO TO statement) change the value of MONEY and the price, the computed GO TO cannot be used when the same differentiations are to be made later in the program. The assigned GO TO is valuable in such a situation because its assignments remain until a new ASSIGN statement is encountered.

The following program segment demonstrates a solution to the problem:

```
C MONEY EQUALS PRICE DIVIDED BY 10 TO PROVIDE 10¢ GROUPINGS
   80 MONEY = PRICE / 10
C BRANCHES FOR ITEMS LESS THAN AND GREATER THAN 90¢
   81 IF (MONEY - 10) 82, 11, 11
C BRANCH ITEMS BY INCREMENTS OF MONEY
   82 GO TO (2, 3, 4, 5, 6, 7, 8, 9, 10), MONEY
C "FALL THROUGH" BRANCH FOR 1¢ - 9¢ ITEMS: ASSIGN VALUE TO M
    1 ASSIGN 41 TO M
      .
      .(calculations)
      .
      GO TO 30
C BRANCH FOR 10¢ - 19¢ ITEMS: MONEY = 1
    2 ASSIGN 42 TO M
        (calculations)
      GO TO 30
C BRANCH FOR 20¢ - 29¢ ITEMS; MONEY = 2
    3 ASSIGN 43 TO M
        (calculations)
      GO TO 30
C BRANCH FOR 30¢ - 39¢ ITEMS; MONEY = 3
    4 ASSIGN 44 TO M
        (calculations)
      GO TO 30
C BRANCH FOR 40¢ - 49¢ ITEMS; MONEY = 4
    5 ASSIGN 45 TO M
        (calculations)
      GO TO 30
C BRANCH FOR 50¢ - 59¢ ITEMS; MONEY = 5
    6 ASSIGN 46 TO M
        (calculations)
      GO TO 30
C BRANCH FOR 60¢ - 69¢ ITEMS; MONEY = 6
    7 ASSIGN 47 TO M
        (calculations)
      GO TO 30
C BRANCH FOR 70¢ - 79¢ ITEMS; MONEY = 7
    8 ASSIGN 48 TO M
        (calculations)
      GO TO 30
C BRANCH FOR 80¢ - 89¢ ITEMS; MONEY = 8
    9 ASSIGN 49 TO M
        (calculations)
      GO TO 30
```

```
C BRANCH FOR 90¢ - 99¢ ITEMS; MONEY = 9
   10 ASSIGN 50 TO M
        (calculations)
      GO TO 30
C BRANCH FOR ITEMS COSTING $1.00 OR MORE
   11 ASSIGN 51 TO M
        (calculations)
C CALCULATIONS FOR ALL ITEMS
   30 (calculations)
                  .
                  .
                  .
C BRANCHING BY ORIGINAL ITEM VALUES
   40 GO TO M, (41, 42,43,44,45,46,47,48,49,50,51)
```

All branches merge for statement 30. Various calculations are performed, and then branching must be done again according to the original grouping. When statement 40 is executed, the program branches to statements assigned to M in the original categories.

REVIEW QUESTIONS

4. How does the form of the assigned GO TO statement differ from that of the computed GO TO statement?
5. What determines the branching in an assigned GO TO statement?

OBJECTIVES REVIEW

Study the objectives at the beginning of this chapter. Check each one to be certain you have achieved it. Restudy the chapter sections related to any objective you cannot perform.

ASSIGNMENTS

Prepare a card layout form, printer spacing chart, and flowchart for one of the following problems. Then write, keypunch, and submit the FORTRAN program.

1. A printed report calculates tax assessments for property in an unincorporated (non-city) area.

Input Records

Fields	Card Columns	
Assessment property number	21-27	I7
Assessed property value (in whole dollars)	30-35	F6.0
Special categories	44	I1

For each $100 of assessed valuation, county taxes are $2.37, school taxes are $4.48, and special district taxes are $0.56. Calculate these taxes for each assessment. Use the assigned GO TO to grant 5%

deduction to special category 1, and 7½% deduction to special category 2. Calculate the combined amount due for each taxpayer, and accumulate totals for each of the three taxes.

The printed report begins with the special heading information (name of county and state) and column headings. Detail lines contain the input fields, the amounts of the three taxes, and the combined amount. If a deduction is given, show 5% deduction with an *, 7½% deduction with **. After the last card is processed, print the totals for each tax, and messages explaining the asterisk messages.

2. A company manufactures nine different product models. Each data card represents one product order.

Input Records

Fields	Card Columns	
Customer account number	23-27	I5
Item model order number	41	I1
Number of items ordered	29-34	I6

The number of items ordered for each model is totaled in a nine-element array. A count is kept of how many orders are received for each model. Each transaction is recorded on a printed report. Use Assigned GO TO statements to print a special message identifying each model.

After all records are processed, the average number ordered for each model is calculated. A summary report is printed with company and column headings and with report date. The total number of items ordered, the number of orders, and the average number per order are given for each product model.

3. A report lists all store sales. Sometimes a special 8% discount is given.

Input Record

Fields	Card Columns	
Purchaser's account number	21-25	I5
Original price	52-57	F6.2
Discount code	48	I1 (1=yes; 0=n

The net price is calculated by subtracting the amount of the discount from the original price. For each sale, a state sales tax of 4.5% is calculated and added to the price to obtain the combined amount. Amount of sales tax and net price are totaled. The printed report contains the company name and location and column headings. Detail lines contain the purchaser's account number, original price, net price if discount is granted, amount of sales tax, and combined amount. Use assigned GO TO statements to branch to different WRITE and FORMAT statements when the discount is or is not given. After the last card is processed, the totals are printed.

Chapter Objectives

1. Be able to write instructions to input format specifications from data cards.
2. Be able to write object-time format specifications in a DATA statement.
3. Be able to write object-time format specifications in type specifications.
4. Be able to write unformatted READ and WRITE statements for tape or disk output.
5. Be able to write a NAMELIST statement.
6. Be able to prepare data to be input with a NAMELIST name.
7. Be able to input or output data with a NAMELIST name.

25

Unformatted READ and WRITE Statements; NAMELIST Statement; Special Techniques to Input Format Specifications

FORTRAN IV has several special forms of input and output statements. None is widely accepted in business data processing, but each has situations for which it is particularly useful. Some of the statements are available only in such extended forms as IBM FORTRAN IV, versions G or H; others are in all standard FORTRAN IV compilers.

Variable or Object-Time Format Specifications

In some computer installations, a program is used frequently, but the input data format is not always the same, or output is arranged in different forms. In such instances, flexibility is obtained in FORTRAN IV, but not in basic FORTRAN, by reading format specifications into storage at object time instead of at compilation time. The format specifications are stored as an array. Then the array name is used instead of a format statement number in READ and WRITE statements within the program.

Object-time format specifications usually are stored in any of three basic ways. The first and most flexible method is to read the format specifications from the first data card or cards.

Format Specifications From Data Cards

Reading format specifications from data cards is the most flexible form because the data card can be changed even when the program is run from an object program instead of from the original FORTRAN source deck.

Certain preliminary steps are necessary, as the following example illustrates:

```
  DIMENSION FRMAT (18), KUSTMR (5)
1 READ (5,2) FRMAT
2 FORMAT (18A4)
3 READ (5,FRMAT) IDNUM, KUSTMR,PREAD,CREAD
```

The DIMENSION statement establishes FRMAT as an eighteen-element array and KUSTMR as a five-element array. FRMAT is the alphameric array storing the format specification codes.

Statement 1 instructs the computer to read array FRMAT according to FORMAT statement 2. Statement 2 declares that FRMAT consists of 18 A4 elements. Thus, the computer reads and stores the first 72 (18×4) columns of the data card as array FRMAT. This data card can be changed each time the program is run.

During one program execution, the first 22 columns of the first data card contain the following:

```
(I5,5A4,F5.1,2X, F5.1)
```

As a result of this input, when statement 3 calls for data to be read according to FRMAT, the data record contains IDNUM in columns 1-5, the five elements of array KUSTMR in columns 6-25, PREAD in columns 26-30, and CREAD in columns 33-37:

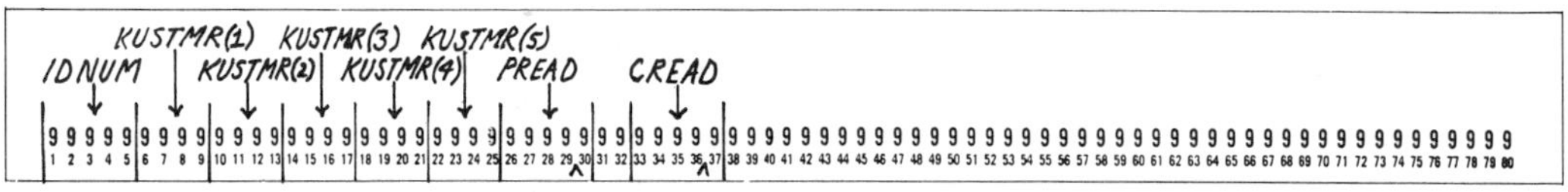

When the program is run another time, the first data card contains the following:

```
(1X,I4,2X,5A4, 3X, F5.1, T50, F5.1)
```

The data record called by statement 3 now contains 4-digit IDNUM in columns 2-5, array KUSTMR in columns 8-27, PREAD in columns 31-35, and CREAD in columns 50-54:

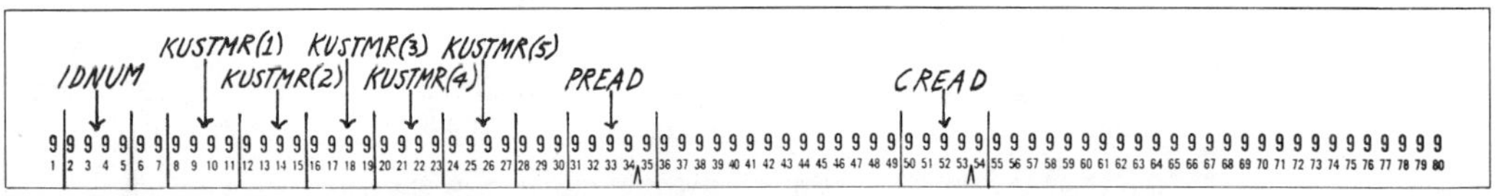

Thus, several different data decks can be processed by the same program, changing only the first data card.

Format specifications read at object time have a few rules that must be followed. First, the specifications must be read in as an array, even if the array contains only one element. Second, the array elements must be alphameric. Third, the format specification codes require the same form as a FORMAT statement except that the statement number and the word FORMAT are not present. Thus, the array consists of at least one pair of parentheses enclosing one or more format codes. Fourth, some forms of FORTRAN IV permit a literal containing two apostrophes only for output. If the object time format code for a READ statement requires a literal field with an internal apostrophe, the H format must be used for the literal.

REVIEW QUESTIONS

1. What type of array must be used when format specifications are read from a data card?
2. How does the variable or object-time format give a program flexibility?

Format Specifications in DATA Statements

The second method of inputting format specifications at object-time utilizes the DATA statement with literals in either apostrophes or the H format. In both cases, the format elements must be enclosed by a pair of parentheses. The format specifications are first input within apostrophes:

```
  DIMENSION FRMAT2 (6), KUSTMR (5)
  DATA FRMAT2 / '(5A4, I5, F5.1, 2X,F5.1)'/
2 READ (5,FRMAT2) KUSTMR, IDNUM, PREAD, CREAD
```

The format specifications for the same fields can be input with the H format specification:

```
  DIMENSION FRMAT3 (8), KUSTMR (5)
  DATA FRMAT3 /32H(1X, I5, 3X, 5A4, F6.1,6X, F6.1)
4 WRITE (6,FRMAT3) IDNUM, KUSTMR, PREAD, CREAD
```

The FORTRAN compiler assumes its standard real or integer field length for each element of the array. Thus, with most models of the IBM S/360 and S/370 computers, A4 is the assumed A field length. FRMAT2 and FRMAT3 require 24 and 32 characters, including the required parentheses. Thus, array FRMAT2 is composed of six A4 fields, and array FRMAT3 contains eight A4 elements.

Format Specifications in Type Specifications

The third way of storing a variable format uses an explicit type specification with the DATA capability. For example, a REAL*8 specification allows 8-character elements in array FRMAT4:

```
REAL*8 FRMAT4 (3) /'(T2,5A4,T5,F5.1,1X,F5.1)'/
```

Because each element in array FRMAT4 is declared 8 bytes in length, the 24 characters of FRMAT4 can be stored in only three elements. The specifications are enclosed by a pair of apostrophes.

Any of the explicit type specifications can be used if the FORTRAN compiler permits this combination of DATA capability and type specification. The IMPLICIT specification, however, cannot be used to establish variable format specification arrays.

REVIEW QUESTIONS

3. How can format elements be specified in a DATA statement?
4. How can format elements be specified in type specifications?
5. Which type specification cannot contain format specifications?

Unformatted Input/Output Statements

Sometimes programs are so large that primary memory space is at a premium. At such times, data fields that are necessary but not needed immediately can be placed in temporary storage on tape or disk. Data written out during a program can be read back and processed during a later part of the program or during another program. This is often accomplished by unformatted READ and WRITE statements for tape or disk

The unformatted WRITE statement looks like the formatted WRITE statement except that the FORMAT statement number is not present. For example, WRITE statement 23 lists variables for identification number (IDNUM) and new balance (BALNEW), and array KUSTMR, dimensioned for five elements. All seven fields are output on tape or disk drive 8:

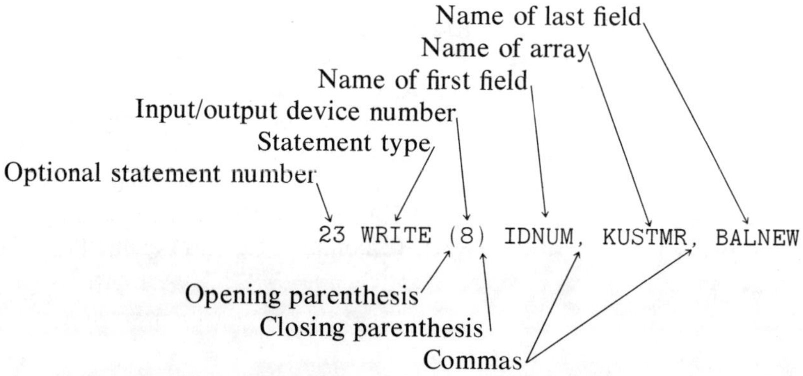

After the word WRITE, only the device reference number is given within the parentheses. The fields are unformatted and are not intended for printer output. Output on the tape or disk device is usable only when retrieved by an unformatted READ statement.

When the data fields are needed later for either printer output or calculations, the unformatted READ statement inputs them back into the computer's main memory. The form can be identical to the WRITE statement except for the change from WRITE to READ:

```
25 READ (8) IDNUM, KUSTMR, BALNEW
```

Statement 25 reads into storage the same data previously output by statement 23. Again a FORMAT statement number is not given.

If the programmer wants to call the input fields by names other than those used in the parallel WRITE statement, the new names will be acceptable so long as the fields match in type and number. To illustrate this, data fields output by statement 23 are input by statement 26 of a different program:

```
26 READ (9) NUM,C1, C2, C3, C4, C5, OLDBAL
```

Statement 26 reads the same data that statement 23 output even though the assigned device number is different, field names are not the same, and the five elements of array KUSTMR are now five separate fields. Whether the device number is the same or different, the programmer (or operator) must see that the tape or disk used for output actually is on the device listed for input.

If an integer variable is established with the value of the input/output device, that variable name can be given instead of the device number in unformatted READ and WRITE statements. For example, integer variable NUM is assigned the number 8; then NUM is enclosed in the parentheses of WRITE statement 24;

```
 1 NUM = 8
   .
   .
   .
24 WRITE (NUM) IDNUM, KUSTMR, OLDBAL
```

With NUM equal to 8, statement 24 directs the output to input/output device 8. This ability to change device assignments with earlier assignment statements gives the program flexibility.

REVIEW QUESTIONS

6. How is the DATA statement used to store object-time formats?

7. What is the difference in specifications between formatted and unformatted READ and WRITE statements?

8. What is the difference in purpose between formatted and unformatted READ and WRITE statements?

9. For which output devices are the unformatted WRITE statement *not* intended?
10. Unformatted READ and WRITE statements are most often directed to which input/output devices?

List-Directed READ and WRITE Statements

Also unformatted are List-Directed READ and WRITE statements. These statements are not available in all versions of FORTRAN IV, but are present in versions G1 and H extended. These highly specialized forms of input and output are not yet standardized throughout the industry. Information regarding them can be obtained from the computer manufacturer.

Asynchronous READ, WRITE, DEFINE FILE, and FIND Statements

Some versions of FORTRAN IV, including H extended, have asynchronous READ, WRITE, and FIND statements (also not standardized) for direct access storage devices such as magnetic disk and drum. These direct access input/output statements enable a programmer to process records either sequentially through a file from the first record to the last, or randomly, going directly to the records to be processed as wanted.

The DEFINE FILE statement must appear in the program before a direct access READ, WRITE, or FIND statement is encountered.

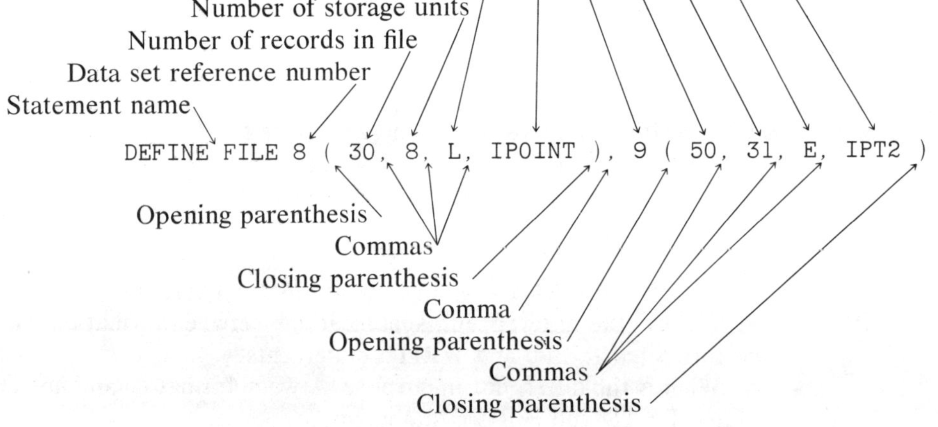

A DEFINE FILE statement can establish one or more files. The example DEFINE FILE statement defines two separate direct access files. The first file is assigned to data set (device) number 8. The second file is assigned to device number 9. The first file contains 30 records, each record containing a maximum of 8 bytes of *internal* storage. The 8 bytes are the combined total of the two fields in each record; one a standard length (4 byte) integer field, and the other a standard length (4 byte) real field. This form of storage is determined by the use of L as the format control code. L indicates that the record can be read either with or without format control, and bytes *in storage* must be given when L is utilized.

Each of the 50 records in the second file contains a maximum of 31 input/output characters. This form of storage unit count is required by the use of E as the format control code. E indicates that a FORMAT statement always will be given with READ and WRITE statements for this file.

IPOINT and IPT2 are nonarray integers that act as pointers to the next available sequential record. They are known as "associated variables." Either before the first direct access input/output statement is encountered, or within the READ or WRITE statement, a numeric value must be established for the associated variable. For example, when records are to be read in a regular progression from the first record (relative record address 1) through an entire file, the following value could be established:

```
10 IPT2 = 1
```

Then the READ instruction can be given:

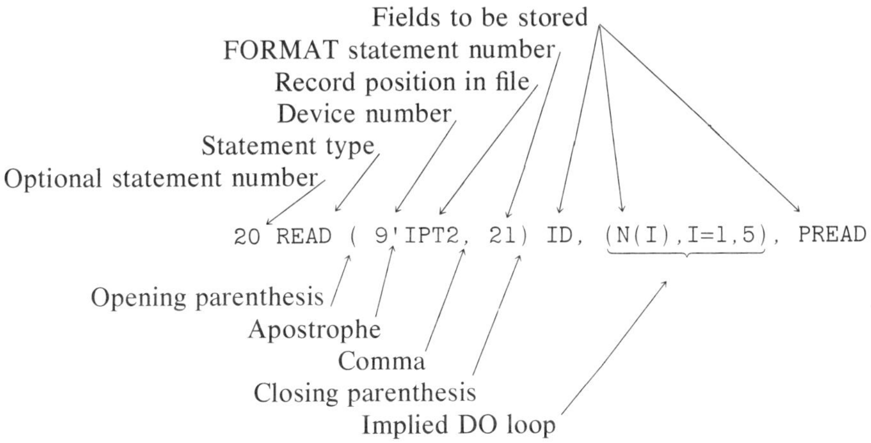

Names of the fields being read need not be the same as the field names used when the file was created, but ordinarily the fields should match in type (integer, real, etc.). For example, the records stored by statement 20 might have been written by statement 22:

```
22 WRITE ( 9'I,21) NUMBER, N,A,M,E,S,PREAD
21 FORMAT ( 15, 5A4, F6.2)
```

The same specifications are used for both the READ and WRITE statements, but field names and arrays may be different.

Each time READ statement 20 is executed, the associated variable IPT2 is automatically established as a value one greater than the record position of the last record read. This incrementing occurs whether one or more records are read by the input statement. Thus, after one execution of statement 20, IPT2 equals 2.

If the programmer wants to read regularly spaced records, such as every sixth record, the associated variable can be used as an adjustable pointer:

```
30 READ ( 9'IPT2 + 5, 31) ID, (N(I), I= 1,5), PREAD
```

After the execution of statement 30, IPT2 is equal to 6 more than it was before the statement execution. (Original value + 5 + 1)

The 31 bytes described in FORMAT statement 21 match the 31 storage units listed in the DEFINE FILE description of data set 9. If L (instead of E) were the format control code, the DEFINE FILE would contain 28 (for seven 4-byte internal storage standard length fields) instead of 31.

If records of a file are to be read randomly, a field name containing the relative record number can be utilized. For example, an inventory number reflects the relative record position number. When information in file 8 is required about an item, the inventory number is input as INNUM. Then the direct access record is called for:

```
40 READ (8'INNUM, 41) ONHAND,ONORDR
41 FORMAT (I6,I6)
```

The eight storage locations in the DEFINE FILE description of data set 8 are internal storage bytes (required by the L format control code), and so they are sufficient for the 12 characters required by FORMAT statement 41 for the two integer fields. The associated variable pointer IPOINT is incremented to one greater than the value of INNUM when statement 40 is executed, but the programmer does not utilize the associated variable in random processing.

Another form of format control is indicated by the code U. The letter U in the DEFINE FILE statement instructs the compiler that format statements will not be issued for any record of the file. When U is the format control code, storage units are given as words (4-byte units).

The FIND statement enables the programmer to increase program execution speed by finding the next record to be input from a direct access storage device while the present record is being processed. This is accomplished by listing the FIND statement some time ahead of the READ statement:

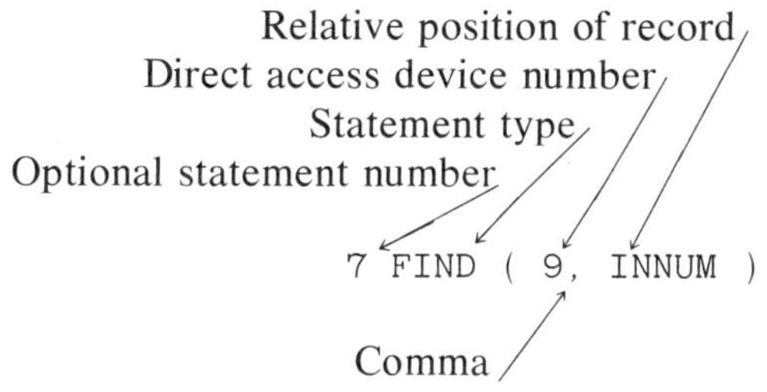

When READ statement 40 is ready for execution, no time will be spent in searching for the record. If the exact position number of a record is known, that number can be used in a FIND statement:

```
8 FIND (9, 21)
```

The twenty-first record on data set 9 will be found by statement 8.

REVIEW QUESTIONS

11. Which input/output device can utilize asynchronous READ and WRITE statements?
12. What are the three format control codes? What does each code indicate?
13. When must a DEFINE FILE statement be used?
14. How are storage units indicated for each format control code in DEFINE FILE statements?
15. What is the advantage of a FIND statement?

NAMELIST Statement

Business data processing ordinarily is concerned with large quantities of data presented on conventionally arranged printed reports. Some FORTRAN IV statements, like unformatted READ and WRITE statements, however, are more useful for interim development than for final form. They might be used for statistical data not intended for standard business report forms, or for storing data necessary later in the program or in a different program.

The NAMELIST specification, which is in this group, is included in many FORTRAN IV compilers. NAMELIST is a specification statement used with a special form of the READ and WRITE statements. It eliminates both a FORMAT statement number and a list of fields. Instead, the NAMELIST name itself represents the list of fields, and the format is set by conventions of the NAMELIST specification. This format lends itself to certain special uses.

A NAMELIST name, which can be used only in input or output statements, is established in a NAMELIST specification:

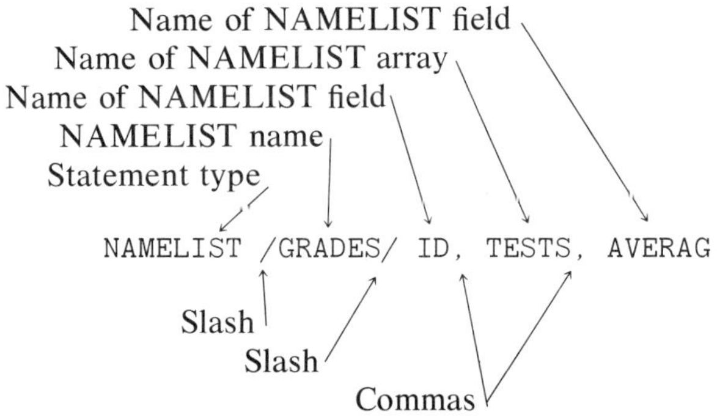

The NAMELIST specification is unnumbered and must come before any statement function or executable statements. It begins with the word NAMELIST in column 7 or later. Then comes the NAMELIST name (GRADES in the example) enclosed in slashes. This NAMELIST name, like other FORTRAN names, must be unique. not used by any variable, array, function, or subroutine. It can be declared only once in the program.

After the second slash come the names of fields included in the NAMELIST name. In the example, GRADES is composed of ID, three-element array TEST, and AVERAG. The field names can be used individually in other calculations and input/output statements. They can also be part of other NAMELIST lists in the same program.

Instead of the separate names, GRADES can now be used in the special NAMELIST form of READ and WRITE statements:

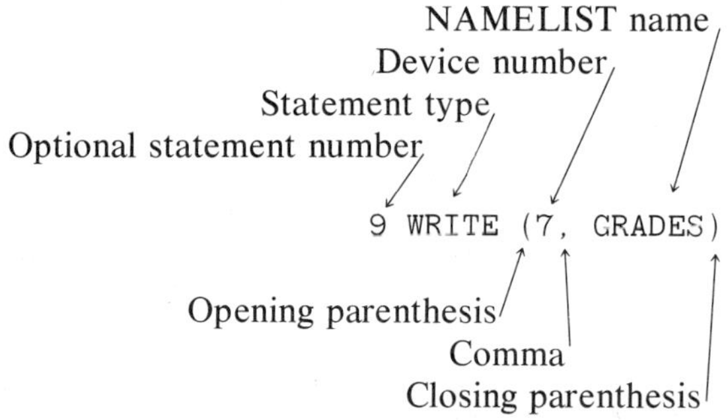

When statement 9 is executed, the fields comprising GRADES are output on device 7 (assumed to be the card punch) in the special NAMELIST format.

NAMELIST Data Format

The NAMELIST form of input and output is different from formatted READ and WRITE specifications. Fields input or output by a NAMELIST name follow special rules:

1. The first character of *every record* (punched card usually) must be blank.
2. The second character of the *first record* of a group of data records must be an ampersand (&).
3. The NAMELIST name follows immediately after the ampersand.
4. At least one blank follows the NAMELIST name.
5. Items of data, in the form of pseudoassignment statements, follow the blank.
6. Each item of data is followed by a comma.
7. The last comma is followed by an ampersand (&) and the word END.
8. Except when an ampersand and END are on a separate card, column 1 is the only blank permitted between the first data item and &END.
9. Alphameric fields are output in their stored numeric form instead of as graphic characters.

When the WRITE statement is executed with a NAMELIST name, *all* variables and arrays in the NAMELIST list are output with both their names and values. On most systems, the first record output contains only a leading blank, an ampersand, and the NAMELIST name. The last record contains only a leading blank, an ampersand, and the word END. The records between contain the variable and array names and values. Statement 9, for example, outputs punched cards in the following form:

```
                        1         2         3         4         5         6
Card columns:  12345678901234567890123456789012345678901234567890123456789012345

    1st card:   &GRADES

    2nd card:   ID=3268,TESTS=90.0,85.0,85.0,AVERAG=90.0,

    3rd card:   &END
```

Thus, the programmer has labeled output (after it has been processed by an interpreter) for study. In addition, because NAMELIST output on punched cards can be input by a READ statement with a NAMELIST, the punched output can be utilized by a later program that inputs with a NAMELIST name.

When a WRITE statement with a NAMELIST outputs to a printer, the printed output follows the same format as the punched NAMELIST output.

REVIEW QUESTIONS

16. Is NAMELIST commonly used in writing standard business reports? Why?
17. The NAMELIST statement must come before what program statements?

18. How many times in a program can a NAMELIST name be declared?
19. Can fields belong to more than one NAMELIST list?
20. In the NAMELIST specification, what encloses the NAMELIST name?

To illustrate the type of use to which NAMELIST output can be put, a program is written for a class whose members have taken a number of tests. The score of correct points for each test is read in for each student. Then the average of all tests for the student is calculated. A report is printed for the instructor and, in addition, a card is output as a record for each student. These cards are punched in NAMELIST format. (Of course, the first and third cards for each student are unnecessary.) After they are processed by an interpreter, the information on the cards is read easily by students.

The logic of the program is flowcharted on page 395.

Input fields are plotted on a multiple card layout form:

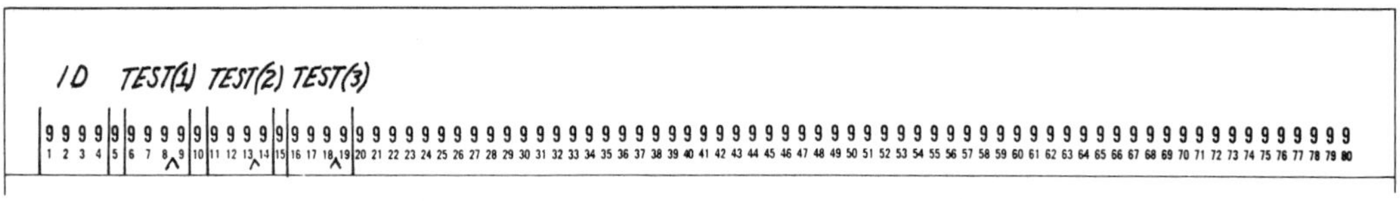

The printed report is planned on a printer spacing chart:

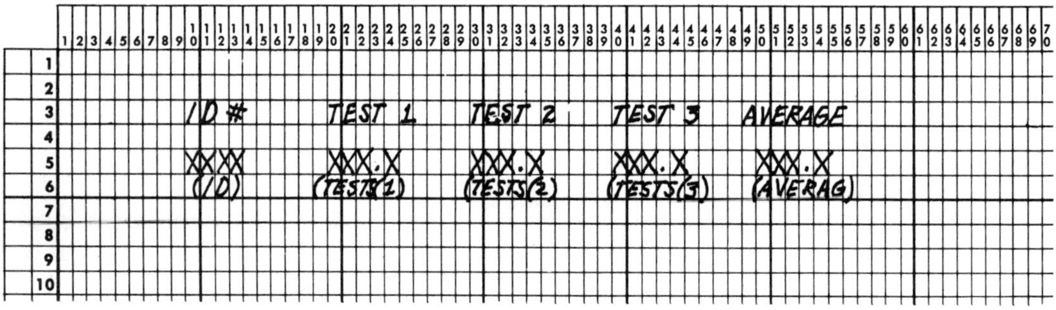

Knowing the form of the NAMELIST output, the programmer next writes the program:

```
  DIMENSION TESTS (3)
  NAMELIST /GRADES/ ID, TESTS,AVERAG
1 WRITE (6,2)
2 FORMAT ('1',T11,'ID #',T21,'TEST 1',T31,'TEST 2',T41,'TEST 3',
 1 T50,'AVERAGE'/)
3 READ (5,4,END=11) ID, TESTS
```

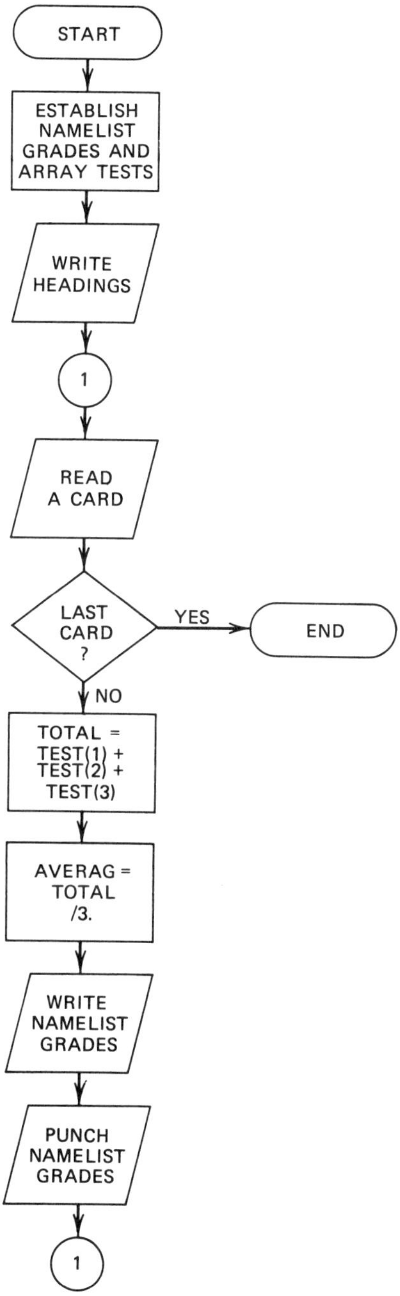
START
ESTABLISH NAMELIST GRADES AND ARRAY TESTS
WRITE HEADINGS
1
READ A CARD
LAST CARD ?
YES
END
NO
TOTAL = TEST(1) + TEST(2) + TEST(3)
AVERAG = TOTAL /3.
WRITE NAMELIST GRADES
PUNCH NAMELIST GRADES
1

```
 4 FORMAT (I4, 3(1X, F4.1))
 5 TOTAL = TESTS (1) + TESTS (2) + TESTS (3)
 6 AVERAG = TOTAL / 3.
 7 WRITE (6,8) ID, TESTS, AVERAG
 8 FORMAT (T11, I4, T21, 4(F5.1, 5X))
 9 WRITE (7, GRADES)
10 GO TO 3
11 CALL EXIT
   END
```

Each student receives his record on a data card in NAMELIST format. The instructor has a printed report.

If the information output on punched cards is required for a later program, the cards can be input by a READ statement using the same NAMELIST list and name:

```
  DIMENSION TESTS (3)
  NAMELIST /GRADES/ ID, TESTS, AVERAG
1 READ (5, GRADES)
```

Paper and magnetic tape, as well as punched cards, can be used with the NAMELIST form of input and output. This form does not permit embedded blanks in either names or values. If blanks are present, they are treated as zeros. Values on the right side of the equal sign can be constants of integer, real, literal, complex, or logical types. Alphameric fields, however, are output in "unreadable" numeric form.

When an array name is not followed by a subscripting integer, the entire array is filled. This was illustrated with array TEST. When the array is multidimensional, it is filled column by column. That is, a 3 × 4 array is filled in the order 1,1; 2,1; 3,1; 1,2; 2,2; 3,2; 1,3; 2,3; 3,3; 1,4; 2,4; 3,4.

The duplication factor can be used when appropriate in establishing such an array. In the following NAMELIST format data, the duplication factor is used for establishing values of five-element array RATE:

```
                         1         2         3         4         5         6
Card columns:   123456789012345678901234567890123456789012345678901234567890

   1st Card:    &LIST1

   2nd Card:    NUM=21212,DEPT=14.,RATE=3*1.0,2.0,3.0,

   3rd card:    &END
```

After these cards are input by a READ statement with the NAMELIST name LIST1, the computer stores the following:

Field Name	Field Contents
NUM	21212
DEPT	14.
RATE(1)	1.0
RATE(2)	1.0
RATE(3)	1.0
RATE(4)	2.0
RATE(5)	3.0

All elements in an array declared with a NAMELIST name need not be input at the same time. For example, data cards read by a NAMELIST input statement could contain the following:

```
                     1         2         3         4         5         6
Card columns: 123456789012345678901234567890123456789012345678901234567890

 &LIST1 NUM=21212,RATE(4)=1.5,RATE(5)=2.5,DEPT=12.0,&END
```

Although the type of input required with NAMELIST formats is impractical for inputting large columns of data, it is useful when only a few fields are read.

A field name can be equivalenced to a name in a NAMELIST list. That equivalenced field name, however, cannot be substituted in NAMELIST input for the name listed in the NAMELIST. In the same way, the NAMELIST list can contain names of fields in the common area, but dummy argument names are not permitted in NAMELIST lists.

REVIEW QUESTIONS

21. What must be in the first column of NAMELIST formatted data?
22. How must NAMELIST data end?
23. Can a NAMELIST field be equivalenced to another field?
24. Can a dummy argument be in a NAMELIST list?
25. On which device is NAMELIST usually output?

OBJECTIVES REVIEW

Study the objectives at the beginning of this chapter. Check each one to be certain that you have achieved it. Restudy the chapter sections related to any objective you cannot perform.

ASSIGNMENTS

Prepare a card layout form, printer spacing chart, and flowchart for one of the following problems. Then write, keypunch, and submit the FORTRAN program.

1. A report of the day's sales is prepared for the sales manager.

Input Records

Fields	Card Columns	
Seller's ID number	21-25	I5
Item sales number	38-40	I3
Number of units sold	74-75	I2
Price per unit	62-66	F5.2
Commission rate	52-53	F2.2

Calculate the total amount of sale and the seller's commission for each record. Count all sales records. Total the amount of all sales and of all sales commissions. After all records are processed, find the average amount of sales and the average commission.

Output. Use unformatted WRITE statement to output detail information to tape or disk. After all records are processed, use unformatted READ statement to input the data for a printed report. Headings contain the company name, company location, and column identification. Detail output lines contain the seller's ID number, item sales number, number of units sold, price per unit, total amount of sale, seller's commission rate, and the seller's commission. Total output lines contain the total amount of all sales, total amount of all sales commissions, average amount of all sales, and average amount of all sales commissions.

2. A teacher wants an analysis of the number of assignments completed and turned in by students in a class.

Input Records

Fields	Card Columns	
Student identification number	21-27	I7
Number of assignments submitted	38-39	I2

The number of assignments is totalled, and students are counted. If 35 or more assignments were submitted, a grade of A is assigned for the homework part of the course. For 28-34 assignments, the grade is B. For 20-27 assignments, the grade is C. Ten through 19 assignments equals D. Nine or fewer assignments receive F grade. After all records are processed, the average number of cards per student is calculated.

Headings of printed report contain name and location of the school, course title, and column identifications. Detail lines print all input fields and the grade for assignments. Using the NAMELIST format, punch a card for each student giving the student identification number and number of assignments submitted. After all records are processed, total lines print the total number of assignments submitted, the number of students counted, and the average number of assignments per student.

3. A company manufactures nine different products. Each data card represents one product order.

Input Records

Fields	Card Columns	
Customer account number	23-27	I5
Product number	41	I1
Number of product items ordered	29-34	I6

The number of items ordered for each product is totalled in a nine-element array. A count is also kept of the number of orders received for each product, regardless of the number of items. Each transaction is recorded on magnetic tape or disk with unformatted WRITE statements. (These will presumably be read back later in unformatted READ statements.)

After all records are processed, the average number ordered for each product is calculated. A summary report is printed with company and column headings. The total number of items ordered, the number of orders for each product, and the average number of items per order are given for each product.

4. The unincorporated sections of a county require a printed and a magnetic tape report of their property taxes. Tax rates are expressed per $100 of assessed valuation of both land and improvements.

Input Records

Fields	Card Columns	
Property owner's name	1-20	A
Property tax book number	23-27	I5
Assessed land value	52-56	F5.0
Assessed improvements value	62-66	F5.0

Calculations. Use a DATA statement to establish the following tax rates: county tax, $2.79; county school tax, $5.26; special district tax, $0.48. Add the assessed land and improvements value to find the total assessed valuation. For each tax, use a statement function to calculate 1/100 the assessment value and multiply that quantity by the appropriate tax rate. Add the three tax amounts to obtain the total tax for each property owner. Total each of the three types of taxes for all property owners. Count the property owners. After all records are processed, calculate the average amount paid for each type of tax.

Printed Report. Headings include county name and state, date of report, title of tax report, and column headings. Detail lines include property owner's name, tax book number, assessed land value, assessed improvements value, three taxes and total tax for the property. After all records are processed, three totals and three averages are printed with explanatory messages.

Tape Report. Tape report is the same as the printed detail line except that the property owners' names are not included. This information is output with an unformatted WRITE statement.

Chapter Objectives

1. Be able to write a DEBUG packet of instructions.
2. Be able to write a DEBUG statement.
3. Be able to write AT statements.
4. Be able to write TRACE ON, TRACE OFF, and DISPLAY option statements.

26

The DEBUG Packet

One of the cliches of computer programming is that a computer does not do what the programmer *wants* it to do but, instead, what he *tells* it to do. This type of implacable logic on the part of the machine often creates a blind spot for the programmer when he tries to correct his program. He knows so well what he meant the machine to do that he overlooks what he actually instructed it to do.

The process of correction is usually called "debugging." To be really effective rather than just making an "educated guess," the programmer needs to follow the movement of his data through the program. Some programs involve so many calculations and manipulations, however, that this is a long and tedious job. Several aids are available in such a situation. WRITE statements may be inserted temporarily at strategic points in the program. The danger in this procedure is that accidentally they may not all be taken out when debugging is completed. The FORTRAN-supplied subroutine PDUMP may also be called, but it usually requires a knowledge of computer storage techniques beyond the scope of the average FORTRAN user.

To help in such predicaments, IBM S/360 and S/370, and a few other FORTRAN IV compilers have a debug packet. This packet requires an AT statement and a DEBUG statement with a choice of options. Normally the debug packet contains at least one of three optional statements: DISPLAY, TRACE ON, and TRACE OFF.

Executable FORTRAN statements can also be part of the packet, although there are a few restrictions on their use. First, the program being debugged cannot branch to a statement within the debug packet, but a branch may be made from the debug packet to any point in the program. Second, if a DO loop is part of the debug packet, the entire DO loop must be contained within the packet. Third, SUBROUTINE, FUNCTION, ENTRY, IMPLICIT, BLOCK DATA and statement function statements cannot be included in a debug packet. However, a debug packet may contain RETURN (for subprograms), STOP, or CALL EXIT statements.

A debug packet must be placed immediately before the program END statement. The AT statements, however, determine when the debugging activity occurs.

The DEBUG Statement

A debug packet of instructions must begin with the DEBUG statement. This statement can be (but seldom is) as brief as the word DEBUG anywhere between columns 7-72. Five options are possible with the DEBUG statement, and normally one, two, or more options are included in the statement. Options may be listed in any order. If more than one option is used, they must be separated by commas. The five DEBUG options are UNIT, SUBCHK, TRACE, INIT, and SUBTRACE.

The UNIT option indicates the output device (data set reference number) on which the DEBUG information is to be output.

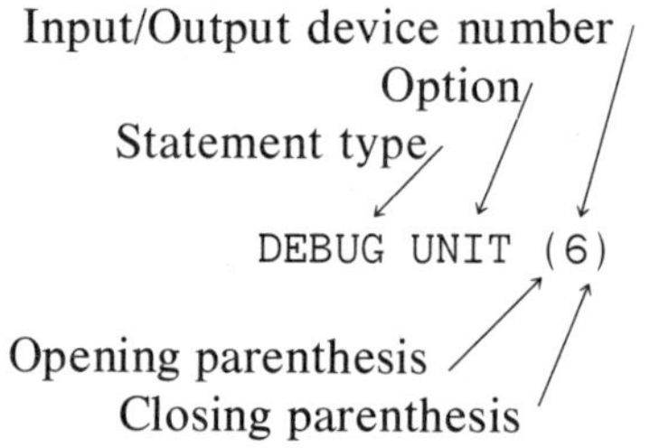

Device numbers are the same as those used in the FORMAT statements. In this example, output from the debug packet will appear on data set 6 (usually the printer under IBM Operating System). If the UNIT option is not given, all debugging data will be output to the standard output device assigned by the system. All debugging output from one FORTRAN program must be output on the same device.

The SUBCHK option checks the validity of subscripts used with array elements during the program. For instance, sometimes a variable used as a subscript has a current value of zero. Because zero cannot be a subscript value, the subscript is invalid. A subscript is also invalid when the value is greater than the number of elements in the array. For example, 8 is not a valid subscript value for an array with six elements.

Especially when the subscript value is calculated, this type of error is difficult to trace. The SUBCHK option, however, sends a message whenever the subscript value is less than 1 or greater than the dimensioned size of the array.

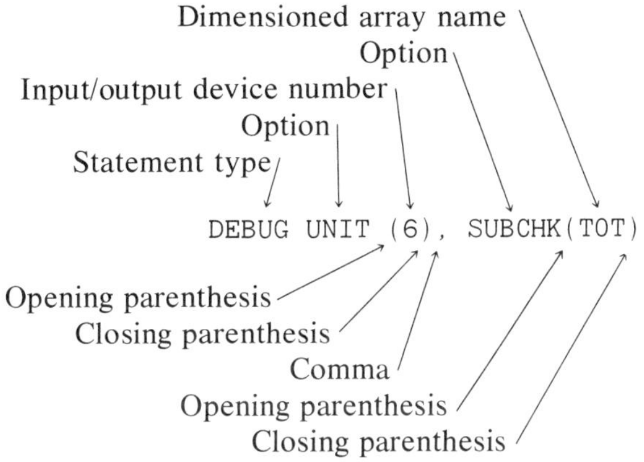

TOT is a four-element array. If all subscript values of TOT are 1, 2, 3, or 4, option SUBCHK will not output a message. If the subscript of TOT contains any other value (either a negative number, 0, or a value greater than 4), a message is output on data set 6:

```
SUBCHK TOT(0)
TOT(0) =  125.0000

SUBCHK TOT(5)
TOT(5) =  200.0000
```

If no array name is given after SUBCHK in the DEBUG statement, *all* arrays in the program are checked for valid subscripts. If the option is not listed, no subscript checking is performed.

When option INIT is listed, it usually is followed by the names of one or more variables and/or arrays in parentheses. For example:

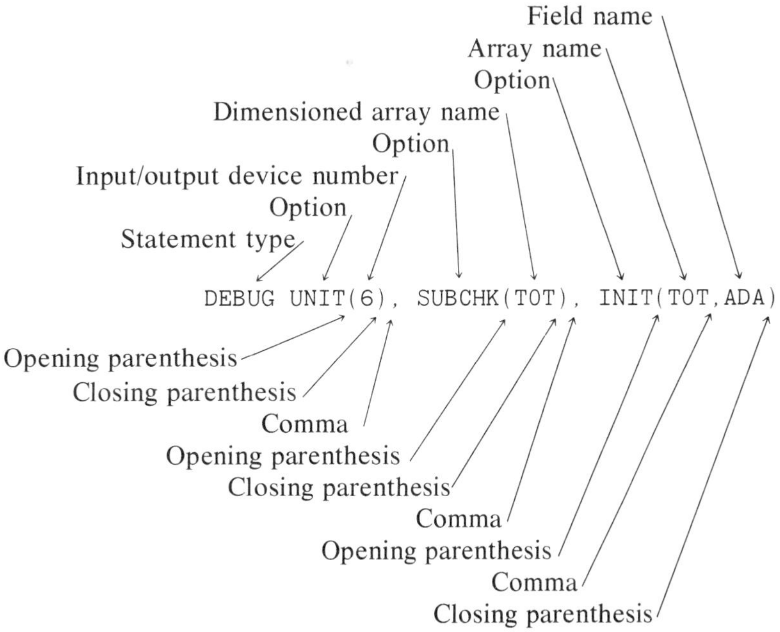

When the value of the field listed in the INIT option changes, its name and value are output beginning in print position 1. For example, variable ADA and then the first element of array TOT are assigned new values. Immediately after each field changes, it is output:

```
ADA =        166.4723
TOT(1) =         27.73427
```

Names and values are displayed whenever the value changes either by calculations, an assignment statement, a READ statement, or an assigned GO TO statement.

If no names are listed in parentheses after the INIT option, the name and value of *every* variable or array element is displayed when it changes. If option INIT is omitted, there is no display when values change.

Option TRACE demonstrates the directional flow of instructions by printing statement numbers as they are executed. Conditional branching instructions such as the IF and computed GO TO statements alter the direction of a program. This affects calculations and other manipulations. If the flow of instructions can be seen, errors often can be more easily pinpointed. A record of statement numbers listed in the order by which they were executed requires at least one TRACE statement, discussed later, and option TRACE in the DEBUG statement:

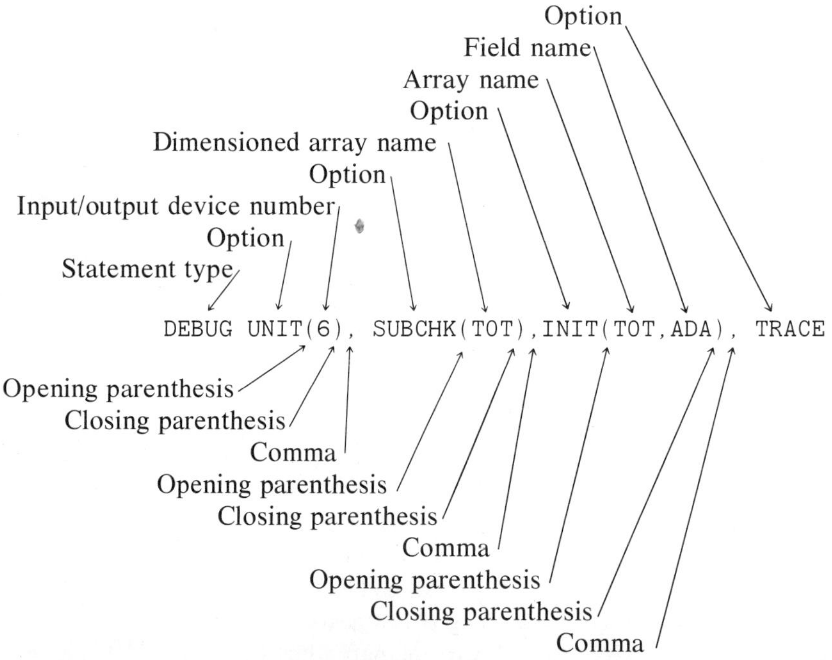

Only numbered statements can be traced. If the TRACE option is omitted, or if statements are unnumbered, no trace can be performed.

Option SUBTRACE specifies that the name of a subprogram be displayed whenever a subroutine is entered. The message RETURN is displayed when subprogram execution is completed.

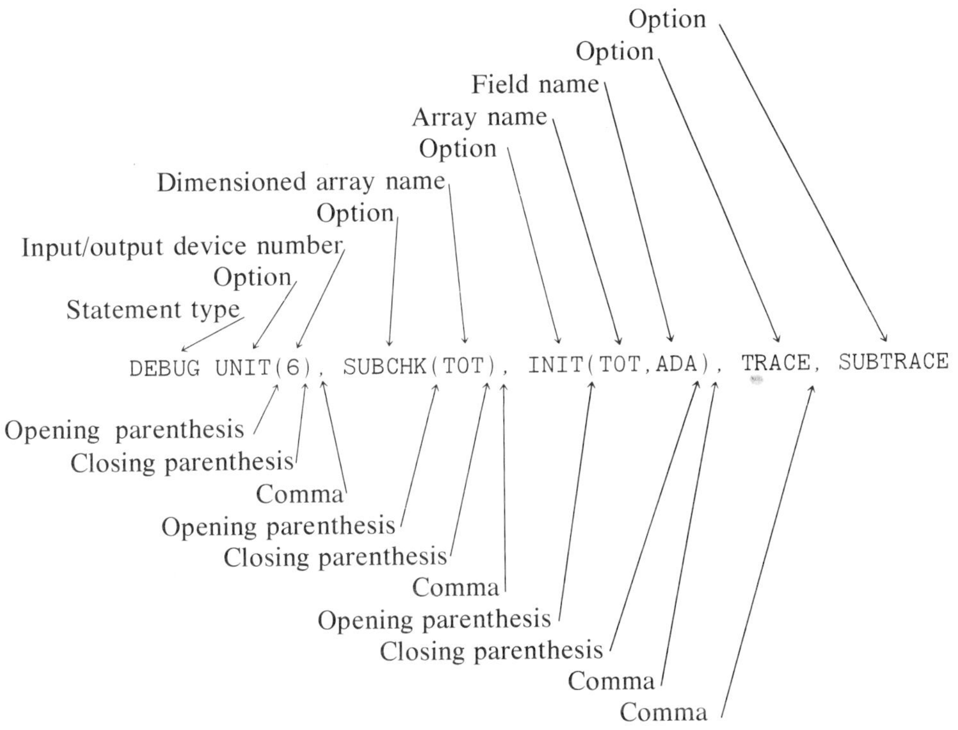

The SUBTRACE option is particularly helpful when a subroutine is entered only under certain conditions as the result of an IF or a computed GO TO statement. Like TRACE, it reveals the flow of the program. The RETURN message is valuable to show that the program is not "caught" in a subprogram from which it cannot escape.

REVIEW QUESTIONS

1. Which two statements are required in a DEBUG packet?
2. How many output devices can be utilized to output debug information from one FORTRAN program?
3. What statement must be the first in a DEBUG packet?
4. When is a subscript invalid?
5. How does knowing the directional flow of a program help in correcting program errors?

AT Statement

An AT statement must follow immediately after the DEBUG statement. The AT statement consists of the word AT in column 7 or later, and then the number of an executable statement.

Number of executable statement
Statement type

```
AT 20
```

The AT statement indicates to the computer the point in the program at which debugging is to begin. This must be immediately before an *executable numbered* statement. In the example, the debugging operation begins just *before* the program executes statement 20. If statement 20 is never encountered, that debug packet is never executed. At least one of the three debugging statements follows the AT statement, and executable FORTRAN statements may also follow the AT statement. The three debug statements are TRACE ON, TRACE OFF, and DISPLAY.

TRACE ON Statement

Beginning with the statement listed in the AT statement, TRACE ON shows program flow by outputting the numbers of all encountered executable statements. If a program is terminated before completion, tracing can reveal the last statement executed, thereby pinpointing the error statement.

Immediately before each numbered executable statement is performed, the statement number is output on the indicated output device. For example,

```
DEBUG UNIT(6),SUBCHK(TOT),INIT(TOT,ADA),TRACE
AT 20
TRACE ON
```

Starting with statement 20, statement numbers are output on data set 6:

```
TRACE 20
TRACE 60
TRACE 20
TRACE 60
TRACE 20
TRACE 60
TRACE 20
TRACE 60
TRACE 20
TRACE 60
```

```
TRACE 20
TRACE 60
TRACE 20
TRACE 60
TRACE 20
TRACE 58
```

If device 6 is the printer, trace messages may be interspersed unintentionally between heading, detail, or total printed lines:

```
TRACE 65
TRACE 50
  YEAR  DEPT  TYPE  CONTACTS  PROJECTED  CONTACTS

TRACE 66
TRACE 3
```

When the error is located, however, the debug packet is easily pulled from the program since all debug instructions are together at the end of the program. Because the debug packet is removed for final processing, errors should not be corrected by FORTRAN statements *within* the packet.

The TRACE ON statement executes only when TRACE is a stated option of the DEBUG statement. A program can contain any number of TRACE ON statements. Each is in effect through any level of subprogram calls and returns, although the trace operates in subprograms only when also specified in the subprogram. TRACE ON cannot appear as part of a LOGICAL IF statement.

TRACE OFF Statement

The TRACE ON statement remains in effect until the program is completed or until a TRACE OFF statement with the number of an executable statement is encountered. For example:

```
DEBUG UNIT(6),SUBCHK(TOT),INIT(TOT,ADA),TRACE
AT 20
TRACE ON
AT 4
TRACE OFF
```

Beginning each time statement 20 is encountered, and continuing until immediately before the execution of statement 4, the number of every executable statement encountered will be output. If the following sequence of instructions is executed, the numbers 20, 21, and 3 will be displayed:

```
                        1 ...
                        2 ...
TRACE ON               20 ...
                       21 ...
                        3 ...
TRACE OFF               4
                       40
```

If the program includes a loop, numbers will be output each time the statement 20 is encountered and will continue until statement 4 is executed. Statement numbers 20, 21, and 3 are listed repeatedly when statements 20 and 4 are both in the loop:

```
                        1 ...
                        2 ...
TRACE ON               20 ...
 each time             21 ...
                        3 ...
TRACE OFF               4 ...
                       40 GO TO 1
                       41 ...
```

The traced numbers need not be coded in sequence:

```
TRACE ON                1 ...
 after first time       2 ...
                        3 ...
TRACE OFF               4 ...
                        5 ...
                        6 ...
TRACE ON               20 ...
 each time             21 GO TO 1
                       22
```

A program may contain more than one TRACE OFF statement. For example:

```
DEBUG UNIT(6), SUBCHK(TOT),INIT(TOT,ADA),TRACE
AT 20
TRACE ON
AT 4
TRACE OFF
AT 24
TRACE OFF
```

If the program branches around both statements 4 and 24, or if the program is terminated so that neither statement 4 nor 24 is encountered, program flow is traced until the end of the program. Like the TRACE ON statement, TRACE OFF cannot be a part of a LOGICAL IF statement.

REVIEW QUESTIONS

6. Which statements can be followed when tracing a program?
7. Why is it important to know when a subroutine is entered?
8. Where is the AT statement placed in a DEBUG packet?
9. Where does a debugging operation begin?

DISPLAY Statement

The DISPLAY statement causes specified variables and arrays to be output immediately *before* executing the statement numbered in the AT statement. The fields appear in the same format as NAMELIST output. For example, assume that ADA is a variable and TOT is a four-element array:

```
DEBUG UNIT(6), SUBCHK(TOT),INIT(TOT,ADA),TRACE
AT 20
TRACE ON
AT 4
TRACE OFF
AT 24
TRACE OFF
AT 6
DISPLAY TOT
```

The contents of all elements of array TOT will be displayed whenever statement 6 is encountered. Output is in the following form:

```
&DBG00#
TOT=  9453.1094    ,    23024.926    ,    611.48633    ,    1574.8887
&END
TOT(3) =    1576.046
   3         ART          (7)     2955.00     ( 59%)        964.56
ADA =    2144.089
&DBG00#
TOT=  9453.1094    ,    23024.926    ,    1576.0461    ,    1574.8887
&END
TOT(3) =    3690.135
   3         BROAD        (6)     3886.00     (100%)       2114.09
ADA =    38.08186
&DBG00#
TOT=  9453.1094    ,    23024.926    ,    3690.1355    ,    1574.8887
&END
```

More than one DISPLAY statement may be included in the debugging instructions of a program. Ordinarily, each is preceded by an AT statement. Different fields can be output with each DISPLAY statement:

```
AT 3
DISPLAY ADA
AT 6
DISPLAY TOT
```

Whenever statement 3 is encountered, variable ADA is output. Whenever statement 6 is encountered, all elements of array TOT are displayed.

The effects of one statement can be shown by using DISPLAY immediately before and after the statement in question. For example, statement 5 follows statement 4. The programmer wants to know the change in contents of field ADA made by calculations in statement 4:

```
1 ...
2 ...
3 ...
4 ADA = CONTAC * A * B * PERCNT
5 ...
6 ...
  DEBUG UNIT (6), TRACE
  AT 4
  DISPLAY ADA
  AT 5
  DISPLAY ADA
  END
```

Because ADA is displayed at both statements 4 and 5, it will be displayed as it is both before and after the execution of statement 4. This technique is often useful in determining if the calculations in a statement are correctly stated.

REVIEW QUESTIONS

10. What is the difficulty in using WRITE statements for debugging?
11. Where in a program is the DEBUG packet placed?
12. What is determined by the AT statement?
13. What are the five DEBUG options? What is the function of each?

OBJECTIVES REVIEW

Study the objectives at the beginning of this chapter. Check each one to be certain that you have achieved it. Restudy the chapter sections related to any objective you cannot perform.

Appendixes

Typical Job Control Cards for IBM S/360 and S/370 OS and DOS Systems

Appendix A:
Part 1: Typical DOS Job Control Cards

```
          1         2         3
123456789012345678901234567890
// JOB JOBNAME
// OPTION LINK
// EXEC FFORTRAN
   (FORTRAN program)
/*
// EXEC LNKEDT
// EXEC
   (data, if present)
/*
/&
```

Part 2: Typical OS Job Control Cards

```
         1         2         3         4         5         6
123456789012345678901234567890123456789012345678901234567890123456
//IC030300 JOB (0303,33,,,,170),'HLSEEDS    30311427F',CLASS=C
//STEP01 EXEC PROC=FORTGCLD
//SYSIN DD *
  (FORTRAN program)
/*
//GO.SYSIN DD *
  (data, if present)
/*
//
```

Appendix B

Data Card Set for Assignment Problems

```
         1         2         3         4         5         6         7         8
12345678901234567890123456789012345678901234567890123456789012345678901234567890
ALMANZA RICHARD     1413408 48050192 23441009F10110024503 1100316000T 1550716740
BROWN ANTHONY       1414516 00041253 26322611F10220062567 2400411595F 1701223741
CHANG JOHN          1417056 52532355 31445722T10320173569 0100914572T 0900815740
CRAIG JEROME        1718954 40020198 31385224T10410152915 1500616549F 1201010740
DAMON JENNIFER      1724319 37040302 02547117T20520021753 0200414512F 1400927741
DAVIDSON PAUL       1724437 40062251 34320514F10620056495 1900412090T 1600315740
ESPINOSA JOHN       1725127 00072338 32547324T10730093805 0600518569T 1300502740
GRAHAM LIZABETH     2130331 35080175 26335621F20810080421 2200317014T 1251211741
HOWARD NATALIE      2130558 50094350 03194810T20920013283 1200412039F 1000804740
ISHIMOTO THOMAS     2134061 20581320 14143414T11020043269 2700312592T 1750417740
JENSEN HENRY        2134147 40042253 25422406F11130024712 0700404012F 1650128740
JOHNS CLAUDIA       2139103 50032315 34320512F21220081516 2020612057T 1450507740
KAMINENTZ MARTIN    2643229 46520198 23942808T11310053925 2608316554T 0900314740
LANG ANTHONY        2644337 49572495 34320325F11420258346 1309612017F 1150729740
LEWIS HOWARD        2645698 45061256 31630013F11520064958 2310414010T 1700212741
MARTINEZ MANUEL     2649007 40052365 00046923T11630122246 0400000196F 1601005740
MILLER LAUREL       2852014 00050105 39320425F21710141527 3004816523T 1250108740
NILES JUDY          2852514 40041365 34320018F21830161400 1411514070T 0900814740
NORTON ELAINE       2854328 00083267 30320108T21920042647 1804312074T 1400213740
OLSON JOHN          2855961 40022506 33780520F12020190802 1015608076F 1600522740
PRESTON CHARLES     3561931 40090161 17855325T12110184992 2910716035F 1350624740
PURCELL MARY        3962563 00030110 31398217T22210060916 1709611552T 1500619740
RIVERA SARAH        3968927 46013205 29395625F22320044462 3104514569F 1650812741
ROSEN MORRIS        3969748 10041303 07231816T12420112743 0302212579F 1700930741
SANDERS ALEXANDER   4275171 40050185 27027415T12510062654 2809614016F 1401024750
SONN WILLIAM        4275455 45072245 39795322T12620132819 0900417565T 1650630740
TYSON PAUL          4276062 40512350 30320809T12730049658 2508318024T 1801218740
UDELL BEATRICE      5384211 40060195 34320610F22810048344 1608412069T 1600420740
VICTOR ROBERT       5385011 47074347 34320522F12930146853 2109716553F 0500615740
WILLS JANICE        5389323 40031405 23443824T23020128568 0501612014T 1401127740
WONG MAY            5389461 28012260 19241712T23120012567 0800214063F 1300321740
```

Appendix C

Program LETTER: Use of the IF and Computed GOTO Statements with Alphameric Fields.

Part 1: Program (using DOS input/output assignments)

```
      DIMENSION LET(26)
      LCOUNT=0
      READ (1,20)LA
   20 FORMAT (1A4)
      READ (1,2) (LET(I),I=1,26)
    2 FORMAT (26A1)
      DO 10 I=1,26
      LTR=LET(I)
      IF (LTR-LA) 8,9,8
    9 GO TO 5
    8 LTEST= (LTR-LA)/16777216
      GO TO(  15,18,15,5,15,15,15,5,23,23,23,23,23,23,23,15,15,15,15,15,
     15,27,22,26,23,23,23,23,23,23,23,23,24,25,5,15,43,15,15,15),LTEST
    5 WRITE (3,50) LTR
   50 FORMAT (T5,'VOWEL', T20, A1)
      GO TO 10
   15 WRITE (3,150) LTR
  150 FORMAT (T5,'CONSONANT', T20, A1)
      GO TO 10
   18 WRITE (3,180)
  180 FORMAT (T5, 'SHOULD BE C')
      GO TO 10
   22 WRITE (3,220) LTR
  220 FORMAT (T5,'SHOULD BE Q', T25, A1)
      GO TO 10
   23 WRITE (3,230) LTR
  230 FORMAT (T5, 'SHOULD BE BLANKS'        T25,A1)
      GO TO 10
   24 WRITE (3,240) LTR
  240 FORMAT (T5, 'SHOULD BE S', T25, A1)
      GO TO 10
   25 WRITE (3,250) LTR
  250 FORMAT (T5, 'SHOULD BE T', T25, A1)
      GO TO 10
   26 WRITE (3,260) LTR
  260 FORMAT (T5, 'SHOULD BE R', T25, A1)
      GO TO 10
   27 WRITE (3,270) LTR
  270 FORMAT (T5,'SHOULD BE P', T25, A1)
      GO TO 10
   43 WRITE (3,430) LTEST
  430 FORMAT (T5, 'SHOULD BE W', T25, A1)
   10 CONTINUE
      END
```

Part 2: Data Cards

```
                  1         2         3         4
columns: 1234567890123456789012345678901234567890

Card 1: A

Card 2: ABCDEFGHIJKLMNOPQRSTUVWXYZ
```

Part 3: Printed Output

```
VOWEL          A
CONSONANT      B
SHOULD BE C
CONSONANT      D
VOWEL          E
CONSONANT      F
CONSONANT      G
CONSONANT      H
VOWEL          I
CONSONANT      J
CONSONANT      K
CONSONANT      L
CONSONANT      M
CONSONANT      N
VOWEL          O
SHOULD BE P           P
SHOULD BE Q           Q
SHOULD BE R           R
SHOULD BE S           S
SHOULD BE T           T
VOWEL          U
CONSONANT      V
SHOULD BE W
CONSONANT      X
CONSONANT      Y
CONSONANT      Z
```

Appendix D

List of Common FORTRAN Mathematical Functions

Function	Definition	Number of Arguments	Type of Argument	Type of Function	Name
Absolute value	$\lvert r \rvert$	1	Real	Real	ABS
			Integer	Integer	IABS
Choosing largest value	$\text{Max}(r_1, r_2, \ldots)$	$\geqslant 2$	Integer	Real	AMAX0
			Real	Real	AMAX1
			Integer	Integer	MAX0
			Real	Integer	MAX1
Choosing smallest value	$\text{Min}(r_1, r_2, \ldots)$	$\geqslant 2$	Integer	Real	AMIN0
			Real	Real	AMIN1
			Integer	Integer	MIN0
			Real	Integer	MIN1
Common logarithm	$\log_{10}(r)$		Real	Real	ALOG10
Exponential	e^r	1	Real	Real	EXP
Fix	Convert from real to integer	1	Real	Integer	IFIX
Float	Convert from integer to real	1	Integer	Real	FLOAT
Natural logarithm	$\log_e(r)$	1	Real	Real	ALOG
Square Root	$\sqrt{r}$	1	Real	Real	SQRT
Trigonometric arctangent (function value returned in radians)	$\arctan(r)$	1	Real	Real	ATAN
Trigonometric cosine (argument in radians)	$\cos(r)$	1	Real	Real	COS
Trigonometric sine (argument in radians)	$\sin(r)$	1	Real	Real	SIN
Trigonometric tangent (argument in radians)	$\tan(r)$	1	Real	Real	TAN
Truncation	Sign of r, times largest integer $\leqslant r$	1	Real	Real	AINT
			Real	Integer	INT

Appendix E

Collating Sequence of EBCDIC Graphic Symbols,
with Hexadecimal, Binary, and Punched Card Representations

Graphic Symbol	Hexadecimal Representation	Binary Representation	Punched Card Column	Decimal Value
(Blank)	40	0100 0000	no punch	64
¢	4A	0100 1010	12-2-8	74
.	4B	0100 1011	12-3-8	75
<	4C	0100 1100	12-4-8	76
(	4D	0100 1101	12-5-8	77
+	4E	0100 1110	12-6-8	78
|(absolute)	4F	0100 1111	12-7-8	79
&	50	0101 0000	12	80
!	5A	0101 1010	11-2-8	90
$	5B	0101 1011	11-3-8	91
*	5C	0101 1100	11-4-8	92
)	5D	0101 1101	11-5-8	93
;	5E	0101 1110	11-6-8	94
−(minus)	60	0110 0000	11	96
/	61	0110 0001	0-1	97
,	6B	0110 1011	0-3-8	107
%	6C	0110 1100	0-4-8	108
_(underscore)	6D	0110 1101	0-5-8	109
>	6E	0110 1110	0-6-8	110
?	6F	0110 1111	0-7-8	111
:	7A	0111 1010	2-8	122
#	7B	0111 1011	3-8	123
@	7C	0111 1100	4-8	124
'	7D	0111 1101	5-8	125
=	7E	0111 1110	6-8	126
"	7F	0111 1111	7-8	127
A	C1	1100 0001	12-1	193
B	C2	1100 0010	12-2	194
C	C3	1100 0011	12-3	195

Graphic Symbol	Hexadecimal Representation	Binary Representation	Punched Card Column	Decimal Value
D	C4	1100 0100	12-4	196
E	C5	1100 0101	12-5	197
F	C6	1100 0110	12-6	198
G	C7	1100 0111	12-7	199
H	C8	1100 1000	12-8	200
I	C9	1100 1001	12-9	201
J	D1	1101 0001	11-1	209
K	D2	1101 0010	11-2	210
L	D3	1101 0011	11-3	211
M	D4	1101 0100	11-4	212
N	D5	1101 0101	11-5	213
O	D6	1101 0110	11-6	214
P	D7	1101 0111	11-7	215
Q	D8	1101 1000	11-8	216
R	D9	1101 1001	11-9	217
S	E2	1110 0010	0-2	226
T	E3	1110 0011	0-3	227
U	E4	1110 0100	0-4	228
V	E5	1110 0101	0-5	229
W	E6	1110 0110	0-6	230
X	E7	1110 0111	0-7	231
Y	E8	1110 1000	0-8	232
Z	E9	1110 1001	0-9	233
0	F0	1111 0000	0	240
1	F1	1111 0001	1	241
2	F2	1111 0010	2	242
3	F3	1111 0011	3	243
4	F4	1111 0100	4	244
5	F5	1111 0101	5	245
6	F6	1111 0110	6	246
7	F7	1111 0111	7	247
8	F8	1111 1000	8	248
9	F9	1111 1001	9	249

Index